Law and Mariage in Medieval
and Early Modern Times

Per Andersen, Kirsi Salonen,
Helle Møller Sigh, and Helle Vogt (eds.)

Law and Mariage in Medieval and Early Modern Times

Proceedings of the Eighth Carlsberg Academy
Conference on Medieval Legal History 2011

DJØF Publishing
Copenhagen 2012

Per Andersen, Kirsi Salonen, Helle Møller Sigh, and Helle Vogt eds.
Law and Mariage in Medieval and Early Modern Times
1. edtion
© 2012 by DJØF Publishing
Jurist- og Økonomforbundets Forlag

Cover: Bo Helsted
Cover illustration: Part of Agnes Slott-Møller's painting "Kong Valdemars Bryllup
med Dronning Dagmar" / "King Valdemar's and Queen Dagmar's Wedding
Celebration" (1932), in Ringsted Rådhus. Photo: Kirsi Salonen

Print & Binding: Toptryk Grafisk, Gråsten

Printed in Denmark 2012
ISBN 978-87-574-2689-2

Sold and distributed in Scandinavia by:
DJØF Publishing
Copenhagen, Denmark
Email: forlag@djoef.dk
www.djoef-forlag.dk

Sold and distributed in North America by:
International Specialized Book Services (ISBS)
Portland, USA
Email: orders@isbs.com
www.isbs.com

Sold in all other countries by:
The Oxford Publicity Partnership Ltd
Towcester, UK
Email: djof@oppuk.co.uk
www.oppuk.co.uk

Distributed in all other countries by:
Marston Book Services
Abingdon, Oxon, UK
Email: trade.orders@marston.co.uk
www.marston.co.uk

CONTENTS

Introduction

Per Andersen, Kirsi Salonen, Helle Møller Sigh, and Helle Vogt

The Eighth Carlsberg Academy Conference on Medieval Legal History, which took place from 4 to 6 May 2011 and was held at the Carlsberg Academy in Copenhagen, brought together scholars from more than ten countries to discuss questions related to 'Law and Marriage in Medieval and Early Modern Times'.

Law and marriage was chosen as the conference theme because matters related to marriage have for some time been the focus of a lively scholarly discussion. This has resulted in the publication of numerous monographs and collections of articles, either organized around a specific topic such as marriage ceremonies or marriage and sex, or geographically focused on marriages or marital traditions in a specific territory or town. The leading idea behind this conference was to bring together scholars from different disciplines, not only to study marriages as legal, theological, and everyday-life phenomena, but also to combine these disciplinary viewpoints. Another important goal of the conference was to bring together not only scholars who could discuss medieval Catholic marriages but also those who could extend the chronological range to early modern times – thus including the effects of the Reformation – and those who could go beyond an ecclesiastical focus to include lay practices as well. The conference seemed fully to succeed in both tasks, since the discussions at the Carlsberg Academy were very vivid and inspiring.

As usual, the conference culminated in publication of the proceedings, which are gathered together in the present book. Although the oral presentations at the conference have been revised and prepared for publication by the authors, these articles have not undergone a formal peer-review process. We have at hand a collection of fifteen articles on varying themes: marriage and canon law, practicing marital law, concepts of marriage, and marital impediments, as well as practical aspects of marriage such as wills, dower, and marital strategies.

In the opening essay, based on his keynote lecture, Philip L. Reynolds asks: *When Medieval Theologians Talked About Marriage, What Were They Really Talking About?* The question addresses the subject matter, configuration, and scope of what theologians during the twelfth through sixteenth centuries wrote about marriage, typically in treatises on marriage as one of the seven sacraments. Taking as his point of departure the premise that the core of this discourse was what the celibate clergy needed to know about marriage in order to minister to the laity – a sacrament from which they were excluded but over which they had oversight and jurisdiction – Reynolds proposes that the discourse located marriage in a certain model of the spiritual and secular realms, represented in part by the Gelasian doctrine. He illumines and substantiates the model by exploring seven historical themes: (1) matrimony as an order integral to the church, albeit the lowest of such orders; (2) the emergence of a discourse on marriage with a specific and enduring structure during the early twelfth century, when theologians prefaced the canonical rules and regulations with an explanation of the place of marriage in the Christian life; (3) the emergence of a list of seven sacraments, the purpose of this list, and the difficulties entailed by the inclusion of marriage as one of the seven; (4) the question whether marriage conferred sacramental grace; (5) the idea that marriage was subject in principle to multiple laws, even though it was wholly subject in actuality to the church; (6) the emergence of the distinction between contract and sacrament; and (7) the intricate jurisdictional considerations involved during the deliberations at Trent in 1563, when the prelates who favoured the decree prohibiting clandestine marriage (*Tametsi*) maintained that although marriage was inalterable as a sacrament, it was alterable as a contract that was subject by its very nature to the public good of the *res publica christiana*, over which the church had assumed jurisdiction in the case of marriage.

Following on from her earlier work on the role of episcopal consultation in the shaping of canon law in the twelfth century, in *The Nature of Alexander III's Contribution to Marriage Law, with Special Reference to 'Licet preter solitum'* Anne Duggan turns the spotlight on Alexander III's contribution to the standardization of the rules relating to Christian marriage. Taking as an example the first four paragraphs of *Licet preter solitum*, which replied in mid-1177 to a series of consultations from Archbishop Romuald of Salerno, she argues that the clarifications and refinements in marriage law which emerged in the course of the twelfth century did not derive from any papal or Curial policy. The clamour for authoritative definition came from regional prelates who required reliable advice on aspects of marriage law which had become controversial in consequence of the teaching in the schools (especially Bologna, Laon, and Paris). Regional prelates played the principal role in determining not only which questions were raised, but which answers became part of the legal tradition.

In his *On an Icelandic Parallel to Codex Justinianus 5.17.10 and Novella 22.6 in the Law Code Grágás*, Hans Henning Hoff examines one particular and exceptional provision on divorce in the Icelandic law code Grágás (1118-1271/1273) according to which a wife could claim a divorce if there were no children after three years of marriage. After describing briefly the multifaceted general rules under which a divorce was possible according to Grágás, Hoff analyses this specific Grágás provision and compares it to *Codex Justinianus* 5.17.10 as it was amended by *Novella* 22.6. The essay concludes that it is very likely that the unusual Grágás provision was influenced by the norms of the Justinianic legislation, and also briefly investigates a possible link between it and the eastern Roman law of Byzantium. Hoff suggests that since the father of the most prominent Icelandic chieftain involved in the revision of the law, Hafliði Másson, had served the Emperor of Byzantium in the eleventh century, it is most likely that Hafliði Másson himself had also been to Byzantium and received there some knowledge about the Justinianic legislation, which was still in force and was being taught to students at that time.

With *Matrimonial Cases Reflected in the Processus iudiciarius secundum stilum Pragensem*, Dominik Budský addresses the practical sides of marriage. His essay deals with a treatise that was relatively well known in Central Europe, *Processus iudiciarius secundum stilum Pragensem*, which was compiled in 1380s by an official of the archbishop of Prague, Nicolaus Puchnik (†1402). Budský argues that references to matrimonial cases occur in several places of the treatise in both a theoretical and a practical way. These are mentioned in the context of interrogatories and varied types of libels such as interrogatory *super matrimonio* and libel *in causa matrimoniali*. Through his analysis of the treatise Budský sheds light on the methods used in the ecclesiastical courts for questioning in matrimonial cases.

Three articles in the collection discuss the concept of marriage. The first of them is Jan Rüdiger's *Married Couples in the Middle Ages? The Case of the Devil's Advocate*. Rüdiger first examines the view, common to social history/social anthropology and legal history/canonistics, that marriage was a key factor in European church teaching, secular lawgiving, and social relations on an everyday level. He then presents his counterargument: How probable is it that an underpopulated, agonistic warrior society, weak on economic resources, would have favoured monogamy over the many advantages of polygyny? Rüdiger suggests that up until the twelfth/thirteenth centuries, 'marriage' was less the inception of a lasting, exclusive relationship than a public acknowledgement of the inception of a relationship that was neither exclusive nor (necessarily) lasting. Rüdiger concludes that in high medieval Europe, men of wealth had relationships with a number of women, some of higher and some of lower status, and that the distinction between *uxor* and *concubina* was a question of who carried the keys and who could see to it that the sons and daughters had an assured future.

Inger Dübeck continues the discussion about the meaning of a marriage in her article *Concubinage and Marriage in Denmark between the Viking Age and the Reformation: A Comparison between Danish and European Medieval Law*. The essay starts by discussing the regulations concerning marriage, cohabitation and concubinage in the Law of Jutland from 1241. Dübeck discusses in particular the rule by which an informal cohabitation with a woman lasting three years, during which time the woman lived as a married woman, eating, drinking and sleeping with the man and with the same duties and responsibility as a wife, would automatically turn the relationship into a consummated marriage. This rule was inconsistent with canon law, but it must have been accepted by the Danish bishops. The rule did not specify if the man and the woman should be of equal or different social status. Later legislation from the early 1580s, Dübeck argues further, leaves the impression that a certain sector of the nobility preferred concubinage with non-noble women, perhaps in accordance with a sort of 'European Common Law' or the European idea of 'morganatic marriage', although legislation showed clearly that the king and other members of the nobility did not accept this practice. The 1582 recess accepted the existence of marriages and even concubinages between noble men and non-noble women, but it deprived the children of such misalliances the right to inherit the noble name or coat of arms or noble land. Dübeck also points out that the nobility did not comply with the new requirements concerning the celebration of marriage, which obliged couples to have a public wedding ceremony before the local vicar in the local church with five witnesses. She concludes that the nobility, instead, continued the old tradition of informal marriages in the presence of good friends as witnesses.

Hiram Kümper's essay tackles the question *Did Medieval Canon Marriage Law Invent our Modern Notion of Rape? Revisiting the Idea of Consent before and after 1200*. He starts by observing a marked distinction between the early medieval concept of *raptus*, which seems to have focused on abduction for the purpose of marriage rather than sexual violence, and its later medieval pendants (*stuprum violentium, rapt, viol, notzog* etc.), which introduced the notion of perpetrating sexual actions against the other's will as a defining factor of the crime. In considering what might have led to this conceptual change, which defined rape in terms much closer to our modern concept of it, Kümper finds the strengthening of the notion of consent in twelfth-century marriage law by canonistic theory. This rise of theoretical issues concerning consent and coercion as problems of determining the will, he goes on to argue, became crucial for the creation of 'modern' secular rape-law from the thirteenth century onwards.

Two essays deal directly with marital impediments. In *Two Models of Incest: Conflict and Confusion in High Medieval Discourse on Kinship and Marriage* Christof Rolker argues that in the Middle Ages there were two very different ways to talk about kin marriage. Following Augustine, one tradition was focused on marriage patterns and the advantages of exogamy for (Christian) society; terms such as *incestum* and references to the biblical prohibitions are strikingly absent from this discourse. These are found only in a rather different discourse, which at the same time is marked by focusing on sexual relations between close relatives. According to Rolker, it is only in the eleventh century that both traditions were conflated, creating the impression that all marriages within the prohibited degrees were 'incestuous'. However, while this was true for mainstream canon law in the century before Gratian, theologians as a rule did not subscribe to this view. Rolker concludes by stressing that divine law on incest and human marriage regulations were two very different things; a recogition of the difference between those thus helped to pave the way for the dramatic reduction of the prohibited degrees by the Lateran Council of 1215.

In *Re-defining Marriage Impediments: Tolerating Dubious Marriages through a Special Declaration from the Apostolic Penitentiary in the Late Middle Ages* Kirsi Salonen examines the regulations of canon law regarding marriage impediments. She argues that even though the impediments were mainly defined by the mid-thirteenth century, development in the interpretation of these regulations continued to take place in the fifteenth and sixteenth centuries. She bases her arguments on the fact that sometimes doubts about the significance of marriage impediments caused problems for couples who intended to marry, or whose marriage was at stake because their union was suddenly considered void. If the local ecclesiastical authorities could not, or did not want to, resolve the dubious marriage cases, the problems were solved by apostolic authority, most often by the Apostolic Penitentiary. Basing her analysis on the source material of the Apostolic Penitentiary, Salonen examines the kinds of cases in which supplicants turned to the authority of the Penitentiary for receiving declarations of tolerances in cases of doubts about marital impediments and how the cases were resolved in the papal curia. She concludes that according to the Penitentiary material, cases related to the impediment of spiritual relationship were the trickiest ones.

The remaining six articles deal with practical and lay aspects of marriages. In *Wills as Testimony of Marriage Contracts in Late Medieval Kracow* Jakub Wysmułek considers the issue of how the notion of a 'last will' is conceptualized. How was a last will understood by medieval citizens? Did it signify a clearly defined legal act, or was it rather a general and not fully defined form of designating donations to be provided after the death of the testator? Although those questions rarely appear in historical researches devoted to last wills, they have great importance for better understanding and interpreting the sources. The article draws attention to the connection between wills, other legal notes (*donationes mortis causa*) designating the survivor's property rights upon the death of a spouse, and marriage contracts, particularly the parts concerning dower. The author argues that last wills, which were often made by relatively young and healthy citizens and validated by the court, included above all a promise of dower to the widow and stipulations concerning the division of property in case the couple had offspring. According to Wysmułek last wills can be best understood as testimonies of contract between the persons involved and not as a preparation for death, driven by fear or by reflections on salvation or damnation of the soul. He argues that among the last wills in the source material from Krakow, the act of making a last will quite often appears as a form of legal confirmation of conditions negotiated by spouses in marital contracts made soon after their marriage. The article concludes that even if this observation refers just to some of the surviving medieval wills, it nevertheless considerably enriches our understanding of them and can help prevent scholars from simplifying the character of this important source material.

Maija Ojala, too, concentrates on the practical side of marriages in her article *Widows' Opportunities to Continue Craft Trade in Northern Baltic Cities during the 15th and 16th Centuries*. She discusses women's opportunities to continue in their craft trade after the death of their husbands and demonstrates that different craft ordinances offered artisan widows a range of possibilities to carry on their business in late medieval cities around the Baltic Sea. In addition she discusses the enforcement of the craft regulations and argues that they should be regarded as offering possibilities and not as mere restrictions against female work.

Paul Brand's essay *Competing for Dower in the English Thirteenth-Century Royal Courts* tackles the practicalities as well. He begins with the assumption that when a married male landowner died in thirteenth-century England, there was normally only a single widow to claim her dower share of the lands which he had held at the time of their marriage or had acquired since. According to Brand, this was the expected consequence, since canon law did not allow a man or woman to be married to more than one partner at a time, and secular law, too, expected that marriages would be monogamous. A second marriage was possible only if the first partner had died or if the first marriage had been formally annulled by the judgment of a competent ecclesiastical court. Yet Brand has discovered that on at least eleven separate occasions between 1221 and 1297 English royal courts (the courts which heard a majority of dower claims) were faced with the competing claims to dower of two women, both of them claiming to have been married to the same recently deceased husband. The author goes on to argue that only in a minority of cases does this seem to have been the result of deception on the part of the husband. More commonly it seems to have been the unintended consequence of the complications of the appellate process of the courts of the church in dealing with matrimonial litigation. On one occasion only both widows succeeded in obtaining dower from the same husband. This seems to have been the result of bad advice received by the husband's heir when settling the claim of one of the widows. On the basis of this Brand concludes that the normal rule (as might be expected) was that only one of the two 'widows' was entitled to dower. In a minority of cases the question of entitlement was settled by a lay jury, but the more common way was through applying a decision made by the relevant ecclesiastical authorities, either reached during the husband's lifetime or made after his death in response to a request from the king's courts.

Thomas Kuehn's contribution, *Dos Non Teneat Locum Legittime: Dowry as a Woman's Inheritance in Early Quattrocento Florence*, continues the discussion about dowry. He states that commonly statutes in medieval Italian communities excluded dowered daughters from inheriting from their fathers, while the patrimony was destined for their brothers or other close agnate males. Women's dowries thus figured as what they could expect from the paternal estate, as their legitimate portion. The usual presumption of historians has been that women's portions were considerably less than those of men. Yet, the author argues, the laws, both the learned civil law and local statutes, did not explicitly equate dowry with the legitimate portion that fell to women by civil law. Using a case study from Florence Kuehn demonstrates that this distinction between dowry and legitimate portion could have real consequences in inheritance disputes. He concludes that depending on the angle of vision, dowry was both more and less than a proportional legitimate share of an estate, as a woman's right to a dowry was close to absolute. She could not be disinherited from it.

Lars Ivar Hansen's article *Marriage among the Land-owning Peasants of Southern Norway: A Device for Social Reproduction of the Peasant Elite* presents some features of the marriage practices and strategies that were implemented by a segment of landowning peasants in southern Norway, through the late medieval and early modern periods. One central aim of the contribution is to highlight how the marriage institution was used within a set of wider, more comprehensive strategies for social reproduction by this segment of peasants, who stood out as a local and regional elite, displaying greater economic and social resources than the majority of peasants. Since they also disposed of a greater amount of 'intellectual capital' in the form of accumulated and traditionally mediated knowledge about legal matters and customary practices, they occupied positions related to local administration and government which were accessible to Norwegian peasants in medieval and early modern times, viz. as legal jurors and local bailiffs. Hansen argues that when implementing their marital strategies, this group had to take account of four basic premises: 1) The bilateral way of reckoning kinship; 2) the inheritance law, as established in the medieval National Law Code of the Norwegian Realm in 1274, and which primarily followed a bilateral pattern, but with some patrilineal elements; 3) the so-called 'residence right' – i.e. the priority held by the oldest son to take over the main residence or patrimonial land, while other heirs had to be satisfied with other, 'loose' shares of land or *mobilia*; and 4) the so-called 'rent ownership system', by which property right was primarily defined as the right to collect rent from land, with no decisive authority over how the land should be cultivated in practice. Using genealogical analysis, as well as analysing father-son relations among the local jurors over time Hansen concludes that this peasant elite used marriage strategies not only to reinforce kinship ties and social networks but also to maintain control over property rights that otherwise would have been lost to younger siblings on the death of a father.

The concluding article, *Clandestine Marriage and Parental Consent in John Calvin's Geneva: The Gradual Synthesis of Theology, Statutes, and Case Law*, is written by John Witte, Jr. According to Witte, parental consent to engagement and marriage was a major reform that the sixteenth-century Protestant Reformation introduced to stamp out the late medieval Catholic toleration of clandestine marriages. John Calvin introduced the doctrine of parental consent to Protestant Geneva both in statutes that he drafted and in cases that he adjudicated as a member of the Consistory court. Witte argues convincingly that Calvin and his fellow reformers insisted on the priority of the father's consent over the mother's consent, but also insisted that even the father could not override his child's own consent to an engagement or marriage contract. Parents and guardians who neglected their duties or abused their authority at this fateful stage of their child's life were severely punished and often forfeited their right to have their child's secret marriage annulled.

*

The conference and the publication of this volume were made possible through generous funding from The Carlsberg Foundation, Ernst og Tove Dobel Andersens Foundation, Knud Højgaard's Foundation, and the 'Netværk for historisk religionsforskning' supported by the Danish Council for Independent Research / Humanities. As organisers and editors we wish to express our special gratitude, once again, to the Carlsberg Academy for providing us with the spectacular venue that gives the conference series its special ambience, namely the mid-nineteenth century villa of the founder of the Carlsberg Breweries, I. C. Jacobsen. As usual, our thanks also go to the caretaker of the estate, Svend Rasmussen, for his patience and invaluable help in making the event run smoothly. We are indebted also to our proof reader and copyeditor, Kate Gilbert, who has with skill transformed these fifteen essays into a more homogeneous volume. And last but not least, our thanks go to our chef, Lino Vogt, and his assistant, Kurt Villads Jensen, who took care of the alimentary needs during the conference.

Aarhus, Copenhagen and Tampere
January 2012

When Medieval Theologians Talked About Marriage, What Were They Really Talking About?

Philip L. Reynolds

1. Introduction

My question is about the subject matter, purpose, configuration of topics, and scope of a certain discourse, namely, what theologians during the twelfth through sixteenth centuries, in their professional capacity as theologians, wrote about marriage. The typical setting of that discourse was a treatise on marriage as one of the seven sacraments, such as one finds in countless commentaries on Peter Lombard's *Sentences* and in the summas of theology.[1]

It might seem odd to introduce some proceedings on the law of marriage by talking about theology, but marriage during the central and late Middle Ages was wholly subject to ecclesiastical jurisdiction, and I am unlikely to court controversy by claiming that if medieval churchmen had been pressed to explain why that had to be so, they would have replied, 'Because marriage is a sacrament'. Whether and how marriage was a sacrament was a theological issue. My question, therefore, is in part about the rationale for the church's jurisdiction, which was a conspicuous fact of medieval life.

---

1. I use the following abbreviations in the notes: BGPh[Th]MA = *Beiträge zur Geschichte der Philosophie [und Theologie] des Mittelalters*; CCL = *Corpus Christianorum, series latina*; CSEL = *Corpus Scriptorum Ecclesiasticorum Latinorum*; PL = J. P. Migne (ed.), *Patrologia Latina*; RThAM = *Recherches de théologie ancienne et médiévale*.

I have two other, more personal reasons for raising the question. First, it is salutary because historians of theology or doctrine all too easily get lost in the details and the arguments *pro* and *contra* and fail to explain what the discourse was all about or why anyone cared. Second, the medieval discourse on the theology of marriage does not match the expectations and concerns of theology students and clergy today, such as those at the theology school where I am privileged to teach. They would expect a theology of marriage to shed light on the difficult art of sustaining a successful marriage, and on that obviously important topic, with a few rare exceptions, the medieval theology of marriage had very little to say. There is pastoral counsel regarding aspects of married life to be found in confessional manuals and sermons, but it is remarkably unrelated either to the contemporaneous theology of marriage as a sacrament or to the scriptural sources of that theology.[2]

The theology in question was not fixed or static. It emerged in its early form during the first half of the twelfth century; it underwent much elaboration and development from around 1200 to 1270; and it was dogmatically formulated for the first time at the Council of Trent in 1563. After that, it took on a 'post-Tridentine' character, as Catholic theologians worked out the implications of Trent's doctrine and tried to tie up the loose ends. There was almost always something happening in the field during that long duration, although there were periods of relative inactivity. I cannot relate the history of marriage as a sacrament here, and I shall not mention at all some of its best-known features, such as the debate about the role of consummation. Instead, I shall begin by proposing a model, and then I shall consider some historical trends and episodes that will illustrate the model and reveal from diverse points of view what medieval theologians were really talking about when they discussed marriage.

2. A model

The discourse of marriage as a sacrament was at its core what the celibate clergy needed to know about marriage. Since this was the only sacrament that they themselves did not receive, what they needed to know was exclusively on behalf of the laity to whom they ministered. The institutional church was responsible for marrying and divorce, and it was required to account for the place of marriage in the Christian life. Looking at marriage

---

2.   S. Farmer, 'Persuasive Voices: Clerical Images of Medieval Wives', *Speculum* 61 (1986), 517-43. R. M. Karras, 'Gendered Sin and Misogyny in John of Bromyard's *Summa predicantium*', *Traditio* 47 (1992), 233-57. R. Schnell, 'The Discourse on Marriage in the Middle Ages', *Speculum* 73 (1998), 771-86.

from the outside, the clergy regarded it as the only acceptable alternative to a celibate vocation, which was preferable. I have said 'at its core' because scholastic theology, wherein the doctrine of marriage as a sacrament emerged and evolved, was never limited to matters of practical expediency. It was an essentially speculative discipline, pursuing the goal of truth about what we should call 'ultimate questions'. Moreover, any question that seemed valid, and was not so particular that it expressed nothing more than idle curiosity, was fair game.

The need outlined above can be articulated as a model that *located* marriage within a certain plan of Christian society. From that location followed the jurisdiction and the professional responsibility of bishops and clergy regarding marriage. On the one hand, being married placed one squarely among secular Christians, since celibacy was the distinguishing feature of the spiritual elite: the pastors and contemplatives. On the other hand, marriage was a vocation within the sacred division of Christianity, a mode of participating in the life of the church. That was the fundamental (though perhaps not sufficient) reason why *getting* married became one of the 'sacraments of the church' during the twelfth century. Inasmuch as one could distinguish between what was due to God and what was due to Caesar in medieval Christendom, marriage was something that one ought to 'render unto God' (Matt. 22:21).

The discourse on marriage also located it within a broader discourse on the sacraments, which in turn was usually located in the division of theology that followed immediately after the incarnation of Jesus Christ (such as in the first part of Book IV of Peter Lombard's *Sentences*). Medieval theologians considered the sacraments to be a prolongation of Christ's incarnation, and they treated the church and the sacraments as coextensive topics. To speak of one was to speak of the other. This close relationship is already apparent, long before the emergence of the seven-sacrament system, in a familiar allegory first expounded by John Chrysostom and Augustine, which elaborates the idea that the marriage of Adam and Eve prefigured the mystical marriage between Christ and the church (Eph. 5:32). Just as Adam fell into a deep sleep and Eve was taken from his side and brought to him as his wife, so Christ died on the cross and blood and water (emblems of eucharist and baptism) flowed from his side.[3] The formation of the church as

---

3.   John Chrysostom, *Catecheses ad illuminandos* 24 (57), 3rd series, *Hom.* 3 'Ad neophytos', 17-18, ed. Wenger, *Sources Chrétiennes* 50, 176. Augustine, *De Genesi contra Manichaeos* 24, PL 34, 215-16; *In Ioannis evangelium* 9.10 and 120.2, CCL 36, 96-97, 661. For medieval examples, see Hugh of Saint-Victor, *De sacramentis christianae fidei* I.6.36, PL 176, 284D, and Bonaventure, *II Sent.* 18.1.1, resp., *Opera Omnia*, vol. 2, eds. PP Collegii S. Bonaventurae (Quaracchi: 1885), 433a.

the bride of Christ (*sponsa Christi*) and the institution of the sacraments, from this point of view, were one and the same event.

3. Holy matrimony

The medieval theology of marriage as a sacrament presupposed that marriage belonged in the church. There was nothing new about that premise, although it took on new significance during the eleventh through twelfth centuries. Augustine had been struck by the fact that whereas the Jews and the Gentiles (he was referring to Mosaic and Roman law) could divorce and remarry, marriage was insoluble in the church – or, as he preferred to put it, 'in the city of God, in his holy mountain' (Psalm 48:1): a pregnant phrase that had eschatological as well as ecclesiological significance in his mind. Augustine called this peculiar feature of Christian marriage the 'good of sacrament' (*bonum sacramenti*). Failing to find any merely human, utilitarian reason for it, he could only suggest that God had chosen to make marriage a sign of 'some greater reality', namely, the mystical marriage between Christ and church, wherein there was no divorce.[4] Again, Isidore of Seville included marriage when writing about the offices in the church. Married folk (*coniugati*) appear here as an ecclesiastical estate (*status*), alongside clerics of various ranks, religious, penitents, and consecrated virgins and widows. After discussing these various estates, Isidore goes on to explain how people enter the church: through the catechumenate, baptism, and so forth.[5]

Christian writers used threefold divisions to illumine the place of marriage within the church and Christian life. Perhaps the oldest is the division of Christians into consecrated virgins, consecrated widows, and married folk. In Jesus' parable of the sower (Mark 4:3-20, etc.), the seed that falls on fertile ground produces yields of thirtyfold, sixtyfold, and a hundredfold. Jerome used this division to elucidate the respective merits of married folk, widows, and virgins respectively.[6] Scholastic theologians were interested in the implication that different ranks of Christians would receive different 'fruits' in the next life, but they used the model chiefly to show that the married and celibate vocations were expressions of a common, underlying vir-

4. Augustine, *De bono coniugali* 7-8(7), CSEL 41, 197; *De nuptiis et concupiscentia* I.10(11), CSEL 32, 222-23.
5. Isidore of Seville, *De ecclesiastis officiis*, ed. Lawson, CCL 113.
6. Jerome, *Adversus Iovinianum* I.3, PL 23, 223B-24A. See also Jerome's commentary on Matthew 13:23 (PL 26, 89A), where he briefly refers to the former passage.

tue (sometimes identified as chastity), albeit in degrees ranging from the merely tolerable to perfection.[7]

Whereas Jerome's model was chiefly moral in its implications, other triple models were more ecclesiological, dividing the members of the church into orders. Such divisions revealed not only the orders' different degrees of excellence but also how they were integral parts of the whole. Two such models, devised respectively by Augustine and Bede, were the chief sources for the medieval versions. Augustine divided Christians into the *continentes* (here representing contemplatives), the *rectores* (bishops, pastors, or ministers), and the married folk. Daniel, Noah, and Job respectively were the types of these three ranks – Job representing married folk because of his trials and tribulations. Again, the women who toiled at the mill (Matt. 24:40), according to Augustine, represented married folk because the turning of the millwheel signified mundane care (cf. 1 Cor. 7:29-34).[8] Whereas Augustine's model was chiefly eschatological (for his point was that some persons from every order would be saved and some damned on the Last Day), Bede's model was more structural and organizational. He interpreted the three floors of the Temple of Solomon allegorically so as to divide the church into three orders: virgins, continents, and married folk, in descending order. Each lower floor was wider than the floor above, partly because the class that it represented was more numerous, but chiefly because the corresponding way of life was less restrictive.[9] Both models appealed to the Carolingian moralists, who liked to think of the church as a great edifice.[10]

Medieval theologians mixed these three models carelessly, and they were both vague and inconsistent about the identity of the two top ranks. But that was only because the details did not matter. The point was to depict the church hierarchically with married folk always at the base: the least

7. Simon of Tournai, *Disp.* 80, q. 1, in J. Warichez (ed.), *Les* Disputationes *de Simon de Tournai* (Louvain: 1932), 231-32; Alexander of Hales, *Quaestiones disputatae 'antequam esset frater'*, eds. PP Collegii S. Bonaventurae, Q. 57, disp. 3.2-3, §§65-79, and Q. 58 (Quaracchi: 1960), 1121-27, 1128-58; Thomas Aquinas, *Summa theol.* I-II.70.3, ad 2m (Ottawa edition, vol. 2 [1931], 1086); Peter John Olivi, *Quaestiones de perfectione evangelica*, q. 6, resp., in A. Emmen, 'Verginità e matrimonio nella valutazione dell'Olivi', *Studi Francescani* 64 (1967), 11-57, at 28-31, §§1-4.
8. G. Folliet, 'Les trois catégories de chrétiens: Étude de ce thème augustinien', *Augustinus Magister*, vol. 2 (Paris: 1954-1955), 631-44. G. Folliet, 'Les trois catégories de chrétiens: Survie d'un thème augustinien', *L'Année théologique augustinienne* 14 (1954), 82-96.
9. Bede, *De templo* I, 7.5, CCL 119A,163.
10. Candidus of Fulda, *Opusculum de passione Domini* 18, PL 106, 95B-C; Christian Stavelot, *Expositio in Matthaeum evangelistam* 62, PL 106, 1412C-D; Smaragdus, *In collectiones epistolarum et evangeliorum de tempore et de sanctis, Dominica II post theophania, in Ioannem*, cap. 2, PL 102, 88D-89A; Jonas of Orléans, *De institutione laicali* II.2, PL 106, 169D.

among Christian vocations, to be sure, but nonetheless an integral part of the whole.

The division of three orders was exclusive as well as inclusive. Ivo of Chartres used Augustine's version in a letter to Louis VI, commending the king for choosing Adélaïde de Maurienne as his wife-to-be and at the same time admonishing him to go through with the proposal. Fearing that a breakup would divide both the nation and the church, Ivo advised that 'every kingdom divided against itself is brought to desolation, and every city or house divided against itself shall not stand' (Matt. 12:25). There were no other ways, Ivo warned, to enter the Kingdom of Heaven: 'Whoever shall not be found in one of these professions will be judged an outlaw by the eternal tribunal and will not have his eternal inheritance'.[11]

The foregoing ideas located marriage in the church, but they did not posit an alternative space within Christendom: a secular realm. To illumine that aspect of the medieval theology of marriage, one must consider the dualistic models favored by medieval churchmen, which were variants or elaborations of the Gelasian doctrine. These posited two realms *within* Christendom, unlike Augustine's two Cities, which divided the world between overlapping godly and ungodly realms. In their basic form, the models postulate two powers under the same God or under Christ: the royal power fosters earthly, this-worldly welfare, whereas the episcopal or priestly power fosters spiritual, next-worldly welfare. The multiple movements of reform and ecclesio-political adjustment during the eleventh century[12] converged to produce an ecclesiastical hierarchy that was segregated from the secular realm (most conspicuously by celibacy) but comparably organized, with a well-developed system of law, judiciaries, and bureaucracy, and with its own canon law to match secular law.

Hugh of Saint-Victor beautifully depicted this augmented version of the Gelasian model in his summa on the sacraments. The church is the body of Christ, of which all Christians are members, but whereas the laity constitute the left side of Christ's body, Hugh explains, the clergy constitute the right. Each side has its ranks of authority and its peculiar duties. The clergy are concerned with spiritual and heavenly things, the laity with corporeal and earthly things. 'Length of days is in her right hand, and in her left hand

---

11. Ivo of Chartres, *Epist. 239*, PL 162, 246C-47C. On the political background to *Epist. 239*, see J. Dufour, 'Louis VI, roi de France (1108-1137), à la lumière des actes royaux et des sources narratives', *Académie des Inscriptions et Belles-Lettres. Comptes rendus des séances, April-June 1990* (Paris: 1990), 456-82, at 465.

12. I refer to what is variously known as the Gregorian (or Papal) Reform (or Revolution). The nomenclature has been the subject of intense and prolonged debate, and none of the four possible combinations is an adequate description. For a survey of the trends and movements involved and of the scholarship thereon, see K. G. Cushing, *Reform and the Papacy in the Eleventh Century* (Manchester: 2005).

riches and honor' (Prov. 3:16). The left is good, therefore, but the right is better.[13]

Hugh goes on to explain why tonsure is the emblem of those on the right. It may signify humility, Hugh concedes, but it is chiefly a crown. The clergy is 'a chosen generation, a royal priesthood, a holy nation, a peculiar people' (1 Pet. 2:9). Moreover, the tonsure is a sign of the clergy's closeness to God and of their mediating function. Nothing should veil a cleric's pate from divine influence, for he is privy to the secrets of God. Clerics are God's messengers to the laity.[14] It is difficult for Hugh to explain why monks are tonsured, for they have no place in this schema. They are admitted to the tonsured clergy only 'by indulgence', so that their cloistered communities can remain self-sufficient and undisturbed.[15]

The clergy are also set apart by their celibacy. Hugh fears the slippery slope. Discussing an ancient debate as to whether consecrated virgins, having lapsed, may validly marry, Hugh reasons that if any such dispensations are made on personal grounds, then any celibate cleric who experiences the urges of sexual desire would lapse and marry, claiming plausibly that it is 'better to marry than to burn' (1 Cor. 7:9). Before long, there would be no celibates left, Hugh argues, and it would become 'impossible for anything to remain stable or established'.[16] Where did marriage belong in this schema? Hugh did not say, but the answer is obvious, if a little complicated. Married persons belonged on the left side, but this model was a chiefly a division of lines and sources of authority, not of persons. The administration and regulation of marriage belonged on the right.

The Gelasian model was insufficient to articulate the conceptions of ecclesiastical power that emerged during the twelfth century, in the wake of the Gregorian reforms. The Gelasian model was dualistic. Without abandoning that model, churchmen superimposed upon it the hierocratic Two Swords model, whereby the secular, royal rulers had a derivative, delegated power bestowed upon them by the church, just as the moon owed its light to the sun. The Pope was both 'royal priest' and 'imperial bishop'.[17] But the hierocratic model, it seems to me, did not explicitly inform the theology of marriage until the sixteenth century, when issues of jurisdiction rose to the very top of the agenda. I shall return to this point at the end of my essay.

---

13. Hugh of Saint-Victor, *De sacramentis christianae fidei* II.2.3, PL 176, 417A-C, and II.2.4, 417D-418D. The likely date of this work is 1130/31-1137.
14. Ibid., II.3.1, 421C. The term *corona* is a common synonym for *tonsura* in medieval Latin.
15. Ibid., II.3.4, 422D.
16. Ibid., II.11.12, 500D: 'nihil deinceps stabile aut ratum esse poterit'.
17. See J. A. Watt, 'Spiritual and Temporal Powers', in J. H. Burns (ed.) *The Cambridge History of Medieval Political Thought c.350-c.1450* (Cambridge: 1988), 367-423; and D. E. Luscombe, 'The Formation of Political Thought in the West', ibid., 157-73, at 165-69.

4. How the shape of the discourse emerged

In retrospect, we can see that what became the discourse on marriage as one of the sacraments originated in the early-twelfth-century sentential litera-ture, during the period in which the episcopate was at last achieving 'the exclusive jurisdiction over all matters pertaining to marriage that it had long claimed as its right'.[18]

The *sententiae* were more or less authoritative opinions on particular theological and canonical topics, 'picked' (*defloratae*) not only from ancient sources – such as Augustine, Isidore, Bede, and the Carolingian exegetes, moralists, and councils – but also from those whom the *Liber Pancrisis* called the *magistri moderni*: masters of the cathedral schools of the Île de France during the early twelfth century, such as William of Champeaux and Anselm of Laon. The *sententiae* survive in great numbers, haphazardly col-lected in miscellanies, deliberately gathered into vaguely systematic florile-gia, and worked up into summary, usually anonymous treatises on particular topics, including marriage.[19]

The literature is fraught with historical problems that have never been fully resolved. Anselm's is the name that appears most frequently when *sen-tentiae* are ascribed to anyone, but the notion that the *sententiae* in general belong to the so-called 'school of Laon' is tenuous.[20] Our best guess is that the *sententiae* became a medium for doing theology during the first quarter of the twelfth century, although it is evident that the habit of collecting and compiling them continued well into the middle of the century. The medium must have originated in the cathedral schools, although the Cistercians fa-vored and collected the literature around mid-century (presumably as a safer alternative to what was then happening in scholastic circles).

Fortunately, the vexing historical problems surrounding the literature as a whole are not of great concern regarding the theology of marriage. The extant sentential literature on that topic comprises a dozen florilegia and

---

18. The phrase is from G. Duby, *Medieval Marriage: Two Models from Twelfth-Century France*, trans. E. Forster (Baltimore: 1978), 20.
19. The retrieval of this literature occurred mainly from the last decade of the nine-teenth century through the mid-twentieth, culminating in O. Lottin, *Psychologie et morale aux XIIe et XIIIe siècles*, vol. 5 (Gembloux: 1959), subtitled 'L'école d'Anselme de Laon et de Guillaume de Champeaux'. Despite the importance of the literature as the first phase in the evolution of scholastic theology, little was written about it after Lottin's cumulative study of 1959 until C. Giraud, *Per verba magi-stri: Anselme de Laon et son école au XIIe siècle* (Turnhout: 2010), a welcome and important reassessment.
20. V. Flint, 'The "School of Laon": A Reconsideration', RThAM 43 (1976), 89-196. M. Colish, 'Another look at the School of Laon', *Archives d'histoire doctrinale et littéraire du Moyen Age* 53 (1986), 7-22, at 11, complained that Flint's 'historical agnosticism' was an over-reaction, but it seems to me that Flint's critique was basi-cally sound and remains valid.

treatises.[21] All are anonymous, and there is no particular reason to associate any them with Anselm, with his students, or even with Laon, but there is a clear historical chain. A seminal sentential treatise on marriage known today by its incipit, *Cum omnia sacramenta*,[22] was dependent both on another such treatise, the *De coniugiis tractantibus* (preserved in the *Liber Pancrisis* and elsewhere)[23] and on the tractate on marriage in a popular florilegium, the *Sententiae Magistri A.*, which in turn was dependent on Ivo of Chartres. Hugh of Saint-Victor, writing in the 1130s, drew extensively on a second, much-revised version of the *Cum omnia sacramenta*.[24] And Peter Lombard drew extensively on Hugh's treatment (as well as on Gratian and on Walter of Mortagne's *De coniugio*) for his treatise on the sacrament of marriage in the *Sentences* (1154-57). We may confidently situate the sentential link in the historical chain of marriage as a sacrament, therefore, between Ivo of Chartres and Hugh of Saint-Victor.

The *sententiae* provided a means of emancipating topics and issues from their haphazard occurrence in Holy Writ (a means later superseded by the much more powerful *quaestio disputata*). Modern scholars are sometimes struck by the practicality of the sentential literature,[25] but it was not focused exclusively on practice or morals. Rather, it seems to have been designed chiefly to teach clerics what they needed to know, that is, to provide them with the rational basis for what they had both to do and to preach.

A new theoretical framework for marriage emerged in this literature. It is especially clear in two influential florilegia: the marriage tractate from the *Sententiae Magistri A.*, and the *In primis hominibus*.[26] The anonymous au-

---

21. For a review of this family of treatises, see H. J. F. Reinhardt, *Die Ehelehre der Schule des Anselm von Laon*, = BGPhThM, nF 14 (Münster: 1974), 10-39. On marriage in the sentential literature, see also H. Zeimentz, *Ehe nach der Lehre de Früscholastik* (Düsseldorf: 1973); and B. Matecki, *Der Traktat 'In primis hominibus'* (Frankfurt a.M.: 2001), 23-45.

22. Edited by F. P. Bliemetzrieder, *Anselms von Laon systematische Sentenzen*, = BGPhMA 18.2-3 (Münster: 1919), 129-51. Bliemetzrieder edited the treatise as part of the co-called *Sententiae Anselmi*, now known to be a much later compilation.

23. Edited by F. P. Bliemetzrieder, 'Paul Fournier und das literarische Werk Ivos von Chartres', *Archiv für katholisches Kirchenrecht* 115 (1935), 53-91, at 73-89.

24. See N. M. Haring, 'The *Sententiae Magistri A.* (Vat. Ms. lat. 4361) and the School of Laon', *Mediaeval Studies* 17 (1955), 1-45. Through an accident of scholarship, the modern edition of the *Cum omnia sacramenta* is divided between two publications. For the first part, see H. Weisweiler, *Das Schrifttum der Schule Anselms von Laon und Wilhelms von Champeaux in deutschen Bibliotheken*, = BGPhThMA 33.1-2 (1936), 33-34. For the second part, see F. P. Bliemetzrieder, 'Théologie et théologiens de l'école épiscopale de Paris avant Pierre Lombard', RThAM 3 (1931), 273-91, at 274-87.

25. Flint, 'School of Laon', 10007; D. E. Luscombe, *The School of Peter Abelard* (Cambridge: 1969), 173.

26. Edited by Reinhardt, *Die Ehelehre*, and Matecki, *Der Traktat*, respectively. See the introductions to these editions on the likely dependence on Augustinian florilegia.

thors began with a hoard of canonical material on the rules and regulations regarding impediments, divorce, the Pauline Privilege, and so forth, taken mainly from Ivo of Chartres; but they prefaced it with freshly harvested, hitherto little cited material from Augustine, which set the rules and regulations in a theological context. This fresh Augustinian material, which they must have drawn from florilegia, was devoted chiefly to two themes: the changing function of marriage in relation to sacred history, running from Paradise and Fall through the incarnation of Jesus Christ; and the three goods of marriage: offspring, faith, and sacrament. Endlessly elaborated, and often interpreted in ways that Augustine could not have foreseen, this fresh material provided a theological framework for understanding the place of marriage in the Christian life, in the integrity of the church, and in God's saving plan.

The authors went to great pains to show that marriage was a legitimate and proper way of life or estate (*status*) that was integral to the church, but they regarded celibacy as the normal and proper way to salvation after the advent of Jesus Christ. Marriage was an anachronism, a remnant of the Old Law, a puzzle for which they had to account. They justified it as a moral fail-safe for those who were not strong enough to cope with celibacy. It was the low road to salvation, permissible for those who were too weak to ascend the heights. This idea is nicely expressed in a gloss of the period on 1 Corinthians 7:9, which survives as an isolated *sententia* (freely translated below):

> 'It is better to marry than to burn' etc. One should distinguish between resistible desire and irresistible desire. By 'desire', I mean the burning [*ardor*] of lust. If it is resistible, it is not a reason for marrying; rather, it should be repressed. But if it is irresistible, then it is better to marry than to burn. For one is good, the other bad.[27]

The primary purpose of marriage in the sentential literature, therefore, was not collaboration or even procreation but *evitatio fornicationis* (the avoidance of fornication).[28] The Modern Masters considered celibacy to be the obvious choice for any Christian. This wholly remedial rationale for marriage waned during the thirteenth century, when theologians came to regard marriage as a legitimate vocation in its own right, albeit one of inferior dignity.

---

27. Oxford, Bodl. Laud Misc. 216, 145va = Lottin, *Psych. et morale* 5, no. 129 (p. 102): 'Item: Melius et nubere etc. Desiderium aliud evitabile, aliud inevitabile – desiderium dico ardor libidinis. Qui si fuerit evitabilis, propter hoc non est nubendum, sed reprimendus est. Si autem fuerit inevitabilis, tunc melius est nubere quam uri; hoc enim bonum, illud malum.'
28. Lottin, no. 401 (p. 102).

Considering themselves to be responsible for explaining and regulating marriage as a sacrament of the church, the Modern Masters struggled to work out the warrants and the implications of such responsibility. For example, they inquired whether infidels could marry at all (that is, whether such putative marriages were valid). According to one *sententia*, Anselm of Laon said No, but Ivo of Chartres and William of Champeaux said Yes.[29] The Modern Masters usually answered this question affirmatively, but the possibility of non-Christian marriage puzzled them and required an explanation.[30]

Again, as well as emphasizing, even celebrating, historical and regional variations in marriage law, the authors ask whether a marriage that the church dissolves exists before it is dissolved – and they answer affirmatively. If the impediment in question involves something repugnant to nature, then one can say that the marriage never existed. But if the impediment is historically adventitious and instituted by the church, as is always the case when a dispensation is possible, then the marriage exists until the church dissolves it.[31] Such speculations, I suggest, served to emphasize the power of the institutional church over marriage.

It would be anachronistic to refer to a doctrine of marriage as one of the sacraments in the sentential literature, but there was a new readiness to apply current sacramental theology and vocabulary to marriage and to illumine marriage by comparing it with other sacraments, albeit in a haphazard, opportunistic fashion. Most remarkable is the opening paragraph of the seminal treatise *Cum omnia sacramenta*, which will recur in the works of Hugh of Saint-Victor and Peter Lombard and in many subsequent treatises on the theology of marriage:

> Whereas all the sacraments originated after sin and because of sin, marriage alone is also said to have been instituted before sin – not as remedy, as the others were, but as an office.[32]

The passage illustrates several themes that are characteristic of the literature. Marriage is set in the context of sacred history, and in particular of the Fall. Hence, there is the distinction between the office (the duty to raise

---

29. Lottin, no. 406 (p. 287).
30. Lottin, no. 131 (pp. 102-03); Oxford, MS Bodl. Laud Misc. 277, 32vb-33ra; Oxford, MS Bodl. Laud Misc. 216, 139va-139vb.
31. *De coniugiis tractantibus*, ed. Bliemetzrieder, 76/16-77/8. *In primis hominibus*, ed. Matecki, 14*/13-15*/1, 30*/3-5. Hugh of Saint-Victor defends the same thesis in *De sacramentis* II.11.4, PL 176, 483B-484B.
32. *Cum omnia sacramenta* (1st recension), 129/24-27; *Cum omnia sacramenta*, 2nd recension, ed. Weisweiler, *Das Schrifttum*, 33/1-3. Cf. *Decretum Dei fuit*, ed. Weisweiler, *Das Schrifttum*, 362/5-6: 'Tunc autem institutum fuit ad officium generandi; modo ad remedium.'

children to worship God) and the remedy against lust, which is the most conspicuous sign that human nature is fallen. The distinction comes from a seminal passage in Augustine's *De Genesi ad litteram*.[33] And there is the possibility of multiple institutions. Most remarkable, though, is the fact that marriage is included among the sacraments as in a numerable category (as one of a class), although there is no indication of what the other sacraments might be or how many there are.

According to the same treatise, the 'reality' (*res*) and sanctity of the sacrament of marriage, which it confers or realizes as well as signifies, is the very fact that spouses are members of the church. To justify this claim, the author invokes the threefold division of Christians, noted above:

> Just as virgins through their virginity, and continents through their conti-
> nence, so good married persons [*coniugati*], through their legitimate union,
> are made members of Christ. Virgins occupy the supreme degree, continents
> the middle one, and married persons the lowest. These are [typified by] the
> three men who alone, Scripture says, will be saved, namely, Daniel, Noah,
> and Job, that is, virgins, continents, and married folk.[34]

Two treatises that were dependent on the *Cum omnia sacramenta* – the second recension of the treatise and the *Decretum Dei fuit* – reproduced this idea with minor modifications.[35] Such variations mattered little. The point was to situate marriage as an *integral* order within the church, but as the *lowest* order. One can see in this literature, then, how the authors used the textual resources available to them to set marriage in the context of a certain theological framework, which both explained it and justified their control over it. Along with the theoretical framework went a distinctive vocabulary and a set of oft-repeated sayings and phrases, largely Augustinian in origin, such as the distinction between office and remedy.

The layout of topics that the anonymous authors and compilers established endured in the theology of marriage as a sacrament through the subsequent centuries. Explanation of how and why marriage was a sacrament came first, with some account of the definition or essence of marriage, the role of marriage in sacred history, and Augustine's three goods. This part may have provided a framework for instruction of the laity and for sexual ethics, but its function seems to have been chiefly theoretical. It explained how and why marriage was a properly Christian vocation, and it justified the church's jurisdiction. Then followed the austerely practical section on

---

33.   Augustine, *De Gen. ad litt.* IX.7, CSEL 28.1, 275/20-21: 'quod sanis esse posset officium, sit aegrotis remedium'.
34.   *Cum omnia sacramenta* (1st recension), ed. Bliemetzrieder, 134/25-135/5.
35.   *Cum omnia sacramenta*, 2nd recension, ed. Bliemetzrieder, 276/28-33; *Decretum Dei fuit*, 367/1-5.

the rules and regulations, most of which was taken up with impediments and the valid reasons for divorce. (The second part was usually much longer than the first, for the rules were complicated.) Whereas the explicitly theological, more speculative part was subject to continuous debate and development throughout the Middle Ages and beyond, the regulative, more practical part changed little (except insofar as the rules had to be adjusted to fit legislative changes, for example following the relaxation of impediments at the Fourth Lateran Council of 1215). I am not suggesting that the theology of marriage was tacked on to the regulative material, without forming an organic whole with it. On the contrary, if the intrusive and overly complicated rules of canon law were the old way of marking out marriage as church territory, the new theological preamble established the context that made sense of that marking out.

The clergy's responsibility regarding marriage – their purview – was limited to the twofold task of explaining the place of marriage in the Christian life and upholding the rules and regulations. (They dealt with relational and sexual issues in the confessional, but the moral philosophy involved owed little to the theology of marriage.) Johann Gropper, a reform-minded cleric and assistant to the Archbishop of Cologne writing shortly before the Council of Trent, illustrates this point for us. Gropper had received no formal training in theology, but that was still not unusual: outside the mendicant orders, theology was an elite discipline studied by very few. Gropper explains that the parish priest's duty is twofold. First, he 'must teach the people about the institution of marriage, its sacramentality and sanctity, and thence about the right use of Christian marriage'. Second, he must advise the people 'so that anyone who wishes to be married should choose a partner with whom marriage is forbidden neither by divine nor by human laws, and with whom he might hope perpetually to lead a holy and indivisible way of life'. The second duty is more pressing, but it may surpass the priest's capacity. The impediments are so fraught with difficulty, Gropper advises, that in this matter, if in no other, the parish priest should be ready to refer questions to his bishop, who alone has judicial authority over marriage.[36]

5. The seven sacraments

The notion that marriage was one of the seven sacraments, as a distinct member of a closed and numerable set, emerged during the first half of the twelfth century. The set was always the same. As soon as theologians began

---

36. Johann Gropper, *De sacramento matrimonii*, from *Enchiridion christianae institutionis in Concilio prouinciali Coloniensi editum* (Paris: 1550), 192v.

to count the sacraments, they posited seven of them, which included marriage, although no one called marriage one of the sacraments or even counted them before the twelfth century.[37]

The term *sacramentum* always had a range of senses in Christian Latin, but in the sense that is most relevant here it had traditionally referred to the rites of a mystery religion. Isidore of Seville was using the term in that sense when he placed the sacraments in the context of a liturgy (*celebratio*). He went on to identify these sacraments as 'baptism and chrism, body and blood'.[38] This was a variant of the standard patristic list found both in the East and in the West. But was it really a list? Isidore may have been referring to three sacraments – baptism, confirmation, and eucharist – but chrism (a mixture of olive oil and balsam) was used for anointing in several rituals, including baptism. Grammatically, his description seems to enumerate either four single entities or two double entities. My point is that Isidore was not counting. Rather, he was thinking of material stuffs that took on special significance and spiritual power in a liturgical context: water, chrism, bread, wine.

The first extant reference to the set of seven appears during the 1140s in a treatise on the sacraments ascribed to a certain Master Simon. Soon afterwards, it appears in an anonymous treatise on the sacraments that is evidently dependent on Master Simon, as well as in the *Sententiae divinitatis* (also anonymous).[39] Peter Lombard, writing in the 1150s, proposed the same set of seven sacraments: 'baptism, confirmation, the bread of blessing (i.e., eucharist), penance, extreme unction, orders, and marriage'.[40] Partly because his *Sentences* became the standard textbook of theology in the thir-

---

37. It is often said in surveys and encyclopedias, even today, that Peter Damian (†1072) posited twelve sacraments, presumably because an eccentric treatise on the twelve sacraments by Nicholas of Clairvaux († after 1176), secretary to St. Bernard, was formerly ascribed to Peter Damian and published among the latter's works in PL 144, 897-902. See J. Ryan, 'Saint Peter Damiani and the Sermons of Nicholas of Clairvaux: A Clarification', *Mediaeval Studies* 9 (1947), 151-61 and J. Leclercq, *Recueil d'études sur saint Bernard et ses écrits,* vol. 1 (Rome: 1962), 47-82. Nicholas's sacraments are baptism, confirmation, the anointing of the sick, the consecration of a bishop, the anointing of a king, the dedication of a church, confession, canons, monks, hermits, nuns, and marriage (but not eucharist!), which correspond to the twelve crosses inscribed on the interior walls during the dedication of church.

38. Isidore of Seville, *Etymologies* VI.19.39.

39. See H. Weisweiler, *Maitre Simon et son groupe* De sacramentis (Louvain: 1937), 2, 82-83; B. Geyer, *Die Sententiae divinitatis: Ein Sentenzenbuch der Gilbertschen Schule*, BGPhMA 7.2-3 (Münster: 1909), 108-09; and É. Dhanis, 'Anciennes formules septénaires des sacrements', *Revue d'histoire ecclésiastique* 26 (1930), 574-608, 916-50, and 27 (1931), 5-26. Dhanis, at 26, 594 ff., seems to have been the first to notice the connection, although he assumed that the seven had first appeared in the *Sententiae divinitatis*.

40. Peter Lombard, *Sent.* IV.2.1.1, in *Sententiae in IV libris distinctae*, vol. 2., eds. PP Collegii S Bonaventurae (Grottaferrata: 1981), 239.

teenth century and the basis of many so-called commentaries (most of which were really summas that used his *Sentences* as a ground plan, although they originated in courses on this textbook), the Lombard's way of organizing sacramental theology became standard. First, one would discuss the sacraments in a general way (*de sacramentis in genere*). Then, one would discuss each of the seven in turn, with marriage almost always coming last: the greatest of the sacraments in signification but the least in dignity, as the masters often remind us. This plan located marriage within a certain stereotyped discourse. It both expressed and formed how scholastic theologians thought about marriage.

Whatever the origin of the seven may have been, Peter Lombard used it to organize the rich sacramental theology that had emerged during the first half of the twelfth century. Theologians had been exploring diverse paradigms and definitions of sacrament, some of which (such as 'sign of a sacred reality') embraced a wide, uncountable range of things. But Hugh of Saint-Victor, who was Peter Lombard's chief source for sacramental theology, resisted that approach. Writing in the 1130s, Hugh developed a salvation history in which the sacraments of the Old Covenant (the rituals, sacrifices, and offerings of the Mosaic law) foreshadowed and were superseded by the more powerful sacraments of the New Covenant. Hugh's treatise on the sacraments was in effect the first summa of theology, for in his mind the topic embraced the entire story of Christ's saving work from beginning to end. Hugh envisaged Christ as a king riding with his knights into battle against the Devil. Some knights (the Jewish patriarchs) precede the King into battle, with banners aflutter. Others (the Apostles) accompany Christ. And other knights (the clergy of the present age) follow after him.[41]

Hugh proposed a paradigm that could be applied, *mutatis mutandis,* to any sacrament worthy of the name. Not every 'sign of a sacred reality' is a sacrament, Hugh points out. A sacrament must involve three features: first, it must be a physical stuff that by its very nature represents a specific healing grace; second, it must have been instituted (typically by Jesus Christ) to signify that grace; third, it must 'contain' that grace as a result of its sanctification, typically by the priest who administers it.[42] Hugh used a medical simile to illustrate his paradigm. Christ is the physician, his medicine is grace, the sacrament is a phial or box containing the medicine, and the minister it the emissary – the paramedic – who brings the phial from the physician to the sick patient.[43] The theme of Christ as the physician of souls (*Christus medicus*) goes back to the early church[44] and is rooted in the New

---

41. Hugh of Saint-Victor, *De sacramentis* I.8.11, PL 176, 312C-D; Prol., c. 2, 183B-C.
42. Ibid., I.9.2, 317C-318B.
43. Ibid., I.9.4, 322A-323C; I.9.3, 320A-320C.
44. See R. Arbesmann, 'The Concept of *Christus medicus* in St. Augustine', *Traditio* 10 (1954), 1-28.

Testament, but Hugh's elaboration of the simile was typical of his period. In a similar vein, Peter Lombard used the parable of the Good Samaritan to introduce his discussion of the sacraments. The Good Samaritan is Christ, and the bandages, oil, and wine with which the Samaritan treats the wounded man are the sacraments.[45] Following the Lombard, the Fourth Lateran Council of 1215 likened the sacrament of penance to a consultation with a skilled physician (*peritus medicus*), who applies wine and oil to the penitent's wounds, and who has to ask the right diagnostic questions in order to apply the proper cure.[46]

These versions of the simile, with their whiff of professional practice, take us to the heart of the matter. The emergence of the sacramental system during the twelfth century was one aspect (arguably the central aspect) of the new emphasis on pastoral care, or *cura animarum* (the care and cure of souls). Instruction (*praedicatio*) was the other chief aspect. The pastoral trend in medieval Christianity attained something of a definitive culmination in the Fourth Lateran Council of 1215.[47] The institutions that we now think of as comprising scholastic culture – the cathedral schools, the universities, and the mendicant *studia* – existed chiefly to provide the necessary training of clerics engaged in such ministry, although they did much else besides. The classic treatise on the subject was the *Liber regulae pastoralis* by Pope Gregory I, but the sacraments were not included in Gregory's account of pastoral care, whereas they were essential to the pastoral work of the bishops, clergy, and friars during the central Middle Ages.[48]

Why *these seven*? Scholastic theologians came up with many ways to demonstrate the necessity of the list *a priori*, but their ingenuity would probably have been equally up to the task of showing why there had to be a different list, perhaps of six or eight sacraments, if that had been *quod erat demonstrandum*. To my mind, the most convincing scholastic demonstration as well as the one with the most historical verisimilitude is that of Thomas Aquinas, O.P., who posits corresponding points of correspondence between the *vita spiritualis* and the *vita corporalis*: baptism corresponds to carnal birth, and so forth.[49] Be that as it may, the list begins to make sense if

---

45. Peter Lombard, *Sent.* IV.1.1 (2:231).
46. *Conc. Lat. IV*, 21, in N. P. Tanner, *Decrees of the Ecumenical Councils*, vol. 1 (London: 1990), 245.
47. See N. P. Tanner, 'Pastoral Care: The Fourth Lateran Council of 1215', in G. R. Evans (ed.), *A History of Pastoral Care* (London: 2000), 112-25.
48. For a summary account of the flourishing of pastoral care in the central Middle Ages, see J. R. Ginther, *The Westminster Handbook to Medieval Theology* (Louisville: 2009), s.v. 'Pastoral Care', 141-43. Pastoral care during the central Middle Ages has become a major focus of interest over the last two decades, but the field has been limited by the lack of any adequate analysis of what the medieval field entailed and, in particular, by the vague assumption that it was more or less coextensive with what we mean by 'pastoral care' in America today, which is not the case.
49. Thomas Aquinas, *Summa theol.* III.65.1, resp. (Ottawa edition, 2847).

one construes it as assembling the chief, indispensible 'sacred medicines' with which the clergy practiced the therapeutic aspect of their craft. The consecration of religious and the anointing of kings are the most conspicuous absences, but these are explicable: the former, because it had nothing to do with priestly ministry to the laity; the latter, because, however interpreted, it would have been too problematic in the wake of the 'papal revolution'.

Why should marriage be included on the list? The inclusion must have owed something to incidental features of congruence, a matter of fit rather than of a common essence. Theologians considered marriage, like all sacraments, to be a remedy against sin, albeit one that contained a moral disease without quite curing it (1 Cor. 7:9). Again, theologians (following Augustine) were emphasizing that marriage, like all sacraments, had to be understood historically: it meant one thing before the Fall, another after the Fall, and yet another after the incarnation of Jesus Christ. Again, marriage was obviously a 'sign of a sacred reality' (*signum sacrae rei*), perhaps the greatest of all such signs (Eph. 5:22-33). And Augustine had used the term *sacramentum* to denote whatever it was about marriage that made it insoluble. Anyone who reads the sentential treatises on marriage can see how the vocabulary and the conceptual apparatus that evolved to explicate sacraments such as baptism and eucharist were readily applicable to marriage, without any sign of special effort or incongruence but also without any attempt to apply to marriage any definitive model or paradigm of the sacraments, or to identify a common essence.

It soon became evident, nonetheless, that marriage did not fit the paradigm easily. The opening statement from the *Cum omnia sacramenta*, quoted above, already notes that marriage was anomalous among the sacraments. They had been instituted as remedies to sin, but marriage had been instituted in Paradise, before sin. During the second quarter of the thirteenth century, theologians began to assemble objections to the inclusion of marriage. Albertus Magnus, O.P., was a pioneer of this technique, although he was not the first to use it.[50] The list of objections continued to grow over the following centuries, but the central problem, put simply, was that marriage did not *look* like a sacrament. According to the paradigm, a sacrament involved some specific stuff that became sanctifying when a minister uttered a prescribed verbal formula over it, which had been instituted by Jesus Christ. The role of the recipient in the act (with the partial exception of penance) was entirely passive: to receive the sacrament from the minister. Augustine had called the two aspects *elementum* and *verbum*, but scholastic theologians, beginning in the thirteenth century, preferred to construe them as

---

50. Albertus Magnus, *IV Sent.* 26.14, q. 1, in *Opera omnia*, ed. A. Borgnet, vol. 30 (Paris: 1894), 120-23.

matter and form, understood in a more or less Aristotelian manner. But there was no material stuff in marriage, and the majority view among theologians, despite wavering and occasional contrary voices, was that no minister or liturgical performance was strictly necessary for a marriage to be valid, sacramental, and insoluble. And although the spouses had to exchange consent, there was no prescribed, essential, inalterable formula, as there was with the other sacraments. Indeed, even non-verbal signs ('nods') would do, for example if the spouses were mute or did not share the same language. Again, a daughter did not have to say anything if her complicity with what her father said was apparently genuine. Discussion of such differences generated several interesting ramifications, some of which had practical consequences, but I cannot go into them here. Suffice to say that for the most part these objections were only dialectical. That is to say, most theologians used them not *assertorie*, to undermine the doctrine, but only as means to test the doctrine and to explicate it by eliciting informative solutions.

If the fit was awkward, why did twelfth-century theologians put marriage on the list, apparently without debate? Presumably because clerics had what we might call 'oversight responsibility' for marriage, and because the hierarchy was judicially responsible for marrying. The episcopate (whether collectively in councils or personally in the Pope) was the legislator, and the episcopal courts tried to enforce the laws. In that sense, at least, marriage fitted the paradigm of a tangible saving means dispensed by the church's ministers to the laity. Thus, Albertus Magnus, responding to the objection that there was no minister of the supposed sacrament, replied that in this case jurisdiction took the place of ministry, for the church's ministers made the rules surrounding the contracting of marriage.[51]

The assimilation of marriage to the sacraments shaped and altered the ways in which scholars thought about marriage, even apart from matters of grace and sanctity. I shall note one such difference here, partly because it presents a stumbling block to the modern reader of medieval theologians on marriage, and partly because it indicates one answer to my question: What were our theologians talking *about*? The definitions of marriage in Roman law and their Christian variants characterized marriage as a condition: a partnership, a *consortium*, a way of life. This seems to be true of the definition from Justinian's *Institutes*, which defined marriage as a joining (*coniunctio*) of a certain sort.[52]

---

51. Albertus Magnus, *De matrimonio* 1.2, ad 3, in the Cologne edition, *Alberti Magni Opera Omnia edenda curavit Institutum Alberti Magni Coloniense*, vol. 26 (Münster: 1958), 156b: 'ideo necesse est, quod quantum ad efficientia [matrimonium] dependeat a contrahentibus. Nihilominus intituta, secundum quae fit contractus, dependent a ministris ecclesiae'.

52. *Inst.* 1.9.1: 'Nuptiae autem sive matrimonium est viri et mulieris coniunctio, individuam consuetudinem vitae retinens'. Modern editions have *continens*, which has

Thirteenth-century theologians cited the definition from the *Institutes* more than any other, and they, too, characterized marriage as a *coniunctio*. But that term was at first equivocal. Some took it to refer to the act of being joined together, others to the enduring union that resulted. Bonaventure, O.F.M., seems to have been the first to have noticed the muddle and to have tried to solve it. Both the act of exchanging consent and the resultant bond (*vinculum*), he explains, can properly be called 'joining' (*coniunctio*), for marriage has both transient and enduring aspects. Bonaventure compares these respectively to the act of ablution and to the enduring character (a permanent 'seal' on the soul) in the sacrament of baptism. He pursues this analysis because he always regards marriage – even when defined as the 'joining of a man and woman' in Roman civil jurisprudence – as a sacrament: as the visible, outward appearance of an invisible, interior mystery. Just as baptism is an outward ablution that signifies an interior cleansing, he explains, so marriage is an outward joining that signifies the mystery of Christ's joining with the church.[53] Most theologians after the middle of the thirteenth century intuitively opted for Bonaventure's first alternative, assuming that the *coniunctio* posited in definitions of marriage denoted not the condition of being married but the transient act of getting married.

Likewise, when theologians after 1200 spoke of the 'sacrament of marriage', they were usually thinking not so much of the condition of *being* married as of the act of *getting* married, just as when they talked about the sacrament of baptism they were thinking of a rite conducted at the font. Duns Scotus, O.F.M., explained that whereas both the sacrament and the contract of marriage were things that existed only in the act of coming into being (*in fieri*), the marriage bond (*vinculum*) that resulted had enduring being (*esse permanens*).[54] Like the modern classes in childbirth that offer no instruction on how to raise a child, the medieval theology of marriage did not get beyond the threshold of married life. To my knowledge, the only theologian who proposed a different view of the sacrament was Robert Bellarmine, a post-Tridentine Jesuit († 1621). From the premise that a sacrament was an outward sign of an inward mystery or grace, Bellarmine deduced that both the visible act of getting married and the visible condition of being married (not the interior bond, which was invisible) might be construed as the sacrament of marriage.[55]

been variously translated, but medieval scholars usually have *retinens*, which they interpret rather literally as 'holding together'.

53. Bonaventure, *IV Sent.* 27.1.1, resp., in *Opera omnia*, vol. 4, eds. PP Collegii S Bonaventurae (Quaracchi: 1889), 676. Bonaventure makes the same point again in 27.2.1, resp. (679).

54. Duns Scotus, *Reportatio Parisiensis, IV Sent.* 28.un., in *Opera omnia*, Vivès edition, vol. 24 (Paris: 1894), 383.

55. Robert Bellarmine, *Controversarium de sacramento matrimonii*, contr. 2, c. 6, in *Opera omnia*, ed. J. Fèvre, vol. 5 (Paris: 1873), 57-59.

6. The question of grace

Whereas the Council of Trent determined that all seven sacraments, including marriage, conferred grace *ex opere operato* and anathematized any who denied it,[56] twelfth-century theologians had assumed, on the contrary, that marriage, unlike the other sacraments, did *not* confer grace. The point was uncontroversial and invariably presented as obvious, not debatable. Consider this vaguely paradoxical statement by Hermann, writing in the 1140s, at the very moment when marriage was being admitted to the seven:

> some [sacraments] are spiritual, others are not. The spiritual sacraments are the major ones, namely, those that avail to salvation. And yet there is one of those [spiritual sacraments] that does not look to salvation and yet is a sacrament of a great reality, namely, marriage. For to take a wife does not have any merit for salvation, yet it is conceded because [it obviates] an unfitness for salvation.[57]

Likewise, although Peter Lombard counted marriage among the sacraments of the New Covenant and stated that what distinguished the sacraments of the New Covenant from those of the Old was their power to cause the grace that they signified, he also said that whereas baptism was both remedial and grace-conferring, marriage was merely remedial.[58]

The position that Hermann and Peter Lombard exemplify remained commonplace and uncontroversial among theologians through the first quarter of the thirteenth century. Theologians of the period reasoned that marriage, precisely because it was merely remedial, was not supernaturally efficacious. They held versions of what I call the preventive theory, according to which marriage prevented the subject from committing sins that would otherwise have occurred (for example, in simple fornication or adultery), without conferring any positive gift or blessing upon the soul. Durandus of Saint-Pourçain, O.P., a fourteenth-century dissenter, provides a good illustration of the preventive model. Suppose that someone gives money to a pauper. The gift of money is 'a remedy for him, lest he be driven by poverty to steal', but it is not a sacrament, and it does not confer grace. In the same

---

56. *Conc. Trid.*, sess. 7, *canones de sacramentis in genere* 6 & 8, in N. J. Tanner (ed.) *Decrees of the Ecumenical Councils*, vol. 2 (London: 1990), 684-85. Ibid., sess. 24, *canones de sacramento matrimonii* 1 (754).
57. Hermann, *Sententiae*, c. 28, PL 178, 1938C.
58. Peter Lombard, *Sent.* IV.2.1.1 (239): 'sacramenta novae legis … sunt baptismus, confirmatio, panis benedictionis (id est eucharistia), poenitentia, unctio extrema, ordo, coniugium. Quorum alia remedium contra peccatum praebent et gratiam adiutricem conferunt, ut baptismus; alia in remedium tantum sunt, ut coniugium; alia gratia et virtute nos fulciunt, ut eucharistia et ordo'.

way, marriage naturally prevents sin, but only by retaining coitus within its proper setting.[59]

What is significant and noteworthy about the prevailing view during the twelfth and early thirteenth centuries is not that theologians held it (for it is easy to see why they did so) but rather that they did not consider it to be a problem. Later theologians argued syllogistically thus: All the sacraments confer grace; but marriage is a sacrament; therefore, marriage confers grace. Peter Lombard seems on a cursory reading to have accepted the premises but not the conclusion of this argument. But a generalization did not have to fit every individual member of the set. Theologians during this earlier period regarded the seven sacraments of the New Law as a functional set with respect to the role of the clergy in relation to the laity. They did not yet think of the seven sacraments as a genus with a common essence. Those theologians of the period, such as Peter Lombard's disciple Peter of Poitiers, who did remark on the apparent inconsistency solved it by denying that marriage was truly and properly one of the sacraments of the New Law. Christ only gave his approval (*approbatio*) to marriage in the gospels, they argued. He could not have instituted it then because it already existed before the incarnation.[60]

For reasons that are unclear, the consensus among professional theologians altered during the second quarter of the thirteenth century. Alexander of Hales was a pivotal figure in the development, although it cannot be attributed to a single person. After around 1260, theologians no longer maintained the preventive theory. It had become unacceptable. There were two major dissenters, however: Peter John Olivi, O.F.M. († 1298), and the above-mentioned Durandus of Pourçain, O.P. († 1334). Both conceded that marriage was a sacrament in some sense but denied that it had 'full univocity' (*plena univocatio*) with the other six sacraments. In other words, it was a sacrament only in a broader, looser sense.

Olivi's point of departure seems to have been his concern that virginity and marriage were estates (*status*) of the church that differed in dignity and merit but represented a common underlying virtue, as Jerome's model revealed. If virginity (i.e., any celibate vocation) was not among the sacraments, then neither was marriage; and vice versa.[61] Pursuing those possibilities, Olivi marshaled arguments to show that marriage did not have 'full un-

59. Durandus, *IV Sent.* 26, q. 3, §16, in *Petri Lombardi sententias theologicas commentarium*, vol. 4 (Venice: 1571), 368rb.
60. Peter of Poitiers, *Sent.* V, c. 14, PL 211, 1257D.
61. See D. Burr, 'The Persecution of Peter Olivi', *Transactions of the American Philosophical Society* 66.5 (1976), 1-98; D. Burr, 'Olivi on Marriage: The Conservative as Prophet', *Journal of Medieval and Renaissance Studies* 2 (1972), 183-204.

ivocity' with what he called the 'sacraments of grace'.[62] Some of these arguments were versions of the dialectical objections pertaining to matter, form, and minister, but Olivi also proposed that marriage did not confer grace *ex opere operato*.[63] Although Olivi later pointed out that he had been speaking for the sake of argument and not *assertorie*, some of his remarks were rash, especially his questioning of the biblical supports for the doctrine of marriage as a sacrament. He suggested that marriage was a sacrament in same sense as sacred signs such as the bronze serpent, the Tabernacle, the ark of Moses were sacraments.[64]

More remarkable than Olivi's inquiry was the reaction that it unleashed. In 1283, the Minister General of the order commissioned a team of Franciscan theologians to examine Olivi's work. They found several errors and doubtful points,[65] which they summarized in a document known as the *Littera septem sigillorum*. This was a list of the correct positions corresponding to Olivi's errors. Among them was this avowal: 'Marriage is a sacrament of the New Law that confers grace. To affirm the contrary is erroneous; to sustain the contrary is heretical; to doubt it is entirely forbidden'.[66] Olivi's position on marriage was one among several errors, but it was the only one treated as potentially heretical in the *Littera septem sigillorum.*

Durandus rashly revisited the same territory, although at first glance he seems to have had no particular motive for doing so other than his contrarian disposition and his dislike of Thomas Aquinas's work. He made two dissenting claims about marriage, insisting on the distinction between them. First, he argued that marriage did not have full univocity with the sacraments of the New Law (i.e., that it was not a sacrament in the proper sense). Second, he claimed that whether marriage conferred sacramental grace was still open to argument and not a matter of faith, although he declined to profess his own opinion. His argument for the second claim is an appeal to divided authority:

> As regards ... [the question, whether marriage confers grace], the jurists hold one position, and the theologians another. The jurists – who know the text of the decrees and decretals by which the view of the Roman church is expressed, and who have expounded and glossed the canons and decretals, and

---

62. Peter John Olivi, *Quaestiones de perfectione evangelica*, q. 6, arg. 24 & ad 24, in A. Emmen, 'Verginità e matrimonio nella valutazione dell'Olivi', *Studi Francescani* 64 (1967), 11-57, at 26 and 51-53.
63. His own term is not *ex opere operato* but *ex vi sacramenti*, which was equivalent if not synonymous.
64. Ibid., 54: 'Non ergo videtur habere aliam rationem sacramenti quam serpens aeneus vel tabernaculum seu archa Moysi, et consimilia: quod tamen ad praesens non assero'.
65. On this process and its consequences, see Burr, 'Persecution of Peter Olivi', 35-44.
66. G. Fussenegger, '*Littera septem sigillorum* contra doctrinam Petri Ionnis Olivi edita', *Archivum Franciscanum Historicum* 47 (1954), 45-53, at 51, no. 6.

some of whom have belonged to the College of Cardinals of the Holy Roman Church – hold that grace is not conferred in the sacrament of matrimony. [….] But modern theologians hold virtually unanimously that grace is conferred through the sacrament of matrimony unless the contractants present an obstacle, just as with the other sacraments, to which marriage is regarded as an equal in this regard. For in their view it is otherwise impossible to maintain that marriage is a sacrament of the New Law.[67]

Note the word 'modern'. Everyone knew that Peter Lombard implied that marriage did not confer grace. In Durandus's view, the doctrine was an innovation of dubious value. That said, although it would seem rash to question today a medieval scholar's account of the opinions of his day, there is reason for us to be suspicious. It is true that the canonists continued to maintain that marriage did not confer grace long after the theologians abandoned it, but the question was theological, not canonical.

What difference did the doctrine make? Why did the question matter? Whether or not one receives supernatural grace seems to be a major issue, but each of the other sacraments was surrounded by a context that gave meaning to the belief that it conferred grace. Baptism was a way of joining a community; penance was a way of unburdening oneself and moving on; eucharist was a communal, encouraging ritual; and so forth. It is less clear what the doctrine of conjugal grace would have meant to married folk, except perhaps to obviate any excuse for separation. William of Auvergne thought that he had found empirical evidence of conjugal grace (which he attributed not to marrying *per se* but to the priestly blessing) in what he had heard in the confessional. He could find no other way to explain why some vigorous, healthy young men were sexually cool toward their pretty wives.[68] Thomas Aquinas reasoned that conjugal grace gave spouses the ability to do what they had the just right (*facultas*) to do – namely, to procreate children – in a fitting way, without sinning: a comforting thought.[69] And Duns Scotus noted that married life was much harder than the religious life. Without grace, he reasoned, it would be impossible to sustain a lifelong marriage.[70]

I wonder, nevertheless, whether the question remained 'merely academic' – a matter of abstruse scholarly speculation – at least until Olivi, and possibly long after that. One fact that raises this doubt is the troubling absence of the topic in some summary accounts of what the clergy needed to know and to teach about marriage. For example, Bonaventure carefully discusses the question of conjugal grace in his commentary on Peter Lom-

---

67. Durandus, *IV Sent.* 26, q. 3, §§ 6 & 8 (Venice: 1571), 4:367v.
68. William of Auvergne, *De sacramento matrimonii*, c. 9, in *Opera omnia*, vol. 1 (Paris: 1674), 524bH-525aC.
69. Thomas Aquinas, *IV Sent.* 26.2.3, resp., in *Opera omnia*, Vivès edition, vol. 11 (Paris: 1874), 73b-74a.
70. Duns Scotus, *Rep. Par., IV Sent.* 28.un. (24:382b).

bard's *Sentences*,[71] composed in the 1250s, but he does not mention it in the chapter on marriage in the *Breviloquium* (c.1256), a compendium of theology that he wrote for his Franciscan students in Paris after completing the commentary.[72] Although Bonaventure's style here is uniquely his own, there is nothing as to content that could not have been written a century earlier. Similarly, there is no mention of grace when Guido of Monte Rochen discusses marriage in his handbook for parish clergy, composed in the 1330s. Guido explains how to get married and who can get married, and he discusses the impediments at length, but his explanation of the nature of marriage and its place in the Christian life is limited to perfunctory, commonplace accounts of the circumstances and reasons for its institution, the proper motives for marrying, and the three goods. Indeed, although marriage is located in the handbook as one of the sacraments, Guido says nothing about marriage precisely *as a sacrament*, let alone about marriage as a means of sacramental grace.[73] Such silences lead me to wonder (I would not put it more strongly than that) whether Durandus's doubt about the theologians' consensus arose not from a discrepancy between the two great scholarly guilds, canonical and theological, but rather from the fact that this staunchly maintained theological tenet had not percolated into pastoral care and parochial instruction.

Trent presented prelates and theologians with a new situation. The objections of Luther and other radicals both to the sacramental system and to the legal power and jurisdiction of the church had made the univocity of all seven sacraments seem to be a cardinal feature of the Catholic faith. The prelates frequently cited Durandus during their deliberations to show that even some Catholics had fallen into the errors now being taught by the Protestants.

7. Multiple realms

The inclusion of marriage among the sacraments of the church obliged theologians to regard marriage as a uniquely complicated sacrament, subject in principle to diverse laws or realms. Each of the other sacraments belonged exclusively in the church, whereas marriage existed among all peoples, even among infidels. Again, whereas each of the other sacraments of the New Law belonged exclusively to the New Law, marriage already existed under the Old Law and, indeed, at the world's beginning, in Paradise.

---

71. Bonaventure, *II Sent.* 26.2.2 (4:667-69).
72. Idem, *Breviloquium* VI.13 (5:279-80).
73. Guido of Monte Rochen, *Manipulus curatorum* (Paris: 1501?), 1.7.2, fols 59r-72r.

Theologians accounted for this complexity in several different ways. I can barely touch on the topic here, but I need to note a broad distinction between two kinds of approach. The Modern Masters of the sentential literature introduced the idea that marriage went through successive institutions (*institutiones*) at different moments in sacred history: in Paradise before sin, after sin, under the Mosaic law, under Christ, and so forth. The precise meaning of the term *institutio* in this context is not always clear. It usually denoted the introduction of some new practice or convention (one could not institute something that already existed), but it was also term a legal term, denoting a law, a regimen, or a regulative principle. Theologians continued to discuss these historically located institutions throughout the Middle Ages, but we can see in the work of Albertus Magnus and Thomas Aquinas the beginnings of a different way of construing the multiplicity of marriage: not in terms of a diachronic sequence of institutions, but in terms of a synchronic array of 'laws': natural law, civil law, and so forth. The term *lex* was used in these latter settings in a rather generous sense that included the New Law of Jesus Christ (also known as the Evangelical Law), as well as the systems and codes of law that legal scholars today would recognize as law.

Albert considers marriage in relation to four such laws. First, the natural law governs sexual procreation for the perpetuation of the species. Historically considered, this law was instituted in Paradise, but it did not end there. Instead, it underlies marriage and the law of marriage in any period. Second, the Mosaic law of marriage established rules about who can marry whom (i.e., the impediments). Third, the New Law of Christ regards marriage chiefly as a remedy against the wounds of concupiscence, making it efficacious *ex opere operato*. Fourth, the civil law of marriage fosters benefits such as the 'honesty' that attends the spouses' mutual consent to marry, the friendship that follows from marriage, and the mutual help that the spouses give each other in sharing the burdens of married life. It is chiefly in this last regard, Albert explains, that the philosophers, such as Aristotle, Aspasius, and Cicero, wrote about marriage.[74] Whereas the first three laws succeed one another historically, the fourth law seems not to belong to any historical sequence. The restriction of civil law to the non-procreative aspects of marriage is puzzling, though, for Albert (like Thomas, his pupil) insisted that the family was the basic building block of the state (the *civitas* or *polis*); and Albert's hugely influential account of the natural law of marriage in relation to the exigencies of procreation consisted mainly of a long quotation from Aspasius's commentary on Aristotle's *Ethics*.[75] That account construes marriage as the proper setting in which to raise human progeny.

74. Albertus Magnus, *IV Sent*. 26.14, q. 1, resp. (Borgnet edition, 30:121b-122a).
75. Albertus Magnus, *IV Sent*. 33.2, resp. (30:290). For the passage in Aspasius (translated by Robert Grosseteste), see P. F. Mercken (ed.), *The Greek Commentaries on*

Thomas Aquinas appropriated Albert's division when he explained the institutions of marriage. Thomas posits five institutions. Marriage was instituted in paradise as an *officium naturae* (i.e., for procreation); after sin as a remedy; under the Mosaic law as regards 'determination of persons'; under Christ as a sacrament of the New Law; and everywhere as an *officium civilitatis*. In the last respect, marriage is regulated by the civil law, which fosters its secondary, non-essential benefits (*utilitates*), such as friendship and mutual service.[76] Here, too, Thomas's fifth 'institution' cannot be identified with an historical event.

Thomas proposes a simpler division in his *Summa contra gentiles*, in the course of a quasi *a priori* demonstration that marriage is a sacrament. This division is primarily synchronic, although it could easily illumine the history of marriage. Thomas starts from the premise that marriage is always a means of perpetuating a human society in the way most likely to preserve and foster well-being. As the means to ensure perpetuity of the species, marriage is an office of nature and is subject to the natural law. As a means to achieve political goods such as the perpetuity and welfare of the state (*civitas*), marriage is subject to civil law. And as a means to achieve the perpetuity of the church, marriage is subject to the church's governance (*regimen*). In is because of this third aspect that marriage must be a sacrament, Thomas deduces, for whatsoever things are 'dispensed to the people by the ministers of the church are sacraments'. Furthermore, that is why the church's priests bless the formation of marriages.[77] Some took Thomas to be saying that the priestly blessing was necessary for marriage to be a sacrament, but his point seems to be rather that the church's judicial supervision of marriage may be subordinated to the broader category of sacerdotal 'dispensation'. Ministers dispense the other sacraments primarily by liturgical performance, whereas they dispense marriage chiefly by *regimen*, and only secondary by liturgical performance.

Neither Albert nor Thomas suggested that Christian marriage might enjoy a kind of 'dual citizenship', whereby it would be subject both to the secular law and to church law. They seem to have assumed instead that the church had assumed control over the secular dimensions of marriage that would otherwise be subject to civil law. Moreover, they probably considered civil law in these contexts not as actual secular jurisdiction but as an epistemic resource: the human wisdom embodied in Justinian's *Corpus iuris civilis* and in the politics and ethics of the pagan philosophers.

---

the *Nicomachean Ethics of Aristotle*, vol. 3 (Leuven: 1991), 182-84. On Albert's use of this source, see P. Blazek, *Die mittelalterliche Rezeption der aristotelischen Philosophie der Ehe* (Leiden: 2007), 123-32.

76. Thomas Aquinas, *IV Sent.* 26.2.2, resp. (Vivès edition, 11:72b-73a).

77. Thomas Aquinas, *Summa contra gentiles* IV.78, Marietti edition, vol. 3 (Turin: 1961), 388-89.

8. Marriage as contract and sacrament

The recognition that marriage was properly and univocally one of the seven sacraments, together with the dialectical objections to the doctrine noted above, brought to light a corollary: that marriage was a unique, hybrid sacrament. Theologians noticed that whereas each of the other sacraments was instituted in its entirety as a sacrament (eucharist was never a meal, for example), marriage had a fully human identity apart from its divinely instituted sacramentality. Thus, a twofold analysis of marriage as a human-divine institution became the key to understanding not only the difference between infidel marriage and Christian marriage but also the internal structure of Christian marriage.

Albertus Magnus and Thomas Aquinas showed that one could provide an adequate, complete rationale for marriage as a human institution that was necessary for natural human well-being, and in particular for the well-being of a state (Aristotle's *polis*), quite apart from its sacramentality. Commenting on Peter Lombard's *Sentences*, therefore, Thomas first treated marriage as an 'office of nature' and only then treated it as a sacrament – an imposed division that had no basis or precedent in the Lombard's text.[78] Moreover, Thomas characterized the human-civil aspect of marriage as the contract, in contradistinction to the divinely given sacrament. Theologians had characterized marriage (or marrying) as a contract before, but Thomas uses the term more frequently and consistently than hitherto, and always to characterize the pre-sacramental aspect of marriage.

The recognition that marriage had this dual identity as contract and as sacrament generated a fissure that would open up from time to time during the late Middle Ages and the Counter-Reformation. Thomas cleverly argued that what he calls the 'material contract' in marriage was related to the sacrament in much the same way as water was related to baptism.[79] But some theologians were inclined to regard the sacramentality of marriage as something like an accidental adornment or superadded bonus.

The latter idea may have generated the possibility that even Christian couples might be able to form the contract without forming the sacrament. For example, Duns Scotus and his followers reasoned that any sacrament of the church required a prescribed verbal formula. Failing that, there would be a valid contract but no sacrament. Such would be the case if two mute Christians married, since they could not utter the form. Just as a mute priest could not confect the eucharist, so mutes could not enter into the sacrament of marriage. The same would be true if the marriage was contracted *inter absentes* through intermediaries, or by an exchange signed letters. Such

---

78. Thomas Aquinas, *IV Sent.* 26.1-2 (11:67-75).
79. Idem., *IV Sent.* 27.1.2, qua 1, resp. & ad 1 (11:83).

couples might still receive grace to support married life (*gratia adiuvans*), but they would not receive grace *ex opere operato*.[80]

The possibility of Christian marriage *inter absentes* was a recurrent theme of such inquiries. Olivi argued that marriage could not be a sacrament properly so-called precisely because it could be contracted *inter absentes* (e.g., through intermediaries or in writing). For example, Olivi explains, the King of Castile's son validly married the King of France's daughter through intermediaries, while the former was in Castile and the latter in France. But a bishop cannot confer orders, confirmation, baptism, extreme unction, or absolution on persons who are in a far-off place, and a priest in Spain cannot confect eucharistic bread in India![81] Olivi overlooked the possibility that a marriage between absent Christians might be a valid contract but not a sacrament. During the sixteenth century, Cardinal Cajetan, too, argued that a marriage *inter absentes* (if they were both Christians) would not be a sacrament, illustrating his argument with the example of penance, but he drew a different conclusion. The crux, in his view, was presence (as in Olivi), and not the verbal form (as in Scotus). A sacrament presupposed personal reception (*passio personalis*). But Cajetan reasoned that such a marriage would be a valid contract, albeit not a sacrament. It could not be a sacrament unless the spouses plighted their troth face to face.[82] A merely contractual marriage between Christians would not be soluble, according to Cajetan, although its durability would fall short of the fully confirmed insolubility of a sacramental marriage. For example, it would easier for the Pope to dissolve a Christian marriage contracted through intermediaries than one contracted face-to-face, since the former owes its permanence not to sacramentality, but to the fact that it is established (*ratum*) in baptism as if in a root (*in radice*). It is 'radically' but not 'formally' established, therefore, whereas marriage contracted between believers in person is established in both ways.[83]

This theme – the separation of contract from sacrament – had a complex history with many variations, and I shall not pursue it further here. The above examples must suffice to illustrate the problems and possibilities that came to the surface when theologians regarded marriage as hybrid contract-sacrament.

80. Duns Scotus, *Rep. Par., IV Sent.* 28.un (24:384-86). See also idem, *Opus Oxon., IV Sent.* 26.un (19:167b-69b).
81. Olivi, *Responsio P. Ioannis ad aliqua dicta*, in D. Laberge, 'Fr. Petri Ioannis Olivi, O.F.M., tria scripta sui ipsius apologetica annorum 1283 et 1285', *Archivum Franciscanum Historicum* 28 (1936), at 374-75.
82. Cajetan, *De sacramentis matrimonii*, Q. 1, printed in the Leonine edition of Thomas Aquinas's *Opera omnia*, vol. 12, 370a.
83. Ibid., 370b.

9. Jurisdiction and the Christian commonwealth

There was obviously an intimate logical connection during the central and late Middle Ages between ecclesiastical jurisdiction over marriage and the doctrine of marriage as a sacrament. Insofar as marriage was a sacrament, it was necessarily subject to church law. Whether the inverse was strictly true was debatable. Durandus of Saint-Pourçain rejected the argument that marriage had to be one of the sacraments because it was wholly subject to ecclesiastical jurisdiction. Even if marriage was not a sacrament in any sense, Durandus argued, it could still be wholly subject to ecclesiastical jurisdiction, provided only that contravention of the rules was spiritually harmful but did not injure the *res publica* as such. In that case, marriage was a matter of individual conscience as far as the republic was concerned, but as a moral matter it could still be subject to church law (which was effectively unrestricted).[84] All sacraments were subject to church law, but not everything subject to church law was a sacrament. But that is an abstract argument. When one considers the matter in historical and cultural context, it is hard to see how the medieval church could have upheld its jurisdiction over marriage without counting marriage as one of the sacraments.

Did the theologians' distinction between contract and sacrament in marriage imply that Christian marriage was a dual citizen, subject to both secular and ecclesiastical jurisdictions? The simple answer as regards the period of this essay is No. As far as I am aware, no theologian who held that Christians could marry contractually without marrying sacramentally suggested that such a marriage would not still be wholly subject to ecclesiastical jurisdiction. That possibility emerged in the modern period in the trend that its Catholic opponents dubbed 'regalism'.[85] It is evident, though, that some theologians during the first half of the sixteenth century questioned whether the church's jurisdiction was exclusive. Johann Gropper notes at the end of his treatise on marriage that human and divine law are so mixed together that it is hard to separate them, and he expresses the hope that the much anticipated general council will explain which aspects of marriage pertain to which law, a project that should be 'light work' for such a body.[86]

Questions about jurisdiction were to the fore at the Council of Trent, with the German princes claiming Christian jurisdiction over their subjects,

---

84. Durandus, *IV Sent.* 26.3, §17 [ad 2c] (368b).
85. See A. Duval, 'Contrat et sacrement de mariage au Concile de Trente', *La Maison-Dieu* 127 (1976), 34-63; J. Denis, 'Evolution historique de la doctrine du mariage-sacrement à partir du XVIIe siècle', in M. Legrain (ed.), *Foi et sacrement de mariage: Recherches et perplexités* (Lyon: 1974), 50-59, at 55-56; and J. C. Murray, 'Leo XIII: Separation of Church and State', *Theological Studies* 14 (1953), 145-214, at 157-61.
86. Gropper, *De sacramento matrimonii*, 192v.

the English king claiming to be head of the English church, and so forth.[87] Moreover, Martin Luther, whose shadow constantly darkened the deliberations over marriage during 1563, denied that the church had any juridical or coercive power over marriage. Indeed, the original, radical version of the Lutheran claims took away from the church any coercive power over anything. There was but one sword.[88]

The last of Trent's dogmatic canons on marriage answered Gropper's question summarily: 'If anyone says that matrimonial cases do not belong [*spectare*] to ecclesiastical judges, let him be anathema'.[89] This canon had been in the first draft of the decrees, and it passed unchanged through the three subsequent drafts without attracting much debate. Nevertheless, those prelates who did mention it were nervous and more or less opposed to it.[90] The Bishop of Orléans touched on one anxiety when he proposed that the canon should be removed 'lest we seem too ambitious' and 'lest we annoy the secular [authorities]'.[91]

Three particular sources of concern came to the surface. First, some proposed that the matter was not suitable for the dogmatic canons, in part because marriage had not always been subject to ecclesiastical jurisdiction. This contention left open the possibility that the decree (*mutatis mutandis*) might be placed among the disciplinary canons instead, which would apply only where they were promulgated.[92] Second, some argued that the scope of the church's jurisdiction would need to be defined, and a division between spiritual and secular domains established. For example, the Bishop of Larino proposed that the canon should specify that it referred to 'matrimonial cases *concerning the sacrament*'.[93] Third, some wanted the canon to be more narrowly stated, for example by anathematizing those who suggested that church courts should defer to secular courts in marriage cases, or who held that secular law had precedence over ecclesiastical law, or who claimed that the church's jurisdiction over marriage was 'tyrannical'.[94]

---

87. J. B. Sequeira, *Tout mariage entre baptisés est-il nécessairement sacramentel?* (Paris: 1985), 169-70.
88. J. W. Witte, Jr., *From Sacrament to Contract* (Louisville: 1997), 47-53.
89. Sess. 24, *Canones de sacramento matrimonii* 12 (ed. Tanner, 755).
90. See G. Le Bras, 'La doctrine du mariage chez les théologiens et les canonistes depuis l'an mille', *Dictionnaire de théologie catholique* 9.2 (Paris: 1927), 2244-46.
91. In *Concilium Tridentinum*, Goerresian Society edition, vol. 9, ed. S. Ehses (Freiburg: 1924), 660/8-10.
92. See proposals by the bishops of Lleida (666/18), Elne (667/10), Nimes (667/41), Alife (675/11), Ross (676/6-7), Ales-Terralba (677/29), Ypres (669/24-25), and Namur (669/40).
93. 662/19-20, 672/31-673/1, 672/13-14. Italics mine.
94. Thus, the Patriarch of Jerusalem (666/32-33), the Archbishop of Barcelona (670/43), and the bishops of Ciudad Rodrigo (668/31-34), Città di Castello (669/4-5), Coimbra (673/15), and Otranto (688/32-34).

The most contested issue during the deliberations of 1563 was the invalidation of clandestine marriage, which all but a few prelates acknowledged would be an innovation. Here, the prelates fell into two irreconcilable parties. The majority (roughly two-thirds) held that the change was not only expedient but possible: that the church did have the power to make it. The minority (roughly one-third) questioned the expedience but maintained above all that the change was impossible, since the church had no power to alter the form of a sacrament once it had been instituted by Jesus Christ. I shall not attempt to summarize here all the issues that surfaced during the prolonged debate of this issue, which ramified in several directions, proceeded at a remarkably high level of theological acumen and erudition, and touched on some of the finer points of legal theory. The point I need to make here is that most prelates of the majority conceded that the church had no power to alter marriage *as a sacrament* but argued, nevertheless, that the church did have the power to alter the conditions of marriage *as a contract.* Thus, they held that the proposed change would not 'touch' the sacrament.[95]

Some of the minority considered that theory to be nonsense, but perhaps they failed to appreciate the subtlety of the argument, which ran as follows: When the contract of marriage became a sacrament of the New Law, it did not lose anything of its contractual nature, just as water retains its natural properties in baptism. Now, although any contract is primarily a result of the free choice of the parties, the very possibility of the contract (for example, regarding the capacity of the parties to enter into it) is regulated by the commonwealth (*res publica*) in the interests of the greater, public good.

The key term in the argument was *res publica*, which (as well as the distinction between contract and sacrament) recurs frequently in the record of the deliberations. For example, the Bishop of León argued that if the commonwealth could override individual interests to pursue the public good, how much more could the church do so, which was invested with 'supernatural power'.[96] Again, the Bishop of Lerus pointed out that Christian marriage did not lose its contractuality (*ratio contracti*) when it acquired its sacramentality (*ratio sacramenti*), and he argued that any contract is subject to the power of the commonwealth (*res publica*) insofar as it serves the larger public good. But whereas marriage outside the Christian commonwealth (*res publica christiana*) is a secular contract, it becomes an ecclesiastical contract in the Christian commonwealth because there it is also invested with sacramentality.[97]

It is not always clear whether the Christian commonwealth to which the prelates referred was the church or the Christian state, but the gist of

95. 650/29-32, 656/22-32, 663/25, 667/32-33, 675/40-42.
96. 665/23-25.
97. 661/8-14.

their case is clear. Since the commonwealth has power to change the conditions for the validity of marriage as a contract, the church, too, has this power, having assumed it either because marriage is also a sacrament, or, more simply, because the church is the superior authority in any truly (rather than heretically) Christian state. The latter line of argument is especially clear in a treatise that one of the leading prelates, Dom Pedro Guerrero, Archbishop of Granada, wrote to explain his position (which does not come across clearly in the recorded proceedings).[98] Since the decree on clandestine marriage (*Tametsi*) was not dogmatic but disciplinary, it was to have been effective only in regions where it was promulgated, namely, in all truly Christian states. It was here that the hierocratic interpretation of sacerdotal and royal power came into its own as the model for locating marriage.

---

98. Ed. J. L. Martín, 'El voto de Don Pedro Guerrero sobre el sacramento del matrimonio en el Concilio de Trento', *Archivo teologico granadino* 44 (1981), 147-219, at 161-66.

THE NATURE OF ALEXANDER III'S CONTRIBUTION TO MARRIAGE LAW, WITH SPECIAL REFERENCE TO *LICET PRETER SOLITUM*

Anne J. Duggan

1. Introduction

The search for Alexander III's 'teaching' on marriage has occupied historians for more than a century, and continues to excite interest. Based on a new approach to the making of 'decretal law', this paper will argue that the focus should be shifted from the hunt for a papal or Curial policy to consideration both of the broader scholarly and legal context and of the pressure from regional bishops and their increasingly learned officials for reliable interpretation of dubious points. Both features are particularly marked in the area of marriage law, where the interactive and consultative aspect of papal-episcopal relations is strikingly evident. There is no doubt that the opinions and judgments contained in Alexander's letters played an important part in the formulation of more consistent regulations for marriage, but I shall argue that the mechanisms of consultation and reception[1] played the principal role in determining not only which questions were raised but which answers became part of the legal tradition.

Alexander III (1159-1181) became pope in the wake of a major transformation in the way that law and theology were studied, taught, and ap-

---

1. In the sense of accepting and applying, which Yves Congar regarded as the characteristic mechanism for the implementation of papal definitions in the early Church: Y. Congar, 'Reception as an Ecclesiological Reality', *Concilium* (English edn) 8 (1972), 43-68, at 45.

plied. In both disciplines, the application of dialectic to the problem of contradiction in the tradition of texts transmitted through some five or six centuries produced lively debate about their interpretation, and this debate created uncertainty in the definition and application of ecclesiastical law or custom. In marriage law the scholarly disputes were exacerbated by diversity of local custom across the Latin West. As more and more marriage disputes came before episcopal courts, regional prelates found themselves confronted by conflicting arguments based on authorities assembled in Gratian's *Decretum* ('Recension II': 1140 x 45)[2] as well as the current teaching in the schools of Bologna, Paris, and elsewhere. Contrary opinions made for exciting debate in the lecture room, but local bishops and ecclesiastical tribunals needed authoritative guidance through what was becoming a labyrinth of contradictory authorities and controversial commentary.

I have written elsewhere about the way in which Øystein of Nidaros in the 1160s and Richard of Canterbury in the mid-1170s furnished themselves with dossiers of papal letters tailored to their particular requirements.[3] That list could be extended to include Eskil Christiansen of Roskilde and Lund,[4] who had been in regular communication with the papacy from at least 1138 until 1177, when he retired to Clairvaux,[5] as well as Absalon of Roskilde (1157/8-1192) and Lund (1177/8-1201),[6] and Stephen of Uppsala (1162-

---

2.   Below, n. 61.

3.   A. J. Duggan, 'The Decretals of Archbishop Øystein of Trondheim (Nidaros)', in U.-R. Blumenthal, K. Pennington, and A. A. Larson (eds.), *Proceedings of the 12th International Congress of Medieval Canon Law, Washington D.C., 2004* (Città del Vaticano: 2008), 491-530; A. J. Duggan, '*De consultationibus tuis*: The Role of Episcopal Consultation in the Shaping of Canon law in the Twelfth Century', in B. C. Brasington and K. G. Cushing (eds.), *Bishops, Texts and the Use of Canon Law in the Earlier Middle Ages: Studies in Honour of Martin Brett* (Aldershot: 2008), 191-214, at 194-98 (Øystein) and 202-04 (Richard).

4.   Bishop of Roskilde (1134-1137), bishop (1137/8-1153), and archbishop (1153-1177) of Lund: *Series episcoporum ecclesiae catholicae occidentalis ab initio usque ad annum MCXCVII*, Series 6/ii, *Lundensis*, ed. H. Kluger (Stuttgart: 1992), 20-28, with full bibliography; *Dansk Biografisk Leksikon* (1980 – 3rd edn), iv, 256-59; *Dictionnaire d'histoire et de géographie ecclésiastiques* 15 (1963), 884-85.

5.   Lund's primacy had been granted by Paschal II in 1104: *Series episcoporum ... Lundensis*, 17; revoked by Innocent II in 1133 during the Anacletan schism (1133-1138): *Series episcoporum*, Series 5/ii, *Hamburg-Bremen*, eds. S. Weinfurter and O. Engels (Stuttgart: 1984), 12-16, 39-40, although it is possible that the letters re-establishing Hamburg's primacy (PL, 179, 179-82 nos 137-41) were not accepted in Scandinavia, for Archbishop Asker of Lund (1089-1137) seems to have acted independently: *Series episcoporum ... Hamburg-Bremen*, 18-19; W. Seegrün, *Das Papsttum und Skandinavien, bis zur Vollendung der nordischen Kirchenorganisation (1164)*. Quellen und Forschungen zur Geschichte Schleswig-Holsteins 51 (Neumünster: 1967), 208-10; restored by Innocent II in 1138: Seegrün, *Das Papsttum*, 139-40; *Series episcoporum ... Lundensis*, 21.

6.   *Series episcoporum ... Lundensis*, 89-93 (Roskilde) and 28-33 (Lund). He was in Paris between 1146 and 1155 (*ibid.*, 90); K. Friis-Jensen and I. Skovgaard-Petersen (eds.), *Archbishop Absalon of Lund and his World* (Roskilde: 2000). For Absalon's continuing links with Paris, and especially Ste-Geneviève, whose abbot was the ca-

1185).[7] For all these prelates, and many others, the papal Curia was a source of support and advice. In addition to constitutional questions of Church order, they sought and received definitions, clarifications, and sometimes relaxations of the requirements of canon law in consideration of the needs of their own provinces. It was in a letter to Øystein, for example, that Alexander relaxed the consanguinity rules for the people living on an island more than twelve days' distant from Norway;[8] and in another that he commented that in ecclesiastical cases the more difficult questions usually arose in relation to matrimony (*quod difficiliores questiones, que in causis ecclesiasticis contingere solent, circa matrimonium emergere consueue-runt*).[9] In responding to such consultations and appeals, the papal Curia had to provide answers on an almost daily basis.

My intention in this paper is modest. By examining the four paragraphs on marriage questions which occur at the beginning of the eleven-point *Licet preter solitum*[10] addressed to Archbishop Romuald II of Salerno (1153-1181/2), probably in mid-1177, I hope to reveal the controversial questions which lie just below the surface of the letter. At the same time, I want to emphasize four critical aspects of this exchange between pope and prelate: that *Licet preter solitum* was a reply to queries raised by Archbishop Romuald; that the questions were posed in the knowledge of the latest canonical jurisprudence; that Alexander's replies were directed specifically to the archbishop of Salerno; and that they represented authoritative counsel rather than magisterial command. Although all eleven *responsa* were circulated across Europe almost immediately and finally received into the *Liber Extra* ('Gregorian decretals') in 1234, they were neither constructed nor received as general mandates.[11]

nonist Stephen of Tournai, cf. C. Vulliez, 'Études sur la correspondence et la carrière d'Étienne d'Orléans dit de Tournai (d. 1203)', in J. Longère (ed.), *L'Abbaye parisienne de Saint-Victor au moyen age* (Paris: 1991), 195-231, esp. 196 and 224-25.

7.   *Suggestum est nobis*, PL 200, 609-10, no. 634 (Benevento 8 Nov. 1169).

8.   *Decretales ineditae saeculi XII*, ed. and revised S. Chodorow and C. Duggan, Monumenta Iuris Canonici (MIC), Series B, 4 (Città del Vaticano: 1982), 149-51 no. 86, at 149. Cf. the similar concession to Stephen of Uppsala: PL 200, 849-52, no. 975.

9.   W. Holtzmann, 'Krone und Kirche in Norwegen im 12. Jahrhundert (Englische Analekten III)', *Deutsches Archiv* 2 (1938), 341-400, at 384-86, no. 2, at 385. For the dating of Øystein's decretals, see A. J. Duggan, 'The Decretals of Archbishop Øystein of Trondheim (Nidaros)', 498-99; A. J. Duggan, 'The English Exile of Archbishop Øystein of Nidaros (1180-83)', in L. Napran and E. van Houts (eds.), *Exile in the Middle Ages: Selected Proceedings from the International Medieval Congress, University of Leeds 8-11 July 2002* (Brussels: 2004), 109-30.

10. WH 620 (§a-d); JL 14091.

11. Below, n. 74.

2. *Licet preter solitum*

No date has been transmitted for this important *responsum*, but its dating and context can be reasonably well established from the *arenga*, in which Pope Alexander referred to his unusually heavy preoccupations (*Licet preter solitum et amplius solito [...] prepeditus*):

> Although we are more than usually [encumbered with various affairs, so that it is not easy for us to reply to anyone's consultations, nevertheless, however much we may be engaged on other things, we are compelled by that special favour which we feel towards you and by fraternal affection to reveal to you in these present letters what we think about those matters on which your prudence has consulted us.][12]

This language echoes the opening of *Quamuis simus*,[13] an important *responsum* sent to Bishop Richard of Winchester from Venice:

> Although we are [involved in many different matters and engaged with many different and weighty responsibilities, apart from our general obligation, the love and affection which we have for you compels us to reply to your consultations, lest we appear to leave undecided[14] those matters which your discretion wished to present to us for clarification.][15]

The similarity between the two *arenge* is so marked that one may conclude that *Licet preter solitum* and *Quamuis simus* were obtained at about the same time. Fortunately *Quamuis simus* was transmitted with a precise date,

---

12. *X* 4.4.3: Licet preter solitum *et amplius solito multis simus et uariis negotiis prepediti ita, quod non sit nobis facile aliquorum consultationibus respondere, illa tamen speciali gratia, quam ad personam tuam habemus, et caritate cogimur fraterna, quid sentiamus de his, super quibus consuluit nos prudentia tua, tibi, quantumcunque aliis simus intenti, presentibus literis aperire.* Text in italics (brackets in the trans.) was omitted from *X*, but supplied in Friedberg's edition. Note that all medieval Latin quotations have been restored to their medieval spellings: 'u' for 'v' and 'e' for 'ae'.

13. WH 761; JL 14156 (§§ a, b, d-f, h), 14152 (§c), 14154 (§g). On the letter, see C. Duggan, 'Papal Judges Delegate and the Making of the "New Law" in the Twelfth Century', in T. N. Bisson (ed.), *Cultures of Power: Lordship, Status, and Process in Twelfth-Century Europe* (Philadelphia: 1995), 172-99, at 178-80; rpt. with the same pagination in C. Duggan, *Decretals and the Creation of 'New Law' in the Twelfth Century: Judges, Judgements, Equity and Law* (Aldershot: 1998), no. I.

14. I am grateful to Dr Paul Brand for suggesting this translation of *indiscussa*.

15. *X* 1.29.6: Quamvis simus *multiplicitate negotiorum impliciti, et grauibus diuersisque sollicitudinibus occupati, nos tamen cogit preter debitum commune tue fraternitatis caritas et dilectio, qua personam tuam diligimus, tuis consultationibus respondere, ne videamur indiscussa relinquere que nobis enodanda tua uoluit discretio presentare.* Text in italics/brackets omitted from *X*, supplied by Friedberg.

'Given at Venice, on the Rialto, 21 July [1177]',[16] which places its issue just three days before the solemn reconciliation between Alexander III and the Romano-German emperor Frederick I outside St Mark's basilica on Sunday 24 July 1177.[17] Serious and complicated indeed were the pope's preoccupations during those July days! Moreover, since Romuald was the head of the Norman-Sicilian delegation which participated in the extended deliberations that produced the Peace of Venice, it is highly likely that he presented his schedule of consultations in person.

The first *consultum* (§a: *X* 4.4.3, *Licet preter solitum*, §*Consultationi tue*) concerned the vexed question of the rôle of consummation in the formation of the bond of matrimony:

> You have asked us whether, if lawful present consent has taken place between a man an a woman, not followed by *carnalis copula*, whether or not an oath was taken, the woman may marry another, or, if she marries another, and *carnalis copula* follows, whether she should be separated from him.[18]

The reply reads:

> On this matter, however, we reply thus to your consultation, that: If there was lawful present consent [made with the usual solemnity, in the presence of a priest or even of a notary, as observed in some places until now, before suitable witnesses], so that one clearly (*expresse*) accepts the other by mutual consent in the customary words (*uerbis consuetis*), each one saying, 'I take thee as mine', whether there is an oath or not, the woman is not allowed to marry another (*alii nubere*), and if she does marry, and physical union follows, she should be separated from him and compelled by ecclesiastical *districtio* to return to the first, although [others think differently] (*quamuis alii aliter sentiant*), [and] otherwise has it [also] formerly been determined by some of our predecessors (*aliter etiam a quibusdam predecessoribus nostris fit aliquando judicatum*).[19]

16. 'Dat. Venetiis in Rivo alto xii kal. aug.': *1 Cant.* 20 (*Cantuariensis prima*: London, Brit. Libr., MS Royal 10.B.iv, fols 42v-57v).
17. Boso, *Vita Alexandri*, in L. Duchesne (ed.), *Le Liber Pontificalis*. Bibliothèque des Écoles françaises d'Athènes et de Rome, 2nd Ser. 3, 3 vols (Paris: 1955-1957 – 2nd edn), ii, 397-446, at 439-40.
18. *X* 4.4.3: *Consuluisti nos siquidem, utrum, si inter uirum et mulierem, prestito vel non prestito sacramento, legitimus consensus interuenerit de presenti, carnali copula non secuta, liceat mulieri alii nubere, uel, si nupserit alii, et carnalis fuerit copula subsecuta, an ab ipso debeat separari* (all omitted from *X,* supplied by Friedberg).
19. *X* 4.4.3 (text in italics/brackets supplied by Friedberg): 'Super hoc autem consultationi tuae taliter respondemus, quod, si inter uirum et mulierem legitimus consensus *sub ea solennitate, quae fieri solet, presente scilicet sacerdote aut etiam notario, sicut etiam in quibusdam locis adhuc obseruatur, coram idoneis testibus,* interueniat de presenti, ita quidem, quod unus alterum in suo mutuo consensu uerbis consuetis expresse recipiat, utroque dicente: 'ego te accipio in meam' et: 'ego te accipio in meum', siue sit iuramentum interpositum siue non, non licet mulieri alii

Behind Romuald's question and Alexander's reply lay about forty years of sharp disagreement between the schools of northern France and Italy, principally Paris and Bologna, about the place of consummation in the formation of marriage. In the long tradition reaching back to Augustine and Ambrose which confirmed the primacy of the consent of the two parties to the validity of a Christian marriage, Leo I's response to Rusticus of Narbonne in 458/459 became critical. He had been asked if a daughter could lawfully be given in marriage to a man who had had a concubine. In his *responsum* Leo had said that she could, since concubinage lacked the nuptial mystery, that is, the sacramental bond between man and wife, marriage and concubinage were entirely different states.[20]

Thus, since the association of marriage (*societas nuptiarum*) was established from the beginning so that, apart from (*preter*) the union of the sexes, marriage should contain within itself the sacrament of Christ and the Church, there is no doubt that that woman [the concubine], in whom it is shown that there was no nuptial mystery (*nuptiale mysterium*) does not belong to matrimony.

In the full context of the question and answer, the meaning was clear enough, but once the statement was extracted and transmitted in collections of canons, the identity of 'that woman' became uncertain. Worse, as Jean Gaudemet demonstrated at Salamanca in 1976, by the beginning of the twelfth century the reading had been further falsified by the intrusion of the little word 'non' in some traditions of the text.[21] Worse still, that version was given wide currency by its presence in *Causa* 27 of Gratian's *Decretum*. There, *Questio* 2 opened with a recapitulation of the traditional doctrine that marriage was made by consent, citing the standard authorities from Isidore of Seville, pseudo-John Chrysostom, Nicholas I, Augustine, and Ambrose,[22] but then it introduced the contrary argument, attributed to no less an authority than St Augustine, that there was no matrimony without sexual union (c.16): 'Non est inter eos matrimonium, quos non copulat conmixtio sexuum....', confirmed by an even more emphatic variant of the

---

nubere. Et si nupserit, etiamsi carnalis copula sit secuta, ab eo separari debet, et, ut ad primum redeat, ecclesiastica districtione compelli, quamuis *alii* aliter *sentiant, et aliter etiam* a quibusdam predecessoribus nostris sit aliquando iudicatum.'

20. JL 544: Leo I to Rusticus, PL 54, 1197-1209, no. 167, at 1204-05: 'Unde cum societas nuptiarum ita ab initio constituta sit, ut preter sexuum conjunctionem haberet in se Christi et Ecclesie sacramentum (Eph. 5:32), dubium non est eam mulierem non pertinere ad matrimonium, in qua docetur nuptiale non fuisse mysterium.'

21. J. Gaudemet, 'Recherche sur les origines historiques de la faculté de rompre le mariage non consommé', in S. Kuttner and K. Pennington (eds.), *Proceedings of the Fifth International Congress of Medieval Canon Law, Salamanca, 21-25 September 1976*, MIC, Ser. C, Subsidia, 6 (Città del Vaticano: 1980), 309-31, at 322-30.

22. *Decretum*, C.27 q.2 cc. 1-3, 5-6, 9, 11-12 ('Recension I'); cc. 4, 7-8, 10, 13-15 ('Recension II'); cc. 4, 7-8 (*paleae*, added later in the twelfth century).

falsified Leo: 'Non dubium est, illam mulierem non pertinere ad matrimonium, cum qua docetur NON fuisse conmixtio sexus',[23] in which 'conmixtio sexus' was substituted for Leo's 'nuptiale mysterium', and this pseudo-Augustine was endorsed in c. 17 by the Leo excerpt itself, complete with the intrusive 'non':

> Cum societas nuptiarum ita a principio sit instituta, ut preter conmixtionem sexuum NON habeant in se nuptie Christi et ecclesie sacramentum, non dubium est, illam mulierem non pertinere ad matrimonium, in qua docetur non fuisse nuptiale misterium.

According to Peter Landau, Gratian received the false reading from Magister A. (perhaps Ailmer of Canterbury, † 1130).[24] From whatever source, Gratian accepted the authority of the false Augustine-Leo and interpreted Leo's 'nuptial mystery' as physical consummation. He then attempted to resolve what he saw as the contradiction in the ancient tradition by arguing that marriage was initiated in the spousal agreement – the consent – and ratified by physical consummation: 'Matrimonium sponsali conuentione initiatur, conmixtione perficitur'. Thus a marriage was *ratum* – ratified and indissoluble – only after physical consummation.[25]

Almost simultaneously, a more consistent teaching was being developed in the theological schools of Paris and Laon, under the influence of Ivo of Chartres († 1115) and Anselm of Laon († 1117).[26] This tradition emphasized the binding character of the consent of the parties and worked out a language to distinguish between engagement and marriage – in Anselm of

---

23. J. Gaudemet, 'Sur trois "Dicta Gratiani" relatifs au "matrimonium ratum"', in H. Wagnon (ed.), *Études de droit et d'histoire: mélanges- Mgr H. Wagnon* (Leuven: 1976), 543-55 (rpt. in J. Gaudemet, *Sociétés et mariage*. Recherches institutionelles 4 [Strasbourg: 1980], 379-91).

24. P. Landau, 'Gratian und die Sententiae Magistri A.', in H. Mordek (ed.), *Aus Archiven und Bibliotheken. Festschrift für Raymund Kottje zum 65 Geburtstag* (Frankfurt am Main: 1992), 311-26, at 313. Ivo of Chartres, *Decretum*, 8.74, had transmitted the correct reading (Martin Brett's draft online edn; cf. PL 161, 566-600), although the intrusive 'non' is found in three MSS of the *Panormia* (attributed to Ivo), 6.23, in Bruce Brasington's draft online edn. Its presence in the printed text in Migne (PL 161, 1248) was an editorial insertion based on Gratian's text made by *Panormia*'s first editor (Sébastien Brant) in 1499, and adopted by Brant's successors. Ivo's authorship of the *Panormia* is doubtful: C. Rolker, *Canon Law and the Letters of Ivo of Chartres* (Cambridge: 2010), esp. 265-72, 'De falsa credita Ivonis Panormia'.

25. *Decretum*, C.27 q.2 c.37 (heading); cf. C.27 q.2 *dictum ante* c. 35: 'Coniugium desponsatione initiatur, commixtione perficitur [...] inter sponsum et sponsam coniugium est, sed initiatum; inter copulatos est coniugium ratum.' This argument was used by Mabel de Francheville in the Anstey case: *The Letters of John of Salisbury*, in *The Early Letters*, ed. and trans. W. J. Millor and H. E. Butler, revised C .N. L. Brooke, Nelson's Medieval Texts (London: 1955; reissued, Oxford: 1986), 231.

26. Fransen, 'La formation', 111-17.

Laon's terms, between the pledge to make a contract (*fides pactionis*) and the pledge of consent itself (*fides consensus*).[27] In the mid- to late 1130s in Paris,[28] Hugh of St-Victor concluded, against the opinions of 'quidam' (probably Gratian and his followers) that a true marriage and a true sacrament of marriage existed, even if no sexual union followed: 'Conjugium tamen verum, et verum conjugii sacramentum esse, etiam si carnale commercium non fuerit subsecutum';[29] and even that clandestine marriages were valid if both parties declared them publicly: 'Tunc siquidem voluntas propria suffragatur et vota legitima succurrunt, cum id quod in occulto fecerunt sponte utrique in manifesto profitentur'.[30] Following a different extract from Leo I, supported by citations from Ambrose and Isidore, he declared that marriage *(coniugium)* was made by the lawful consent lawfully made by a man and woman to observe a shared companionship for life.[31] The effect of the consent was immediate, whether or not consummation followed:

> we say that marriage exists from the moment when such consent is made between a man and a woman, so that even if carnal union follows, nothing more is added to the sacrament of marriage.[32]

He then went on to develop what became the classic distinction between an espousal that promised marriage in the future and one by which sacramental marriage was effected immediately.

> To promise to do something is very far from doing something. He who promises does not do, but he who does already does what he does. [...] Therefore he who promises that he will take a wife has not yet taken a wife, and she who promises that she will marry has not yet married, nor is she yet a wife, but ought to be in the future.[33]

The existence of pre-existing promises could not invalidate later actual marriages, nor could subsequent actions invalidate

27. Fransen, 'La formation', 113, citing F. L. Ganshof, 'Note sur deux textes de droit canonique dans le "Liber Floridus"', in *Etudes d'histoire du droit canonique dédiés à Gabriel le Bras* 1 (Paris: 1965), 105-15.
28. D. van den Eynde, *Essai sur la succession et la date des écrits de Hugues de Saint-Victor*, Spicilegium Pontificii Athenaei Antoniani 13 (Rome: 1960), 100-03.
29. *De sacramentis,* xi.3 (PL 176, 482).
30. *De sacramentis,* xi.6 (PL 176, 489).
31. *De sacramentis,* xi.4 (PL 176, 484-85).
32. *De sacramentis,* xi.5 (PL 176, 485).
33. *De sacramentis,* xi.5 (PL 176, 486). For the argument that the idea originated with Anselm of Laon († 1117), see H. J. F. Reinhardt, *Die Ehelehre der Schule des Anselm von Laon. Eine theologie- und kirchenrechtsgeschichtliche Untersuchung zu den Ehetexten der frühen Pariser Schule des 12. Jahrhunderts* (Münster: 1974), 78-86.

the sacrament of marriage [...] confirmed by the testimony of present consent, because whatever follows such consent in another association, even with carnal congress or the procreation of children, should be wholly null.[34]

It was the present lawful consent of the parties alone that made a sacramental marriage. All other customs, including the exercise of parental power, the bestowal of a ring, the giving of dowry or dower by father or husband, and priestly blessing, were secondary.[35] And Hugh even gave an example of the words of binding present consent:

> When he says, 'I take thee as mine, that thou mayst be my wife and I in turn thy husband', and she similarly says, 'I take thee as mine, that I may be thy wife and thou in turn my husband', or something similar, in which even if they do not use the same words, they nevertheless take them to mean this.[36]

This line of argument reached its culmination in the work of Peter Lombard, also in Paris, whose *Sentences* comprise a survey of Christian theology. Writing between 1155 and 1158 in the full knowledge of Gratian's 'Recension II', he, like Hugh of St-Victor, distinguished between engagement and marriage[37] and confirmed the binding quality of present consent, whether or not preceded or followed by consummation: 'Efficiens autem causa Matrimonii est consensus, non quilibet, sed per verba expressus, nec de futuro, sed de presenti.'[38] Meanwhile, Pope Innocent II had issued an important *consilium* to Henry of Winchester between 1138 and 1141 in the Sackville marriage case. Innocent declared the validity of the first of William de Sackville's two marriages in words which suggested that present consent was the determining factor:

---

34. *De sacramentis,* xi. 5 (176, 486).
35. *De sacramentis,* xi. 5 (PL 176, 487). Pope Nicholas I (858-867) had listed such customs in the schedule of 106 *responsa* relating to Catholic practices which he sent to the Bulgarian prince Boris I in 866. Emphasizing that the consent of the parties was sufficient, he described such solemnities desirable but not absolutely necessary, especially where the poor could not afford them: 'peccatum autem esse, si hec cuncta in nuptiali foedere non interveniant, non dicimus' (PL 119, 978-1016, no. 97, at 980).
36. *De sacramentis,* xi. 5 (PL 176, 488).
37. Peter Lombard, *Sententiarum libri quatuor,* 4.26-37 (PL 192, 908-32), at 4.27.9 (PL 192, 913). For the modern edition, see *Magistri Petri Lombardi Parisiensis Episcopi, Sententie in IV Libris Distinctae,* 2 vols, Spicilegium Bonaventurianum 5 (Grottaferrata: 1981).
38. Peter Lombard, *Sententiarum,* 4.27.3 (PL 192, 910-11).

> Because lawful consent had taken place, I declare that the woman [...] became a wife from the moment she consented by voluntary agreement (*spontanea pactione*) to be a wife. For it was not promised for the future, but confirmed in the present (*Non enim futurum promittebatur, sed presens firmabatur*).[39]

Although the consent theory was gaining ground, the dispute remained undecided. In Bologna, Rufinus sprang fiercely to the defence of the Master's teaching in 1164,[40] and the question was further invigorated by the appearance of a new authority, attributed to Pope Benedict VIII (1012-1024), which ridiculed the idea that mere words could make a couple one flesh and thus create the permanent bond of marriage.[41] This newly minted authority

39. *Super eo quod*: WH 1016; JL 8274; *App.* 6.31, from the version in Henry of Winchester's *Nouerit discretio* to Theobald of Canterbury: L. Voss, *Heinrich von Blois Bischof von Winchester (1129-71)* (Berlin: 1932), 166-67 no. 7a; *English Lawsuits*, II, 387-88 no. 408A. Cf. Richard of Anstey's appeal: *English Lawsuits*, II, 387-95 no. 408B at 389; *The Letters of John of Salisbury*, i, 227-37 no. 131, at 228-29. C. Donahue, Jr. challenged the authenticity of *Non enim* [...] *firmabatur* in 'Johannes Faventinus on Marriage (With an Appendix Revisiting the Question of the Dating of Alexander III's Marriage Decretals)', in W. P. Müller and M. E. Sommar (eds.), *Medieval Church Law and the Origins of the Western Legal Tradition: A Tribute to Kenneth Pennington* (Washington D.C.: 2006), 179-97; cf. A. J. Duggan, 'The Dauvillier-Donahue Theory', forthcoming in 'Master of the Decretals: A Reassessment of Alexander III's Contribution to Canon law', in P. D. Clarke and A. J. Duggan (eds.), *Pope Alexander III (1159-81). The Art of Survival* (Farnham: 2012), chapt. 13, at 388-92.

40. *Die Summa decretorum des Magister Rufinus*, ed. H. Singer (Paderborn: 1902; rpt. 1963), 440-42, attacking the 'inanis glorie aucupes' (440-41) who had dared to oppose Gratian on this point. For a beautiful translation of the passage, which he thinks, probably rightly, was directed against Peter Lombard, see Donahue, 'Johannes Faventinus on Marriage', 181-82, although he allows that some unidentified Bolognese master or masters might have been the target. In support of the consummation theory, Rufinus may even have forged the decretal *Si de uniuersis,* attributed to Alexander I, pope and martyr (?109-?119), cited *Summa ... Rufinus*, 448-49; cf. Singer's introduction, *ibid.*, cviii and n. 70. That 'authority' appears also in the *Summa* of Johannes Faventinus (J. F. von Schulte, 'Die Rechtshandschriften der Stiftsbibliotheken von Göttweig, Heiligenkreuz, Klosterbeuburg, Melk, Schotten in Wien', *Sitzungsberichte der kais. Akademie der Wissenschaften in Wien, Phil.-hist. Klasse* 57 [1867 (1868)], 559-616, at 589, 590) and in *Lipsiensis* 59.6.

41. *Lex diuine*: JL 3773; WH 610. Appendices to Gratian, e.g.: Graz, Univ.-Bibl., III.69, fols 283v-284v, no. 10; Harvard Law Library, MS 64, last two folios, no. 25; cf. *Decretum*, C.27 q.2 c.18 (*palea*), '[...] non aliter uirum et mulierem posse fieri unam carnem, nisi carnali copula sibi cohereant. Qui ergo nequaquam mixtus est extranee mulieri federe nuptiali, quo pacto per nuda sponsionis uerba possunt una caro fieri, nullatenus ualemus intueri. Propinquitas enim sanguinis uerbis dicitur, non uerbis efficitur.' Weigand noted it in 20 *Decretum* MSS: R. Weigand, 'Die Fälschungen als Paleae im Dekret Gratians', in H. Fuhrmann (ed.), *Fälschungen im Mittelalter,* ii: *Gefälschte Rechtstexte der bestrafte Fälscher.* MGH Schriften 33 (Hannover: 1988), 301-18, at 313 and n. 54. Huguccio commented (1188 x 90), 'Hec palea uidetur multum contraria eis que diximus' (Bibliotheca Apostolica Vaticana, ms Vat. lat. 1280, fol. 271vb).

circulated in some copies of Gratian in the 1160s and 1170s and was accepted as a *palea* in the vulgate edition.[42]

It seems to me that Romuald of Salerno's first question in *Licet preter solitum* was prompted by this debate, which the concoction of 'Benedict VIII' had re-ignited. Instead of waiting for the schools to work out a solution, the archbishop sought and received a clear *responsum* from Pope Alexander tailored to the form of the question.

Consultant and respondent were fully aware of the intellectual and legal background. Alexander's Curia used Gratian's *Decretum* on a daily basis and the work was already widely distributed across the whole of Europe,[43] but they were also aware of the current debates in the schools. It is likely, indeed, that Romuald cited Gratian's authorities: 'Augustine' and 'Leo' and the newly added 'Benedict', as well as the supporting opinions, and it was to these that the *responsum* alluded in its conclusion: 'although others think differently and otherwise also has it formerly been judged by some of our predecessors (*quamvis alii aliter sentiant, et aliter etiam a quibusdam predecessoribus nostris sit aliquando iudicatum*)'.

The second question (§b: *X* 3.32.2, *Verum post* [*illum*] *consensum*), supplementary to the first, was equally informed by the ambiguities in the *Decretum*. Although Gratian arrayed a chain of authorities (*Decretum*, C.27 q.2 cc.19-26) to demonstrate that 'what God has joined no man should put asunder', so that although the parties can choose mutually to enter religion, neither can do so without the other's consent because they have become one flesh, and if they do they are to be restored to their spouses,[44] the *dictum post* c.26 appended the exception that '*Sponsi* can observe continence, even

---

42. Writing in England between 1166 and 1170 in the context of this debate, the Roman legist Vacarius wrote that it was the lawful union of husband and wife, not their physical union, that made them one flesh: *Magistri Vacarii Summa de matrimonio*, ed. F. W. Maitland (London: 1898), 23, §20 (rpt. from the *Law Quarterly Review* 13 ([1897], 133-43 and 270-87, at 279): 'Et ita duo non commixtione carnali sed coniunctione legitima sunt una caro'. His treatment of the contradictions in the canonical tradition cannot be treated here, but after examining the pseudonymous Augustine, Leo, Benedict, and others (23-5, §§21-23; *LQR* 279-81), he concluded (25, §23 *ad fin.*; *LQR* 281) that the 'more learned fathers of the Church (*periciores auctores ecclesie*) had the better argument when they taught that 'consent alone constitutes marriage, as long as each accepted the other (*quod solo consensu fiat coniugium, dum se mutuo accipiunt*), an opinion which accords with reason and the civil law (*que sententia et rationi congruit et iuri ciuili*).

43. M. Pacaut, *Alexandre III: Étude sur la conception du pouvoir pontifical dans sa pensée et dans son oeuvre* (Paris: 1956), 313-36; P. Landau, 'Gratian and the *Decretum Gratiani*', in W. Hartmann and K. Pennington (eds.), *The History of Medieval Canon Law in the Classical Period, 1140-1234. From Gratian to the Decretals of Pope Gregory IX* (Washington D.C.: 2008), 22-54, at 48-49: the decade 1150-1160 witnessed the beginning of a Europe-wide reception which reached its apex by about 1180.

44. *Decretum*, C.27 q.2 cc.19-26.

without consulting those they have espoused (*quas sibi desponsauerunt*)',[45] supported by cc. 27 and 28 (attributed to Popes Eusebius (falsely) and Gregory I (597-604).[46] Following these, the *dictum post* c.28 explained that the fact that *sponsi* could unilaterally take vows of continence or enter a religious community proved that they were not married: 'patet, quod inter sponsum et sponsam coniugium non est', and referred back to the pseudo-Augustine and pseudo-Leo (cc. 16 and 17), which concerned marriage, not betrothal, so that it appeared to support his consummation theory.

Gregory's original letter had referred to an engaged woman (*desponsata*), citing the 'legal decrees (*decreta legalia*)' which allowed *sponsi* to adopt the religious life without penalty. In permitting either or both *sponsi* to enter a monastery, the *Codex Justinianus* 1.3.54.3 required only that the *sponsa* returned the *arra* which the *sponsus* had conferred on her in contemplation of a future marriage.[47] In Justinianic law the difference between *sponsalia* (engagement) and *matrimonium* or *nuptiae* (marriage) was clearly delineated[48] in a manner not very different from Anselm of Laon, Hugh of St-Victor, and Peter Lombard: an engagement was not a marriage, and could be rescinded by either or both parties. Pope Alexander, indeed, confirmed as much in response to a consultation presented in person by Bishop Bartholomew of Exeter in November 1164. Promises to marry, even those sealed with an oath, were not binding. The parties should be advised to keep their promises, but:

> If they are unwilling to accept one another, it seems that this [breach of promise] can be tolerated [...] lest worse should happen – for instance, that someone should marry a person whom he/she will always hate.[49]

45. *Decretum*, C.27 q.2 d.p.c.26: 'Sponsi uero, etiam inconsultis, quas sibi desponsauerunt [...] continentiam posse seruare.'
46. The 'Eusebius' (c.27) is falsely attributed; that to Gregory I (c.28) is authentic: PL 77, 876-77, vii. 23.
47. *Codex* 1.3.54 §3: 'si quis sponsus vel sponsa desideraverit saeculi istius vitam contemnens in sanctimonialium conversatione vivere, sponsus quidem omnia, quae ararum nomine futuri causa coniugii dedisset, sine ulla imminutione recipiat, sponsa autem non duplum, sicut hactenus, sed hoc tantum sponso restituat, quod ararum acceperat nomine, et nihil amplius reddere compellatur, nisi quod probata fuerit accepisse.' The following *lex* allowed married persons unilaterally to enter religion: 1.3.54 §4.
48. *Digest* 23.1.1: 'Sponsalia sunt mentio et repromissio nuptiarum futurarum (Sponsalia are the promise and the counterpromise for a future marriage)'; *Digest* 23.2.1: 'Nuptiae sunt coniunctio maris et feminae et consortium omnis vitae, divini et humani iuris communicatio'.
49. *Super eo quod*, §c: WH 1013; *X* 4.1.2 (attributed to Innocent III!): 'Si autem se adinuicem admittere noluerint; ne forte deterius inde contingat, ut talem scilicet ducat, quam *semper* odio habet: uidetur, quod [...] hoc possit in patientia tolerari.' For the letter, cf. C. Duggan, 'Decretals of Alexander III to England', in F. Liotta (ed.), *Miscellanea Rolando Bandinelli, Papa Alessandro III*. Accademia Senesi degli Intronati (Siena: 1986), 85-151, at 104-05 no. 82; rpt. with the same pagina-

Although the distinction between engagement and marriage was generally established by the end of Alexander's pontificate,[50] and long engagements were not uncommon,[51] some confusion remained. At different times and in different places *sponsus/sponsa* could mean either an engaged or a married person, and one of Alexander III's late decretals used all three words, *coniugium, matrimonium, sponsalia*, for marriage.[52] In Gratian's hands, as we have seen, Gregory I's betrothed woman (*desponsata*) became a married woman, and her freedom to repudiate her betrothal to enter a monastery in Naples was interpreted to imply that no marriage existed between a man and wife until physical union had occurred – an interpretation supported by cross-reference to the pseudo-Augustine and pseudo-Leo.

How much of this ambiguity was understood by either the pope or the archbishop is uncertain. It is highly likely, however, that Romuald wanted an authoritative rebuttal of Gratian's inference. Alexander's response that after lawful present consent one party could enter a monastery leaving the other free to re-marry if marital relations had not taken place, because they had not become one flesh,[53] went some way towards solving the dilemma, but the solution was at best paradoxical. In this case, Alexander and his advisers may have been swayed by the authority of the Gregorian text, as transmitted by Gratian, in the mistaken belief that it referred to a married woman and not to a fiancée, and explained the dissolution of the bond of matrimony with the pseudo-Benedict argument that the couple did not become one flesh until they had been joined in sexual union.

Contradictions in Gratian also lay behind the third question posed by Romuald (§c; *X* 4.11.1, *Utrum autem filii*): Could the sons and daughters of co-sponsors marry one another, whether born before or after their parents

---

tion in Duggan, *Decretals and the Creation of 'New Law'*, no. III. For the date, see A. J. Duggan, 'The Effect of Alexander III's "Rules on the Formation of Marriage" in Angevin England', *Anglo-Norman Studies* 33 (2011), 1-22, at 9 n. 45.

50. Book VI of the *Appendix Concilii Lateranensis* (*c.* 1179-1184) was entitled, 'De sponsalibus et matrimonio contrahendo uel jam contracto', and *Compilatio prima* (1189-1190) and the *Liber Extra* (1234) opened their Book IV on matrimony with the title 'De sponsalibus et matrimonio'.

51. The three younger sons of Henry II of England had very long engagements: Richard and Alice of France, more than 20 years (1169-1191), but no marriage ensued; Geoffrey and Constance of Brittany, 15 years (1166-1181), before their marriage in 1181; John and Isabella of Gloucester, 13 years (1176-1189), before their short-lived marriage in 1189.

52. *Solet frequenter* (to Archbishop Roger of York): WH 990; JL 14162; *1 Comp.* 4.4.(4); cf. Duggan, 'Decretals of Alexander III', 143 no. 990.

53. *Licer preter solitum*, §b: 'Verum post *illum* consensum legitimum de presenti licitum est alteri, altero etiam repugnante eligere monasterium, sicut *etiam* sancti quidam de nuptiis uocati fuerunt, dummodo carnalis commixtio non interuenerit inter eos, et alteri remanenti, si commonitus continentiam seruare noluerit, licitum est ad secunda uota transire, quia, quum non fuissent una caro simul effecti, satis potest unus ad Deum transire, et alter in seculo remanere.'

became spiritually related through sponsorship?[54] Just as familial relationship was a bar to matrimony, so was the spiritual relationship established
when a man or a woman raised a child from the sacred font at baptism or
'stood behind' an adolescent at confirmation. If two or more persons performed this function together, they became spiritually related not only to
their god-children but also as god-parents to one another, and there was an
established tradition which prohibited marriage between their children,
since they had been made spiritual siblings with one another as well as with
the god-child. Gratian (C.30 q.3 cc.4-5) presented contradictory canons respectively from Urban II and Paschal II.[55] Alexander's reply not only
acknowledged the diversity of customs in different regions (*canones
secundum diuersorum locorum consuetudines contrarii inueniuntur*) but
cited Gratian's two authorities in reverse order, though without naming
either the source or the authors. The first (Paschal II, 1099-1118) declared
that children born after their respective parents had become god-parents
could not marry one another; the second (Urban II, 1088-1099) that they
could, whether born before or after their parents' spiritual compaternity was
established, although they could not marry the god-child.[56] He then declared
his preference for the second: 'it seems more tolerable to us (*tolerabilius*)
that the second later canon should be followed (*Unde tolerabilius nobis
uidetur, ut secundum posteriorem canonem debeat obseruari)*', adding the
significant qualification, 'unless the custom of the church is known to have
it differently, which would cause scandal.(*nisi consuetudo ecclesie, que
scandalum generet, aliter se habere noscatur)*', almost certainly a reply to a
question raised by Romuald in relation to the customs observed in his own
church.

The fourth question (§d: *X* 4.11.2, *Si uir uel mulier*), also concerned
supervenient spiritual relationship. What was to happen if a husband or wife
knowingly or unknowingly raised his/her own child from the baptismal

---

54. *Licet preter solitum*, §c: 'Utrum autem filii aut filie ante uel post compaternitatem
geniti possint adinuicem copulari'.
55. *Decretum*, C.30 q.3 c.4 (Urban II): 'et quod spiritualium parentum filii uel filie,
ante uel post conpaternitatem genite, possunt legitime coniungi, preter illam personam, qua conpatres sunt effecti'; c.5 (Paschal II): 'Post susceptum uero de fonte filium uel filiam spiritualem, qui ex conpatre uel conmatre nati fuerint, matrimonio
coniungi non possunt'.
56. *Licet preter solitum*, §c; X 4.11.1: 'Et licet primus canon exinde editus [Paschal II]
natos post compaternitatem adinuicem copulari prohibeat, alter tamen canon post-
erius editus [Urban II] primum uidetur corrigere, per quem statuitur, ut, siue ante
siue post compaternitatem geniti sunt, simul possint coniungi, excepta illa persona
duntaxat, per quam ad compaternitatem uenitur.' John Noonan pointed out long
ago that Alexander was mistaken in the chronological order, since Paschal followed Urban, and not *vice versa*: J. T. Noonan, Jr., 'Who was Rolandus?', in K.
Pennington and R. Somerville (eds.), *Law, Church, and Society. Essays in Honor
of Stephan Kuttner* (Philadelphia: 1977), 21-48, at 25-27.

font? Once again, the canonical tradition transmitted by Gratian was complicated. Although Gratian concluded in a *dictum* (*post* c.10) that whether a woman knowingly or unknowingly became a sponsor to her own child or stepchild she was not to be separated from her husband, and *vice versa*,[57] his cited authorities said different things.[58] These, and the prevailing custom in his own province provoked Romuald's consultation, which the papal response echoed. Acknowledging that it was generally established (presumably in the province of Salerno) that such persons should be separated (*quamuis generaliter sit institutum, ut debeant separari*), Alexander declared that *alii*, with better and more humane understanding (*sentientes potius uel humanius*) had decreed otherwise. In saying this, he was probably thinking of Gratian's c.3 (Nicholas I) and c.4 (Council of Chalon-sur-Saône, 813), as well as his *dictum post* c.10. 'Therefore', he concluded,

> It seems to us that whether they do this out of ignorance or malice they should not be separated one from the other, nor should either withhold the marital debt from the other, unless they can be persuaded to remain continent: because, if it is done from ignorance, they would seem to be excused by their ignorance; if from malice, their fraud and trickery should not benefit them.[59]

3. Conclusion

The pattern of raising contentious questions in order to obtain an interpretation based on the collective wisdom of the papal Curia became a regular

57. *Decretum*, C.30 q.1 d.p.c.10: 'His itaque auctoritatibus apparet, quod siue proprium, siue tantummodo uiri filium mulier de sacro fonte susceperit, non ideo a uiro suo est separanda. Quod et de uiro similiter oportet intelligi.'

58. The first four canons on the subject in Gratian's C.30 q.1 demonstrate the contradictions: a spouse who received his/her child from the baptismal waters (c.1) and a father who acted as sponsor at his stepchild's confirmation (c.2) were to be barred from marital relations, but a woman who so raised her stepson was not barred (c.3: Pope Nicholas I); and a woman who deliberately sponsored a stepchild at confirmation was not freed from the responsibility of marriage (c.4: Council of Chalon-sur-Saône, 813). Rufinus had commented on the discrepancies in his *Summa* (c. 1164), before agreeing that married couples should not be denied marital relations, unless they had mutually agreed to the action in order to live continently: *Die Summa decretorum des Magister Rufinus*, ed. H. Singer (Paderborn: 1902; rpt. Aalen: 1963), 460.

59. *Licet preter solitum*, §d: *X* 4.11.2: 'Ideoque nobis videtur, quod, siue ex ignorantia siue ex malitia id fecerint, non sunt ab inuicem separandi, nec alter alteri debitum debet subtrahere, nisi ad continentiam servandam possint induci: quia, si ex ignorantia id factum est, eos ignorantia excusare uidetur; si ex malitia, eis sua fraus non debet patrocinari uel dolus.' The reference to malice, fraud, and trickery alluded to *Decretum,* C.30 q.1 c.4, where a woman deliberately contrived to establish compaternity with the intention of securing a formal separation.

part of the process of judicial and legal refinement, and this process involved bishops and their advisers, the papal Curia, and the masters in the
schools. It is in this dynamic context that Alexander III's contribution to the
development of the law relating to marriage should be seen.

The theological roots were in northern France; the legal roots in the
recovery of Justinianic law, and its study, across a wide swath of southern
Europe,[60] which in turn stimulated advances in canonical jurisprudence. At
the same time, the pressure for an educated clerical class to service the expanding episcopal, papal, and secular administrations created a demand for
advanced learning which produced the explosion in schools and students
through the twelfth century. In canon law, the most important event was the
compilation of the *Concordia discordantia canonum* by Gratian in Bologna,
about which there continues to be fierce debate.[61] From a relatively modest
beginning in the mid-1120s the compendium of ecclesiastical decrees grew
from about 1,860 *capitula* to more than double that number (3,945) by the
mid-1140s, and, under its popular title *Decreta* or *Decretum*, it rapidly cap-
tured the field. Peter Landau saw evidence of its use in the papal Curia as
early as 1143-1144;[62] it can be traced in litigation from at least 1150;[63] and
it passed into the mainstream of legal learning and practice across Europe in
the following thirty years. Although Gratian's work became the primary
source of authoritative legal texts and definitions, its uncertainties and am-

---

60. Catalonia, Septimania, Provence, Lombardy, Tuscany, and Latium.
61. Anders Winroth argues for two distinct recensions by two distinct authors in 1139
     and 1145 x 58: 'The Two Recensions of Gratian's Decretum', *Zeitschrift der Sa-
     vigny-Stiftung für Rechtsgeschichte, kanonistishe Abteilung* 83 (1997), 22-31; A.
     Winroth, *The Making of Gratian's* Decretum (Cambridge: 2000), esp. 142-44.
     Landau, 'Gratian and the *Decretum Gratiani*', esp. 24-25, accepts the two-
     recension model of Winroth, but dates them 1139 and 'around 1145'; K. Penning-
     ton, 'The "Big Bang": Roman Law in the Early Twelfth Century', *Rivista interna-
     zionale di diritto comune* 18 (2007), 43-70, at 45-46 and 53, pushes the composi-
     tion back to the 1120s for 'Recension I'; the 1130s for an intermediate version
     (Florence, Biblioteca Nazionale Centrale, Conventi soppressi A.1.402); and *c.* 1140
     for 'Recension II'; and Spanish scholars have advanced the concept of an evolving
     texte vivant, developing in as many as seven or eight stages (*etapas*): C. Larrainzar,
     'La formación del Decreto de Graciano por etapas', *Zeitschrift der Savigny-Stiftung
     für Rechtsgeschichte, kanonistishe Abteilung* 87 (2001), 5-83; C. Larrainzar, 'La
     investigación actual sobre el Decreto de Graciano', *Zeitschrift der Savigny-Stiftung
     für Rechtsgeschichte, kanonistishe Abteilung* 90 (2004), 27-59; J. M. Viejo-
     Ximénez, 'La composizione del decreto di Graziano', in S. A. Szuromi (ed.), *Me-
     dieval Canon Law Collections and European Ius commune (Középkori kánonjogi
     gyűjtemények és az európai ius commune)* (Budapest: 2006), 97-169; J. M. Viejo-
     Ximénez, 'La composition de C. 28 del decreto de Graciano', in B. d'Alteroche et
     al. (eds.), *Mélanges en l'honneur d'Anne Lefebvre-Teillard* (Paris: 2009), 1007-29,
     esp. 1008-09.
62. P. Landau, 'Papst Cölestin II. und die Anfänge des kanonischen Eheprozessrechts',
     De processibus matrimonialibus 13 (2006), 57-71, at 68-71.
63. P. Nardi, 'Fonti canoniche in una sentenza senese del 1150', *Studia Gratiana* 29
     (1998), 661-70, at 664.

biguities produced problems of interpretation which could not be resolved by dialectical means alone. The *capitulum* in 'Recension II' on servile marriage (C.29 q.2 c.8), for example, was far from clear. In it, the question whether the male serf (*seruus*) of one master could marry the female serf (*ancilla*) of another was answered with a canon from the Carolingian Council of Chalon-sur-Saône (813).[64] This had declared that marriages between serfs, even of those with different lords, could not be dissolved, but it added that 'this is to be observed in respect of marriages where there was a lawful union, especially with the lords' consent (*et per uoluntatem dominorum*)'.[65] As Peter Lombard pointed out in 1155-1158, that rider could be interpreted to mean that serfs' marriages were invalid without their lords' permission, although some (*quidam*) argued the opposite.[66] This was the context of a *consultatio* sent from Archbishop Eberhard I of Salzburg (1147-1164) to Alexander III's predecessor Adrian IV, between 1154 and 1159.[67] The result was the seminal declaration in *Dignum est* of the absolute right of *serui* to marry.[68] Although sent only to Salzburg, it circulated in decretal collections and was cited in a *summa* on the *Decretum* by Simon of Bisignano before 1179,[69] and was received into the *Liber Extra*.[70]

64. A. Winroth, 'Neither Slave nor Free. Theology and Law in Gratian's Thoughts on the Definition of Marriage and Unfree Persons', in *Medieval Church Law*, 97-109, at 107.

65. *Decretum*, C.29 q.2 c.8 (not in Recension I). For the view that the insertion of this *capitulum* supports the argument that two different authors (the first a pastor, possibly a bishop, the second a professional jurist) were responsible for 'Recensions' I and II, see A. Winroth, 'Marital Consent in Gratian's *Decretum*', in M. Brett and K. G. Cushing (eds.), *Readers, Texts and Compilers in the Earlier Middle Ages. Studies in Medieval Canon Law in Honour of Linda Fowler-Magerl* (Aldershot: 2009), 111-21, at 116-21; A. Winroth, 'Neither Slave nor Free', 108-09; cf. A. J. Duggan, '*Servus servorum Dei*', in B. Bolton and A. J. Duggan (eds.), *Adrian IV. The English Pope (1154-1159). Studies and Texts* (Aldershot: 2003), 181-210, at 189-90 and 204.

66. Peter Lombard, *Sententiarum libri quatuor*, 4.26-37 (PL 192, 908-32), at 4.36.2 (PL 192, 930); cf. *Magistri Petri Lombardi Parisiensis Episcopi, Sententiae in IV Libris Distinctae*, 2 vols, Spicilegium Bonaventurianum 5 (Grottaferrata: 1981), ii.

67. On Eberhard, see W. Stelzer, *Gelehrtes Recht in Österreich. Von den Anfängen bis zum frühen 14. Jahrhundert*, Mitteilungen des Instituts für Österreichische Geschichtsforschung, Erg.Bd. 26 (Vienna: 1982), 17-21.

68. *Dignum est*: WH 344; JL 10445; full text *App.* 45.7: P. Landau, 'Hadrians IV. Dekretale 'Dignum est' (*X* 4.9.1) und die Eheschliessung Unfreier in der Diskussion von Kanonisten und Theologen des 12. und 13. Jahrhunderts', *Studia Gratiana* 12 (1967) = *Collectanea S. Kuttner*, ii, 511-53; Duggan, '*Servus servorum Dei*', 189-90 and 204. Archbishop Eberhardt donated copies of Peter Lombard's work to the Benedictine monastery of Admont in 1164 (Admont, Stiftsbibliothek codd. 36 and 52): Stelzer, *Gelehrtes Recht in Österreich*, 19, n. 7.

69. T. P. McLaughlin, 'The Extravagantes in the Summa of Simon of Bisignano', *Medieval Studies* 20 (1958), 167-75, at 170 no. 4. For the full text, see the electronic edn, *Summa in Decretum Simonis Bisinianensis*, ed. P. V. Aimone, http://www.unifr.ch/cdc/summa_simonis_de.php (accessed 22 Nov. 2011); for au-

About twenty years later Romuald of Salerno's *Licet preter solitum* entered the same tradition even more swiftly. The complete letter had reached Canterbury within at most four years, where it was included in the collection of decretals assembled probably by the distinguished canonist Master Gerard Pucelle.[71] Almost immediately it was segmented and distributed according to subject through the *Appendix concilii Lateranensis*, compiled probably in Lincoln between 1179 and 1181-1184;[72] within about eleven years the segments had reached Bernard of Pavia's *Breviarium* (*Compilatio prima:* 1189-1190),[73] and so passed with minor adjustments into the *Liber Extra.*[74] Meanwhile, Simon of Bisignano referred to it in his *Summa* on the *Decretum* before the end of 1179[75] and it was cited in *Reverentia sacrorum canonum*, an anonymous *summa* compiled in Cologne in the mid-1180s.[76]

There was nothing new in this process of consultation and circulation. The earliest 'decretal', *Directa ad decessorem nostrum*, was a *responsum*, or rather a series of *responsa*, sent by Siricius I (384-398) to Himerius of Tarragona in 385.[77] What was new was the scale of the enterprise and its

---

thorship, date (March 1177–March 1179), decretal citation, manuscript survival, and relationship with the *Summa Lipsiensis*, see *ibid.*, ii, iv-xcix.

70. *X* 4.9.1.
71. *1 Cant.* 56. For Gerard Pucelle, see now Duggan, '*De consultationibus tuis*', 202-03; P. Landau, 'Gérard Pucelle und die Dekretsumme *Reverentia sacrorum canonum*: zur Kölner Kanonistik im 12. Jahrhundert', in *Mélanges...Lefebvre-Teillard*, 624-38. In addition to *Quamuis simus*, at least rescripts were obtained at Venice by English envoys, any one of whom could have acquired a copy of *Licet preter solitum*: cf. *Suggestum est auribus*, to Archbishop Roger and the (dean and) chapter of York, 25 June (WH 998; JL 13882; *X* 3.38.20; C. Duggan, 'Decretals of Alexander III', 44-45); *Continebatur in litteris*, to Bishop Roger of Worcester, Rialto, 13 May x 15 Oct. 1177 (WH 201; JL 14033; *X* 3.10.2); *Significavit nobis O.*, to Abbot Robert of Fountains and Master Vacarius, Rialto, 30 June 1177 (WH 973; JL 13937; *App.* 6.13; *X* 4.7.2); *Conquestus est nobis H.*, to the bishops of Exeter and Worcester, Rialto, 5 July 1177 (WH 150; JL 14167; *X* 4.17.1).
72. *App.* 6.8, 5.1, 32.1, 31.2 (on marriage), 8.8, 6.4, 6.5, 8.9, 38.1, 26.6, 26.7. For the suggestion that its compiler was the Bologna-trained jurist Master Peter de Melide, see A. J. Duggan, 'Making Law or Not? Papal Decretals in the Twelfth Century', in P. Erdő and S. A. Szuromi (eds.), *Proceedings of the Thirteenth International Congress of Medieval Canon Law, Esztergom 2008*. MIC, Ser. C, Subsidia 14 (Città del Vaticano: 2010), 41-70, at 46 n. 35.
73. *1 Comp.* 4.4.3, 3.28.2, 4.11.1, 4.11.2 (on marriage), 2.13.14, 2.1.6, 5.12.1, 2.13.15, 2.18.6, 1.12.1 = 5.12.2, 5.10.8.
74. *X* 4.4.3, 3.32.2, 4.11.1, 4.11.2 (on marriage), 2.20.14, 2.1.4, 5.14.2, 2.20.15, 2.26.4, 1.20.1, 5.12.17.
75. McLaughlin, 'Extravagantes', no. 47 (a), for marriage.
76. Landau, 'Gérard Pucelle und die Dekretsumme *Reverentia sacrorum canonum*', 634-36 no. 25.
77. JK 255; PL 13, 1131-46, no. 1, at 1133, 'Portamus onera omnium qui gravantur: quin immo haec portat in nobis beatus apostolus Petrus, qui nos in omnibus, ut confidimus, administrationis suae protegit et tuetur haeredes.' See D. Jasper, 'The Beginning of the Decretal Tradition. Papal Letters from the Origin of the Genre

consequences for the development of canon law in the second half of the twelfth century: and both were manifestations of the professionalization of canonical jurisprudence. Access to skilled counsel and representation encouraged what can only be described as an explosion of appeals from the late 1150s onwards, and the increasingly professional treatment of cases in ecclesiastical courts simultaneously raised questions of process, definition, and jurisdiction for which bishops from Trondheim to Salerno sought clarification *sub certa forma rescriptorum*.[78] It was these interactive processes of consultation, circulation, and reception, replicated many hundreds if not thousands of times through Alexander III's pontificate, that created the basis of the new 'decretal law'. Because of their relevance to current questions, teaching and practising lawyers began to insert transcripts of new decretals into their copies of Gratian,[79] or to assemble collections of such material for use in analogous cases.[80]

The impetration of *Licet preter solitum* and its subsequent treatment by professional jurists is a particularly arresting illustration of the whole process. What it reveals is not an Alexandrine drive to standardize 'the law' in any particular, but willingness to give the support of his authority to what was deemed to be the better judgment, in the current state of understanding both of theology and of the application of that theology in the rules that constituted canon law. He was as mindful as any of the burden of tradition; mindful, too, that the best minds of the day were moving towards a more coherent interpretation of the contradictions in that tradition, but in matters as sensitive as marriage the settled practices of the different populations

through the Pontificate of Stephen V', in D. Jasper and H. Fuhrmann (eds.), *Papal Letters in the Early Middle Ages* (Washington D.C.: 2001), 7-81, at 13 n. 38.

78. O. Hageneder, 'Forma und formare. Begriffsgeschichtliche Überlegungen zur Terminologie der Papsturkunden', in T. Kölzer et al. (eds.), *De litteris, manuscriptis, inscriptionibus... Festschrift zum 65. Geburtstag von Walter Koch* (Vienna, etc.: 2007), 89-96, esp. 94-96

79. Copies of a consultation from Bishop Amandus of Bisceglie and the corresponding *responsum* from Pope Adrian IV, *Litteras quas pro negotio*, issued from the Lateran on 2 Jan. 1157 x 1159 (WH 627a) were inserted in the margin of Florence, Bibl. Naz. Cent., Conv. Sopp. 1.402, fol. 8rb, one of the earliest surviving manuscripts of 'Recension I', described by Pennington, above n. 61, as 'an intermediate stage'.

80. The early stages of this practice are particularly well recorded for England during the pontificate of Alexander III in the works of Bartholomew of Exeter, Roger of Worcester, Baldwin of Forde/Worcester/Canterbury, and Richard of Canterbury. See esp. C. Duggan, *Twelfth-Century Decretal Collections and their Importance in English History* (London: 1963), 66-117; C. Duggan, 'Decretal Collections from Gratian's *Decretum* to the *Compilationes antiquae*: The Making of the New Case Law', in *Medieval Canon Law in the Classical Period*, 246-92; A. Morey, *Bartholomew of Exeter, Bishop and Canonist: A study in the twelfth century* (Cambridge: 1937); M. G. Cheney, *Roger, Bishop of Worcester, 1164-79* (Oxford: 1980); A. J. Duggan, '*De consultationibus tuis*', 191-214; A. J. Duggan, 'Making Law or Not?' (above, n. 72).

across the Latin West could not simply be torn up. *Licet preter solitum* is characterized by the vocabulary of discretion and discussion. The words *uidetur* (it seems) or *uidetur nobis* (it seems to us) appear twice in the four paragraphs discussed here. Local custom also appears twice, and Alexander allowed that the milder interpretation of the rule on supervenient spiritual relationship, which he favoured, could be set aside if the local church thought otherwise, since it might cause scandal, that is, disturb the moral susceptibilities of the people and lead them astray.[81]

One will therefore seek in vain for an Alexandrine code of marriage law. The subject was not even mentioned in the two councils which he summoned (Tours, 1163; Third Lateran, 1179). It was not by decree, then, but through the multiple exchanges between regional prelates and the Curia that the rules for marriage were progressively refined through Alexander's pontificate, and that refinement was made in the context of the learned law, knowledge of which had penetrated to the remotest regions.

81.   Above, at n. 56.

Abbreviations

App.	*Appendix concilii Lateranensis*: *Concilia omnia tam generalia quam particularia...*, ed. P. Crabbe, 2nd edn (Cologne, 1551), ii, 820-944; rpt. in *Sacrorum conciliorum nova et amplissima collectio*, ed. J. D. Mansi, cont. I. B. Martin and L. Petit, 53 vols. (Florence/Venice: 1759-1798; Paris: 1901-1927; rpt. Graz: 1960-1961), xxii, 248-453.
Codex	*Codex Iustinianus*
1 Comp.	*Compilatio prima*: *Quinque compilationes antiquae necnon collectio canonum Lipsiensis,* ed. E. Friedberg (Leipzig, 1882; rpt. Graz 1956), 1-65.
Decretum	*Decretum Gratiani*; *Corpus Iuris Canonici*, ed. E. Friedberg, 2 vols (Leipzig, 1879-1881), i.
Digest	*The Digest of Justinian*, ed. T. Mommsen and P. Krueger, with an English translation, ed. A. Watson, 4 vols (Philadelphia, 1985).
JL	P. Jaffé, *Regesta Pontificum Romanorum ad annum 1198*, ed. S. Loewenfeld, F. Kaltenbrunner, and P. W. Ewald, 2 vols (Leipzig, 1885-1888).
Lipsiensis	*Quinque compilationes antiquae necnon collectio canonum Lipsiensis,* ed. E. Friedberg (Leipzig, 1882; rpt. Graz 1956), 189-208.
PL	*Patrologiae cursus completus, series latina* (*Patrologia latina*), 221 vols, ed. J. P. Migne (Paris, 1841-1864).
WH	Decretal number assigned by W. Holtzmann.
X	*Liber Extra/Decretales Gregorii IX*: *Corpus Iuris Canonici*, ed. E. Friedberg, 2 vols (Leipzig, 1879-1881), ii.

ON AN ICELANDIC PARALLEL
TO *CODEX JUSTINIANUS* 5.17.10
AND *NOVELLA* 22.6
IN THE LAW CODE GRÁGÁS

Hans Henning Hoff

1. Introduction

The medieval Icelandic law code known as *Grágás*[1] was in force from the summer of 1118, when it was accepted at the General Assembly (*Alþingi*), until 1271-1273, when it was superseded in several steps by the law code *Járnsíða*. The section of *Grágás* dealing with engagement and marriage (*Festa Þáttr*, the 'Betrothals Section') also includes quite a number of provisions about divorce. This paper will briefly describe the provisions making a divorce possible under Icelandic law from the Commonwealth period

1. The manuscript *Konungsbók* (Gl. kgl. Saml. 1157 fol., written circa 1250) has been edited in two volumes as *Grágás, Islændernes lovbog i fristatens tid, udgived efter det kongelige Bibliotheks Haandskrift* by Vilhjálmur Finsen (Copenhagen: 1852; rpt. Odense: 1974), cited as *Grágás* Ia and Ib; the manuscript *Staðarhólsbók* (AM 334 fol., written circa 1271) has been edited by Vilhjálmur Finsen as *Grágás efter det Arnamagnæanske Haandskrift Nr. 334 fol., Staðarhólsbók* (Copenhagen: 1879; rpt. Odense: 1974), cited as *Grágás* II. Fragments of other manuscripts were published by Vilhjálmur Finsen as *Grágás: Stykker, som findes i det Arnamagnæanske Haandskrift Nr. 351 fol., Skálholtsbók og en Række andere Haandskrifter* (Copenhagen: 1883; rpt. Odense: 1974), cited as *Grágás* III. All translations of *Grágás* into English are taken from (or based on, if taken from *Staðarhólsbók*) *Laws of Early Iceland I-II Grágás: The Codex* regius *of Grágás with* material from other manuscripts, trans. Andrew Dennis, Peter Foote, and Richard Perkins (Winnipeg: 1980 and 2000), cited as *Laws of Early Iceland* I and II respectively.

(*Þjóðveldisöld*), and will then turn to one particular provision, which resembles a provision from the *Codex Justinianus* and the Justinianic *Novella* that followed it.

2. Fundamental rules on divorce in *Grágás*

The general rule regarding divorce can be found in the Betrothals Section of *Grágás* at the beginning of the first chapter which deals with divorce. This is chapter 14 of 58 chapters contained in that section in the manuscript *Staðarhólsbók*:

Hiona scilnaðr scal huergi vera a landi her nema þar er byscop lofar. nema þviat eins at þav sciliz fyrir omegðar sakir eða þav viNiz a þann a verka. er hin meire sár metaz.[2]

There shall be no separation of man and wife here in the country unless a bishop gives leave, save only when they separate on account of dependents or when one of them inflicts an injury deemed a major wound on the other.[3]

The provision directly following this general rule in the same chapter explains in more detail what it means to separate (that is, get divorced) on account of dependants (*sciliaz fyrir ómegðar sakir*):

Þar er hiú ii.[av] ero. oc a annat þeirra fe eN annat ecki. nu coma omagaR a hendur þvi er fe lavst er. eða hafa comit fyR oc eytt féno. þa á þat þeirra er fe a eptir. at segia til bvom sinom oc nefna vatta. at ec vil scilia við felaga miN. fyrir þær sakir at ec vil eigi omaga felaga mins láta eyða fe míno.[4]

Where there are man and wife and one of them has means and the other none, and dependents now become the responsibility of the one without means, or they have already become a responsibility and have used up what means there were, then the one with means left has the right to announce before five neighbours of theirs, naming witnesses, that 'I wish to separate from my partner because I will not let my partner's dependents use up my means'.[5]

---

2. *Grágás* II, c. 134, 168.12-14; cf. also *Grágás* Ib, c. 149, 39.24-40.02; *Grágás* Ib, Belgdalsbók A.M. 347 fol. (c. 40, p. 236); *Grágás* III, Skálholtsbók (c. 17, 35), A.M. 125A 4to (c. 17, 420), A.M. 173D (c. 5, 457).
3. *Laws of Early Iceland* II, 63. What is called 'separation' in the translation rather seems to be a divorce in legal terms, as the frequently used words *scilnaðr* and *lögscilnaðr* are quite clear in this regard: cf. the definitions of 'divorce' and 'separation' in B. F. Garner (ed.), *Black's Law Dictionary* (St. Paul: 1999 – 8th edn), 515, 1396. However, as this translation has been done by three native speakers, their translation shall remain unaltered.
4. *Grágás* II, c. 134, 168.14-19, cf. *Grágás* Ib, c. 149, 40.02-07.
5. *Laws of Early Iceland* II, 63.

A relative who was the next in line to support the dependants was also entitled to proclaim a divorce:

Ef scilnaðr verðr gøʀ með hionom .ii.^{eim} af þeim söcom at þav hafa eigi fe til at føra omaga sina fram. oc a þat að hallda hvárt sem þav ráða þat siálf eða sa maðr er omagar þeirra horfa til handa. Sa maðr scal svo at því fara. at ganga iþing brecco. þa er hann hefir vm nótt verit a því socnar þingi er hann heyr siálfr. sva at meire lutr þingheyianda heyre. oc nefna ser vatta. at því at hann segir scilit með þeim oc nefna þav bæði; af því at hann vill eigi føra fram omaga þeirra. oc mæla þat svo fremmi er eiɴ er comiɴ a fe hans þeirra omagi.[6]

If a separation of man and wife is brought about because they do not have the means to maintain their dependents, then that is to be binding whether it is instituted by themselves or by the man who has responsibility for their dependents in prospect. Such a man is to proceed like this: go onto the assembly slope when he has been overnight at the prosecution assembly in which he himself participates, and in the hearing of a majority of the assembly participants name witnesses to witness that he declares that they are separated - and name them both - because he will not maintain their dependents - and say this - only when one of their dependents has already become a charge on his means.[7]

The younger manuscript of *Grágás, Staðarhólsbók* has a novel (Icelandic: *nýmæli*) which abolishes the possibility to separate because of depedents one was obligated to support. Not only does the manuscript *Staðarhólsbók* contain the better text of many provisions, but from the following novel it is evident that the manuscript contains provisions which can´t have been in force at the same time.

Þat er mælt at huergi scal hiona scilnaðr vera fyrir fatøkis sakar hvartki sa er þav raða siálf ne frændr þeirra. Scipta scal omögum þeirra oc föra frændom sem aðr var mælt. Eigi scolo þav scyld at scilia reckio sina fyrir þeim söcom. Ef at réttum tölum verðr aɴað hióna fe lavst. þa scolo omagar þes er fe lavst er koma a fe þes er feit hefir.[8]

It is prescribed that there shall nowhere be separation of man and wife on account of poverty, whether instituted by themselves or by their kinsmen. Their dependents are to be allocated and delivered to kinsmen as prescribed earlier. They are not required to give up the marriage bed on that account. If by a correct calculation either husband or wife is found to be without means, then the dependents of the one without means are to become a charge on the property of the one who has means.[9]

As this provision is not contained in the manuscript *Konungsbók,* it seems likely that it was adopted after 1250, a dating which would also be in accor-

6. *Grágás* II, c. 134, 169.12-22; cf. *Grágás* Ib, c. 149, 40.20-41.02.
7. *Laws of Early Iceland* II, 63-64.
8. *Grágás* II, c. 170, 203.05-10.
9. *Laws of Early Iceland* II, 271 (Addition 232).

dance with the ever-increasing influence of the church during the twelfth and thirteenth centuries. Around 1250 both bishops in Iceland were Norwegians, and they thus might have been more directly influenced by the archbishop in Niðarós (Trondheim).[10]

According to both the earlier and later mansucript versions of *Grágás*, divorce was possible without the bishop's leave, if a kinship was discovered which was so close that a divorce would have to be proclaimed if applied for:

Ef frændzemi su kømr upp með hium .ii.[eim] at þav ætti at sciliaz ef þav være sótt vm. þa mego þav sciliaz at o sekio fyrir lof by-scops framm.[11]

If such a degree of kinship comes to light between man and wife that they would have to separate if they were prosecuted for it, then they have the right to separate without prior leave from the bishop and incur no penalty if they do.[12]

Another rather specific provision enabled a wife to proclaim a divorce:

Ef maðr vill feria konu sina navðga af landi brott heþan. þa a hon at segia scilit við með þeim ef hon vill. [...] Hon þarf eigi að vanda vatta til þess aNan veg. enn nefna þa menn er vátt bærir ero. at þvi at hon segir scilit við hann. Þeir scolo eigi segiaz or þvi vette. enn um raða hagiN þeirra. scal um þessar sakir svo fara sem byscop lo-far.[13]

If a man tries to take his wife out of the country under compulsion, then she has the right to declare their separation if she wishes. [...] She need not select witnesses for that otherwise than by naming men who are qualified to witness that she separates from him. They are not to excuse themselves from acting as witnesses. As for their married state, it shall be as the bishop gives leave.[14]

Even though the divorce was subject to the bishop's approval in this case, it should in practice have been easy to obtain if the wife was able to produce the necessary evidence.

According to the cases described above, then, a divorce was possible if dependants were consuming the property of the couple (until the novel in Staðarhólsbók was enacted after ca. 1250); if one partner inflicted a severe injury on the other; if too close a kinship was discovered between them; or if the husband forced his wife to leave the country with him against her will. However – as has already been indicated in the general rule cited above – in addition to these quite clear cases allowing for a divorce, there was one

10. Cf. M. Stefánsson, 'Kirkjuvald eflist', in *Saga Íslands II*, ed. S. Líndal (Reykjavík: 1975), 55, 139-141.
11. *Grágás* II c. 134, 168.24-169.03; cf. *Grágás* Ib, c. 149, 40.13-15.
12. *Laws of Early Iceland* II, 63.
13. *Grágás* II. c. 139, 172.12-13+18-22; cf. *Grágás* Ib, c. 151, 44.05-07+12-16.
14. Cf. *Laws of Early Iceland* II, 66.

rather unspecific provision providing for the possibility on more general grounds. In this case, the bishop had to be consulted:

Þar er hiu .ii.av vilia sciliaz. oc a þat þeirra er scilnað vill gera at bioða hino til byscops fundar. eigi siðaR en vii. vikor ero af sumre. ef til þings scal fara til fundar hans. [...]

Nu scolo þav bera mál sín fyrir byscop þaN er ifir þeim fiorðungi er sem þav eru or; fösto dag þaN er fyRi er i þingi. en byscop scal segia þeim þuat dagiN eptir. hvat hann lofar. EN ef byscop sceR ecki ór vm scilnað þeirra. þa scal heimta fe hennar sem hann hefði lofað scilnað.[15]

Where a man and a wife wish to separate, then the one who wants to bring about the separation has to invite the other to a meeting with the bishop, after no more than seven weeks of summer have passed if it is a question of going to the assembly in order to see him. [...]

Now they are to bring their affairs before the bishop of the Quarter from which they come on the first Friday of the assembly, and the bishop is to tell them on the Saturday what he gives them leave to do. But if the bishop does not decide upon their separation, then her property shall be claimed as if he had given leave to separate.[16]

From this provision it is quite clear that it was at the bishop's sole discretion to proclaim a divorce.

Despite the rather restrictive approach of most of the provisions cited so far, there is one more provision which might well be the reason for the fact that in reality, divorces seem not to have been very unusual during the Icelandic Commonwealth period. This provision entitled the bishop to proclaim a divorce if a couple was repeatedly at odds with one another:

Þar er hiu verða eigi samhuga. þa er byscopi rétt at lofa kononni fiar heimtingar allar undan boanda sinom. þott hann geri eigi lögscilnað þeirra ef honom þickia for urtir til þes. Sva scal fe hennar heimta sem byscop mælir fyrir. hvart sem þat er et næsta vár eða siðaR. Kona þarf eigi at lata stefna bönda sinom til byscops fundar. um þetta mál. oc þviat eins ef hon vill lög scilnað gera lata.[17]

Where man and wife prove to be at variance, then if the bishop thinks there is good cause it is lawful for him, even without bringing about their legal separation, to give the woman leave to claim all her property out of her husband's hands. Her property is to be claimed as the bishop ordains, whether it is done in the following spring or later. Only if she wishes to have their legal separation brought about need a woman have her husband summoned to a meeting with the bishop in the matter.[18]

15. *Grágás* II, c. 135, 170.02-04+08-13; cf. a bit different *Grágás* Ib, c. 151, 42.05-08+13-23.
16. Cf. *Laws of Early Iceland* II, 64-65 (some part of the translation is modified here as this is a translation of the *Konungsbók* manuscript).
17. *Grágás* II, c. 171, 204.02-08; cf. *Grágás* Ib, c. 149, 41.10-17.
18. *Laws of Early Iceland* II, 64 with Addition 234, 272. A more precise translation of the first sentence would be: 'Where man and wife prove to be at variance, the bishop is entitled to allow the wife to claim all her property out of her husband's

One of the main legal consequences of a divorce, besides of course the possibility of marrying someone else, seems to have been the wife's right to claim her property out of the hands of her husband. However, in some cases the latter was also possible without formally dissolving the marriage, as the provision above indicates.

In *Staðarhólsbók*, the chapter directly following the provision on divorce cited above at note 15, there is a chapter consisting of only one sentence, which is very unusual given the often very extensive chapters in *Grágás*.

Ef karl maðr huilir eigi isama sæing kono sinni vi. missere fyRir orøkðar sakir. þa eigo frændr fiar heimtingar hennar oc sva retta far enda a hon sialf se sit at varðveita.[19]	If on account of negligence a man does not sleep in the same bed as his wife for six seasons, then any claim she has to property and to personal compensation lies with her kinsmen, but she herself has the right to take care of her own property.[20]

In medieval Iceland, there were only two seasons (*misseri*) each year, summer and winter. Therefore a 'season' designates a six-month period, and six seasons comprise a period of three years. Even though this peculiar provision is part of a longer chapter in *Konungsbók*, in this manuscript it starts with a larger letter than an ordinary new sentence. This provision is amended by one other provision contained in a different chapter in *Staðarhólsbók* (not contained in *Konungsbók* or other manuscripts):

Kona sialf er iafnan aðili at fiár heimtingum sinum við buanda sinn hueriom sem handsalat var i mund malum. hvart sem er at byscop lofar henni fiarheimting. eða orøkiz boandi hennar við hana svo at hann huílir vi. misseri fyrir utan reckio hennar. af urøkðum.[21]	The woman herself is always the principal in claims for her own property from her husband, those that were formally guaranteed to her in the bride-price agreement, whether it is so that the bishop gives her leave to make the claim or that her husband out of neglect sleeps elsewhere than in her bed for six seasons.[22]

What is unfortunately not clear from the provision about the three-year period and the wife's property rights is whether it only entitled the wife to

hands even if he does not proclaim their [legal] divorce, if he thinks there are obstacles for this'. The last sentence should more precisely be translated in the following way: 'A woman does not need to have her husband summoned to a meeting with the bishop in the matter unless she wishes to have a [legal] divorce proclaimed'.

19. *Grágás* II, c. 136, 170.20-171.02; in *Konungsbók* this provision is part of chapter 158, cf. *Grágás* Ib, c. 158, 55.05-08.
20. *Laws of Early Iceland* II, 77.
21. *Grágás* II, c. 168, 200.02-06.
22. *Laws of Early Iceland* II, 272.

claim her property back, or whether this provision automatically meant that the wife could be divorced from her husband. The context seems to indicate the latter, as the right to reclaim the wife's property is one of the main legal consequences of the provisions allowing for a divorce. However, this is not certain, as there are – as has been shown above – also provisions stressing that a wife was in some cases entitled to claim her property back without a divorce formally being proclaimed. If this provision allows for a divorce, the rationale for it seems to be that the legislator of *Grágás* wanted to ensure that a wife had the possibility of procreating legal heirs. This seems to be the most likely interpretation.[23]

3. Similar provision in the legislation of Justinian

Codex Justinianus 5.17.10 includes a provision resembling in several ways the Icelandic provision just mentioned:

In causis iam dudum specialiter definitis, ex quibus recte mittuntur repudia, illam addimus, ut, si maritus uxori ab initio matrimonii usque ad duos continuos annos computandos coire minime propter naturalem imbecillitatem valeat, possit, mulier vel eius parentes sine periculo dotis amittendae repudium marito mittere, ita tamen, ut ante nuptias donatio eidem marito servetur.[24]

To the causes formerly specifically defined for which bills of divorce are legally send [sic], we add another, namely, that if the husband is unable for two continuous years after the beginning of the marriage to cohabit with his wife on account of impotency, the woman or her parents may send a bill of divorce to the husband without the loss of the dowry, provided, however, that the husband shall retain the prenuptial gift.[25]

By virtue of *Novella* 22.6 the two-year period was later extended to three years:

Per occasionem quoque necessariam et non irrationalbilem distrahitur matrimonium, quando aliquis impotens fuerit coire mulieri, quando aliquis viris data sunt, sed

A just cause for divorce is given when the husband is impotent, and shows himself to be so for a period of two years, as that period was defined by a former law, from the

23. Cf. also V. Finsen, ´Fremstilling af den islandske Familieret efter Grágás´, in *Annaler for Nordisk Oldkyndighed of Historie* 1849, 150, 274 and J.F.G. Schlegel, ´Commentatio historica et critica de Codicis Grágás origine, nomine, fontibus, indole et fatis´ in *Codex Juris Islandorum Antiquissimuss, qui nominatur Grágás* I, Copenhagen 1829, 14, 121-122.
24. *Corpus Iuris Civilis* II, *Codex Iustinianus*, ed. P. Krüger (Berlin: 1954; rpr. Hildesheim 1997), 5.17.10 Imp. Iustinianus A. Menae PP.
25. 'Annotated Justinian Code', 2nd edn, ed. and trans. F. H. Blume and T. Kearly, published online at http://uwacadweb.uwyo.edu/blume&justinian/default.asp and accessed 29 Oct. 2011, *Codex* 5.17.10.

biennium quidem secundum de hoc a nobis pridem scriptam legem transcurrat ex nuptiarum tempore, ille vero quia pro veritate est vir non ostendat. Licebit enim mulieri aut eius patribus disiungere matrimonium et mittere repudium, vel si noluerit hoc maritus. Et hic siquidem dos, si qua est omnino data dos, sequitur mulierem, et reddit hanc vir, si eam contigit, accipi, propter nuptias autem seu ante nuptias donatio manet apud virum nihil de suo damnificandum. Hanc itaque legem corrigimus brevi quadam adiectione: non enim biennium numerari solum ex ipso tempore copulationis, sed triennium volumus. Edocti namque sumus ex his quae inter haec provenerunt, quosdam amplius quam biennium temporis non valentes postea potentes ostensos ministrare filiorum procreationi.[26]

time of the marriage. For the wife, or her parents, may dissolve the marriage and send a bill of divorce against the consent of the husband. In such case, the dowry belongs to the wife and must be returned to her by the husband. But the prenuptial gift of the gift on account of marriage remains with the husband, and he shall suffer no loss in his property. We must, however, correct this law by a small addition, and make the period of impotency from the time of marriage three years instead of two. For we have learned in the meantime that men that were impotent for a longer period than two years, became subsequently able to procreate children.[27]

The woman's right to reclaim her property (her dowry) is generally accepted in *Codex Justinianus* 5.12.31:

Cum quidam dotes pro mulieribus dabant sive matres sive alii cognati vel extranei, recte quidem eas mariti sine monumentorum observatione suscipiebant: cum autem mulier redhibitionem casus stipulabatur et huiusmodi fortuitus casus evenisset, ipsa mulier utpote a se non facta donatione propter hoc, quod monumenta deerant, necessitatem habebant actiones huiusmodi casus ad eum qui dotem dedit per cessionem transferre vel ipsas res reddere: et ita inveniebatur forsitan post prolixa matrimonii annorum curricula et liberos forte editos infelix mulier indotata.

Sancimus itaque in huiusmodi omnibus casibus nullis monumentis rem indigere, sed in omni persona ratas esse huiusmodi

Although some persons, whether mothers, or other cognate relatives or outsiders, have customarily given dowries for women, men could legally marry them without registration of the gift. But when a woman had the return of her dowry promised to her by stipulation, upon the happening of a certain event, and this event came to pass, the woman was frequently compelled, where the dowry was not given by her, to transfer the right of action for the return of dowry to the person who gave it, or to return the property personally, because the gift was not registered, and thus an unhappy woman was perchance, found without dowry, after many years of matrimony, and after she had, perchance raised children. 1. We therefore ordain that in none of such

---

26. *Corpus Iuris Civilis* III, *Novellae*, ed. R. Schöll and W. Kroll (Berlin: 1954), 150-151.
27. 'Annotated Justinian Code [Novels]', ed. and trans. Blume and Kearly, published online at http://uwacadweb.uwyo.edu/blume&justinian/Novels1_40.asp, and accessed 24 Nov. 2011, *Novel 22.6*.

donationes et mulierem dotem suam ipsam habere, cum fortuitus casus hoc lucrum ei addiderit, et firmiter hoc apud eam permanere, nisi ipse, qui ab initio dotem dederit, sibi dari huiusmodi stipulatus est: tunc etenim, cum neque ab initio suspicio aliqua liberorum concurrit, sed sibi omnem rem ille qui dotem dedit pepigerit, huiusmodi tractatus habere locum non potest. Atqui in aliis omnibus casibus, in quibus ipse non stipulatus est, tristitiae suae mulier hoc proprium habeat solacium per actionem dotis.[28]

cases shall registration be necessary, but such gifts shall be valid to all persons, and the woman shall have her dowry, if the contemplated event gives it to her, and she shall remain the owner thereof unless the party who originally gave the dowry caused a stipulation to be exacted to the effect that the dowry should be returned to him when such event should happen; for when no thought has been given to children originally, but the party who gave the dowry exacted the promise of the return of the property to himself, the matter cannot be treated as above. 2. But in all other cases, in which the giver has no stipulation [for return of the property to him] the woman shall have a solace for her sadness through [her right to] an action on the dowry.[29]

These provisions enacted by Justinian are to be found in almost all compilations with relevant legal provisions for practical use in the Byzantine Empire, and it is therefore very likely that they were still very well known in eleventh-century Byzantium. In the *Basilika*, this provision forms *B.* 28.7.4[30]; in the *Ecloga* it is contained in 2.9.3;[31] and the version of the very same provision in *Procheiros Nomos* 11.2 runs as follows:

> A marriage is necessarily dissolved, and for valid reason, when a man is unable to cohabit with his wife or exercise the function of nature, or if he is so apart from his wife for three years. The wife and her parents can then dissolve the cohabitation and procure a divorce, even if the husband does not wish it. In that case if dower has been paid it shall revert to the wife and the husband shall lose it. But the prenuptial gift shall belong to him and he shall not be deprived thereof.[32]

The wording at the beginning of this provision according to which the marriage is 'necessarily' dissolved might be the reason that the provision in *Grágás* does not expressly state that after three years the divorce 'can' be proclaimed. Because the provision in the law of Byzantium apparently sup-

28. *Codex* 5.12.31 §1-2, Imp. Iustinianus A. Iuliano PP.
29. 'Annotated Justinian Code', ed. and trans. Blume and Kearly, *Codex* 5.12.31 §1-2.
30. Basilicorum libri LX series A, ed. Scheltema and van der Wal, (Groningen: 1962) vol. 4, 1362
31. *Ecloga: Das Gesetzbuch Leons III. und Konstantinos' V*, ed. L. Burgmann, Forschungen zur byzantinischen Rechtsgeschichte 10 (Frankfurt a.M.: 1983).
32. *Procheiros Nomos*, trans. E. Hanson Freshfield (Cambridge: 1928) c. XI.2, 82.

poses that divorce inevitably occurs under these circumstances, it appears likely that this consequence was also intended by the corresponding provision in *Grágás*, in particular because this provision appears in a context where all provisions deal with divorce. It can hardly be regarded as coincidence that the two provisions about divorce and separating the property of husband and wife both have this very special element: that the couple did not have intercourse which led to children for exactly the same period of three years.

4. Possible influence of *Codex Justinianus* 5.17.10 and *Novella* 22.6 on *Grágás*

In medieval Icelandic historiography one of the oldest and most reliable sources we have, written c. 1120-1130, is the 'Book of Icelanders' (*Íslendingabók*) of Ari 'The Wise' Þorgilsson. In this short, concise history of Iceland from its settlement until Ari's own era, the author mentions the important role played by one Hafliði Másson as the Icelandic laws were being written down for the first time in the winter of 1117/1118 at his farm in northern Iceland. From the wording used in *Íslendingabók*, it can be concluded that the laws were not only written down as they were, but also reviewed and amended at the same time.[33]

Even today, Hafliði's most important role in reviewing and writing down the Icelandic laws for the first time if frequently overlooked. As the law code forming the bulk of what is now called *Grágás* was compiled, it was named the law code, which Hafliði had compiled. Therefore the contribution of the lawspeaker, Bergþórr Hrafnsson, and other distinguished men familiar with law who were also members of the commission must have been rather modest and limited to the oral laws already in existence. It was even at Hafliði's estate that the codification took place, and the *Íslendingabók* of Ari the Wise particularly stresses the role of Hafliði, of course along with that of Bergþórr, the officiating lawspeaker.[34] But why should Hafliði, who had never been a lawspeaker himself, have been such an important figure in codifying the Icelandic laws?

The oldest chronicle with sagas about the Norwegian kings, *Morkinskinna*, includes a very short episode in the saga about Harald Hardrada (*Haraldr harðráði*), the king of Norway who was killed in 1066 at the Battle of Stamford Bridge. In the description of Harald's arrival in

33. Cf. H. H. Hoff, 'Das Verhältnis der Grágás zu den Isländersagas und den sogenannten Gegenwartssagas', in H.-G. Hermann et al. (eds.), *Von den Leges Barbarorum bis zum ius barbarum des Nationalsozialismus: Festschrift für Hermann Nehlsen zum 70. Geburtstag* (Köln, Weimar and Wien: 2008), 531, 538-539.
34. Cf. Ari the Wise, *Íslendingabók*, Íslensk fornrit I (Reykjavík: 1986), 23.

Byzantium – a minor episode which does not matter at all for the overall story – Hafliði's father is mentioned:

En mikill fjöldi var þar áður fyrir Norðmanna, er þeir kalla Væringja. Þar var sá maðr íslenskur, er Már hét ok var Húnröðarson, faðir Hafliða Mássonar, ok var þar ágætr sveitarhöfðingi. Honum var mikill grunur á um menn þessa ina útlendu hvárt allt myndi eftir því sem þeir sögðu. Ok síðan hitti hann að máli Halldór Snorrason, er þá var með Haraldi, er kallaðisk Norðbrikt, ok vildi Már tala við Harald, en Haraldr vildi ekki við hann eiga, og fékk Már ekki þar af. Ok síðan rézk hann ór Miklagarði og þótti einskis ørvænt nema nokkur stórræði kœmi upp af stundu.[35]

A great multitude of Norsemen were already there and were called Væringjar. There was an Icelander named Már, who was the son of Húnröðr and the father of Hafliði Másson. He was a distiguished chieftain. He was very suspicious about whether everything these foreigners said was true. He made it a point to speak with Halldór Snorrason, who was in the company of Haraldr who called himself Norðbrikt. Már wanted to speak with Haraldr, but Haraldr wanted nothing to do with him. Már got nowhere with him. Then he left Constantinople, thinking it was not unlikely that major events were in the offing.[36]

This raises the possibility that Hafliði Másson might have followed the example of his father and other Scandinavians and entered into the service of the Emperor of Byzantium as part of the so-calledknown as the 'Varangian Guard'. Unlike in western Europe at that time, in eleventh-century Byzantium the legal heritage of Justinian was still alive. At mid-century in particular, there was an increased interest in studying law; and contempory sources even record complaints that every soldier wanted to become a lawyer or jurist.[37] This makes it even more possible that a young Icelander might have received some legal education before entering the Varangian Guard protecting the Emperor in the palace and in the battlefield.

Even though it is difficult to tell whether the obvious parallel between *Grágás*, *Codex* 5.17.10 and *Novella* 22.6 results from a direct influence from Byzantium via Hafliði Másson, the provisions are strikingly similar. This is very unlikely to be a coincidence.[38] As the main person in reviewing

35. *Morkinskinna*, ed. Á. Jakobsson and Þ. I. Guðjónsson, Íslensk fornrit XXIII.1 (Reykjavík: 2011), 88-89.
36. *Morkinskinna*, trans. T. M. Andersson and K. E. Gade (Ithaca and London: 2000), 132.
37. Cf. Johannes Scylitzes, *Excerpta ex breviario historico Ioannis Scylitzae curopalatae, excipientia ubi Cedrenus disinit*, ed. Immanuel Becker, *Corpus scriptorum historiae byzantinae* 4 – Georgius Cedrenus II (Bonn: 1839), 639 (652) (with Latin translation); and Michael Attaleiates, *Michaelis Attaliotae Historia*, ed. Immanuel Becker, *Corpus scriptorum historiae byzantinae* 36 (Bonn: 1853), 76 (with Latin translation).
38. Konrad Maurer has described the *Grágás* provision in some detail in his *Vorlesungen über altnordische Rechtsgeschichte*, vol. II Über Altnordische

and writing down the laws in Iceland in the winter of 1117/1118 Hafliði Másson was at that time most probably around sixty years old.[39] It seems unlikely that he studied law in Italy as a young man, since at that time (approximately 1070-1080) it was rare for a student to travel there from so far abroad. Because he already had family ties with Byzantium, it seems much more likely that he himself went there as well. If so, he was well placed to import many provisions from Justinianic legislation to Iceland at the beginning of the twelfth century.[40]

Kirchenverfassung und Eherecht (rpr. Osnabrück: 1966), 620 and 626, but does not mention its parallel in Roman law.

39. Hafliði was born c. 1050-1060 and died in 1130; his father, Már Húnröðarson, left Byzantium c. 1034/1035.

40. For more detail and with far more examples from different fields of law, see H. H. Hoff, *Hafliði Másson und die Einflüsse des römischen Rechts in der Grágás*. Ergänzungsbände zum Reallexikon der Germanischen Altertumskunde (Berlin and New York: 2012).

MATRIMONIAL CASES REFLECTED IN THE *PROCESSUS IUDICIARIUS SECUNDUM STILUM PRAGENSEM*

Dominik Budský

1. The author

The treatise *Processus iudiciarius secundum stilum Pragensem*[1] originated in the late 1380s in Prague. Its author, Nicolaus Puchnik († 1402), was a theoretically trained lawyer from a family of minor castellans in South Bohemia[2] who practised as a judge. A key moment in Puchnik's career came in the year 1383, when he obtained the Licenciate in Decrees[3] after having lectured in Canon Law at the University of Prague for just a single year. In 1383 Puchnik also received his first administrative position, when he was appointed to the officiality by Archbishop John of Jenstein.[4] The two

---

1.   This paper originated in part as a result of grant project n. 285111 GAUK, '*Processus iudiciarius secundum stilum Pragensem* by Nicolaus Puchnik', to produce a complete critical edition of the treatise. The present author is currently preparing a Ph.D. thesis on the same topic at the Catholic Theological Faculty of Charles University in Prague, under the supervision of prof. PhDr. Zdeňka Hledíková, CSc.
2.   A. Sedláček, *Hrady, zámky a tvrze Královstvi českého* [The Castles, Chateaux and Citadels of the Kingdom of Bohemia] I-XV (Prague: 1993-1998), vol. XI, 266.
3.   Z. Hledíková, 'Úřad generálních vikářů pražského arcibiskupa v době předhusitské' [The Office of Vicar-General of the Prague Archbishop in the Pre-Hussite Period], *AUC–Phil. et Hist., Monographia* 41 (1971), 127-28.
4.   Z. Hledíková, 'Úřad generálních vikářů', 127-28. As Licentiate of Decrees Puchnik is first mentioned in the officiality sentence of 31 July 1383, which also announces that Puchnik has assumed the office of Master Bores, Archdeacon of Horšovský Týn: *Regesta Boehemiae et Moraviae aetatis Wenceslai IV.*, vol. V/1-1, eds. K. Beránek and V. Beránková (Prague: 2006), 86, no. 148 (hereafter *RBMV* V/I-1). This is Puchnik's first appearance in the function of official.

achievements were probably closely related: Jenstein may have chosen Puchnik because he was both well educated and still a young adept.

With the beginning of the last decade of the fourteenth century, Nicholas continued to move closer to the centre of church politics, where he was to remain until the end of his life. In August 1392 he attained the position of Vicar-General.[5] His dual responsibilities as official and as Vicar-General till May/June 1394 must have meant that he had to manage a heavy workload, a supposition borne out by numerous entries in the Court Acts, or *Libri erectionum*.[6] This means that he was occupied almost daily with one or another office, often in cases which lasted for years.

A particularly painful moment in the life of Nicholas Puchnik came in March 1393, when he was caught up in the dispute between Archbishop John of Jenstein and Emperor Wenceslas IV. Because of his position as Vicar-General, and as a result of this quarrel, he was tortured under the supervision of the emperor himself.[7] In the second half of the 1390s, Puchnik was dismissed from the office of Vicar-General after the accession of the new archbishop, Olbram of Škvorec (1396-1402). Olbram was probably led by the wishes of Wenceslas IV, who must have regarded Nicholas as potentially dangerous. Although the change was due to take place on 25 January 1398,[8] Puchnik nevertheless was still called upon often to act as Vicar-General, as attested by many entries of the Court Acts (especially in

---

5. To determine the exact date when he started to administer the office of Vicar-General is not easy, because Puchnik is often mentioned just with the title of official or Vicar-General. As the Vicar-General he is mentioned for the first time on 26 August 1392: *Acta iudiciaria consistorii Pragensis,* vol. I-VII, ed. F. Tadra (Prague: 1893-1901), here III, 78 (hereafter *AI*). In previous records he is always mentioned only in connection with the function of the officiality. His designation to the office of Vicar-General is recorded in 1395: see *Libri erectionum archidiocesis Pragensis saeculo XIV et XV* vol. I-VI, ed. A. Podlaha (Prague: 1875-1927), here IV, 456-58 (hereafter *LE*). However, it is likely that in August 1392, after having represented John of Pomuk in the office of Vicar-General (3 August 1392, *RBMV* V/I-1, 195, no. 431), he became Pomuk's colleague (second Vicar-General) and from 26 August 1392, he had begun to administer the office of Vicar-General itself (*AI* III, 78).

6. The Court Acts of the Prague consistory ('Acta iudiciaria conssitorii Pragensis') are protocolary records (minutes) describing the progress of individual trials litigated before the court of the Vicar-General. This court and its acts began in 1373, whereas the court of the Prague officiality had begun more than a century before. The agenda of both courts was very similar and their jurisdictions largely overlapped, although in principle marital disputes were litigated by the official's court only. Nicholas Puchnik was one of the few who combined both judicial functions in one person. For the preservation of documents of the officiality see Z. Hledíková, 'Několik zlomků soudních písemností z církevní praxe druhé poloviny 14. a počátku 15. století' [A Few Fragments of Court Documents from the Church Practice of the Second Half of the 14th and early 15th Century], *Táborský archiv* 12 (2001-2003), 25-55, including a series of several fragments of the officiality's index.

7. J. Polc, *Svatý Jan Nepomucký* [Saint John of Pomuk] (Prague: 1993).

8. *AI* III, 317.

later 1398 and 1401).[9] Clearly Olbram's act of dismissal was not carried out, but the lack of sources makes it difficult to ascertain whether this was because of the weakening power of the monarch, or Puchnik's entrenched position, or because the archbishop himself had changed his mind. At the apex of his career, Puchnik was elected Olbram's successor as Archbishop of Prague in May/mid-June 1402 by the Metropolitan Canonry.[10] Because the monarch had been imprisoned since March of that year, the canonry may have had a relatively free hand in this election. Otherwise it would have been difficult to select one of the witnesses of Wenceslas's fury, a person for whom he certainly had no great affection. It is also worthy of notice that the half-brother and rival of Wenceslas, Sigmund of Luxembourg, supposedly approved of the election.[11]

Nicholas Puchnik became the *archiepiscopus electus* – the elected Archbishop of Prague – for a short time, but he did not live long enough to get definitive confirmation or to be installed. On 28 July he published a document in which he promised to pay the *servicium* including debts of Olbram of Škvorec.[12] However, he must have died sometime between that date and 10 September, because in the following papers dated 10 September 1402, published by the administrator of the archdiocese Jaroslav of Pořešín,[13] he was remembered as *quondam archiepiscopus*. He was buried in the cathedral of St Vitus on 19 September 1402.[14] Some sources claim that Puchnik's death came as the result of poisoning or some other type of violence, but of course there is no proof of this.

2. The genesis of the work, its meaning and use

Nicholas Puchnik was very well educated for the task of creating his treatise, both theoretically (the Licenciate of Decrees) and practically (the officiality). He is the first known author in Bohemia to write on canon procedural law, in an era when canon law was taught at the University of Prague

---

9.   In 1398 for instance: *RBMV* V/I-2, 18, no. 628; *AI* III, 370; in 1399, *Regesta Boehemiae et Moraviae aetatis Wenceslai IV.*, ed. V. Jenšovská, vol. I/7 (Prague: 1981), 1706. In 1400, see *Archiv pražské metropolitní kapituly I (–1419), Katalog listin a listů* [The Archives of Prague Metropolitan Canonry I (–1419), Catalogue of Documents and Papers], eds. J. Eršil and J. Pražák (Prague: 1956), 186, no. 667; *RBMV* V/I-2, 40, no. 686; and many other records up to 1402.
10. According to the *Monumenta Vaticana res gestas Bohemicas illustrantia*, ed. K. Krofta, vol. V (Prague: 1903), 1124-25 (hereafter *MBV*), the benefices vacated upon his election were reserved to Anton, cardinal of St Cecily.
11. A. Sedláček, *Hrady, zámky* vol. VII, 161, mentions this, unfortunately without reference to any sources.
12. *MBV* V, 1127.
13. *RBMV* V/I-2, 73, n. 771.
14. *AI* IV, 164. The particular place is unknown.

in lectures based on papal law books, the *Clementinae* and the *Liber Sextus*.[15] Puchnik must have recognised the obvious lack of a manual to explain not only the legal norms, but also the rules of procedure. There were hearings in dozens of cases before the courts of the Prague officiality and Vicar-General almost every day, often lasting months or even years, and such a manual would help not only law students but also the staffs of both courts, plaintiffs, and defendants to navigate through the maze of procedural steps. In contrast to other commonly used procedural treatises (e.g. that of Johannis Andreae[16]), Puchnik's writing had the advantage of not only clearness and practicality but also his practice of quoting many formulas used in the documents issued at the different stages of cases. It also contained an important addition *secundum stilum Pragensem*, which clearly distinguished it from all other procedural treatises. This appendix represents a description of legal specifics (customs) as they were actually practised before the court of the Prague official.[17] The proof of the frequent use of this treatise is the occurrence of manuscript copies throughout the territory of wider Central Europe. Even today there survive or there is evidence of no fewer than fifteen copies,[18] e.g. in Germany (Rostock, Berlin, Leipzig, Munich), Poland (Gdańsk, Wroclaw, Kraków), and Austria (Graz). Because of the Hussite movement and following war, only one copy is to be found in the Czech Republic (Olomouc).

3. *Processus* and matrimonial cases

The treatise reflects matrimonial cases in several places, of course in a theoretical way. The usual structure of each chapter is to describe and explain the procedural conduct of a case and then to illustrate it with the help of juristic formulas quoted from documents used in such a case, systematically added at the end of each chapter. The matrimonial cases occur in these chapters:

---

15. J. Kejř, *Dějiny pražské právnické univerzity* [The History of Prague law university] (Prague: 1995), 54.
16. For comprehensive information, see L. Fowler-Magerl, '*Ordines iudiciarii*' *and* '*Libelli de ordine iudiciorum*': *From the Middle of the Twelfth to the End of the Fifteenth Century*, Typologie des sources du moyen âge occidental 63 (Turnhout: 1994), 10-15 (literature).
17. Fowler-Magerl, *Ordines iudiciarii*, 71, (typology of *Ordines*) includes this treatise in the group 'Short *ordines* intended for the courts of the local judges ordinary'. I believe this categorization should be augmented by highlighting the *Processus*'s importance for teaching canon law at the university.
18. P. Spunar, *Repertorium auctorum Bohemorum provectum idearum post Universitatem Pragensem conditam illustrans* (Wroclaw et al.: 1985), 157 mentions only six copies. The same incorrect information is in Fowler-Magerl, *Ordines iudiciarii*, 71.

a) *Sex modi quibus posiciones actoris repelluntur* (Six ways by which the articles of the plaintiff may be rejected by the defendant) The first way suggests that the plaintiff's claim cannot contain verbs with negative formulations, but only positive verbal expressions:

> Tu dicis, quod tecum contraxi matrimonium tali die et in tali loco, ego dico et probare volo, quod illo die et ante et post illum diem eram continue in alio loco.

b) *Interrogatoria supra diversis materiis: super matrimonio* (Interrogatories according to different types of cases: in matrimonial disputes). The questions are above all directed towards which words were used in contracting a marriage; who were witnesses; whether the procedure was meant or was not meant as a joke; whether anyone was forced; or whether the marriage was arranged by friends. Other questions are directed towards the age of the spouses, the period of the wedding, the time of joining the marriage, clothing, etc.

> Primo igitur super matrimonio talia interrogatoria formentur salvis interrogatoriis prelibatis. Interrogentur testes, quibus verbis matrimonium contraxe[ve]runt et quis prius verba matrimonii expressit et utrum verba expresserunt animo contrahendi vel iocose vel ludendo, utrum sponte vel libere contraxe[ve]runt, vel utrum aliquis metus, vel [co]accio intercessit vel an semel autem plures iterando contractum contraxerunt, utrum tractatus amicorum precessit matrimonium. Item quot annorum fuerint contrahentes, quando contraxeverunt, utrum aliqua contractio est subsecuta et utrum contrahentes sedebant vel stabant et quibus vestibus inducti [sunt].

c) *Replicatio* (The plaintiff's response to the objections of the defendant): 'Tres enim sunt cause favorabiles puta matrimonialis, liberalis et testamentalis, in quibus iudex debet favere actori pocius, quam reo etc'.

d) *Formae libellorum* (Different types of libels according to the subject-matter of a case): *libellus in causa matrimoniali* (a matrimonial case). A wife requests confirmation of a legitimate marriage with a man who has married another woman as well. Simultaneously she asks for a declaration of nullity of this new marriage.

> Libellus super matrimonio. Coram vobis etc. B. contra P. proponit et dicit, quod licet dicta B. cum dicto P. et dictus P. cum dicta B. matrimonium verum et legitimum bannis premissis et in facie ecclesie per verba de presenti contraxerint et se affectione carnali pertractaverint per XX annos. Tamen dictus P. a dicta B. divertens aliam Dorotheam supraduxit, cum qua adulterari non veretur. Quare dicta B. petit decrevi, declarari et pronunciari inter se et dictum P. verum et legitimum fuisse matrimonium ac inter dictam D. et P. nullum fuisse nec esse [matrimonium] vestra diffinitiva sentencia mediante.

4. Summary and conclusion

Marriage is logically mentioned mainly in two chapters of the treatise, interrogatories and libels. It is reflected in a theoretical way but is also connected to the practical purpose of the treatise. Puchnik's *Processus* was the remarkable, universally used treatise which found its way into the countries neighbouring Bohemia, thanks in part to academic peregrination but also in large extent to its usefulness. The treatise, which was used for decades, has a clear and transparent structure, which only underlines its practicality and didactic tendency.

MARRIED COUPLES IN THE MIDDLE AGES? THE CASE OF THE DEVIL'S ADVOCATE

Jan Rüdiger

1. Stating the case

I have assigned myself an uncomfortable position to take. The devil certainly makes a hard case and probably an ungrateful defendant. I am consoling myself with the knowledge that the role of the Devil's Advocate is, or used to be until fairly recently, an essential one in a canonisation process. And while the subject of our conference – medieval marriage – hardly needs a process to enter into a canon, the simile allows me at least to retain the position of one of us. I have no desire to pose as an iconoclast.

That said, I find it intriguing that the role of the Devil's Advocate presupposes complicity with opposing counsel. The idea is that the person who, in a Roman Catholic canonisation process, argues *against* sanctity actually, personally agrees with everyone else present that the saint-to-be really ought to be a saint and only takes his rôle as a matter of argument. I am about to argue the case against the idea that Marriage and the Married Couple were universal phenomena in the Western Middle Ages. I am not sure that I myself am taking that stance only for the sake of the argument. So I ask you to consider the case with an open mind, while I too am prepared to be convinced. The devil, after all, has lost many cases at the Vatican.

I should like first to present my case as a hypothesis; then argue it on some very few examples; then rehearse the argument; then invite comment and adverse examples. My own examples are only by way of illustration; after all, the strength of an argument is not that you can find evidence to support it but that you can find no evidence to contradict it. I am aware that any such evidence, as it might be supplied in later debate on this hypothesis, will affect its tenability.

My hypothesis is that 'the married couple' was an outlandish and rare concept in the social practices of Western European lay societies, all milieux, until the twelfth or thirteenth century, according to region. I understand 'marriage' as a formally contracted, potentially sexual, exclusive union of one man and one woman of some intended durability – viz., in the sense it is commonly used. By 'social practices' I mean less the occurrence of events, such as a feast or a ceremony, denoting 'marriage', than its supposed consequence, the establishment of a lasting two-person partnership – the 'married couple', usually thought to be at the core of medieval households. I should like to suggest that at the core (if that is a meaningful simile at all) there was a person – usually a man – entertaining social relationships with a number of men and women around him, some more and some less dependent and/or subordinate, making up the household or primary social group, and that many of the man–woman relationships thus constituted had, or were presumed to have, a sexual side to them. In short, medieval Europe was a largely polygynous society.

2. Marriage in medieval history[1]

Scholarship, otherwise widely divergent in premises and outlook, is overwhelmingly in favour of considering monogamous marriage to be one of the consistent features of the last two millennia or so of European history. A wealth of studies in the legal tradition, from the mid-nineteenth century on, have repeatedly underlined the importance of formally contracted marriage, whatever form it took at different points, to central areas of society: the conception of legitimate offspring; intergenerational transmission of goods, material and immaterial; the organisation of the household; the forging of alliances between kin groups (and creation of other liens of parentage); and questions of honour and shame, decency and (in infringement) immorality.[2] In short, there seems to be no doubt that Europeans have for a very long

1. Part of what follows is an extended and reworked version of the argument presented in an earlier Danish-language publication: J. Rüdiger, 'Ægteskab – fandtes det? Jon Loptssons kvinder', in H. J. Orning, K. Esmark and L. Hermanson (eds.), *Gaver, ritualer, konflikter. Et rettsantropologisk perspektiv på nordisk middelalder* (Oslo: 2010), 77-105. That article also provides a case study to illustrate the argument.
2. For a useful summary of the trends in research 'twenty-five years after the Goody thesis' see B. Jussen, 'Perspektiven der Verwandtschaftsforschung fünfundzwanzig Jahre nach Jack Goodys "Entwicklung von Ehe und Familie in Europa"', in K.-H. Spieß (ed.), *Die Familie in der Gesellschaft des Mittelalters*. Vorträge und Forschungen 71 (Ostfildern: 2009), 275-324.

time made marriage a key concept of a number of discourses, and innumerable instances of practice.

The rise of historical research inspired by ethnology has been a stimulating challenge to the older tradition of legal history, with its focus on institutions and its privileging of normative sources. Many assumptions about the pertinence of prescripts have been lastingly corrected; indeed the idea of 'legal anthropology' is to add an ethnologically informed focus on practice to the older focus on written law, and to try to get a glimpse of how seemingly anarchical practice expressed, indeed created, an order of its own. It is not surprising that studies of the ninth through twelfth centuries, a period previously labelled 'feudal anarchy', were the field in which medieval historians first, and perhaps with most impact, tried out approaches borrowed from ethnology and social anthropology. Marc Bloch's *premier âge féodal* became the arena for the most innovative research in the 1970s and 80s. Ethnologist Jack Goody's influential *The Development of the Family and Marriage in Europe* (1983) and historian Georges Duby's study of marriage in feudal France, *Le chevalier, la femme et le prêtre* (1981), proved to be enormously consequential to further studies of medieval societies with an *Annales* slant. Goody's main thesis is that 'the Church' brought about some fundamental changes from late Antiquity onwards, accentuating the already significant difference between, on the one side, Europe and the Mediterranean, and on the other side, many other societies, such as sub-Saharan Africa. Consequently, Christian Europe departed yet more sharply from a situation that, seen in a supra-regional context, was already markedly particular.[3] Goody highlights four areas in the field of kinship structures in which the Church worked fundamental changes: the suppression of endogamy (relationships contracted within the same group, such as cousins intermarrying); the suppression of the levirate (a widow marrying a close relative, for example a brother, of her deceased husband) which had been fairly common in Antiquity as well as being a requirement of Mosaic Law; the disappearance of adoption; and the discouragement of polygynous practices ('concubinage') in favour of permanent monogamous relationships.

Georges Duby's great theme was the clash between two models of marriage, the 'lay' and the 'clerical' one.[4] During the course of the eleventh

---

3.   J. Goody, *The Development of the Family and Marriage in Europe* (Cambridge: 1983); cf. in a similar vein J. Goody, *The European Family: An Historical and Anthropological Essay* (Oxford: 2000).

4.   G. Duby, *Le chevalier, la femme et le prêtre. Le mariage dans la France féodale* (Paris: 1981), as well as several other works by the same author; cf. G. Duby, *Mâle moyen âge. De l'amour et autres essais* (Paris: 1988); G. Duby, *Dames du douzième siècle*, 3 vols (Paris: 1995-1996). Duby's views are also apparent in the relevant volumes of two influential general histories, both of which he co-edited, G. Duby (ed.), *Histoire de la vie privée 2: De l'Europe féodale à la Renaissance* (Paris: 1985), and G. Duby, 'Il modello cortese', in C. Klapisch-Zuber (ed.), *Storia*

century, clerics began to enforce a new and radical remodelling of marriage, which according to the new doctrine was to be a union of souls, echoing the marriage of Christ to his Church, and bearing the same hallmarks of voluntariness and permanence. Consent of the two persons involved, man and woman, was sufficient; although a public contraction of marriage was desirable in order to keep things tidy and avoid all the pitfalls of clandestinity, at the end of the day *consensus facit nuptiam*; the declaration of wills of man and woman alone made a marriage valid and permanent. This threatened, according to Duby, a well-established lay model of marriage, which was one of the main instruments for social groups (heavily organised along kinship lines as they were) to conclude alliances, settle disputes, or both. Duby and other historians working in the field have provided numerous impressive examples of individual fates that took a dramatic turn when the two models clashed.[5]

For all their obvious dissimilarities in approach and outlook, there is one thing Duby and Goody have in common: Whatever form it takes ('lay' or 'clerical' for instance), the ubiquity of marriage as such is taken for granted. For Duby, the entire kinship system, indeed 'the whole society' is based on marriage, described as 'the cornerstone of social structure'.[6] Goody the ethnologist, in trying to refute some of the more radical historicisations of *mentalité*, goes so far as to claim that 'a conjugal relationship which is defined by relatively exclusive sexual and marital rights' is a practically universal phenomenon,[7] and that in pre-modern Europe, 'at the core of the network of kin relationships there was always a conjugal pair who formed the basis of a nuclear family or household'.[8] Historians of the Middle Ages seem on the whole to follow this powerful double example, however much they otherwise might disagree with Duby or Goody (or both). Hans-Werner Goetz, in his widely disseminated *Leben im Mittelalter* (1986), roundly declares: 'Gründungsmoment und Grundlage der Familie bildete die Ehe.'[9] The social history of women was (and is) customarily or-

delle donne in Occidente 2: Il medioevo (Rome and Bari: 1990), 310-29. All of these works have been translated into several other European languages.

5. Duby, *Chevalier*, 142-50; Duby, *Mâle moyen âge*, 50-73; Duby, *Dames*, vol. 1, passim.

6. Duby, *Chevalier*, 23: 'la clé de voûte de l'édifice social'.

7. Goody, *European Family*, 4.

8. Ibid., 59. Cf. similar views in D. Barthélemy, 'La vie privée dans les maisonnées aristocratiques de la France féodale', *Histoire de la vie privée 2*, 96-162; C. Brooke, *The Medieval Idea of Marriage* (Oxford: 1989); L. Betzig, 'Medieval Monogamy', *Journal of Family History* 20 (1995), 181-215; L. Otis-Cour, *Lust und Liebe. Geschichte der Paarbeziehungen im Mittelalter* (Frankfurt am Main: 2000); D. d'Avray, *Medieval Marriage: Symbolism and Society* (London: 2005), allowing for the discursive nature of the concept of marriage.

9. H.-W. Goetz, *Leben im Mittelalter vom 7. bis zum 13. Jahrhundert* (München: 1986), 39.

ganised along the themes of life stages and the leeways and opportunities they offered women, featuring at least a prominent chapter on marriage in its different forms.[10] Marriage looms less large in the social history of men in the Middle Ages, which is normally organised much along the lines of the life stages as defined by individual prowess and social power: child, youth, adulthood, old age. Yet in this narrative too, marriage has its fixed place; it marks the passage from youth into adulthood – a transition nowhere described more compellingly than by Georges Duby himself, in his account of the life of William Marshall, the celebrated twelfth-century erstwhile fortune hunter who went on to become regent of England.[11] William Marshall's desperate hanging around in the ante-rooms at the new King Richard Lionheart's court trying to find out whether the young king would make good the promise of his ageing father to hand over to William a bride, and the wealth and status that came with her, marks a high point of Duby's narrative and warns even the most sceptical mind that marriage could certainly make or break a man.

In the face of this overwhelming evidence, Duby's setting marriage as a serious matter off against pre- and extra-marital dalliances which young and not-so-young members of the military élite allowed themselves with pretty women of the peasantry, or indeed their own households, seems quite obviously convincing. A similar dichotomy, and the tendency to pass over those other women rather sweepingly, is pervasive in almost all research. The fact that medieval husbands, especially among the military élites, behaved in anything but a strictly monogamous fashion is freely admitted. Yet nothing much is made of this fact, which is glossed over nonchalantly in most works, as though there was nothing surprising about it. '[M]en of wealth often kept women of inferior social status as concubines', writes James Brundage in his standard work on medieval sexuality and society, 'feeling that it was less scandalous and more convenient to retain attractive young women as companions than to marry them.'[12] The idea is that sexual attractiveness (on the part of the woman) and lust or sexual prowess (on the part of the man) are the self-evident, indeed more or less the only possible reasons for all non-marital relationships, and therefore practically an anthropological constant: men just are like that, and if they happen to be well-

---

10. Cf. E. Ennen, *Frauen im Mittelalter* (München: 1984), beginning with two chapters on the position of women in law and in marriage respectively before the chronological part starts with the Merovingians, as though those were quasi-timeless basic conditions for women's lives.
11. G. Duby, *Guillaume le Maréchal ou le meilleur chevalier du monde* (Paris: 1984).
12. J. L. Brundage, *Law, Sex and Christian Society in Medieval Europe* (Chicago and London: 1987), 297.

placed to do so they indulge in sporting with 'the prey', as Duby somewhat uncharitably calls women in the chivalrous society.[13]

3. The semantics of the couple

Like the dichotomy itself, the different characteristics of marriage and non-marital relationships have a long intellectual tradition. 'I have myself experienced the distance between duly contracted marriage, which is an agreement entered into for the sake of generating offspring, and a relationship based on lust' (*pactum libidinosi amoris*) reads the 'confession' of St Augustine of Hippo from around A.D. 400[14], in what was to become arguably the most influential text for the medieval history of man-to-woman relationships. Augustine repeatedly establishes his dichotomy: 'I was then not so much a friend of marriage but a slave of my lust' ('non amator coniugii sed libidinis servus eram'),[15] is how he describes his earlier life, when he was living together with a series of women in wait for his betrothed bride to come of age. The Augustine tradition thus associated marriage, itself legitimised by St Paul as the proper way of dealing with sexual desire ('burning'), with the worthy causes of secular society – specifically the generation of legitimate offspring – and posited it against *libidinosus amor*, lust and lasciviousness, which necessarily went with concubines. What had been different forms of contractual relationships in Roman society and law,[16] separated by degrees of formality and social recognition but not normally by different moral valorisations, became the governing dichotomy in the semantics of man-to-woman relationships. 'Aliud est uxor, aliud concubina', as Pope Gregory the Great had it: one thing is a wife, another one a concubine. The idea is pervasive in medieval writing on the topic. *Concubina* became a passepartout word, to be used in quite varying circumstances, from royal women in contested relationships to churchmen's wives in the anti-'Nicolaitist' movement of eleventh-century church reformers for celibacy among the secular clergy to downright prostitutes. The common denominator for this use, spanning as it did a wide range of different relationships (covering the whole society, in fact), was by the eleventh century an almost

---

13. Duby, *Mâle moyen âge*, 47.
14. Augustine, *Confessionum libri XIII*, ed. L. M. J. Verheijen, *Corpus Christianorum series latina* 27 (Turnhout: 1990), IV 2,2.
15. Ibid. 2,5.
16. H.-J. Becker, 'Die nichteheliche Lebensgemeinschaft (Konkubinat) in der Rechtsgeschichte', in G. Landwehr et al. (eds.), *Die nichteheliche Lebensgemeinschaft* (Göttingen: 1978), 13-18; P. Veyne, 'L'empire romain', *Histoire de la vie privée 1: De l'empire romain à l'an mil* (Paris: 1985), 19-224; S. Treggiari, Iusti coniuges *from the Time of Cicero to the Time of Ulpian* (Oxford: 1991).

purely moral one: 'Concubinage' was, in one way or another, imperfect and improper, and it was, as attested by St Augustine, basically libidinous.

The overwhelming evidence of the use of this dichotomy in medieval sources, most of which are imbued with the Patristic tradition, has (understandably) shaped modern perceptions of man–woman relationships. It is, however, necessary to discriminate between the different 'uses' of the terms and the dichotomy: in a word, the semantics. Their pervasiveness in quite a number of discourses, from moral theology and church law to political propaganda, is quite obvious and shrouds a little the fact that medieval authors themselves were quite aware of the fact that it could be difficult to trace the dichotomy down to actual social practice and apply it to individuals and their sexual relationships. St Augustine himself was nonplussed by observing that Scripture itself was unclear in the matter, since for instance the bondswomen with whom Abraham had children were interchangeably designated *uxor* and *concubina*. Sara, however, he noted with apparent relief, was only called *uxor*.[17] The redactors of church law felt equally unable to draw the line. As early as A.D. 400, the First Council of Toledo decreed that if a married man (the canon avoids a term for marriage and terms it 'a believer having a wife', 'uxorem habens fidelis') kept a concubine, he was to be excluded from communion. If, however, he kept the concubine instead of a wife ('pro uxore concubinam habet'), things were all right: 'as long as he contents himself with the relationship to one woman, either wife or concubine, as he prefers' ('tantum ut unius mulieris, aut uxoris aut concubinae, ut ei placuerit, sit coniunctione contentus').[18] The formula was repeated again and again in councils, and found its way almost unchanged into Gratian's *Decretum*, the most influential twelfth-century collection of Church law,[19] driving home the point that at the heart of Church teaching was not marriage, but monogamy: 'It is not allowed for a Christian to have even two women at the same time, let alone more.'[20] Under this premise, the legal mind was forced to admit that the boundary between marriage and non-marriage could indeed become blurred. If the necessary characteristics of the 'new', Reformist marriage – above all, mutual consent and permanence – were in place, then that 'makes her a wife, even if Law calls her a concubine'.[21] These finer points of Church law were, however, lost in a well-

---

17. Augustinus, *De Civitate Dei* 16,34, on Gen 25.
18. I Tol c.17, quoted after G. C. Caselli, 'Concubina pro uxore. Osservazioni in merito al c. 17 del primo concilio di Toledo', *Rivista di Storia del Diritto Italiano* 37-38 (1964-1965), 163-211, at 182.
19. *Decretum*, D.34 c.4: 'tamen ut unius mulieris, aut uxoris aut concubinae, sit coniunctione contentus'.
20. *Decretum*, D.34 c.5: 'Christiano, non dicam plurimas, sed nec duas simul habere licitum est'.
21. *Decretum*, D.34, 'secunda pars: hanc coniugem facit affectus, concubinam vero lex nominat.'

established semantics of concubinage in common Church usage, though they did leave their mark on contemporary lawgiving, such as the Jutish Law from 1241, according to which a 'slegfred' (*sløkæfrith*, the Danish equivalent of *concubina* for the purpose) was to be considered a wife when she had openly shared table and bed with a man for three years and was known to carry the keys of the house – pragmatic, visible signs of permanence and mutual consent as markers of 'marriage' by the standards of Church law.[22]

4. Polygyny in the medieval North: an overview of scholarship

The notorious matter-of-factness of Merovingian and Carolingian polygyny appears to have been on its way out by the ninth century.[23] In the high Middle Ages, kings in all parts of Francia, as well as their English and Spanish counterparts, were only rarely (and exceptionally) seen in polygynous situations. While extra-marital unions of princes were to remain a recurrent feature of European history all through the Middle Ages and beyond (take the famous courtesans of Renaissance Italy and the powerful mistresses at the courts of the Valois and Bourbon kings in early modern France), bringing with them such emblematic figures as the 'royal bastard', these unions were quite a long way removed from the unabashed straightforwardness with which early medieval kings acquired their women. At least, that is the image conveyed by narrative sources and supported by documentary evidence from the Frankish part of the continent. It would maybe be more accurate to say that post-Carolingian societies became very reluctant to mention polygyny. This overall Frankland monogamism, which puts its mark on both 'clerical' and 'secular' sources, makes it quite difficult to assess the extent of everyday élite polygyny in high medieval Europe, but one thing is clear:

22. *Jyske Lov, text 1: NkS 295 8*, ed. P. Skautrup, *Danmarks gamle Landskabslove med Kirkelovene* 2 (København: 1933), 68-69 (I §27): 'Hwa sum hauær slækæfrith i garth mæth sik. oc gangær openbarlich mæth ath souæ. oc hauær laas oc lykki. oc søkær atæ oc dryk mæth opænbarlich i thre wintær. hvn skal wæræ athalkunæ oc ræt hwsfrø.' Cf. I. M. Jensen, 'Landskabslovene som kilde til kvinders stilling i 1100-1200-tallet', *Kvinder i middelalderen* (København: 1982), 61-68; N. Damsholt, *Kvindebilledet i dansk højmiddelalder* (København: 1985); T. Nors, 'Kampen om ægteskabet', *Den jyske Historiker* 42 (1987), 28-46.
23. Cf. S. F. Wemple, *Women in Frankish Society: Marriage and the Cloister, 500-900* (Philadelphia: 1981); P. Stafford, *Queens, Concubines and Dowagers: The King's Wife in the Early Middle Ages* (London: 1983); D. Herlihy, Opera muliebria: *Women and Work in Medieval Europe* (New York: 1990); R. Le Jan, *Famille et pouvoir dans le monde franc (VIIe-Xe siècles). Essai d'anthropologie sociale* (Paris: 1995); A. Esmyol, *Geliebte oder Ehefrau? Konkubinen im frühen Mittelalter* (Köln: 2002).

Outside of moral theology and invective, royal and aristocratic polygyny had ceased to be a matter of discourse.

As any reader of Saxo or the sagas knows, things are different in the North. Scandinavian historiography, both Latin and Norse, abounds with tales of kings who keep many women, serially or simultaneously.[24] Indeed, kings are so openly polygynous, and the fact that they are is related so complacently by the authors, that the question imposes itself: why?

Having done away with the idea, dear to eighteenth- and nineteenth-century essayists, of a progressive refinement of mores (or, with a negative slant, a progressive decline of sexual liberty), modern scholarship now assigns a prominent role in Viking society to traditional lay marriage. In fact, in studies of women in the Viking and Northern Middle Ages, marriage in its different forms is now placed just as centrally as it is in medieval women's studies in general.[25] The ubiquity of *frillur*[26] alongside 'proper' wives is then explained as either an ornamental élite phenomenon not really

24. For the image of women in the sagas, cf. E. Mundal, 'Kvinnebiletet i nokre mello-maldergenrar. Eit oposisjonelt kvinnesyn?' *Edda* 82 (1982), 341-71; E. Mundal, 'The Position of Women in Old Norse Society and the Basis for their Power', *NORA – Nordic Journal for Women's Studies* 1-2 (1994), 3-11; E. Mundal, 'Korleis påverka kristninga og kyrkja kjønnsrollemønstra?', in N. Lund (ed.), *Viking og Hvidekrist. Norden og Europa i den sene vikingetid og tidligste middelalder* (København: 2000), 41-58; A. S. Arnórsdóttir, *Kvinner og 'krigsmenn'. Kjønnenes stilling i det islandske samfunnet på 1100- og 1200-tallet* (MA thesis, University of Bergen: 1990) [= *Konur og vigamenn. Staða kynjanna á Íslandi á 12. og 13. öld* (Reykjavík: 1995)]; J. Jochens, 'Old Norse sources on Women', in J. T. Rosenthal (ed.), *Medieval Women and the Sources of Medieval History* (Athens, GA. and London: 1990), 155-88; J. Jochens, *Women in Old Norse Society* (Ithaca and London: 1995); J. Jochens, *Old Norse Images of Women* (Philadelphia: 1996); H. Kress, 'Gægur er þér í augum. Konur í sjónmáli Íslendingasagna', in G. Karlsson and H. Þorláksson (eds.), *Yfir Íslandssála. Afmælisrit til heiðurs Magnúsi Stefánssyni* (Reykjavík: 1992), 77-94. Many works on women in the Viking and Middle Ages use the sagas to some extent; cf. J. Jesch, *Women in the Viking Age* (Woodbridge: 1991); B. Sawyer, *Kvinnor och familj i det forn- och medeltida Skandinavien* (Trondheim: 1998 – 2nd edn); B. Bandlien, *Å finne den rette. Kjærlighet, individ og samfunn i norrøn middelalder* (Oslo: 2001). With a focus on Latin material from Scandinavia: B. Strand, *Kvinnor och män i Gesta Danorum* (Göteborg: 1980); Damsholt, *Kvindebilledet*; T. Nors, 'Saxos særheder', *Den jyske Historiker* 41 (1987), 19-35.

25. Cf. L. Carlsson, *'Jag giver dig min dotter'. Trolovning och äktenskap i den svenska kvinnans äldre historia*. Skrifter udgivna av Institut för Rättshistorisk Forskning, Rättshistorisk bibliotek 18-20, 2 vols (Stockholm: 1965-1972); E. Roesdahl, *The Vikings* (Harmondsworth: 1987), 59-61; J. Jochens, '"Með jákvæði hennar sjálfrar": Consent as Signifier in the Old Norse World', in A. E. Laiou (ed.), *Consent and Coercion to Sex and Marriage* (Washington DC: 1993), 271-89; Sawyer, *Kvinnor och familj*, 38-40.

26. Old Norse *friðla/frilla*, pl. *-ur* (modern Scandinavian *'frille/-a'*) is commonly rendered by 'concubine'. This may be accurate, especially in contexts marked by the 'Augustinian divide', whereas in other contexts we may think of the ethnological term 'co-wife'. An impressive study is A. Magnúsdottír, *Frillor och fruar. Politik och samlevnad på Island 1120-1400* (Göteborg: 2001).

impinging on the core of the cellular household (which would correspond to Duby's or Brundage's view), or alternatively as a holdover from a Dark Age past, doomed to disappear in the long run.

This idea of a passage from an older society featuring (among other things) widespread polygyny to a new one where polygyny slowly but steadily disappeared is very much at the base of general views of the history of man–woman relationships in the North. As we can see, it follows the general European narrative described above, with a lag of three to four centuries, which again makes it nicely compatible with the 'Europeanisation' paradigm, the current version of progressism. This approach is sometimes explicitly spelled out, but more often, and perhaps more effectively, it is conveyed by the use of such small words as 'still' or 'already', shaping as they do our ideas about social change. But what basis do we have to claim that polygyny was *still* a social fact in twelfth-century Scandinavia? Or that polygyny had anything to do at all with heathen society, for that matter? After all, most sources (and practically all of the narrative material) about the pre-Christian period belong to the twelfth and thirteenth centuries, when the heathen past was definitely past. This is Christian literature.

The perils of using sagas as sources for the time they purport to narrate has of course been a subject of scholarly debate for a century, and it is unnecessary to take it up here. I merely want to point out that unlike many political, economic and cultural features (royal power, law regions, landownership, cult organisation), sexual mores, including polygyny, seem to be regarded as surprisingly unproblematical in this sense. Norway's founder king Harald Finehair was a man with at least sixteen children; a man who according to the skald Þjóðólf of Kvinesdalen had nine wives from all parts of Norway and dismissed them for the Jutish princess Ragnhild when he had the chance; a man indeed whose conquest of all Norway was prompted by the challenge issued by a Vestland chieftain's daughter whom he wasn't powerful enough to fetch to his bed: she said he could come back when he had managed to establish the kind of kingship that Gorm had built for himself in Denmark.[27] While the fact that the grand unifying figure of Norwegian national history was so openly polygynous was nasty enough as it was for Norwegian bourgeois sensibilities to stomach, at least he was safely removed into heathen times, and so was polygyny in general.

Moral judgements may have changed during the past four decades or so, as our own society has become less and less monogamous (and Christian), but the chronological equation in which polygyny=heathen and monogamy=Christian is by and large still held to be valid. Now, while there is no doubt that monogamy was indeed a Christian project, we do not know

---

27. Snorri Sturluson, *Heimskringla*, ed. B. Aðalbjarnarson, 3 vols, *Íslenzk fornrit* 26-28 (Reykjavík: 1941-1951); *Haralds saga hárfagra* chs. 3-4, 9, 20.

whether polygyny was specifically linked to pre-Christian society – except in the minds of theologians, for whom polygyny and polytheism were indicative of one another.[28] As regards social practice, we are simply in no position to judge whether, say, the lands of future Denmark or Norway were markedly polygynous in the eighth century. The few indications we have, such as the famous observation of Ibn Faḍlān about Norse travellers fondling their slave girls in public,[29] in fact do point to forms of ostentatious élite polygyny, but it is precisely the forms, and not polygyny in itself (current in both Muslim and Frankish as well as Byzantine higher circles), that arouses the interest of the Arab observers. Famous quotes often repeated in research, such as Dudo of Saint-Quentin's tale of how Nordic polygyny led to overpopulation and hence to the Viking expansion,[30] are of course more valuable as evidence for ideas about the correspondence of barbarism, unbridled sensuality and unbridled violence current in ninth-century Frankish intellectual milieux, plus knowledge of the learned *vagina gentium* imagery, than for actual sociography of early Viking Scandinavia. It is a different matter with Adam of Bremen, who is quite aware of the social context of resource polygyny: 'Every one of them has, according to his faculties, two, three or even more women at once'.[31] So at least for the eleventh century, we can be fairly confident about élite polygyny – but here again, we learn nothing much about the social context. Rune stones, which frequently show us women in a position to erect memorials for their men, cannot tell us what kind of relationship ('marriage'?) the woman and man in question had, how it was contracted, and whether it was an exclusive one. The evidence from the sagas is completely puzzling for anyone who looks for a chronological order in sexual relations. While not quite as formidable as insatiable Harald Finehair, polygynous kings are very much in evidence all through the kings' sagas (in the case of *Heimskringla*, right down to Magnus Erlingsson, *kvin-*

28. Key references are 1 Kings 11 (Solomon's wives introducing idolatry); Hos. 1 and Ezra 23 (fornication) and the New Testament analogy bride=Church (for which, see above).

29. *Ibn Faḍlāns Reisebericht*, ed. A. Zeki Validi Toğan, Abhandlungen für die Kunde des Morgenlandes 24/3 (Leipzig: 1939), ch. 83; cf. R. M. Karras, *Slavery and Society in Medieval Scandinavia* (New Haven and London: 1988); R. M. Karras, 'Concubinage and slavery in the Viking Age', *Scandinavian Studies* 62 (1990), 141-62.

30. Dudo of Saint-Quentin, *De moribus et actis primorum Normanniae ducum*, ed. J. Lair, *Mémoires de la Société des Antiquaires de Normandie* 23 (Caen: 1865), I 1: 'ilae namque gentes, petulanti nimium luxu exardescentes, feminasque quamplurimas singulari turpitudine stuprantes commiscendo, illinc soboles innumeros obscena illiciti connubii commixtione patrando generant.'

31. Adam of Bremen, *Gesta Hammaburgensis ecclesiae pontificum*, ed. B. Schmeidler, *Monumenta Germaniae Historica in usum scholarum* (Hannover and Leipzig: 1917), IV 21 (on *Sueonia*/Svealand): 'quisque secundum facultatem suorum virium duas aut tres et amplius simul habet.'

namaðr mikill ('a big one for women').[32] The more overtly partisan works such as *Sverris saga* or *Hákonar saga Hákonarsonar* are more reticent and only mention them at any length if absolutely unavoidable – as in the case of the birth of those two kings, both of them born out of temporary and clearly extra-marital unions. In the sagas of Icelanders, which are primarily set in the ninth through eleventh centuries and where one would consequently expect a great deal of polygyny, it is curiously all but absent: There is only a handful of *frillur*, mostly in the context of the story of their sons, against a background of nicely cellular couples. In contrast, the contemporary sagas (narrations about current or recent events in thirteenth-century Iceland) abound with relationships to *frillur*, most of them recounted quite incidentally and matter-of-factly.[33] The overall impression is that (1) we can more or less safely assume the existence of élite polygyny in the Viking Age but do not know anything more precisely about it, and (2) élite polygyny certainly was a living social fact in twelfth- and thirteenth-century Scandinavia, and we know quite a lot about it – indeed, thanks to the sagas' loquacity, more than about polygyny in any other part of high medieval Europe.[34]

So what place is there for marriage in a generally polygynous system? There can be many different ones. In present-day Europe, marriage coexists quite well with both polygynous and polyandrous practices. Normally, their incidence will fit into a life-stage model: Young unmarried men and women are (at any rate according to the image our culture likes to project of itself through novels, films, and TV serials) the most likely to experiment with a fairly quick succession of relationships, or with conducting them simultaneously, without excluding the possibility – and above all, the ideal – of a stable, monogamous relationship. Romantic love, as 'invented' in the twelfth century[35] and given its present shape in the decades after 1800, remains the mentalitarian standard model of human relationship (alongside its concomi-

---

32. *Heimskringla - Magnúss saga Erlingssonar*, ch. 37. Cf. Bandlien, *Å finne den rette*, 53, on the derogatory use of the term 'women's man', akin to 'drunkard', both of which are used in the older *Sverris saga* to describe the same king Magnus, the enemy of the eponymous hero Sverrir. But in *Heimskringla* Snorri uses the word in the *epílogos* to sum up a king after his death in a clearly non-critical sense. Putting aside the question of a possibly intended inversion of the older verdict by Snorri, that master of oblique criticism, it appears that a penchant for women and drink was in itself neither a positive nor a negative quality, the assessment depending on the mastery of the self in indulging in either.
33. See Magnúsdóttir, *Frillor och fruar*, for detailed analyses.
34. I develop these ideas more fully in my Habilitationsschrift J. Rüdiger, *Der König und seine Frauen. Polygynie und politische Kultur in Europa (9.-13. Jahrhundert)* (Humboldt University, Berlin: 2006); German edition to be published by Akademie-Verlag, Berlin; English translation in preparation with Brill, Leiden.
35. Cf. Stendhal, *De l'amour* (Paris: 1822), ch. 51, who was possibly the first in a long line of moderns to argue this.

tant form, the core family), with two notable recent changes: it need no longer be a heterosexual one; and marriage is no longer required. On the other hand, if it *is* contracted, marriage normally presupposes romantic love. So strong is the hold of a sensibility that is strongly Romantic, but ultimately stems from the revolutionary twelfth-century change in Church teaching that brought about the principle of marriage by consent, that we culturally ('instinctively') disapprove of marriage contracted for non-romantic reasons, such as social advancement or material improvement. A good part of the present-day debate about 'forced marriages' among immigrants is influenced by the idea that any marriage not based on mutual consent is plainly wrong. All in all, we know from our own experience that a society can perfectly well practice, and accept, polygyny/-andry and at the same time practice, and promote, monogamy. (The speciality of present-day society would be that monogamy has become somewhat removed from marriage, given that 'affairs' are now much more easily condoned than they were a few decades earlier, while romantic love remains solidly monogamous, and 'unfaithfulness' is considered a terminal felony in love – indeed, it still evokes much the same vocabulary as medieval writers would use for both secular felony and religious apostasy).

To sum up: Over the past millennium and a half, and even at times when marriage was less optional than it is today and more of the social and economic status depended on marital status, polygynous behaviour – if not polyandry, definitely more stigmatised until quite recently – was widespread, generally known, and culturally negotiated. From countless detailed or generalising mentions of *concubinae, frillur, cyfes, barraganas, soignants* (to name but a few terms[36]) we know that it was no different in the Middle Ages. Of course, the place of marriage in this system varied greatly over space, time, and social milieu.

5. The social semantics of polygyny

The claim that marriage can (and normally does) exist in a polygynous context calls for a word about terminology. Marriage is, as pointed out above, one of the forms that sexual relations can take in a society which practises both monogyny and polygyny. It is important not to mix up mono-/poly*gamy* (being married to one/many), and mono-/poly*gyny* (having relationships with one/many women).[37] There is a widespread use in scholarly

36. Latin, Norse, Anglo-Saxon, Castilian, and French respectively.
37. Polyandry (for a woman to have relationships with several men) did not exist as a commonly approved practice in the Medieval West, although it did haunt the (male?) imagination.

literature of poly*gyny* as one of the two forms poly*gamy* can take (namely, for a man to be married to more than one woman, as opposed to its notional counterpart poly*andry*, for a woman to be married to more than one man).[38] I suggest that this use should be avoided, however, because it leaves no space for the socially relevant plurality of sexual relationships which we do not see as marriages. The term 'polygyny' would effectively be unfit for any medieval or modern European context, since Christian Europe so emphatically rejects multiple marriages (bigamy and on up), so 'polygyny' in the sense of 'marriage to several wives at once' would be a contradiction in terms.

Instead, by 'polygyny' I mean a state where a man entertains socially relevant sexual relationships with several women, actually or notionally at the same time ('simultaneous' as opposed to 'serial' polygyny). A 'socially relevant' relationship is one that observers removed from the actual context in time or space find important enough to take note of. (For medieval history, this part of the definition is redundant because if we know about a relationship at all in any detail, this already proves it was considered relevant, since it was observed, related, and recorded.) The advantage of this definition is that it can do without the arbitrary imposition of minimum requirements for a relationship to be included, such as a certain duration, certain formal features such as a ceremony, the transfer of goods, or even sexual consummation – we neither can nor need prove that the partners actually slept together if we concentrate on the surrounding society's opinion that they may have.

This definition is quite at variance for instance with the one proposed in the new edition of *Reallexikon der germanischen Altertumskunde*, which does operate by such minimum requirements.[39] It is, however, essential not

38. Cf. M. Clunies Ross, 'Concubinage in Anglo-Saxon England', *Past and Present* 108 (1985), 3-34; P. Bretschneider, *Polygyny: A Cross-Cultural Study* (Uppsala: 1995). Clunies Ross and Karras, 'Concubinage', prefer to use the term 'poly*coity*' (from 'coitus') to denote multiple sexual relationships. I prefer 'polygyny'(/-andry), however, because here the emphasis is on the social, not the sexual nature of the relationship. Indeed, it is not necessary for such relationships to be effective that they actually have a sexual side to them, but only that people think they may have.

39. H. Reichert, s.v. 'Nebenfrau', *Reallexikon der Germanischen Altertumskunde* 21 (Berlin and New York: 2002), 18: 'Der Begriff N[ebenfrau] bezeichnet Frauen in polygynen Eheformen von Ges[ellschaften], in denen die Rechtsordnung gestattet, daß ein Mann neben einer Hauptehe gleichzeitig eine oder mehrere weitere Bindungen von geringerem Rechtsstatus oder gleichrangige Ehen nebeneinander eingeht. Dadurch unterscheidet sich die Polygynie einerseits von Konkubinaten, das sind Einehen mit geringeren Regelungen als das matrimonium, insbesondere im Scheidungs- und Erbrecht (Lebensgemeinschaften), andererseits von kurzfristig wechselnden oder illegalen sexuellen Beziehungen während einer Einehe.' Reichert goes on to admit that by this definition, '[d]as Ausmaß der echten Polygynie ist ungewiß' because neither ecclesiastical sources nor chronicles differentiate

to let any arbitrary exclusions dim perceptions. A relationship can be important, its consequences considerable for the two persons involved and a lot of others besides, even if (to take a crass example) it only lasts for some moments, as in the case of King Sigurd Munn who on his itinerary through Norway sometime around 1140 enjoyed the hospitality of a farmer, allowing himself to include in the hospitality a slave girl grinding corn whose song had attracted him.[40] In this case, the relation had considerable political ramifications, because the boy born out of this very short-lived union was adopted by one of the contending factions as their pretender to kingship, and did indeed hold the throne for a brief spell as Håkon Herdebrei ('the broad-shouldered', r. 1157/61–1162). His foster-father the farmer and his foster-brothers the farmer's sons rose to (and fell from) power with him. Now it would of course be possible to appraise the political relevance of the king's taking advantage of the slave girl without considering it in terms of polygyny. After all, the custom, generally accepted in Norway and to a lesser extent in Denmark, that a son generated by a king had a claim to kingship regardless of who the mother was (the *Geblütsrecht* of earlier German legal history)[41], meant that in the medieval North, every sexual relationship of a king could produce a possible pretender. However, the relationship itself, brief though it was, had a wider-reaching social effect quite apart from the fact that a son was born from it. Taking a woman of the household as his mate while on *veitsla* – one of the visits on the never-ending itinerary through the kingdom by which a high medieval king asserted his rule and subjects' hospitality was mandatory, whether willingly extended or not[42] –

neatly between the different forms of relationship. I prefer to view this less as a failure on the part of medieval authors to live up to modern standards of legalism than an accurate image of distinctions that were blurred at the time.

40. *Heimskringla - Haraldssona saga*, ch. 18. 'Sex hospitality' is a frequent theme in medieval literature; see Ennen, *Frauen*, 41, and A. Guerreau-Jalabert, *Index des motifs narratifs dans les romans arthuriens français en vers (XIIe-XIIIe siècles)*. Publications romanes et françaises 202 (Genève: 1992), motif T281, for examples.

41. Its classical formulation is in Gregory of Tours, *Libri historiarum X*, ed. R. Buchner, 2 vols (Darmstadt: 1977 – 5th edn), V, 20: 'disregarding the descent of the women, they consider as kings' sons [all children] generated by kings' ('praetermissis nunc generibus feminarum, regis vocitantur liberi, qui de regibus fuerant procreati'); cf. E. Hoffmann, *Königserhebung und Thronfolgeordnung in Dänemark bis zum Ausgang des Mittelalters* (Berlin and New York: 1976); J. Jochens, 'The Politics of Reproduction: Medieval Norwegian Kingship', *American Historical Review* 92 (1987), 327-49. Such kings, which it would evidently be meaningless to call 'illegitimate' because they clearly were not, are frequent in eleventh- to thirteenth-century Norway, and in Denmark up to the mid-twelfth century.

42. For Norway especially, see the recent study by H. J. Orning, *Unpredictability and Presence: Norwegian Kingship in the High Middle Ages*. The Northern World 38 (Leiden: 2008). But Western European kingship was not all that dissimilar up until at least the thirteenth century. In fact, throughout Latin Europe, the end of élite polygyny as a feature of political culture and the centralisation, local and institutional, of princely power more or less coincide.

was part of this assertion. How in individual cases the king enacted his claim, and how the household reacted, was one of the crucial moments in which royal power was negotiated.[43] So the relationship was part of royal polygyny; it came with a political surplus and must be seen as part of the actions with which a king and his followers acted out 'power'. There is no reason to exclude it from the overall picture just because it was, in itself, just a short (and probably, on the part of the woman, forced) sexual act: it did have a modifying effect on social relations.

6. 'Main' and other women: The evidence of the law books

Having made this point about polygyny and its political relevance, I return to marriage and the question of its place within the system. That place must be quite removed from the kind of relationship King Sigurd Munn had with the slave girl. In effect, if we imagine different kinds of man-to-woman relationships along a scale of social standing, they would be very much at opposite ends of the scale. There can hardly be a less respectable way of having a relationship with a woman than the one Sigurd Munn had in the mill-house, whereas full formal marriage is about the 'highest', most solemn form society knows.

Now this is my very point: In most medieval lay societies up until the mid-thirteenth century, full formal marriage is a purely relational maximum. The only meaningful way of using the term 'marriage' in the description of a society is, as we have done above for 'polygynous relationship', to do away with set criteria. If they were applied, we would find ourselves using labels like 'imperfect marriage', 'nearly full marriage', and similar expressions. Instead, the question is rather an ethnological one: Does a given society hold the idea that along the scale of possible forms of man-woman relations, there is one type of relationship, high up on the scale, which is considered the absolute maximum?

Our own society does; you cannot be anything more than married. (You can combine civil and church marriage, of course, but once you are married in either form, you cannot be more than that.) Imperial Roman society did too, though by degrees; there were several forms of recognised legal marriage which varied according to required forms, cultic rites, economic consequences and dissolubility. According to scholarship, the medieval North did, as well: beside and beyond polygynous behaviour, with slave girls or with classy *frillur* of long standing, there was a secular model of marriage, involving the passage of the woman into a new kinship structure

---

43.   See Rüdiger, *Der König und seine Frauen*, for a discussion of instances.

(without complete dissolution of previous bonds), requiring the consent of a number of adult males, the transfer of goods, and (less tangibly) a shift in social relationships between two kin groups. There is no need to go out of one's way to find evidence for it. The two most prestigious source types from the high Middle Ages, the sagas (especially, as pointed out above, the sagas of Icelanders) and the regional laws (*landskabslovene*), appear to deal with 'secular marriage' at some length.[44] Or do they? The laws make a harder case than the historical narratives because they pretend to contain hard-and-fast rules, while the saga style generally shuns clear-cut terminology. For instance, if I am not mistaken, there is no single term applied to the relationship of such classic 'married couples' as, say, Egil and Ásgerð in *Egils saga*, or Njál and Bergþóra in *Njáls saga*.[45] Conversely, a first glance at the Elder Gulating Law from western Norway, which may in part date back at least to the mid-twelfth century but which in its known form is not much older than 1200,[46] shows two things: (1) there is a clear difference

44. Cf. Bandlien, *Å finne den rette*; Jochens, *Women*; I. Holtan, *Ekteskap, frillelevnad og hor i norsk høgmellomalder* (Oslo: 1996).
45. Translation can be misleading, since they frequently use the vocabulary of marriage where the original is much less explicit. The saga vocabulary includes the use of verbs such as *taka*, 'take' and *fá*, 'receive', which are used for all kinds of man-to-woman relationships (and, of course, all sorts of transmission of goods). The translators' tendency to interpret the more solemn and high-status relationships as marriages and the dictionaries' tendency to gloss them accordingly can sometimes form an argumentative circle. To give just one famous example: In the heroic speech accounting for her decision to stay with Njál as he is about to be burnt inside his farmstead by his enemies (ch. 130 of *Njáls saga*), Bergþóra says: 'ek var ung gefin Njáli', (literally: 'young was I given to Njál'). These two are often seen as a model saga married couple; the major dictionaries interpret the expression 'to give (*gefa*) a woman to a man' as the sagas' term for marriage (cf. W. Baetke, *Wörterbuch zur altnordischen Prosaliteratur* (Berlin: 1965) s.v.;R. Cleasby and G. Vigfússon, *An Icelandic-English Dictionary* (Oxford: 1874), s.v.; J. Fritzner, *Ordbog over det gamle norske Sprog* (Oslo: 1863-1896), s.v. I have come across only one word which appears to denote the inception of a specific sort of relationship akin to marriage: the reciprocal verb *kvángast* (*qwænnæs* in *Jyske Lov* I §12 and passim), which, as it is derived from *kvenna*, 'woman', is thus 'to get oneself with woman'.There does not seem to be a noun denoting the ensuing relationship (as opposed to the event) corresponding to *coniugium* etc.
46. It is doubtful whether any parts of the laws go back to the earlier eleventh century, as they claim. The first fragments are from ca. 1200; the main body is attested by the earlier thirteenth century. Especially when discussing single words and phrases as opposed to general content, it will be wise to be very careful in dating any part of the laws to much before 1200 unless there is evidence for it. Cf. K. Venås, 'Kvinne og mann i Gulatingslova. Etter en idé av Lis Jacobsen', in B. Eithun et al. (eds.), *Festskrift til Finn Hødnebø 29. desember 1989* (Oslo: 1989), 285-303; M. Rindal, 'Dei norske mellomalderlovene', in M. Rindal (ed.), *Skriftlege kjelder til kunnskap om nordisk mellomalder* (Oslo: 1995), 7-20; R. Røsstad, *Á tveim tungum. Om stil og stilvariasjon i norrønt lovmål* (Oslo: 1997); K. Helle, 'Lov og rett i middelalderen', in E. Mundal and I. Øye (eds.), *Norm og praksis i middelaldersamfunnet* (Bergen: 1999), 7-22; L. I. Hansen, '"Ætten" i de eldste landskapslovene – realitet, konstruksjon og strategi', ibid., 23-55; B. Sawyer, 'Son skal taka arv etter

between marriage and other relationships, and (2) the difference corresponds to the 'Augustinian' dichotomy, adapted to the living conditions of West Norwegian farmsteads where the head of the household has free access to the bodies of his dependant women. The 'lay' model of marriage according to Duby is easily recognised in the Gulating stipulation against bigamy: 'Every man shall own [only] one woman, whom he has bought with brideprice and settlement' ('várr scal hverr eina kono eiga, þa er hann hever mundi keypt oc maldaga').[47] The paragraph also bans multiple sexual relationships in the household: 'If a man has his slave woman alongside his wife/woman' ('ef maðr hever ambótt sina við sina kono').[48] The wording is quite close to the corresponding passages in Canon law: 'If a believer who has a wife [also] has a concubine [...]' ('si quis habens uxorem fidelis concubinam habet[...]'), and so is the sanction: public penitence for the man, to which the Gulating Law adds payment of 12 øre to the bishop. The Frostating Law of Trøndelag even has the expression *gera brullaup* ('do the bride's run', meaning marriage in modern Scandinavian) for the ceremony that marks the difference between the two relationships. Interestingly enough, however, this occurs in a paragraph about the respective inheritance rights of children born to a couple before they 'made the bride's run' and those born afterwards. The Frostating Law's answer is: no difference.[49] So at closer inspection, the categorical distinction becomes blurred and tends to vanish in a haze. The same goes for terminology. The Danish and Swedish laws use words like 'slegfred' (*slækæfrith*), clearly a vernacular term, where Church Law has *concubina*; but *uxor* is rendered by 'main woman' or 'eminent woman' (*aþalkuna*)[50] – as though there were others besides her as a rule. Other sexual relations ('hverja sem hann hefir við konu sína', 'whatever other woman he has besides his wife') are frowned upon but taken for granted. The impression is that although the 'Augustinian dichotomy' is mirrored in the law books, the mirror's frame has a polygynous gilding to it.

far sin', ibid., 56-79; and generally E. Sjöholm, *Sveriges medeltidslagar. Europeisk rättstradition i politisk omvandling* (Lund: 1988).

47. Elder Gulating Law § 25; corresponding expression in Frostating Law III 13. The Gulating Law continues with a reprisal of Canon law stipulations on bigamy: If a man has taken two women 'with brideprice and settlement', he must discharge the one he has 'bought' last.

48. Ibid. The word for the bondswoman living in the house is *arinelja*, 'hearth-co-woman' or 'the rival by the fireside' (if 'rival' she is, which in a polygynous setting need not be the case).

49. Elder Frostating Law III 11.

50. *Aðalkuna* and its variants are also in frequent in other law books; cf. Law of Jutland I 27; Scanian Law III 16; East Gautish Law AB 13; Valdemars Law of Zealand, Arvebogen og Orbodemål I 18.

At any rate, the earlier laws are by and large untouched by the more revolutionary innovations of recent church teaching.[51]

All over the relevant chapters of the law book one finds the contrast
between seemingly clear-cut terms and blurred practical applications. On
one hand, the law books continue the dichotomy to include the offspring of
marital vs. non-marital unions by designating a child as *skilgetinn*, 'properly
conceived', literally 'conceived in a way that makes a difference' (this is
also the word used by Magnus Erlingsson in his abortive attempt to
strengthen his weak claim to kingship by introducing a strict law of legitimate succession in Norway around 1163[52]) and opposing this to *laungetinn*,
'secretly or improperly conceived'; and by coining a terminology of 'cor-
ner-children' and 'bush-children' (*hornungir, hrísungir*) for children born of
the illicit union of a free man and an unfree woman or vice versa. But beyond all these legalistic niceties, when it comes down to the decisive question of the inheritance rights of children from different kinds of union, the
categories melt away before the eye of the beholder. First, there is ample
occasion for these children to be accepted on equal terms in the kin group:
the co-optation into the group goes by the name of *ættleðning* ('kin-
leading'). Secondly, despite an impressive attempt at introducing quite a
rigmarole of ostensibly ancient rituals with Old Testament overtones – including, in one version, the cutting of a ceremonial shoe of ox hide into
which the participants must step one by one (cf. Ruth 4:7) – what it boils
down to is that the father, seconded by the other powerful males of the kin
group, is quite free to co-opt whomever of his sons he pleases. The concept
is not unlike the French *laudatio parentum*, the (normally but not invariably) formal right of the male relatives to give their assent to the more vital
forms of alienation of property: it allows ample space for individual
manœvring while at the same time arranging for safeguarding the interests
of those with whom group solidarity goes deepest.

As a result, any son born out of any union could become fully equal
with the sons born of a 'marriage' – a fact which effectively countermands
any stipulation about the illegitimacy of having 'other women alongside the
main one'. What remains is a differentiation of degrees. Some children are
born with the proverbial silver spoon in their mouths, others have a more
precarious status, and it is up to the big men in the kin group to decide

---

51. Though the affectation of ignorance can be a powerful strategy of social rhetorics,
aiming at a situation where what seemingly is ignored can in fact safely be ignored.
52. Gulating Law 1. Magnus's claim was dubious since while his mother was a king's
daughter, his father was not of royal birth. Female descent, though not unheard of
(the most famous case being the eleventh-century Danish king Svend Estridsen),
seems to have put any claimant at a disadvantage.

whether or not to include them as peers.[53] This differentiation of degrees corresponds to what was said above about the differences in status of the relationships a man might have with different women. The point is that even the law books, which otherwise mouth the 'Augustinian dichotomy', will not draw a categorical line. There are women who are joined to their men with much solemnity, and who for a number of reasons (among them the self-assurance that comes with form) would be hard to sidestep. And there are others. But there is no dividing line between one kind and the others. What remains is a gradation in formality – the one described by the laws, and hinted at in the sagas.

7. 'Retrospect marriage'

But what about inheritance? One of the most important facets of 'marriage' as opposed to other sexual unions is that it is supposed to confer 'legitimacy' and therefore inheritance rights upon the children born of such a union.[54] Law books are on the whole more widely concerned with children and inheritance than with the union of the parents themselves. And while here, too, closer inspection reveals that 'illegitimate children' are not nearly as categorically excluded from inheritance as it would at first seem, I am willing to concede that 'illegitimacy' would constitute, if nothing else, a serious handicap when it came to inheritance prospects. But I strongly suspect that actual practice allowed for much more leeway on the part of the men and women concerned than law book regulation would have it. Here I must ask my readers and colleagues to further the discussion by checking the following argument against their own source material, as I have done on the basis of my limited acquaintance with Nordic and West Frankland evidence. Mine is in fact a plausibility argument: How probable is it that long before the advent of the institutionalised state, any given society will allow its manœuvring space for on-the-spot decisions to be circumscribed by decisions made several decades earlier?

The traditional argument can be summed up as follows: 'Children born of a marriage have exclusive, or at least greater, rights to inheritance than children born of concubines, etc.' But given the general uncertainty as to

53. There is a moving tale in *Vatnsdœla saga* (ch. 42) about how far a boy would go to make his father, in whose house he is openly living, publicly acknowledge paternity and thereby admit him into the inner circle of the kin group: At his father's instigation, he picks up an axe and kills a guest. 'Now he himself has introduced himself into our kin', says the father, commenting on the *ættleiðing* process.
54. In fact, this point was put forward during the discussion of this paper at the Carlsberg Academy conference in the afternoon session of 4 May 2011. In the following I supply a paragraph or so summing up my counter-argument.

what precisely made it possible to say of any two people that they were married, except for general consent on the part of the surrounding society that this was indeed the case, I suspect that in many cases, the question ran rather the other way around: 'Children seen to make successful exclusive, or greater, claims to inheritance must be legitimate – and therefore, if anyone is interested, their parents must have been married'.

This is a caricatural way of putting it, I grant. But at the same time I feel it does carry conviction. Competition for inheritance, both material and immaterial, must have been among the most important issues in the agonistic warrior societies of the early and high medieval West. In the absence of any transpersonal, overarching, generally accepted and powerful set of laws (such as those provided by late medieval and modern legislators), able-minded and -bodied sons cannot always have been content with stepping back into the 'rank and file' just because it was generally assumed that their own parents had been united by less of a public ceremony than their siblings' parents. Quite apart from the question of how far the memory of whether 'marriage' rites had actually taken place can have been transmitted over several decades without being altered by dynamic re-fashioning, the idea that everyone just accepted marital legitimacy even if it hit themselves and their interests hard rather makes ninth- or eleventh-century power brokers look a little too meek.

I suspect[55] that competition was more acerbated and more open than that. Did Charlemagne really exclude his 'illegitimate' sons, born of 'concubines', from inheritance and focus on the 'legitimate' offspring only? Or did he focus on the prospectively most successful offspring, making them 'legitimate' by the fact that he pointed them out as his heirs (while being forced to revise his decisions occasionally)? Did one son inherit the power of an Icelandic chieftain (Jón Loptsson, † 1197) more or less undivided because his mother was married to his father, whereas he himself (Sæmund Jónsson, † 1222) in his turn left his power divided between four or five sons because he never contracted marriage but only had sons with concubines? Or was it the other way around: In one generation, there was a clear winner in the power struggle after Jón's death, so status was conferred on Sæmund and his mother (incidentally not a high-born woman at all), whereas in a deadlock, none of Sæmund's sons could make a claim to sole legitimacy, and therefore, none of the mothers could lay claim to having been 'married' to the father?[56] In many cases, 'silver-spoon' sons will have been the prospectively most successful candidates anyway, simply because they were better related and possibly had been brought up close to power in the first place. It was less easy to sidestep a king's grandson than a peasant's one.

55. For evidence see Rüdiger, *Der König und seine Frauen* and Rüdiger, *Ægteskab*.
56. For a full discussion, see Rüdiger, *Ægteskab*.

But that is a difference of degrees, just as in the argument rehearsed above about high-born and well-related woman finding it easier to claim control of the household ('key and locks').

This view can be referred to by the neologism of 'retrospect marriage': The course of events, ongoing practice, successful competition on the part of the women and their children, and windfalls such as sudden reversals of alliance (making formerly high-end relationships obsolete, or vice versa), could at any given moment result in changing ideas about who was on top. The moment the father died was payday, and whatever situation was then current would to a considerable extent determine the settlement – after which the question of erstwhile 'legitimacy', unless contested in a pro-tracted power struggle, would quickly cease to be of much practical rele-vance. Often things would have been over in a matter of days or weeks. If these events were then recorded in a Latinate mode, the Augustinian idiom would apply, thereby clothing lay élite practice in the language of monoga-mism (*uxor*/*concubina*) with the benefit of hindsight. And I agree that in the long run, especially in west central Europe after the eleventh century, the idiom was to prove a powerful modifier of practice. But up until then, con-cepts of monogamism and the ensuing forms of discourse were perhaps the main difference between the *umm-walād* ('the [ruling] son's mother'), that towering figure of the tenth- and eleventh-century courts of Muslim al-Andalus, and the successful mothers in the Christian parts of the West. Like other legal forms, marriage was less a state than an event, or rather, a long story of uncertain outcome.

As Dominique Barthélemy has reminded us, 'a right is less an abstract concept than a series of concrete manifestations, occasional but regular. This is why the political system does not reveal itself truthfully in an image immobilised at a given moment; it consists of sequences, of a succession of characteristic situations, duly memorised by the contemporaries'.[57] When a dispute over succession is settled by recourse to a law's differentiation be-tween a 'slegfred' and an 'adelkone', or when a man and a woman appear in a church to do public penitence and pay their 12 øre to the priest, marriage exists – there and then. When King Harald Hardrada (the 'Hard-Ruler'), on returning from his Byzantine career, establishes Þóra, the sister of several of his most valued Norwegian allies, in his household alongside the Novgorod king's daughter Elizabeth, and in due course treats his sons by her as his heirs, then marriage does not exist. When King Olav 'Skötkonung' in Svealand behaves in a similar way but clerics such as Adam of Bremen take exception, and maybe influence the concubine's son's chances of success as

---

57. D. Barthélemy, 'Les comtes, les sires et les 'nobles de châteaux' dans la Touraine du XIe siècle', in E. Mornet (ed.), *Campagnes médiévales: L'homme et son space. Études offertes à Robert Fossier* (Paris: 1995), 439-53, at 447 [my translation].

a ruler, then marriage exists – insofar as opposition to the ruler is based on advocacy of the Augustinian dichotomy.[58] Only a comprehensive assessment of the sources can give us an indication of which 'truth', at any given moment in any regional or social context, was more influential. But the evidence given does not really allow us to uphold the assumption that monogamous marriage – the married couple – was a universal and perennial phenomenon without alternatives. I rather suspect it was a fairly novel introduction into medieval societies which, along with other novelties of the central Middle Ages, went on to carry the day.

8. Summary of the argument

May I sum up my case: Scholarship leaves no doubt that Europeans have for a very long time made marriage a key concept as well as a key social practice. Much attention has been given, and continues to be given, to different *concepts* of marriage. Evolutionary models have by and large given way to views stressing innovation and conflict, intellectual debate and social strategies. But to my knowledge – though here of course I may be wrong – the debate has always focused on the *changes* brought about by theology, church legislation, Canon and secular law, and their respective reception and acceptance by different parts of the medieval West. Marriage by consent, indissolubility and the various stages of incest legislation are seen as the most contentious issues. Explicitly stated or by implication, then, it is assumed that pre-reform or 'secular' marriage differed from the reformist model in these respect, viz. that it was a matter for social groups – two kinship groups or 'families', whatever that means in any given context – to arrange; that it often went with transfer or exchange of property; that it could be dissolved by means such as repudiation or separation; and that endogamy from the second degree onwards was widely acceptable. Before and beside that, other sexual relationships could and did occur; they were of no significance socially apart from the unrest that 'bastards' might introduce into succession.

I have a suspicion that St Augustine, glorying in the chastisement of his own *pactum libidinosi amoris* and setting it off against duly contracted Roman marriage, has much to answer for this view. No doubt the Church, prompted by St Paul and ultimately Adam and Eve, has always championed monogamy. But I believe that the radical fusion of monogamy and marriage that created so much unrest in the High Middle Ages did not mean *change*

---

58. The instances are in *Heimskringla - Haralds saga Sigurðarsonar*, chs. 17; 33; 51ff, and Adam of Bremen, *Gesta Hammaburgensis ecclesiae pontificum*, II 39; 59.

but in fact the *introduction* of marriage as a special, exclusive relationship forming a couple.

My assumption is that prior to that, the dichotomy 'marriage/all other forms of sexual relationships', as formulated by St Augustine, much church law and most modern scholarship, was not a feature of Western societies. Society was not constructed around 'the couple'. It consisted of single men – and very rarely, women – presiding over a minimum of surplus resources with which to maintain other human beings. Often, that would in fact mean that a man kept one women, and they would have children. But given the necessary resources, there might as well be several (or conversely, no) women to a man.[59]

If one affects ignorance of the subsequent history of marriage, and indeed its biblical and Roman antecedents, in the attempt to fake an anthropologist's view of medieval Western European subsistence economy farming or coastal societies with an agonistic warrior élite and no institutionalised forms of social mobility, then the question would be: How probable is it that of all resources and status markers, from cattle and farmsteads to ships and armour, only and precisely the 'exchange of women'[60] would be an exception to the rules of accumulation and distribution common to these societies? There is no apparent reason why men and women should fail to profit from the opportunities polygyny offers them, which may be condensed into five headwords[61] :

1 – generation: the multiform chances of having offspring

2 – habitus: quite apart from any considerations about what store is put by virility, in a society with a dearth of vital resources, polygyny is a status marker

3 – expression: man-to-woman-relationships can be made to express, according to context, alliance, domination, subjugation, or any blend of these

4 – agon: few other fields of competition are so easily 'read' by those in the face of whom men, or women, compete

5 – performance: this is shaky ground, but there is reason to assu-me that while sexual union can be read 'semantically', as a sign of, say, subjugation (and don't we modern Europeans know it), in many Early European contexts the identity of signifier and signified was much less arbitrary than

---

59. For Carolingian peasant households, see the argument recently advanced by L. Kuchenbuch, "'..mit Weib und Kind und...'": Die Familien der Mediävistik zwischen den Verheirateten und ihren Verwandten in Alteuropa', in K.-H. Spieß (ed.), *Die Familie in der Gesellschaft des Mittelalters*. Vorträge und Forschungen 71 (Ostfildern: 2009), 325-76.

60. To borrow the classic expression of Marcel Mauss, which has been the object of much criticism since, not all of it gender-motivated.

61. As developed in Rüdiger, *Der König und seine Frauen*.

that. Though the *hieros gamos* concept – the idea that the inception of a sexual relationship is not merely an expression of rule, but is tantamount to its coming into effect – is, as far as high medieval sources go, only explicit at any length in Irish narratives, we can glimpse intimations of it in other regions, from Scandinavia to the Mediterranean.

On all these counts, monogamy brings about a drastic reduction in flexibility and range of options. It is very possible that societies accept that reduction in favour of monogamy; late medieval and modern Europe has on the whole done just that. But it wants explanation, not presupposition. I am afraid the Devil's Advocate would have to ask opposing counsel to explain his reasons for assuming that early Europe, too, practised a kind of monogamous marriage set apart from all other forms of sexual behaviour.

If we look at earlier Europe as a basically polygynous society, we are allowing for a multitude of social levels of man-to-woman relationships. Some of them are low-status, and some of them are high-status – that is the Gulating Law case of the woman 'bought by agreement'. My point is that the status of these relationships is not determined by their form – that is, a high-status 'wife' has not high status because contrary to those bondswomen or occasional flings with the daughters of the peasantry she is 'married' to the man — but she is 'married', including ceremony and public visibility, because she has high status. Polygyny implies a range of relationships of different status and prestige. What we commonly regard as 'lay marriage' is the relational maximum: *aðalkona*, the woman on top.

My argument against using the term 'marriage' for such a high-status union is twofold: first, there is no categorical difference between those relationships, though there can be considerable difference in status, and accordingly, in living conditions. Secondly, there is always only a relative status, no absolute maximum. There can always be a bigger haul. King Magnus Barefoot, who ruled in Norway for a brief but successful period in the late eleventh century, started with relationships to girls in his father's *hirð*, the itinerary companionship. On his father's death, he was amongst the most successful contenders for succession and made good his domination of Trøndelag by acquiring two daughters of a local chieftain – whether by threat or alliance we cannot tell, but either way, the 'expressive' potential of these unions is clear. When he was firmly in control, he reached even further, and acquired a Swedish king's daughter as part of a larger peace settlement.[62] We tend to look at that king's daughter as King Magnus's 'wife' and the others as 'concubines', but that is Augustinian parlance. She was simply the most prestigious one, and the one the king would have to place in the high seat at banquets. She could be fairly sure of her position because

---

62. This is his story as told by Snorri Sturluson in *Heimskringla - Magnúss saga berfœtts*.

given the circumstances she would be hard to top. But it could always happen, as it did in the case, alluded to above, of Elizabeth/*Ellisif*, the first royal spouse of Magnus's grandfather, King Harald Hardrada († 1066), acquired by the then-promising young pretender with Byzantine wealth and experience to back him on making his bid for kingship in Norway. He was later caused to strike a deal with a faction of mighty Trøndelag chieftains, in the course of which he acquired one of their women. The sagas show both women on an equal footing, which makes modern scholarship view him as that rare bird, a Christian king and a bigamist. But he wasn't, or not specifically; he was as polygynous as the rest of them, only in his case there was no one clear top woman on the relational scale.

The nearest thing to status difference within this polygynous continuum we can really see is the way the relationship was started. That's the point about law expressions like Gulating *keypt með máldaga*, 'bought on agreement'. As everywhere else in these extremely status-conscious face-to-face societies, the decisive operator was whether one was in a position to have one's way.[63] For a man to have a woman taken away from one, or for a woman to be taken away, whether by plunder or bullying, was degrading, and settled the future status as low. To be acquired by agreement, and to have this agreement made public by ceremonies like the formalised *brúðlaup* and its many European counterparts, implied high status. There might be future situations where a still more prestigious woman might enter the household, but it was a good starting point for establishing oneself in a society where, for lack of formal and categorical hierarchy, competition among women was every bit as sharp as that among men.

To conclude, let me sketch the transition worked by the introduction of marriage into Western Europe around 1100. In a small part of the continent, mainly parts of Frankland, the endeavours of the Church to translate its theological ideal into social practice concurred with secular trends that went

---

63. *Ráða* (modern 'råde/-a'), 'to have one's way' is probably the single most important term of Nordic political language in the Middle Ages; cf. J. Rüdiger, *Did Charlemagne Know Carolingian Kingship Theory?* (Stockholm: 2011). If a powerful man acquired a woman without her group's/relatives' consent (*ekki at frændaráði*), then social relationships are quite impressively stated and were possibly altered by the fact, as happens in the case of a *frillutak* ('acquisition/robbery of a co-wife' or 'of a concubine') told in *Egils saga*, chs. 7 and 32; cf. E. Ebel, *Der Konkubinat nach altwestnordischen Quellen. Philologische Studien zur sogenannten "Friedelehe"*. Ergänzungsbände zum Reallexikon der Germanischen Altertumskunde 8 (Berlin and New York: 1993), 30-62. It is not the fact that she was a *frilla* but that her acquisition was a power display which can be construed as ignominous. Characteristically, the saga's account of the law suit ensuing over the inheritance of the erstwhile raptor is clearly in favour of the 'ignominious' daughter, who is in fact Egil's high-minded 'main wife' Ásgerð, a strong saga woman if ever there was one. Her own and her children's characters bear witness to the legitimacy of her property claims.

towards a 'vertebration', a fixation of status of women, with a view towards ensuring fixed succession. Far from being a clash between an older lay and a recently introduced clerical model of marriage, twelfth-century Frankland monogamism developed concurrently in a lay and a clerical mode, which tended to fuse, and did. The clash was between both types of monogamism on the one side, and open polygynous competition on the other side. The kings of France and Denmark used monogamism as a way of establishing clear-cut succession with considerable success. Other parts of Europe remained wary of the new ways for the time being. In early twelfth-century Norway, King Magnus Barefoot's several sons, none of them borne by his 'wife' the Swedish king's daughter, arranged for a surprisingly stable joint rule, while in Normandy and England, where the élite was now embracing monogamism, none of the surviving sons of King Henry I († 1130), able though they were, could succeed their father – not even Robert of Gloucester, the main power broker of his day. What stood in their way was the fact that Henry I had contracted one royal alliance, now justly considered 'marriage', which would have conferred the necessary legitimacy on the son who never lived to see the day, having gone down with the 'White Ship' in 1120. An unclear situation of legitimate succession and fifteen years of devastating factional war between the daughter and a male relative of Henry I were the result. The new model had come to stay. Within a century, it had introduced marriage to practically all of Europe.

Concubinage and Marriage in Denmark Between the Viking Age and the Reformation

A Comparison between Danish and European Medieval Law

Inger Dübeck

1. Introduction

The Law of Jutland, book I, chapter 27[1] was the first secular regulation for Jutland and Funen concerning marriage as well as cohabitation and concubinage. It was formulated by Gunner (c. 1152-1252), the Bishop of Viborg, but was given by the king, Valdemar II, and his council of high nobility and bishops. Gunner had studied in Paris during the late twelfth century and had probably met or known some of the early Decretists, possibly even Huggucio, who is known to have accepted that concubinage was 'nothing more or less than a *de facto* marriage'[2]. Concubinage was a common custom of life in Europe during the twelfth century. Many writers found that concubinage with marital affection ought to be considered a marriage.

Chapter 27 has the following question: 'For how long a time can a man keep a concubine?' It gives this answer:

> If someone has a concubine living on his farm during three winters and openly has sexual intercourse with her, and she rules over locks and keys and eats and drinks with him, then she shall be his wedded wife.

1. *Danmarks gamle Landskabslove*, vol. 2, Jyske Lov, ed. J. Brøndum-Nielsen et al. (Copenhagen: 1933) (hereafter *LJ*).
2. J. A. Brundage, *Law, Sex and Christian Society in Medieval Europe* (Chicago and London: 1987), 297-99.

Chapter 33 opens with this question: 'How to be married?' It continues with this answer:

> The man who will take a woman as wife shall ask for her by her father or son, if he is full grown, or her brother. If she has no relatives then he shall receive her from her nearest kinsman, but she must consent herself. If she has no relatives she can ask whom she wants to give her away...

The Law of Jutland also had two rules concerning concubine children, in chapters 21 and 25 of book I, which show us that such children might meet problems if they wanted to inherit the father's estate. The Decretists had not been able to agree on the status of concubine children, but most of them classified such children as natural and stipulated that they had to be legitimized by a formal act in order to be able to inherit the father's estate. With respect to secular inheritance rules, concubine children were adjudged to be illegitimate until they obtained civil legitimacy. But even after the father's legitimation of them, they would still be illegitimate for ecclesiastical purposes. Chapter 21 states that the father of a concubine child should take it to the court, and register that the child was his and that he had conveyed so much as he liked of his property to the child. Then the child would keep so much and no more. But if he acknowledged paternity of the child by a legitimacy declaration, then the child would inherit half a share in relation to legitimate children. If there were no legitimate children, then the registered child would inherit the father's entire estate.

Chapter 25 on children of adulterous relations denied bastard children such possibilities. The first rule included in this chapter says that bastard children cannot inherit from their father, even if he registered them in court and surrendered as much as he might, unless he gave the gifts into their hands before he died. The second rule states that concubine children will be legitimate if the father marries their mother, even if they were born before the marriage. The rule is in accordance with a principle of canon law: 'legitimatio per subsequens matrimonium'.[3]

2. European law on concubinage between 800 and 1600

Among the Northwestern Franks and the Normans the bishops had, as early as 829, declared that no man might have more than one partner, although they were prepared to tolerate concubinage as a substitute for marriage. If a man dropped his concubine, he was free to marry, because this would not be

---

3. *Liber Extra*, book IV, tit. 17, ch. 6, *Marriage Canons from the Decretum of Gratian and The Decretals, Sext, Clementines and Extravagantes* trans. J. T. Noonan, Jr., ed. A. Thompson, O.P. (Oregon: 1994), 155.

a remarrying. But Frankish marriage law accepted a sort of second-class marriage, the so- called *Friedelehe* known from German law, which constituted a legal cohabitation. The *Friedelehe* did not give the husband a personal right over the woman, and the children were not accepted as legitimate.[4] In the Nordic countries, especially in Denmark and Norway, we find sources which give us a hint of the existence of some sort of concubinage practice, or *Friedelehe*, as early as the centuries between 800 and 1000, although written sources are scarce. Among these hints is the Danish and Nordic word for a concubine: *frille*, which probably derived from the Old German word *fridila*, which referred to the woman in a Frankish *Friedelehe*.[5]

Concubinage was a well-known practice in all medieval European societies, in Anglo-Saxon and Nordic countries, too, first and foremost among feudal and military leaders in the early aristocracy. The early canonists found concubinage immoral, though not illegal, and would not accept that such couples should be looked upon as married. Georges Duby was of the opinion that such flexibility in matrimonial relations proved useful for the aristocracy of northwestern France in the tenth and eleventh centuries, suggesting that the influx of Scandinavians might have promoted its revival under the name of marriage 'in the Danish manner' (*more danico*). The children of wives *more danico* were regarded as only second-class heirs, like the children of *Friedelfrauen* in the Frankish period. The practice of concubinage lasted as long as it served family interests. It protected inheritance to some degree.[6]

The Church in Norway tried to make such connections illegal, although unmarried cohabitation was not expressly prohibited, but it was accepted in the secular legislation if the relationship was undisguised and public. If such cohabitation continued for a period of twenty years, as stated in the Gulatingslag, chapter 125, it was automatically transformed into a legal marriage and the children into legitimate heirs. The Gulatingslag may probably be dated to the first half of the twelfth century,[7] and as such it was older than the Danish Law of Jutland. The only difference between the two rules was the time limit, which in Norway was twenty years of cohabitation, whereas in Denmark it was only three.[8] In both cases, unmarried cohabitation was transformed automatically into a legal marriage after the prescribed time. Similar regulations were given by later Norwegian rulers, while in Ice-

---

4.   G. Duby, *The Knight, the Lady and the Priest: The Making of Modern Marriage in Medieval France* (Chicago: 1993), 41-43.
5.   *Ordbog over det danske Sprog,* 'Frille', vol. 6 (Copenhagen: 1994); *Den Danske Ordbog,* 'Frille' (Copenhagen: 2004).
6.   Duby, *The Knight, the Lady and the Priest,* 40-44.
7.   Fr. Brandt, *Forelæsninger over Den Norske Retshistorie I* (Kristiania: 1880), 25-26, 109-110.
8.   *LJ* I, 27.

landic sagas concubinage was depicted as a normal practice of the aristocracy, both secular and clerical.

Clandestine marriage in Western Europe was, like concubinage, a problem not only for the church but also for secular governments. The canonists claimed that in order to be legitimate marriages had to be celebrated publicly, but as there were six dispensations from this requirement, it was difficult in many situations for secular authorities as well as individuals to be sure if a man and a woman were married or not. The dispensations applied to: 1) Marriage between great nobles, in respect of the families and kinship; 2) Marriage between a person of noble rank and a non-noble, because of the social scandal; 3) Marriage between a rich person and a poor one, for the same reason; 4) Marriages in which one of the parties was very old; 5) Marriages in which the parties had already exchanged informal consent but were afraid of parental wrath; and 6) Situations in which a couple already had lived together for a long time and wished to regularize their relationship. Clandestine weddings were commonplace, and an organized trade made it possible to be married by a clergyman who was prepared to do the nuptial blessing without witnesses.[9]

The famous Roman law teacher Bartolus († 1337) is representative of the secular legal position that simple cohabitation by partners of equal social status established a presumptive marriage in civil law. Unlike the canonists, he did not claim a promise of future marriage,[10] preferring instead to view concubinage relations as quasi-marriages with legitimate children. Bartolus may have had a certain influence on secular municipal authorities, but this was not the case in towns that were under such clerical authorities as bishops or archbishops. From the thirteenth and early fourteenth centuries on in such cities, the municipal authorities began to enact statutes forbidding concubinage under the threat of punishment. In some countries, moreover, we find that the royal legislation accepted concubinage under certain conditions, contrary to the regulations of the municipal statutes.

This seems to have been the case in Spain, where both church and state seemed to have tolerated *barragania* among the laity, as indicated by royal legislation from 1263.[11] *Barragania* was a concubinage relationship between two free persons with full majority, for instance between two single persons or a widow and a widower. The women in such relations were typically female public dealers, hucksters, innkeepers or other independent persons.

---

9. Brundage, *Law, Sex and Christian Society*, 442-43.
10. Ibid., 436 and 444.
11. Las Siete Partidas, I. 4.14 pr.1-2. See Brundage, *Law, Sex and Christian Society*, 446; E. Ruiz-Galvez Priego, *Statut socio-juridique de la femme en Espagne au XVIème siècle* (Paris: 1982), 113-53.

In Denmark in the same period we find on the one hand the Law of Jutland, royal legislation that allowed for the legitimation of concubinage, and on the other chapter 35 of the Municipal Statute for Copenhagen given by the bishop in 1294, according to which a person who was sentenced for 'publice tenere concubinam' should be punished according to the arbitrary decision of the bishop. The Bishop of Roskilde was the master and owner of Copenhagen.[12]

3. Danish legal opinion in the fifteenth century

No written court books or other written sources or acts from ecclesiastical or secular courts or institutions have been preserved from the period before the fifteenth century, when it becomes possible to find a few decisions. Among these, the 'Glosses to The Law of Jutland' written by Knud Mikkelsen are of great interest. This legal scholar, who was appointed Bishop of Viborg in 1451, had studied in Germany, received a degree in canon and civil law (*doctor juris utriusque*) from the University of Erfurt, and was appointed to various diplomatic missions by the Danish king Christian I. He probably died around 1478-1488. He is also one of the few learned persons from the fifteenth century who have left some literary legal works to enlighten us today about the status of legal thinking in medieval Denmark.

Knud Mikkelsen meticulously examined the laws of the Danish realm (*leges municipalis regni dacie*) in order to show in which respects they agreed with imperial Roman and canon law and in which respects they contradicted or were inconsistent with them. In cases of contradiction or inconsistency he did not want to alter the Danish legislation, because the Law of Jutland was accepted by and given by the king and the bishops and the secular high aristocracy. He would alter Danish legislation, if the Danish laws expressed a mistake or delusion, and if the difference between Danish legislation and Roman law was caused by dissimilarities in the two realms caused by different times and different places.

His translation into Latin of the Law of Jutland and his glosses to this law book were made in accordance with the scholastic method and practice in Europe, based on his understanding of Roman and canon law, and he commented on individual rules with reference to the *Corpus Iuris Civilis* and the *Corpus Iuris Canonici*. It may be of interest to learn Knud's opinion of the concubine rule set forth in *LJ* I, 27. His translation of the chapter into Latin was as follows:

12. *Københavns Stadsret*, text I, ch. 35; text II, ch. 2, *Danmarks Gamle Købstadlovgivning*, vol. III, ed. E. Kroman (Copenhagen: 1955), 21, 32.

Quamdiu quis debet tenere secum concubinam suam. Quicumque habuerit secum concubinam in curia et audit cum ea manifeste dormitum, et ipsa habet seras et claues, et commedit cum ea et bibit manifeste in tribus annis, hiis elapsis ipsa debet esse legitima.

He glossed it in this way:

'Quicumque habuerit. Facit l.in concubinatu ff de concubinis (*Dig.* 25, 7,3), quia lex presumit, quod sit uxor, dummodo sit ingenue et non uiuit inhoneste, ut in l.in libere ff de ritu nupciarum (*Dig.* 23.2.24). Set non ponitur tempus pro illa presumpcione, sicut hic. Secundum canones cessat illa presumptio nisi matrimonium fuerit publice contractum, ut xxx q v c I (*Decretum* C. 30 qu.5, c.1) in fine. Uide ibi glo et de clam despon c cum inhibitio (*Liber Extra*, book 4, tit. III, c. 3 concerning clandestine betrothal).[13]

According to Knud's interpretation of *LJ* I, 27, if such marriages were not carried out publicly they should not be considered lawful, but rather were to be looked upon as adultery, fornication or debauchery, in accordance with canon law. He was in this way expressing the mainstream late-medieval opinions of European canonists on clandestine marriages. But personally he seems to have accepted that cohabitation with a woman under the given conditions was acceptable not only *de facto*, but also legally as a marriage, and was not fornication if she had not to earn her living with her body but was a person with the duties and rights of a normal married wife as they related to housekeeping and cohabitation with her husband ('… and she rules over locks and keys and eats and drinks with him…').

Knud's glosses to the Law of Jutland were well known and used in practice during the fifteenth and sixteenth centuries, not only because of their comparisons with Roman and canon law, but especially because his comparisons influenced the interpretation of the rules in the Law of Jutland itself, the other Danish provincial law books, and the coronation charters and constitutions of Danish kings from Erik Glipping in 1282 to Queen Margrethe I in 1376. Of great interest for legal historians are his quotations from customary law, *generalis consuetudo* and *usus modernus et communis*. His quotations from the provincial Viborg High Court and the King's Court have given rise to the greatest interest, however, because the court practice itself from this period has disappeared.[14]

13. *Danmarks Gamle Landskabslove*, vol. IV, Jyske Lov, Texts 5-6, ed. S. Iuul and P. Jørgensen (Copenhagen: 1945), 40-41.
14. L. Holberg, *Dansk og fremmed Ret. Knud Mikkelsen og hans Glosser til Jydske Lov* (Copenhagen: 1891), 1-22.

4. Reformation, concubinage and legal changes in Denmark

The close personal connections between Martin Luther (1483-1546), Philip Melanchthon (1497-1560), Johannes Bugenhagen (1485-1558) and the Danish king Christian III (1503-1559) meant that Luther's writings were well known in Denmark among theologians and the learned aristocracy. Many of Luther's texts criticized the Pope and the double standard for sexual activities among the clergy of the Roman Catholic Church at all levels. He attacked the lower-level clergy for their heterosexual concubinage, and the papal court for same-sex activities.[15] Luther wanted to do away with marriage practices that had been developed during the Middle Ages, such as *de facto* marriage through concubinage. Everyone should marry, he believed, the sooner after puberty the better. Though not a sacrament, marriage was the ideal state for almost everyone. Luther regarded sexual morality as extremely important, which is why he spoke and wrote about sex regularly throughout his long career.[16]

In a letter to a government official at Warburg and Eisenach dated 27 June 1540 Luther had this to say about the bigamy of Philip of Hesse, whose second wedding had taken place the preceding March, attended by Philip Melanchton and Martin Bucer:

> I do not know of anything better than that you would write to the emperor, that Philip of Hesse intends to write to the emperor himself regarding this matter and say that he has taken a concubine and intends to send her away again, as other princes and lords have also done before. Such a letter would raise a fuss [...] but people would come to some agreement [...] And the matter would be made secret [...] if the emperor was to regard her as a concubine, however, no one would dare to speak about it in any other ways.[17]

From his *Table Talk*, the following remarks are taken:

> About clerical concubinage someone said to Luther that if there was a reformation of the canons in Zeitz and Naumburg, they would be forced to dismiss their 'cooks' and send them away. They would concede this for only two weeks, for they could not do without them for any longer, or hold themselves back. Thus they took them back again. But the 'cooks' did not want to come back to them, but they promised them that they would support and protect them. And they bought new clothes for them, so that people did not recognize them. And people said that a locksmith was supposed to have said that he had had much work during these two weeks, day and night, just making keys. For every woman wanted a key to the parsonage now that they [the canons] had sent their whores away.[18]

---

15. S. C. Karant-Nunn and M. E. Wiesner-Hanks, *Luther on Women: A Sourcebook* (Cambridge: 2003), 137-39.
16. Ibid., 137-41.
17. Ibid., 163.
18. Ibid., 165.

Luther reacted angrily to this story. Another story which incensed him concerned the emperor Charles V, who had made Pope Alexander VII's nephew, Alessandro de' Medici, Duke of Florence in 1530 and arranged for him to marry his illegitimate daughter Margaret. Luther believed that Alessandro was the son of the future Pope Clement VII and a whore.[19]

Until the sixteenth century there were no formal secular prohibitions against lay concubinage, except for the few municipal rules, which contained a threat of punishment. With the Reformation in 1536 the Danish church turned into a national Lutheran-Evangelical Church, which gave rise to a different view of marriage in relation to the possibility of divorce, and to an austere and rigorous view of unmarried relations. The requirement of celibacy for clergymen and vicars was rejected. Indeed, the church now expected them to marry; and as to lay people, noble or common, the church would no longer allow cohabitation outside marriage. Not only did concubinage become socially unacceptable during the late sixteenth century, it came to be regarded as a crime, and was legislated against as such for the next three centuries.

The first Protestant bishop of Zealand, Peter Palladius (1503-1560), openly warned the population against fornication and a life of sin or loose living, decreeing that 'No one may live together as in a marriage, unless they can prove that they are married'. He warned ungodly noblemen in particular to avoid such behavior, and the new Church ordinance from 1539 declared that such 'loose livers' should be 'confounded'.[20]

The highly educated theologian and Professor Niels Hemmingsen (1513-1600) at the University of Copenhagen wrote a book on marriage in a Danish and a Latin version. It was printed in 1572, the Latin version – entitled *Libellus de conjugio, repudio et divortio* – published in Leipzig and the Danish one in Copenhagen with the terser title of *Om ægteskab* (*On Marriage*).[21] Here Hemmingsen discussed the problem of whether a nobleman who had many children with his noble wife might, after her death, marry a non-noble woman, on condition that the children of his first marriage should be heirs to his family's landed property while the children of the non-noble woman would have to be satisfied with the movable property only; and if such a solution might be formally contracted between the two parties and accepted by family and friends. His answer was that it is not part of the concept of marriage that an inheritance must be divided equally, and that such an arrangement was not against the Law of God. But in order to avoid strife, he continued, the authorities should accept, and the children and kin-

19. Ibid., 166-67.
20. Peder Palladius, *En Visitatsbog*, ed. M. S. Lausten (Copenhagen: 2003), 154.
21. Niels Hemmingsen, *Vejledning i ægteskabssager 1572*, trans. and comm. R. Mott (Copenhagen: 1987).

dred should consent to, the arrangement.[22] Although Hemmingsen did not explicitly associate this question with *LJ* I, 27, he might have had European morganatic marriage in mind. It was not a part of Danish law, but the principles were known by those of the Danish nobility which had studied Roman law or were close connected with members of the nobility in Germany and France.

In the practical daily life of the Danish aristocracy, concubinage with lower-class women continued in spite of the new religious strictures. Such well-known men as Tycho Brahe (1546-1601), Arild Huitfeldt (1546-1609), and Johan Friis (1494-1570) are known to have lived in unmarried relations.[23] Possibly this practice became more common in the the East-Danish province Sealand and Scania during the early sixteenth century. Some of the late-medieval texts of the Law of Scania incorporate some rules from The Law of Jutland, among these *LJ* I, 27.[24] There might have been different motivations for this choice of lifestyle. Of these, probably the question of inheritance to and ownership of the landed property of noble families was the most important. The following description of legal practice shows that the nobility in fact continued to look upon these relations as morganatic marriages in accordance with classical feudal European principles.

5. Legal practice in the High Court and the King's Court

Legal practice in the King's Court (in Danish: *Kongens Retterting*) during the reign of the first Lutheran king, Christian III (1534-59), seems to document that concubinage was still an acceptable route to marriage and legitimacy. A decision of the Royal Court from 19 September 1538, in which the king himself acted as a judge together with members of the Royal Council,[25] shows how *LJ* I, 27 was understood in the time before the new marriage legislation of the early 1580s. A woman in the town of Nyborg had lived for nine years with a tailor, who before being killed in war had formally married her before a vicar. The man's brother, wishing to appropriate what the widow and her two children had inherited, attempted to have her declared a

---

22. Ibid., 156, no. 441.
23. T. F. Troels-Lund, *Dagligliv i Norden i det sekstende Aarhundrede*, vol. XII (Copenhagen: 1914), 171, 181, 183-84.
24. The Law of Scania, Text I ('Istud sequens capitulum cepi ex lege Valdemari regis que data [est] in Vordingborg'), and Texts II and III, in *Danmarks gamle Landskabslove, Skånske Lov, Første Hefte* (Copenhagen: 1920), 400-01; and Første Bind, Syvende Hefte (Copenhagen: 1930), 771-72.
25. *Udvalg af Gamle Danske Domme afsagte paa Kongens Retterting og paa Landsting*, Anden Samling, Udgivet af J. L. A. Kolderup-Rosenvinge (Copenhagen: 1844), 81-82.

concubine, with no right to inheritance for herself or the children. The court accepted the condition of three years' cohabitation concerning *LJ* I, 27 as enough for a legal marriage, and that the woman was fully entitled to the inheritance and that the children were automatically legitimated.

Another case from the King's Court shows that it was possible to abuse the intention behind *LJ* I, 27 in order to prove that a formal legal marriage had not taken place and that the woman should be considered a concubine of lower rank than the man. The marriage in question, which was celebrated in Scotland with Scottish witnesses only, was between a Danish nobleman, Mogens Løvenbalk, and a Scottish noblewoman, Genett Craigengelt. The couple settled in Jutland in his mansion, Tjele, and produced two children, a son, Knud, and a girl, before Mogens died in 1536. Eighteen years later Knud and his mother summoned the nobleman named Erik Skram, a High Court Judge in Jutland, who was married to Mogens' sister, to the Kings Court claiming that Erik had appropriated Knud's and his sister's rightful inheritance and demanding its return. Knud produced several sealed letters with declarations from his mother's Scottish family – including its head, the Earl of Montrose, whom he had visited – to prove that his mother had been lawfully married to his father in Scotland. He also presented documentation from the priests at St Ninian's Church in Leith, where the wedding ceremony had taken place.

Erik Skram and his wife countered that the marriage of Mogens Løvenbalk was not valid, because Genett had only been his concubine. They contended that Løvenbalk had treated the Scottish woman as a concubine during all their time of cohabitation, but not in the sense of *LJ* I, 27, because no one had ever seen her eat or drink with him or seen her manage the home as a wife with jurisdiction over keys and locks. Furthermore, they claimed, Løvenbalk had given Genett and the children silver, gold, money, jewels, furniture, cattle and household movables during his lifetime, in exchange for more than twenty or thirty thousand guilder, and in the deed of gift had referred to her as 'his woman Genett, who was living with him'. Skram was of the opinion that if Genett had been Mogens' lawful wedded wife, he would have let her keep the land and mansion; that she herself should have claimed more at a meeting in Copenhagen with the king and some of the members of the Council of the Realm soon after her husband's death; and that the son, Knud Løvenbalk as a man of age himself should have claimed his right of succession under *LJ* I, 22 concerning inheritance and debt on the same occasion (at which time he was only around ten years old!).

As Genett Craigengelt had not claimed more land or valuables (properties) at the Copenhagen meeting in the presence of members of the Council of the Realm, Erik Skram maintained that he had taken the mansion and the land as his wife's legitimate heritage. In his view, Genett had accepted the compromise proposed at the Copenhagen meeting, by which she was to pay him more land (for two mortgage deeds on two farms) and movables as additional payment (for his wife). Erik Skram further asserted that Danish law gave him a right to take and use the land of the manor, because Knud Løvenbalk had not claimed his right before the time limit of fifteen days concerning claims for payment of debts under *LJ* I, 22.

The king and Royal Court evidently were unpersuaded by the evidence from Scotland produced by Knud Løvenbalk. Nor did they call the then still-living Genett († 1567) as a witness to comment on the Scottish letters. Although Knud admitted that his father did not treat his mother as he should have, he also produced documents to prove that his father on his deathbed had confessed before God and the world that Genett was his lawful wedded wife. He also claimed that the contract which his mother had made in Copenhagen when he and his sister were small children should not be considered valid. The king and the Royal Court nevertheless upheld the claims of Erik Skram and his wife. A postscript to this decision, however, tells us that Knud Løvenbalk received a *responsum* from the University of Wittenberg confirming his position on the marriage status of his mother and his own legitimacy. He then in 1567 asked the new king, Frederik II (1559-1588), to help him. The king received a *responsum* from the University of Copenhagen, which in the same way confirmed the views of Knud. The two children of Mogens Løvenbalk, Knud and his sister, were given the right to wear the coat of arms of the family Løvenbalk, and the children of Erik Skram were instructed to accept them as family and to surrender part of the land to them.[26]

Erik Skram, himself a judge (though not in this case) conducted the case for his wife as if the relationship between her brother and and Genett had been, not a concubinage according to *LJ* I, 27, which would have lead to a lawful marriage after three years, but a concubinage between two persons of different social rank: like a European morganatic marriage. This claim was unsupportable, because Genett was *de facto* a member of the high Scottish nobility. Nevertheless Skram was successful in misinforming the King´s Court. The king and his court were easy targets for his manipulations because the king and the entire Danish nobility opposed any transfer of Danish noble land into the hands of foreigners, especially to a supposedly non-noble woman and her bastard children.

Why Genett was treated so badly by her husband is difficult to understand. Perhaps she had problems learning the Danish language, especially in the Jutland dialect; perhaps she was a shy person who had problems meeting strangers; or maybe she suffered from some nervous disease. Perhaps she

---

26. *Danske Domme 1375-1662*, vol. II: 1554-1569 (Copenhagen: 1979), no. 208, 27-35.

was rebuffed or snubbed for being a Roman Catholic and a foreigner. It is not possible to say.

A court decision from the Viborg High Court in 1568 declared that a boy born of two parents who had lived together for more than twenty years in accordance with the conditions set forth in *LJ* I, 27 was a concubine child, and not a bastard child as was claimed by his opponent. Jørgen Hansen, son of the nobleman Hans Skeel, did not plead upon *LJ* I, 27 concerning his mother, although she would have been taken for a lawful wedded wife after just three years of cohabitation. The reason for this was probably that the father already was betrothed to a noblewoman, Karen Skram, daughter of Peter Skram, the admiral of the Danish navy. The court instead found the solution in *LJ* I, 25 together with *LJ* I, 27 and dismissed the claim of the plaintiff, declaring that Jørgen Hansen ought not to be deprived of his honor and respect as a concubine child.[27]

6. Social life and sexual behavior in sixteenth- and seventeenth-century Denmark – Nobility, burghers and farmers

The legal practice in the higher courts does not tell us much about the routine practices of daily life. Whereas early recesses in these courts prescribed serious punishment for sexual offences in accordance with official royal and religious views, among ordinary people unmarried sexuality and bastard children were acceptable as social consequences. In the countryside a practice developed whereby fines could be paid to the King's local lord lieutenant for such offences, and for poorer people the amount of the fines could be determined by the solvency of the offender. These fines formed a steady and certain source of income for the Crown and for the University of Copenhagen.[28] For their part the burghers in the towns had over the centuries developed a sociable and convivial culture within their different guilds, companies and corporations, with their own internal fines for immoral conduct. Even the first generation of Lutheran vicars, despite being newly allowed to marry, did not live up to the expected moral claims, but were often discovered in various sexual immoralities.[29]

The Lutheran-sanctioned Marriage Ordinance of 19 June 1582 stipulated that marriages should take place in public before a local priest and five witnesses. The nobility felt offended by this new regulation, partly because it set aside the concubine rule in *LJ* I, 27 specifying three years' cohabitation and the privilege of celebrating marriage as an informal – and in prac-

27. Ibid., no. 335, 317-19.
28. Troels-Lund, *Dagligliv i Norden*, 171-76.
29. Ibid., 185-86, 194-97.

tice, sometimes clandestine – act. Moreover, they did not wish to be dependent upon the local vicar, who was not a member of the aristocracy. After the Reformation the nobility had gained a much stronger position in the Council of the Realm and in the higher courts, because the former Catholic bishops had been removed and had not been replaced in the Council of the Realm by the new Protestant bishops or superintendents. In the long run the high nobility gained the right to informal, clandestine marriages as part of their privileges, but ultimately with the new stipulation that the witnesses were required to secure publication and registration of the marriage.

7. Frederik II and his legislation on marriage

In medieval canon law, consensus between the man and woman was the decisive condition for a valid marriage. This could take the form of either *sponsalia de presenti*, which established the marriage automatically when the parties declared themselves married, or *sponsalia de futuro*, a declaration of betrothal followed by sexual intercourse. This remarkable independence from legal strictures meant that neither society in general nor the church in particular found it easy to determine the point at which a marriage could be said to have taken place. During the Counter-Reformation, however, the conditions for a valid marriage were tightened considerably. The decree *De clandestinis* or *Tametsi* issued by the Council of Trent in 1563 mandated that henceforth marriages not solemnized before the parish priest and at least two witnesses would be declared invalid.

The principles of canon law had been followed in late-medieval Danish marriage law, and they were recognized in early Protestant practice. Although the new rules forbidding informal or clandestine marriages from the Council of Trent 1563 were not promulgated in Lutheran Denmark, the Danish king and his council may be said to have followed the same principles when they introduced the Ordinance of 19 June 1582 some two decades later. The Ordinance bound betrothal to a special form with the requirement that it should take place before a vicar and five witnesses (chapter 1, article 5). In addition, chapter 1, article 2 stipulated, under threat of punishment, that the betrothed couple should not have intercourse before they were married in the church. The intention of the Ordinance was to abolish the old customs, which might result in a clandestine marriage. It bore a notable similarity to the Council of Trent's decree, not only as to the presence of witnesses (albeit five rather than two), but also as to the requirement that a cleric be present in order to establish a legal marriage.[30]

---

30.   E. Andersen, *Ægteskabsret I* (Copenhagen: 1954), 24-25.

The legislation from the early 1580s leaves us with the impression that a certain sector of the nobility still preferred concubinage with ordinary women[31] as a sort of 'European Common Law' over ordinary marriage. Two sources in particular tell us that such relations were common among unmarried noblemen. The first of these, the royal letter of 11 June 1580 concerning those who cohabit with unmarried women, had the consequence that many noblemen married their non-noble concubines, rather than letting them go and freeing themselves from the engagement, contrary to the king's command and intention and the intention of Luther as mentioned in his letter of 27 June 1540.

The second source was the recess of 19 June 1582, which stated that noblemen who took concubines or married non-noble women might not let the children of such relations be treated like noble heirs as to landed property and noble rights, but could leave them only movables and money. This document was prepared by the Council of the Realm, all of whose members countersigned the document and together with the king affixed their seals to it as a special guarantee. The 1582 recess had only two articles, which stated 1) That children of a non-noble woman were not to be accepted as belonging to the nobility, and 2) That such children would not be entitled to a noble name or a noble coat of arms. The father was, however, allowed to give his children money and movables. With this recess the feudal ideas of morganatic marriages or the special 'European Common Law Concubinage' with ordinary women and the status of children of non-noble rank as concubine children were codified in the Danish legislation. Even though the children of Løvenbalk and Genett Craigengelt were accepted eventually as legitimate children and lawful members of the Danish nobility, no doubt their case helped to inspire the formulation of the 1582 recess.

8. Class prejudice and marriage law between the seventeenth and nineteenth centuries

Among the privileges claimed by the higher nobility was the right to marry at home in their mansions with good friends as witnesses, independent of a vicar of a lower social class in the parish church. Consequently, they maintained that chapter 1, article 5 of the 1582 Marriage Ordinance should be understood as applying only to the lower classes, while the nobility had their privileges from the medieval dispensations from canon law relating to

---

31. Concerning a sort of 'European Common Law' as substantiated by M. Lupoi in 'A European Common Law before Bologna?', in Per Andersen et al. (eds.), *Law before Gratian. Law in Western Europe c. 500-1100. Proceedings of the Third Conference on Medieval Legal History 2006* (Copenhagen: 2007), 17-20.

the marriage of great nobles.[32] This formal legal problem was not solved until 1683, with the comprehensive law book called 'The Danish Law' given by Christian V. In book III, chapter 16, article 11 of this book concerning marriage, we find a clear distinction between ordinary people on the one hand and members of the nobility and the higher ranks on the other. For the ordinary people the old requirements of five witnesses and the vicar were repeated from the 1582 Marriage Ordinance. As a special addition to this main rule, however, an exception was given in the second section to the effect that noble people and other people of high rank might establish a marriage with six private friends as witnesses to their consent (in Danish, the saying of '*Ja-Ord* ,' 'Yes I will'). In the comments to the Law Book we do not find reference to any special source as an explanation for this distinction. But in the published preparatory works for the Danish Law Book, we find a special remark concerning the establishing of marriages saying that the king, who was no longer a chosen king, but since 1660 a hereditary absolute monarch had approved this special arrangement.[33]

In 1685 the king gave Denmark and Norway a comprehensive new church ritual, in which the marriage rules from the Danish Law Book for both the common people and the nobility and people of higher ranks were repeated. A few years later, on 6 February 1694, a special act was given concerning consensus marriages for these high social classes. It stated that this privilege had been misused, and as a consequence the witnesses from now on would be required to give a written confirmation to the confessor of the couple, who in turn would have to inform the bishop, and – especially important – enter the message in the church register. This registration alone made the informal betrothal into a valid marriage.

In his presentation of the Danish family law from the nineteenth century J. H. Deuntzer found that these special betrothals were very seldom used in practice.[34] The first democratic constitution of Denmark from 1849 took into account the new political changes, and in article 92 all privileges for the nobility and people of ranks were abolished, including the special marriage rules. From this we can surmise that the rules concerning informal or clandestine marriages for the nobility were taken seriously and most likely had been prasticised in some way during the sixteenth and seventeenth centuries, and less often in the eighteenth and nineteenth centuries.

---

32. See above, n. 12
33. *Forarbejder til Danske Lov*, eds. V. A. Secher and Chr. Støchel, vol. II (Copenhagen: 1893-1894), 358, 525.
34. J. H. Deuntzer, *Den danske Familieret* (Copenhagen: 1899), 17-18.

DID MEDIEVAL CANON LAW INVENT OUR MODERN NOTION OF RAPE? REVISITING THE IDEA OF CONSENT BEFORE AND AFTER 1200

Hiram Kümper

1. Introduction

At first sight, rape seems to be a disturbingly stable crime, as it can be observed in almost any human culture at any time or place. This is both true and false at the same time. For although there have been acts of sexual violence throughout time and in all places, the conceptualization of such acts has differed markedly. In this paper I will argue that our modern notion of rape as a sexual act committed against the will of the victim was born only in the twelfth century. Moreover, I will try to find its birthplace.

I will bring forward my argument in three steps. First, I will survey a variety of laws and other legal texts that deal with issues of sexual violence from the earlier Middle Ages – that is, the sixth to the twelfth century. Second, I will survey similar but later texts, some from the twelfth but most from the thirteenth century. The pictures that emerge from these two eras differ significantly from one another, as we will see. Finally, I will ask the most significant question that emerges from this observation: What might have happened in between?

But first of all, let me make some general remarks on the current state of research on sexual violence and its juridical prosecution in the Middle Ages. Interest in sexual violence among historians has been growing since roughly the 1980s,[1] spurred by the publication of American journalist Susan Brownmiller's polemical and highly influential work *Against Our Will* in 1975.[2] Traditional legal history had and still has its problems with writing the history/-ies of rape, as normative sources and actual legal practice seem to have differed significantly from each other – at least in the later Middle Ages, where we have enough court records to come to such a conclusion. Strangely, legal history is probably the most laggard of all the scholarly disciplines in investigating this topic. One of the most active fields of research, on the other hand, has been literary studies, in which scholars have explored a plethora of rape-narratives in all kinds of literary genres.[3] So far only a few of them, however, have successfully combined questions and sources for both legal and literary history. One such is Corinne Saunders's substantial book on rape in medieval English literature, which also takes into account a vast body of sources from both traditional and learned laws as well as religious writings.[4] As for canon law, the eminent scholar James Brundage has published several smaller pieces on the place of rape in canonists' writings.[5] They are complemented by studies in penitential literature, which in the last decades Pierre J. Payer has studied with great attention.[6]

1. For one of the first important collections of articles, see R. Porter and S. Tomaselli (eds.), *Rape: An Historical and Cultural Enquiry* (Oxford: 1990), esp. Roy Porter's essay, 'Rape – Does It Have a Historical Meaning?', 216-36.
2. S. Brownmiller, *Against Our Will. Men, Women and Rape* (New York: 1975). Brownmiller's influence on academic historiography in the United States is discussed by S. P. Pistono, 'Susan Brownmiller and the History of Rape', *Women's Studies* 14 (1988), 265-76.
3. From the vast body of literature I shall only refer here to L. A. Higgins and B. R. Silver (eds.), *Rape and Representation* (New York: 1990) and E. Robertson and C. M. Rose (eds.), *Representing Rape in Medieval and Early Modern Literature* (New York and Houndmills: 2001). Just recently published: A. Classen, *Sexual Violence and Rape in the Middle Ages: A Critical Discourse in Premodern German and European Literature* (Berlin and New York: 2011).
4. C. Saunders, *Rape and Ravishment in the Literature of Medieval England* (Cambridge: 2001).
5. J. A. Brundage, 'Rape and Marriage in the Medieval Canon Law', *Revue de droit canonique* 28 (1978), 62-75; also cf. J. A. Brundage, *Law, Sex, and Christian Society in Medieval Europe* (Chicago and London: 1987), s.v. 'rape' (index, p. 655); and J. A. Brundage, 'Sin, Crime and the Pleasures of the Flesh: The Medieval Church Judges Sexual Offences', in J. L. Nelson and P. A. Linehan (eds.), *The Medieval World* (London: 2003), 294-307.
6. See, for example, P. J. Payer, *Sex and the Penitentials: The Development of a Sexual Code 550-1150* (Toronto: 1985) and *Sex and the New Medieval Literature of Confession, 1150-1300* (Turnhout: 2009), which together form a comprehensive survey of the genre.

2. Rape in Early Medieval sources: a brief survey

The earlier Middle Ages saw *raptus* as a social rather than an exclusivly sexual crime. From ancient laws, primarily Roman law, they inherited the blurry distinction between the taking away of a woman for the purpose of marriage, which at times might also have been a consensual elopement of the partners against their parents' will, and the violation of a woman's sexual integrity.[7]

At least in Merovingian times, women evidently could bring their own cases to court and sometimes, when it was judged appropriate, could receive compensation; this included cases of *raptus*.[8] Possibly this means of recourse became less available to them in the Carolingian period. In any case, legal writings more commonly addressed the rights of the women's peers, her parents, or her guardian than those of the woman herself. The first place to go when searching for such normative rulings is the so-called *leges barbarorum*, of which the following table gives a small selection.[9]

Table 1: Rape in early medieval *leges barbarorum* (a selection)

Pactus legis Salicae (507/11) c. 16 § 2[10]	Si quis cum ingenua puella per virtutem moechatus fuerit ... MMD denarios qui faciunt solidos LXII semin culpabilis iudicetur.	If anyone forcibly engages in sex with a free-born girl ... let him held be liable for 2500 denarii, which make sixty-two and one half solidi.[11]
Leges Burgundionum (6th century) c. 30 § 1	Quicumque ingenuus ancillae violentiam fecerit, et vis potuerit adprobari, inferat ei, cuius ancilla est, solidos XII.	Whatever native freeman does violence to a maidservant, and force can be proved, let him pay twelve solidi to him to whom the maidservant belongs.[12]
Edictus Rothari (643)	Si uir mulieri uiolentias fecerit, et inuitam tullerit uxorem, sit	If a man does violence to a woman, and takes her as his

---

7. S. F. Wemple, 'Consent and Dissent to Sexual Intercourse in Germanic Societies from the Fifth to the Tenth Century', in A. E. Laiou (ed.), *Consent and Coercion to Sex and Marriage in Ancient and Medieval Societies* (Washington, D.C.: 1993), 227-43.

8. Some interesting cases from the seventh century are given by Marculf in his *Formulae*: see *The Formularies of Angers and Marculf: Two Merovingian Legal Handbooks*, ed. A. Rio (Liverpool: 2008), 305 (index, s.v. 'disputes, over raptus').

9. All Latin quotations are from the edition of the *Monumenta Germaniae Historica* (hereafter *MGH*), vol. 2 of the *Leges*.

10. Identical with *Lex Salica*, c. 14 § 13.

11. *Laws of the Salian and Ripuarian Franks*, trans. by T. J. Rivers (New York: 1986), 59.

12. *The Burgundian Code. Book of Constitutions or Law of Gundobad. Additional Enactments*, trans. by K. Fisher Drew (Philadelphia: 1972), 44. Note that Drew translates *ancilla* as 'maidservant', while Rivers (n. 14) uses 'chambermaid'.

c. 187	culpabilis solidos nongentos, mediatatem regi et medietatem parentibus mulieris.	wife against her will, he has to pay 900 shillings, one half to the king and the other half to the woman's parents.
Leges Alamannorum (7th century) c. 75 § 1	Si quis cum alicuius ancilla vestiaria concupuerit contra voluntatem eius, cum 6 solidis conponat.	If anyone lies with someone's chambermaid against her (?) will, let him compensate with six solidi.[13]
Lex Visigothorum (506) III 4 § 14	Si viduam qusique vel virginem ingenuam violenter adulterandam conpresserit vel stupri forsitam conmixtione polluerit, si ingenuus est, centum flagellis cesus illi continuo, cui violentus extitit, serviturus tradatur [...]	If a free-born or unfree man forces adultery upon a free-born virgin or widow, or if he defiles her by nefarious intercourse, he shall receive 100 lashes – if he is a free man – and shall be given to his victim as a servant [...]

The *leges*, with their complex catalogues of crimes and penances (*compositiones*), require a far more thorough discussion than is possible here. As even this cursory look makes clear, however, the early medieval *leges barbarorum* do not share our modern concept of rape, inasmuch as the lack of consent on the victim's side does not play a role in the constitution of *raptus*. The few and debatable exceptions where the will is explicitly in question influence the qualification of the deed, its aggravation or its mitigation, but are not a vital condition for its constitution.

This notion is substantiated by other sources from the earlier Middle Ages. Pentitentials, for instance, usually impose penance upon the victims of sexual violence, obviously in a purifying manner, for fornication has taken place – even if by violent force. Although these penances are lighter than the ones given those who fornicate voluntarily, the absence of consent affects only the duration, not the existence of the penitential state. This obviously parallels the ideas we have witnessed in secular penal laws. One of the more illustrative examples comes from the Carolingian *Paenitentiale Pseudo-Theodori*:

> Si qua christiana femina a perfidis Iudaeis munera suscepit ac cum eis uoluntarie fornicationem fecerit, annum integrum separatur ab ecclesia et cum magna tribulatione uiuat, deinde viiii annos peniteat. Si autem liberos generat, xii annos peniteat. Si uero inuita passa est, v annos peniteat ...

> (If a Christian woman takes money from unbelieving Jews and fornicates with them voluntarily, she will be excommunicated from the Church for one

---

13. *Laws of the Alamans and Bavarians*, trans. with an introduction by T. J. Rivers (Philadelphia: 1977), 94. It is even possible – though highly unlikely – that '*voluntatem eius*' means *his* (i.e. the chambermaid's master's) rather than *her* will here.

year and will live with great tribulation; thereafter she will do penance for nine years. If she produces children, she will do penance for twelve years. But if she suffered [this] truly unwillingly, she will do penance for five years ...)[14]

This is not the place to discuss whether it might be significant that of all sorts of possible cases it is inter-religious sexual intercourse that is discussed here. The main point in my argument would rather be that it is the will and its absence (*vero invita*) that aggravates or mitigates the sin in this example, while it would not constitute it.

As we have seen, there is a terminological problem with *raptus*. A second, no less problematic term that is frequently used to indicate acts of sexual violence is *oppressio*. It is usually used in rather short rulings and indicates violence, although it does not specify of what kind. We will find this term still in use considerably later. A peace ruling for Saxony of the German king Henry [VII] from 1221, for instance, plainly states:

Raptus sive oppressio virginis vel mulieris per capitis decolacionem punietur.

(Rape or the oppression of virgins or [other] women is punished by decapitation.)[15]

The pressing problem with the crime of *raptus* in the earlier Middle Ages, however, does not seem to have been rape (in our modern sense), but rather abduction. Hinkmar of Reims, for instance, discusses the problem at length in his *De coercendo raptu puellarum et sanctimonialium*.[16] This certainly matches well with the observation from the *leges barbarorum*. Here as elsewhere we find consent as an issue – but it is hardly ever the woman's consent that is in question; it is that of her parents or guardian.[17]

When we skip a few centuries, however, we will find this remarkably changed.

14. *Paenitentiale Pseudo-Theodori*, ed. C. van Rhijn (Turnhout: 2009), 17 (X. 37). Translation is mine.
15. *MGH, Constitutiones,* vol. 2, 394-395, no. 280. Translation is mine.
16. *Patrologia Latina* 125, cols 1017-36. Also cf. R. Stone, 'The Invention of a Theology of Abduction: Hincmar of Rheims on Raptus', *Journal of Ecclesiastical History* 60 (2009), 433-48.
17. For example, see the capitulary of Louis the Pious in *MGH, Capitularia,* vol. 1, 315 (no. 156), cap. 1.

3. Rape in thirteenth-century sources

The *Sachsenspiegel* ('Saxon Mirror'), written by Eike of Repgow in c. 1225, states the lack of consent as a distinct condition:

> An varendeme wive unde an siner amien mach die man not dun unde sin lif verwerken, of he sie ane iren dank beleget.

> (A man may commit rape with a common woman or his concubine and therefore receive the death penalty if he sleeps with her without her consent.)[18]

This ruling is especially significant for its emphasis on consent as compared to other and even later laws. Even women who are supposed to have generally consented to sexual intercourse, such as prostitutes or concubines (*amies*), may withdraw their consent in any given situation, and therefore can potentially be victims of rape if intercourse goes ahead without it, even when the offense is committed by their former sexual partners.

The law-book of the imperial town of Mühlhausen in Thuringia, written at roughly the same time, states:

> Liet ein man bi einimi wiebisnamin an urin danc undi widir urin willin is uri dan leit, so sal su sich weri mit gescrei undi sal iz danach zu hant cundigi mit zurizzinir waitz undi mit giwundin hendin undi mit weniningen oigin undi mit bustrubitemi hairi. Mit den vier sachin sal alliz diz sicreigi miti volgi biz an den richteri, sua su den vindit.

> (If a man lies with a woman without her consent and against her will, and if she does not want this, she shall defend herself with clamour, and afterwards she shall immediately declare it [the deed] with torn clothes and with hand-wringing and with tears and with disheveled hair. And having these four things presented everyone shall follow her to the judge, wherever she may find him.)[19]

These two are the first occurences in German law – whether written in German or in Latin – that explicitly hold the lack of consent to be an intrin-

---

18. *Des Sachsenspiegels erster Theil oder das Landrecht*, ed. C. G. Homeyer (Berlin: 1863 – 3rd edn), 342 (Landrecht III 46 §1). An English translation is found in *The Saxon Mirror: A 'Sachsenspiegel' of the Fourteenth Century*, ed. and trans. M. Dobozy (Philadelphia: 1999), 127. Dobozy, however, 'modernizes' in terms of modern rape legislation when she translates thus: 'It is possible to receive the death penalty for having intercourse with an itinerant woman or one's lover against her will'.

19. *Das Mühlhäuser Reichsrechtsbuch aus dem Anfang des 13. Jahrhunderts, Deutschlands ältestes Rechtsbuch: Nach den altmitteldeutschen Handschriften herausgegeben, eingeleitet und übersetzt*, ed. H. Meyer (Weimar: 1936 – 3rd edn), 106-11. The translation is mine.

sic element of the crime of rape.[20] But this is by no means an exclusively German phenomenon. All over Europe in the thirteenth century, seemingly out of nowhere, legal writings implement this new condition in their rulings on fornication by violent force. In France,[21] for instance, the famous *coutumier* Philippe de Beaumanoir wrote in his *Coutumes de Beauvasis* (1283):

> Femme eforcier si est quant aucuns prent a force carnele compaignie a feme contre la volonté de le feme, et sor ce qu'ele fet tout son poir du deffendre soi.

> (Rape is when someone has carnal intercourse by force with a woman against her will and when she does what she can to defend herself.)[22]

In England, Henry Bracton's *De legibus et consuetudinibus Angliae* appeared in the 1220s, more or less contemporaneously with Eike's *Sachsenspiegel*. One passage of the classical edition reads:

> Raptus mulieris ne fiat defendit tam lex humana quam divina. ... Si autem contra voluntatem eius iactet eam ad terram, forisfaciat gratiam suam ... Et si meretrix fuerit ante, tunc non fuit meretrix, cum nequitiae eius reclamando consentire noluit.

> (Man-made as well as divine laws forbid the rape of woman [...] If he throws her upon the ground against her will, he forfeits the king's grace [...] And if she was a whore before, she was not a whore then, since by crying out against his wicked deed she refused her consent.)[23]

Editor Samuel E. Thorne marks this as a possible later edition. But even if so, it still fits quite well in a larly thirteenth-century context. Other legal

20. A comprehensive study of rape in medieval Germany, especially before c. 1300, remains a desideratum. More general catalogues of laws and penalities are provided by R. His, *Das Strafrecht des deutschen Mittelalters*, vol. 2 (Weimar: 1928), 150-62; and E. Schubert, *Räuber, Henker, arme Sünder: Verbrechen und Strafe im Mittelalter* (Darmstadt: 2007), 211-14.

21. On rape jurisdiction in medieval France, see A. Porteau-Bitker, 'La justice laïque et le viol'; N. Gonthier, 'Les victimes de viol devant les tribunaux à fin du Moyen Âge d'après les sources dijonnaises et lyonnaises', *Criminologie* 27:2 (1994), 9-32. Also of particular interest is a study by the literary scholar K. Gravdal, *Ravishing Maidens: Writing Rape in Medieval French Literature and Law* (Philadelphia: 1991), esp. 1-20. On consent issues (not only concerning rape) see especially K. Varty, 'The Giving and Withholding of Consent in Late Twelfth-Century French Literature', *Reading Medieval Studies* 12 (1986), 27-49.

22. *Coutumes de Beauvaisis: Texte critique publié avec une introduction, un glossaire et une table analytique*, ed. A. M. Salmon, vol. 1 (Paris: 1899), 469-70 (c. 829). English translation: *The Coutumes de Beauvaisis of Philippe de Beaumanoir*, ed. F. R. P. Akehurst (Philadelphia: 1992).

23. *Bracton on the Laws and Customs of England*, ed. G. E. Woodbine and S. E. Thorne, vol. 2 (Cambridge, MA: 1968), 418-19. Note the striking parallel to Eike's *Sachsenspiegel* in the last sentence!

writings, such as the famous Statutes of Westminster (1275 and 1285) and a few 'private' law-books from the later thirteenth century (*Fleta*, *Britton*, and the *Mirror of Justices*) also express the idea of consent – whether taken up from Bracton or from somewhere else is another question, one that does not play a major role in my argument here.[24]

Once the idea of consent had permeated legal texts and rulings concerning rape, we will find it only few decades later as an argumentative figure in early surviving court records. In a 1393 rape case in Paris, for instance, which Walter Prevenier has brought to scholarly attention, the widow Ysablet des Champions voiced her lack of consent in an almost formulaic way. 'You may do with me what you will, for I am not mistress of my own body at present and cannot stand in the way of your desires', Ysablet testified to having screamed, 'but all that you have done, are doing, and will do to me is contrary to my desire and will.'[25] This is just one of many examples we can find throughout Western Europe. People knew how to tell their stories in court.[26] Indeed, Philippe de Beaumanoir had already worried about this fact and therefore presented a 'blueprint' of a defence for alleged rapists as early as 1283.[27] As late as the seventeenth century the English Lord Chief Justice Sir Matthew Hale, for long 'the most quoted authority on the law of rape'[28] in England, even down to the twenti-

---

24. The British Isles are the single best studied region with respect to rape legislation during the Middle Ages. See, for example, J. M. Carter, *Rape in Medieval England: An Historical and Sociological Study* (Lanham: 1985); A. Musson, 'Crossing Boundaries: Attitudes to Rape in Late Medieval England', in A. Musson (ed.), *Boundaries of the Law: Geography, Gender, and Jurisdiction in Medieval and Early Modern Europe* (Aldershot: 2005), 84-101; K. Phillips, 'Written on the Body: Reading Rape from the Twelfth to Fifteenth Centuries', in N. J. Menuge (ed.), *Medieval Women and the Law* (Woodbridge: 2000), 125-44; E. Hawkes, 'Bibliography of Legal Records Related to Rape and Ravishment in Medieval England', *Medieval Feminist Newsletter* 21 (1996), 15-18; R. Kittel, 'Rape in Thirteenth-Century England: A Study of the Common Law Courts', in D. K. Weisberg (ed.), *Women and the Law: A Social Historical Perspective*, vol. 2 (Cambridge, MA: 1982), 101-16; J. G. Bellamy, *The Criminal Trial in Later Medieval England: Felony before the Courts from Edward I to the Sixteenth Century* (Toronto: 1998), App. I, 162-86.
25. W. Prevenier, 'Violence against Women in a Medieval Metropolis: Paris around 1400', in D. Nicholas and B. Barhrach (eds.), *Law, Custom and the Social Fabric in Medieval Europe: Essays in Honor of Bryce Lyon* (Kalamazoo: 1990), 263-84, at 264.
26. The classic study of such narratives remains N. Zemon Davis, *Fiction in the Archives: Pardon Tales and their Tellers* (Stanford: 1987); on rape narratives, see 36-37. See also J. S. Cockburn, 'Early Modern Assize Records as Historical Evidence', *Journal of the Society of Archivists* 5 (1975), 215-31 (esp. for English records); and – with special reference to rape cases – M. Naessens, 'Sexuality in Court: Emotional Perpetrators and Victims versus a Rational Judicial System?', in E. Lecuppre-Desjardin and A.-L. Van Bruane (eds.), *Emotions in the Heart of the City: 14th – 16th Century* (Turnhout: 2005), 119-56.
27. Salmon, *Coutumes de Beauvasis*, 469-70 (c. 829).
28. B. Toner, *The Facts of Rape* (New York: 1977), 95.

eth century, once called rape 'an accusation easily to be made and hard to be proved, and harder to be defended by the party accused, tho never so innocent'.[29]

The aforesaid is certainly not to suggest that all of sudden a cogent and perfectly uniform rape law emerged in thirteenth-century Europe. Some legal writings from the thirteenth and even fourteenth centuries still held fast to the traditional idea of *raptus*, where the use of force remained a qualifying, not a constituting element. Good examples of such traditional rulings can be found in many of the Iberian *fueros*.[30] But the sheer number of new legal writings that convey this new, somewhat 'modern' idea of rape with the lack of consent and its juridical diagnosis as its central elements, are beyond doubt significantly widespread and cannot be explained by random emergence. This observation leads to the following pressing question:

4. What might have happened in between?

If there is a reason for this striking change in rape jurisdiction, it must have been something that affected more than a single region or a single kingdom. Otherwise it cannot be explained why rape laws changed so markedly in so many different regions nearly synchronically during only a few of decades. And of course, as legal historians well know, such a pan-European event did indeed take place during the 'long' twelfth century: the spread of the learned *Ius commune*, of Roman and canon law.

Roman law soon drops out as a likely candidate in the process, however. In fact, this is where the ambiguity of '*raptus*' – sometimes sexual violence and sometimes abduction for the purpose of marriage – stems from. According to Olivia Robinson, in Roman law rape 'in the modern sense seems [...] not to have been a matter of great social concern', and indeed only 'abduction was seen as a serious problem'.[31] Legal sources outlawed the use of force and fear to accomplish sexual relations and made this use of violence (*vis*) a capital public crime. But actually later medieval law, as we

---

29. M. Hale, *History of the Pleas of the Crown*, vol. 1 (London: 1763), *635
30. For instance, see the *Siete Partidas* (completed c. 1265): *Las Siete Partidas*, vol. 5, ed. and trans. S. P. Scott, repr. ed. R. I. Burns (Philadelphia: 2001), 1425. On the prosecution of rape in the medieval Iberian Peninsula, see R. Córdoba de la Llave, 'Criminalidad sexual en la Edad Media: Fuentes, estudios y perspectivas', in C. Barros (ed.), *Historia a debate* 4 (Santiago de Compostela: 1995), 49-61; I. Bazán Díaz, 'El estupro: Sexualidad delictiva en la Baja Edad Media y primera Edad Moderna', *Mélanges de la Casa de Velázquez* 33 (2003), 13-46.
31. O. F. Robinson, 'Unpardonable Crimes: Fourth Century Attitudes', in O. F. Robinson and J. W. Cairns (eds.), *Critical Studies in Ancient Law, Comparative Law and Legal History* (Oxford: 2001), 117-26, at 124. By and large, this observation can indeed be enlarged well beyond the fourth century.

have come to know it from the thirteenth-century panorama above, learned little from Roman law in this respect.[32] That leads us to canon law.

At first glance, canon law is not a promising place to look for regulations on matters of penal law – especially not in terms of capital crimes such as murder, homicide or rape. Medieval canonists, however, did develop teachings also on this matter, some of which turned out to be exceptionally influential.[33] One of those, I would argue, also touches upon the way rape was handled in secular law. Moreoever, it was not the canonists' actual discussion of rape that ultimately became so influential in the handling of rape in secular jurisdictions, but the more indirect effect of the legal principles they introduced into the discussion.

This is not to say *raptus* was not discussed by the canonists, by Gratian and his commentators. Gratian in his *Decretum*, however, largely stuck to the idea of displacement as the central element of *raptus*:

> Cum ergo hec illicito coitu sit corrupta, cumque ita sit abducta, id est a domo patris ducta, quod de eius nuptiis nichil actum ante fuerit, raptam appellandam negari non potest. Sed non omnis illicitus coitus, nec cuiuslibet illicita defloratio raptus appellatur. Aliud enim est fornicatio, aliud stuprum, aliud adulterium, aliud incestus, aliud raptus.

> (Therefore when she is corrupted through illicit intercourse, and when she is abducted, that is, led from her father's home, insofar as no act of marriage with her has previously been performed, it cannot be denied that she must be called ravished [*raptam*]. But not every type of illicit coitus nor illicit defloration of any woman is termed *raptus*. For fornication is one thing, defilement [*stuprum*] another, adultery another, incest another, *raptus* another.)[34]

This notion – clearly inherited from Roman law[35] – was taken up and differentiated by Gratian's commentators. Some even defined *raptus* exclusively as of the carrying off of a woman from one place to the other, with no attention given to the degree of violence: 'A rapist of a woman is not called he who carnally knows her by force but he who carries her from one place to

---

32. This is heavily simplified. For a more detailed discussion, see C. Saunders, 'Classical Paradigms of Rape in the Middle Ages', in S. Deace and K. F. Pierce (eds.), *Rape in Antiquity: Sexual Violence in the Greek and Roman World* (London: 2002), 243-66.

33. See the thoughtful study of L. Kéry, *Gottesfurcht und irdische Straf: Der Beitrag des mittelalterlichen Kirchenrechts zur Entstehung des öffentlichen Strafrechts* (Cologne and Vienna: 2006).

34. *Decretum* C. 36.1.2 – *Corpus iuris canonici: Editio Lipsiensis secunda post Aemilii Ludovici Richteri curas ad librorum manu scriptorum et Editionis Romanae*, vol. 1, ed. E. Friedberg (Leipzig: 1879), 1288. Translation by Saunders, *Rape*, 77-78.

35. Cf. *Dig.* 47.9.3.5 or *Cod.* 9.20.1.

another with force and knows her carnally', Albericus de Rosciate said in the fourteenth century.[36]

As is well known, marriage law underwent a profound re-evaluation and more binding formulation in the long twelfth century, with Gratian and his *Decretum*, the decretalists, and Pope Alexander III as prominent figures in this process.[37] To cut a long and complex story audaciously short: In contrast to earlier debates, freely exchanged words of present consent ('I take you to be my wife/ husband'), rather than consummation and parental consent, were established as the main criterion for a valid marriage. Consent in cases of *raptus* played only a small role in the *Decretum* and the writings of the first generation of its commentators. Still, in the thirteenth century Henricus de Segusio, otherwise known as Hostiensis, starts his discussion of the *poena raptorum corporum* in his *Summa aurea* (sometimes known as *Summa super titulis Decretalium*) with the observation:

> Illud autem secundum legem non distinguitur an mulier volens fuerit, an in- uita, sponsa propria, an aliena coniugata, vel non: sed acerbius punitur hoc crimen adulterii adlectione.

> (But this is not distinguished according to the law: if the woman is willing or unwilling, [if she is the perpetrator's] fiancée or another man's betrothed, or not: but this crime is punished more severely when combined with adultery.)[38]

But at the same time, things gradually changed, when an increasing number of canonists began to apply legal figures and principles they knew from other contexts in their commentaries on the law of *raptus*. At a second glance this seems even rather natural, for one of the prominent places where canonists discussed the crime of *raptus* were debates over the validity of marriages between *raptor* and *raptam*. In this respect, the most important legal figure canonists introduced into the law of *raptus* was the measure of

36. Quoted by G. Dahm, *Das Strafrecht Italiens im ausgehenden Mittelalter: Untersuchungen über die Beziehung zwischen Theorie und Praxis im Strafrecht des Spätmittelalters, namentlich im XIV. Jahrhundert* (Berlin: 1931), 428: 'Raptor mulieris non dicitur ille, qui per vim eam cognoscit, sed ille, qui abducit per vim de loco ad locum et eam carnaliter cognoscit'. Similarily Albertus Gandinus, one of the earliest and most influential canonists to treat issues of penal law: cf. his *De multis questionibus*, in *Albertus Gandinus und das Strafrecht der Scholastik,* vol. 2, ed. H. Kantorowicz (Berlin: 1907), 398-99.

37. The body of literature on this process is vast, so I will refer the reader only to the helpful overview by P. J. Reynolds, 'Marrying and its Documentation in Pre-Modern Europe: Consent, Celebration, and Property', in P. J. Reynolds (ed.), *To Have and to Hold: Marrying and its Documentation in Western Christendom, 400-1600* (Cambridge: 2007), 1-42.

38. *Henrici Cardinalis Hostiensis Summa aurea: interjectae recens fuerit erudita ex summa Martini abbatis, Azonis et Accursii* [...] (Venice: 1570), fol. 412v.

resistance a woman had to show against her *raptor*: it required a force sufficient to move a 'constant man' (*vir constans*) to do something against his
explicit will. This legal figure was already known in marriage law, where it
measured the force that had been applied to coerce one of the partners into
marriage, and could lead to an annulment of the marriage.[39] Now it also
constituted the boundary between rape and fornication.

This is only just the beginning of a complex process of gradual deve-
lopement towards our modern notion of rape, for the conflicting intersection
of physical force and the individual will increasingly haunted medieval canonists and the rising discipline of moral theology. We cannot yet see the
exact path this development took through the great variety of *summae*,
glosses, and commentaries, many of them not printed since the early modern period, none of them translated. But we can have a dim idea which direction to take in future research. It seems highly probable that modern rape
law was conceptualized in tight parallel to marriage law – a field of legal
practice which influenced traditional secular law throughout Europe considerably earlier than most other fields of canon law, for it most frequently
affected everyday life and fell completely under the jurisdiction of church
officials.

The institutionalization of marriage law in general and of marital consent in particular during the twelfth century, I would propose, therefore led
to the invention of our modern notion of rape in the following decades, with
lack of consent as its core element. I hope to prove that in more detail in the
future.

39. On the figure of the *vir constans* see R.e Balbi, 'Il criterio del 'vir constans' nella
teorica canonistica della 'coactio' come vizio del consenso matrimoniale: Dalla de-
cretistica classica al 'Liber Extra' di Gregorio IX', *Ius ecclesiae* 19 (2007), 309-31;
and – for its influence on modern legal cultures – H. Eidenmüller, 'Druckmittel bei
Vertragsverhandlungen', in R. Zimmermann (ed.), *Störungen der Willensbildung
bei Vertragsschluss* (Tübingen: 2007), 103-24, esp. 109-13.

Two Models of Incest: Conflict and Confusion in High Medieval Discourse on Kinship and Marriage

Christof Rolker

> Jesus Christ ordered every Christian
> Not to marry his kin
> You cannot take kin to within the fourth degree
> Otherwise it will be buggery.[1]

1. Introduction

The lines from *Yde et Olive*, a thirteenth-century *chanson de geste*, clearly refer to the canonical marriage prohibitions as formulated by the Fourth Lateran Council in 1215.[2] At the same time, however, there are striking differences between the *chanson* and the synodal decrees. While in *Yde et Olive* the prohibited degrees are described as being instituted by Christ himself, and thus as immutable divine legislation, the Lateran Council famously argued that in reducing the prohibited degrees from seven to four it was

---

Abbreviations: C. J. = *Codex Justiniani*; CCCM = *Corpus Christianorum, Continuatio Medievalis*; CCSL = *Corpus Christianorum, Series Latina*; PG = *Patrologia Graeca*; PL = *Patrologia Latina*.

1.   *Esclarmonde, Clarisse et Florent, Yde et Olive: Drei Fortsetzungen der Chanson von Huon de Bordeaux*, ed. M. Schweigel, Ausgaben und Abhandlungen aus dem Gebiete der romanischen Philologie 83 (Marburg: 1889), lines 6448-51: 'Tous crestïens Jesucris commanda / Ca son parage ne se mariast pas / Tu ne le pues avoir dusques en qart, / U autrement bougrenie sera.' The translation is that of Darron Burrows, as quoted in D. Watt, 'Behaving like a man? Incest, lesbian desire, and gender play in *Yde et Olive* and its adaptations', *Comparative Literature* 50 (1998), 265-85, at 268.
2.   *Decrees of the Ecumenical Councils*, ed. and trans. N. P. Tanner, 2 vols. (London: 1990), vol. 1, 257-58.

simply changing 'human legislation' (*statuta humana*), adjusting it to changing needs of society. Violation of these laws was not 'buggery', but according to papal practice could be dealt with by dispensation.

These differences point to the well-known paradoxes surrounding medieval marriage prohibitions. On the one hand, transgressing them was to commit incest – one of the most horrible crimes possible, as both secular and clerical authors asserted. On the other hand, so many marriages violated at least one of the numerous prohibitions that one cannot help but think that such marriages were socially acceptable. Likewise, the rhetoric of divine law and God's wrath stands in stark contrast to the cool negotiations over dispensations of all kinds. For the modern reader at least, it is also puzzling to encounter a legal category that encompassed such diverse elements as father/daughter incest, the abduction of nuns and marriages between third cousins twice removed.

In the present paper, I will address these paradoxes by looking at two very dissimilar branches of the medieval discourse on endogamy and exogamy, and more specifically at different justifications of marriage prohibitions as found in systematic canon law collections of the eleventh and twelfth centuries. At this time, the prohibitions had grown to their most extreme form. Banning, *inter alia*, marriages within the seventh degree according to canonical computation, the law as contained in these collections was excessive compared to any ancient or modern marriage law, and even compared to early medieval canon law or indeed canon law after 1215. The first of two important, but very different traditions relating to marriages among relatives is the view of kin marriage as incest and thus as an abomination, as a violation of divine precept. The other tradition is a discourse on the advantages of exogamy, as articulated perhaps most famously in St Augustine's *City of God*. Although both traditions can be and have been used to justify the same legislation, I want to stress how strikingly different they were, before looking at the effects produced by the conflation of both traditions in the eleventh and early twelfth centuries. As I want to argue, the systematic collections produced a new reading of the old texts by presenting them in a different way, both changing the law and presenting it as unchangeable. Finally, I want to argue that nonetheless there were contemporary approaches which, using very similar sources, developed models that did not justify the legal *status quo* but rather questioned it.

2. Purity and pollution: incest as an abomination

Let us first concentrate on the heated discourse on incest as an abomination, which played such a prominent role in medieval marriage law as well as in literary imagination.[3] For this branch of the medieval discourse on the marriage prohibitions, the biblical ban on incest is of course of paramount importance. In Leviticus 18, sexual relations with a small number of relatives (including a few in-laws) are condemned as an abomination by God himself. As is repeatedly pointed out, the incest prohibitions mark the difference between the chosen people and the gentiles (Lev. 18:3, 21, 27-28), and indeed incest is linked to blasphemy (Lev. 18:20). At the same time, incest is prohibited in the same context and also in the same language as a number of other sexual offences including sex with a menstruating woman, sodomy and bestiality. The marriage prohibitions as contained in Leviticus are thus incest prohibitions: transgression of this law is clearly a sexual offence, a violation of divine order and a threat to purity.

From a medieval perspective, a second source for the discourse on incest as a abomination was Roman law. While there are of course important differences from the Old Testament prohibitions, let alone from medieval legislation, the relevant legislation was cast in similarly strong language. Incest for the Romans was *nefas*, a violation of divine order.[4] Although the relevant laws apparently were rarely applied, and kin marriages contracted in good faith were dealt with rather lightly,[5] the high tone of these laws should not be underestimated. The extension of the term *incestum* to the unchastity of a Vestal is important evidence that such unions were regarded as sacrilege. In this context, it is also important to note that incest was part and parcel of 'othering'. Just as in Leviticus the prohibited acts are attributed to the Egyptians, there are both Greek and Roman traditions to associate incest with various 'barbarians'.[6] Literary sources are likewise indicative of the horror with which sexual unions between close relatives were regarded: Divine punishment or at least a violent death in some form is the usual fate of

---

3.   For the latter, see E. Archibald, *Incest and the Medieval Imagination* (Oxford: 2001). For canon law, see J. A. Brundage, *Law, Sex and Christian Society in Medieval Europe* (Chicago and London: 1987), ch. 5; M. de Jong, 'An Unsolved Riddle: Early Medieval Incest Legislation', in I. Wood (ed.), *Franks and Alamanni in the Merovingian Period: An Ethnographic Perspective*. Studies in Historical Archaeoethnology 3 (Woodbridge: 1998), 107-40; M. H. Gelting, 'Marriage, Peace and the Canonical Incest Prohibitions: Making Sense of an Absurdity?', in M. Korpiola (ed.), *Nordic Perspectives on Medieval Canon Law*. Publications of Matthias Calonius Society 2 (Helsinki: 1999), 93-124; and most recently K. Ubl, *Inzestverbot und Gesetzgebung: Die Konstruktion eines Verbrechens (300-1100)*. Millenium-Studien 20 (Berlin: 2009).
4.   P. Moreau, *Incestus et prohibitae nuptiae: Conception romaine de l'inceste et histoire des prohibitions matrimoniales pour cause de parenté dans la Rome antique*. Collection d'études anciennes, Série latine 62 (Paris: 2002), 29-105, esp. 43-52.
5.   J. F. Gardner, *Women in Roman Law and Society* (London: 1986), 125-27.
6.   Brundage, *Law, Sex and Christian Society*, 14; Moreau, *Incestus*, 88-90.

the perpetrator in incest stories such as that of Apollonius of Tyre, which remained popular throughout the Middle Ages.[7]

Concerning the question of which unions were actually called incest, these authorities differed substantially. Nonetheless, they form a fairly uniform discourse in the sense that it is more about sex than marriage, and that incest is always seen as a violation of divine order, not just human law. It is this language we find in early medieval legislation on the prohibited degrees. From the sixth century onwards, the councils directly refer to Leviticus to justify marriage prohibitions;[8] the Second Council of Toledo (531 or perhaps 527)[9] interpreted Leviticus 18:6 ('omnis homo ad proxy-mam sanguinis sui non accedat ut revelet turpitudinem eius') so as to justify extending marriage prohibitions to 'all' kin.[10] More generally, several early medieval councils employed a language of purity and pollution when dealing with the prohibited degrees.[11] This is also true for the early medieval penitentials, where sexual contacts between relatives are treated in the context of sexual sins and other polluting acts. In canon law, the term *incestum* was applied not only to unions between relatives (whether by blood or by marriage) but also to other sexual offences, including sex between godparent and godchild and intercourse with consecrated virgins. This all strongly indicates that in these sources, the discourse on marriage prohibitions was actually more about sex than about marriage, and it also highlights the spiritual dimension. Those who transgressed these boundaries were threatened with divine punishment, as both conciliar acts and hagiography show.

One may still legitimately ask how much of this is due to 'genuine fear' of incest or how much of this is 'propaganda'. It is in any case remarkable that the early medieval incest discourse itself is fairly consistent, as both old and new prohibitions are talked about in terms of purity and pollu-

---

7.   Archibald, *Incest*; C. Kiening, 'Familienroman und Heilsgeschichte', in K.-H. Spieß (ed.), *Die Familie in der Gesellschaft des Mittelalters*. Vorträge und Forschungen 71 (Ostfildern: 2009), 51-76.

8.   R. Weigand, 'Die Ausdehnung der Ehehindernisse der Verwandschaft', *Zeitschrift der Savigny-Stiftung für Rechtsgeschichte, kanonistische Abteilung* 111 (1994), 1-17, at 2-3.

9.   The dating is difficult. According to the statutes (see http://www.benedictus.mgh.de/quellen/chga/chga_044t.htm) the second council was held in the fifth year of the reign of Amalric (suggesting 531) in the fifth *aera* (suggesting 527).

10. *La colección canónica Hispana*, ed. G. Martínez Díez and F. Rodríguez, 6 in 7 vols., Monumenta Hispaniae sacra, Series canonica 1-6 (Madrid: 1966-2002), vol. 4, 352-53. On the content and context of these prohibitions, see Ubl, *Inzestverbot*, 200-08.

11. In addition to de Jong, 'Unsolved Riddle' and Gelting, 'Marriage', see A. G. Remensnyder, 'Pollution, Purity and Peace: An Aspect of Social Reform between the Late Tenth Century and 1076', in T. Head and R. Landes (eds.), *The Peace of God: Social Violence and Religious Response in France around the Year 1000* (Ithaca: 1992), 280-307.

tion. Even if not expressing 'genuine fear', this vocabulary was certainly apt to inspire such fear, and this may not only have helped to win acceptance for the new prohibitions but also have fostered their further expansion. Given the growing disparity among the actual laws, let alone the diversity of the manuscript tradition,[12] the tone of this discourse may well have inspired bishops to act according to the principle 'better safe than sorry'.

3. 'The greatest amount of *caritas* for the greatest number of people': Exogamy and the economy of affection

Compared to this 'heated' incest discourse, the second tradition I want to discuss is a strikingly cool line of reasoning on endogamy and exogamy. The best-known example is a passage in Augustine's *City of God*, but there are both earlier and later authors arguing along the same lines.[13] John Chrysostom, for one, developed a model very similar to that of Augustine.[14] What these authors have in common is that they talk not so much about sex, but rather analyse matrimony as a means to multiply social bonds. While Augustine links exogamy to *caritas*, his argument is neither based on the Bible nor specifically Christian. Exogamy in this model is superior to endogamy in connecting more people by mutual affection. As Augustine put it, endogamy was avoided,[15]

> [...] not that one man should combine many relationships in his sole person, but that those relationships should be distributed among individuals, and should bind social life more effectively by involving a greater number of persons in them. Thus, 'father' and 'father-in-law' are the names of two different relationships; and so the ties of affection (*caritas*) extend to a greater number of persons when each has one man as his father and another as his father-in-law.

The positive effects of exogamous marriage can thus be measured and indeed counted. The fewer relationships united in one person, and the more

---

12. See Weigand, 'Ausdehnung der Ehehindernisse', 2-3, esp. notes 2 and 7, for early examples.
13. M. Verbaarschot, 'De iuridica natura impedimenti consanguinitatis in theologia et in iure canonico a S. Petro Damiano usque ad Decretales Gregorii IX (ca. 1063-1234)', *Ephemerides theologicae Lovanienses* 30 (1954), 697-739; Moreau, *Incestus*, 125-27; Ubl, *Inzestverbot*, 56-62.
14. *In epistulam ad Corinthos I homilia XXXIV* (PG 61, 289-91), on which see Verbaarschot, 'De iuridica natura', 699.
15. Augustinus, *De civitate Dei libri XXII*, eds. B. Dombart and A. Kalb, 2 vols, CCSL 47/48 (Turnhout: 1955), here *De civitate Dei* xv, 16 (CCSL 48, 476-79); the translation is taken from Augustine, *The City of God against the Pagans*, trans. R. W. Dyson (Cambridge: 1998), 664-65.

persons related to each other, the better. As Jeremy Bentham might have said, exogamy serves to produce 'the greatest amount of *caritas* for the greatest number of people'. The key argument against endogamy is that it is 'unnecessary', as spouses related by blood are already connected by mutual affection, and more *caritas*-efficient marriage strategies are available. If incest in this model was a sin, it was so because it was a waste of the scarce good of *caritas*.

A second important aspect of this model, apart from the cool (utilitarian) mode of speaking, is that it is linked to a very wide definition of kinship. Common descent always creates at least some affection that only gradually fades away. Yet crucially, this kinship is not identified with the prohibited degrees. Cousin marriage, Augustine affirms, was recently forbidden,[16] but more distant relatives are nonetheless kin. In other words, the prohibited degrees are much more narrowly defined than kinship, and in any case are subject to change. Indeed, as Augustine argues at some length, the ban on cousin marriages was only based on changing custom (*consuetudo, mos*); he praises both pagans and Christians for developing customs that are morally superior to positive law. Thus, the ban on cousin marriage is based on natural law and custom, but like all human legislation it may well change – as indeed happened at least twice in Augustine's lifetime.[17]

For the medieval reception of this model, it is crucial that a version of it was repeated by Isidore in his *Etymologies*.[18] This version provided an important inspiration for the high medieval canon law on the prohibited degrees and was regularly (if incorrectly) quoted to justify the seventh degree in canonical computation. However, it is also important that Isidore did not use terms like 'incest' when discussing the prohibited degrees, and vice-versa.[19] Instead of linking the prohibited degrees to the biblical incest prohibitions, Isidore repeated Augustine when he stated that *propinquitas* among blood relatives 'fades away' the more distant the relation is, but is 'called back' by matrimony.[20] Like Augustine, he did not think that relation by

---

16. Augustine refers to cousin marriage as banned 'hoc tempore'; from this and a small number of similar references it has been inferred that Theodosius († 395) issued such a ban in 385. However, cousin marriage was legal again in 405 (C. J. 5, 4, 19). See S. Treggiari, *Roman Marriage: Iusti Coniuges from the Time of Cicero to the Time of Ulpian* (Oxford: 1991), 114.
17. See previous note.
18. Isidore, *Etymologiae* ix, 6: 'De cognatis et agnatis' as quoted below (n. 18). All Isidore quotations are from *Isidori Hispalensis episcopi etymologiarum sive originum libri XX*, ed. W. M. Lindsay, 2 vols. (Oxford: 1911) [s.p.].
19. See Isidore, *Etymologiae* v, 26 on the term *incestus*, but with no reference to specific degrees of kinship; the discussion of consanguinity in *Etymologiae* ix, 6, on the other hand, does not even mention incest.
20. Isidore, *Etymologiae* ix, 6: 'Haec consanguinitas dum se paulatim propaginum ordinibus dirimens usque ad ultimum gradum subtraxerit, et propinquitas esse desierit, eam rursus lex matrimonii vinculo repetit, et quodam modo revocat fu-

blood precludes marriage in all cases, as both his text and the tables of consanguinity confirm.[21]

4. Conflating traditions in the eleventh and twelfth centuries

The difference between these two models seems clear enough. Given the stress on 'ritual purity' in recent scholarship on medieval incest legislation, it is worth mentioning that both traditions were well known in the Middle Ages. Evidently, both could be used to justify the ever-expanding incest prohibitions. The point is, however, that for centuries they were normally not combined. Early medieval incest legislation followed the tradition of Roman law in using the language of purity and pollution, and sometimes referred to the biblical incest prohibitions to justify marriage prohibitions. Augustine's *City of God*, on the other hand, was very widely known but before the eleventh century was never quoted by popes or councils legislating on incest, nor was the chapter quoted above copied into any canon law collection. Some authors, such as Jonas of Orléans († 841), drew on both traditions in their discussion of the prohibited degrees,[22] but this seems to have been without much effect on canon law.

This only changed in the eleventh century, perhaps most famously with Peter Damian's letter on the degrees of kinship, in which he both quoted a definition of kinship very similar to that found in Augustine (and Isidore) and condemned marriage with even very distant relatives as a most horrible crime.[23] While there is some discussion about what Peter Damian actually meant to say, and some of his arguments are clearly flawed,[24] it is worth mentioning that his approach of combining Augustine/Isidore with the early medieval incest prohibitions was in tune with mainstream canon law. More specifically, his approach was manifestly inspired by the collection of Burchard of Worms, of which he must have been one of the

gientem.' Cf. *De civitate Dei* xv, 16 (eds. Dombart and Kalb, CCSL 48, 476): 'Fuit autem antiquis patribus religiosae curae, ne ipsa propinquitas se paulatim propaginum ordinibus dirimens longius abiret et propinquitas esse desisteret, eam nondum longe positam rursus matrimonii vinculo conligare et quodammodo revocare fugientem.'

21. The tables show more degrees of kinship than the prohibited ones; see H. Schadt, *Die Darstellungen der Arbores consanguinitatis und der Arbores affinitatis: Bildschemata in juristischen Handschriften* (Tübingen: 1982).
22. *De institutione laicali* (PL 106, 121-278, here at 183).
23. Letter 19, ed. *Die Briefe des Petrus Damiani*, ed. K. Reindel, MGH, Briefe der deutschen Kaiserzeit 4, 4 vols. (Munich: 1983-1993), vol. 1, 179-99; cf. letter 102, ed. Reindel, vol. 3, 132.
24. Ubl, *Inzestverbot*, 451-60.

first Italian readers;[25] and later collections in their choice of material made similar choices to those of Peter Damian.

It is therefore the systematic canon law collections of the eleventh and early twelfth centuries that I now want to turn to. I will mainly concentrate on the *Decretum* of Burchard of Worms from the early eleventh century and the *Panormia* compiled a century later in northern France. Both works were very popular, indeed the most popular systematic canon law collections before Gratian. Apart from their very considerable direct influence, they also provided material for many other collections, and as I will argue, even beyond this the very structure of these collections is an important aspect in understanding 'the law' on endogamy and exogamy.

5. Burchard of Worms: incest and innovation

Recent scholarship has highlighted the paramount importance of Burchard of Worms († 1025) in the history of medieval marriage legislation.[26] According to Karl Ubl, Burchard compiled his collection as a 'handbook for the incest campaign of Emperor Henry II' and more or less single-handedly expanded the prohibited degrees of kinship to the seventh degree in canonical computation.[27] Even if one does not subscribe to this interpretation, there can be little doubt that Burchard took a vivid interest in incest legislation. Book seven on incest seems to have been planned at an early stage of the work,[28] and it was evidently important to Burchard. In the course of its compilation, he manipulated several proof-texts it contains,[29] and in doing so both reduced the contradictions between them and at the same time came to a stricter interpretation of the law.[30] At the very least, his

25. J. J. Ryan, *Saint Peter Damiani and His Canonical Sources: A Preliminary Study in the Antecedents of the Gregorian Reform*, Pontifical Institute of Medieval Studies Studies and Texts 2 (Toronto: 1956), 161; D. Jasper, 'Burchards Dekret in der Sicht der Gregorianer', in W. Hartmann (ed.), *Bischof Burchard von Worms*. Quellen und Abhandlungen zur mittelrheinischen Kirchengeschichte 100 (Mainz: 2000), 167-98, at 169-70.

26. P. Corbet, *Autour de Burchard de Worm: L'église allemande et les interdits de parenté (IXème–XIIème siècle)*, Ius Commune, Sonderhefte 142 (Frankfurt: 2001); Ubl, *Inzestverbot*, ch. 7.

27. Ubl, *Inzestverbot*, 426-35, at 435.

28. Comparing the earliest manuscripts, Hoffmann and Pokorny found evidence of substantial reworking of almost all books, but the only change to Burchard's book seven was the addition of the two last canons: H. Hoffmann and R. Pokorny, *Das Dekret des Bischofs Burchard von Worms: Textstufen - Frühe Verbreitung - Vorlagen*, MGH, Hilfsmittel 12 (Munich: 1991), 40-86, esp. 41, 70-71, 73, 81-82.

29. Corbet, *Burchard de Worms*, 89-91.

30. This fits the general trend of Burchard's work; see G. Austin, *Shaping Church Law around the Year 1000: The* Decretum *of Burchard of Worms*, Church, Faith and Culture in the Middle Ages (Farnham and Burlington: 2009).

collection played a very important role in establishing the seventh degree of consanguinity and canonical computation as the legal standard.

How did Burchard deal with the two models of incest discussed above? Much like Peter Damian in the middle of the century, Burchard combined the two traditions, by employing Isidore's version of the Augustinian model and mixing it ingeniously with the early medieval incest prohibitions. More specifically, he quoted Isidore to argue that family affection 'fades away' the more distant the relation by blood becomes, but is 'restored' by matrimony. At the same time, he assembled a wide range of sources that condemn kin marriage as incest. Crucially, however, he also manipulated the tradition on two important points. First, he defined kinship much more widely than Isidore had done;[31] and secondly, he identified this 'kinship' with the prohibited degrees. In part, Burchard changed the law by manipulating the actual wording of his proof-texts.[32] However, I would like to draw attention to another, more subtle way in which Burchard changed the law.[33] My argument here is that the structure of his collection and the arrangement of the canons strongly affected the way his proof-texts worked. This to me seems relevant to understanding more than Burchard alone. While only few compilers of later canon law collections manipulated their texts as directly as Burchard did, my arguments about the arrangement of canons can be applied to many other systematic canon law collections.

The first, but fundamental decision of Burchard was to dedicate a separate book to the prohibited degrees, and to give it the title *De incesta copulatione*.[34] The collection of such substantial material under this heading was an innovation,[35] and it influences the reading of canons found in this book. The very unity of the book suggests that there was something like a uniform

31. On this crucial point, see Ubl, *Inzestverbot*, ch. 7. For Burchard's stemma, see Schadt, *Darstellungen*, 109-10 and Corbet, *Burchard de Worms*, 95-98.
32. Corbet, *Burchard de Worms*, 89-95.
33. For an inspiring discussion of the effects produced by different arrangements of proof-texts in pre-Gratian canon law collections, see A. Thier, 'Dynamische Schriftlichkeit: Zur Normbildung in den vorgratianischen Kanonessammlungen', *Zeitschrift der Savigny-Stiftung für Rechtsgeschichte, kanonistische Abteilung* 124 (2007), 1-33.
34. See L. Fowler-Magerl, *Clavis canonum: Selected Canon Law Collections before 1140: Access with Data Processing*, MGH, Hilfsmittel 21 (Munich: 2005). The *Clavis* database is now available online: http://www.mgh.de/ext/clavis/. My thanks to Greta Austin for checking the *editio princeps* and Burchard manuscripts not available to me.
35. The Freising *Collectio duodecim partium*, which is very closely related to Burchard, is the only other collection to have a separate book on 'incest'. Earlier systematic collections do gather canons on incest, and in their rubrics and sub-titles also use terms like '*incestus*', but not in the same way as Burchard did. To take two major collections as an example: in the *Collectio vetus Gallica* seven canons are grouped together under the heading 'De incestis et adulteris et qui uxores suas demittunt', while in the *Dacheriana*, the incest prohibitions are in the first book, *De penitentia*. For these and further examples, see Fowler-Magerl, *Clavis*.

crime of incest, and more specifically suggests that the canons condemning incest as an abomination are talking about the same matters as the canons that define kinship as extending to the seventh degree of consanguinity. Burchard thus conflated two traditions that hitherto had been separate. Those early medieval councils that so strongly expressed fear of incest as a source of ritual impurity were referring to incest prohibitions significantly more limited than those Burchard propagated, while his authorities in favour of the very wide definition of kinship were not equally concerned with purity and pollution, if at all.[36] In Burchard's book seven, however, the divergent traditions are combined under the heading of 'incest', thus giving the very strong impression that the violation of these excessive prohibitions was indeed a horrible sexual crime.

The second aspect is also related to the systematic character of Burchard's collection. As one would expect from a systematic collection, it does not give any clue to the chronology of the material it presents. In the case of incest legislation, this is an important piece of information. As will be discussed later, the changing nature of this legislation was an important argument in the debates over dispensation from and finally reduction of the prohibitions. The reader of Burchard's *Decretum*, however, while confronted with a large number of authorities mainly asserting the seventh degree, can in no way guess at any historical development of these texts. This impression is partly due to Burchard's suppression of some material and the manipulation of other texts, but again the arrangement itself is crucial in suggesting that the law on incest had never substantially changed.

At the same time, Burchard of course omits the original context of his material, which in many cases would have led the reader to very different conclusions from that of the relevant excerpt. For example, if one reads the acts of the Second Council of Toledo in context, it is quite clear that the bishops defined kinship, including the prohibited degrees of kinship, in Roman law terms.[37] If reduced to a few lines of condemnation of incestuous unions[38] and presented in the midst of authorities banning marriage to the seventh degree of kinship,[39] however, this fragment becomes yet another proof-text for a position that would have been utterly incomprehensible to the bishops gathered in Toledo. On the other hand, the quotation from Leviticus 18:6 contained in this short Toledo fragment in itself influences the understanding of the surrounding canons. By alluding to Leviticus before quoting Isidore's rather wide definition of kinship, Burchard also makes

---

36. Isidore's definition of kinship is taken from Roman inheritance law, and thus quite independent even from Roman marriage law, let alone the medieval incest legislation; see above (n. 18).
37. Ubl, *Inzestverbot*, 200-02.
38. Burchard, *Decretum* vii, 6 (PL 140, 780-81).
39. Burchard, *Decretum* vii, 2 and 10-16 (PL 140, 779-82).

Isidore appear to talk about kin marriage as an 'abomination'. Yet as mentioned above, Isidore in his discussion of the prohibited degrees would never have quoted Leviticus, nor have called perpetrators of this laws 'incestuous'. In these cases, the *mise en page* led to a remarkable reciprocal effect on how the proof-texts were most likely understood. The reading of texts from either tradition was substantially shaped by the presence of those from the other tradition, merging both into one model.

In the end, the book title, the suppression of the original context and the re-contextualizing of the authorities may have been as important as the selection of texts; and in my opinion these strategies are more important than Burchard's occasional manipulation of the actual proof-texts and their inscriptions. Important as these manipulations were for defining which unions were affected in practice, the importance of the more subtle changes that led to the re-definition of all endogamy as 'incest' can hardly be overestimated. It was this aspect of Burchard's work that fueled the eleventh-century debates, contributing to the highly sexualized rhetoric of reform.[40]

6. The *Panormia*: a new reading of Augustine

The second canon law collection I want to examine is the famous *Panormia*, compiled around the year 1115 in northern France.[41] To judge by the number of extant manuscripts, it was the single most successful of these collections. Another reason why an analysis of Burchard and the *Panormia* together is likely to give an accurate picture of 'the' canon law in the century before Gratian is that both collections were not only copied, but can be shown to have been used in many contexts. For Burchard's *Decretum*, from very early on there is ample evidence that it was particularly valued in the conducting of councils. Bishop Eberhard of Constance († 1046) recorded in his copy that disputes at synods were 'not easily settled without the author-

---

40.　On this rhetoric, see Remensnyder, 'Pollution'; K. G. Cushing, *Reform and the Papacy in the Eleventh Century: Spirituality and Social Change*, Manchester Medieval Studies (Manchester and New York: 2005), ch. 6; and most recently M. McLaughlin, *Sex, Gender, and Episcopal Authority in an Age of Reform, 1000–1122* (Cambridge: 2010).

41.　On the collection, see M. Brett, 'Creeping up on the Panormia', in R. H. Helmholz, P. Mikat, J. Müller and M. Stolleis (eds.), *Grundlagen des Rechts: Festschrift für Peter Landau*. Rechts- und Staatswissenschaftliche Veröffentlichungen der Görres-Gesellschaft N. F. 91 (Paderborn: 2000), 205-70. For the ongoing edition by Brett and Brasington, see http://project.knowledgeforge.net/ivo/. On the relation between Ivo of Chartres and the *Panormia*, see C. Rolker, *Canon Law and the Letters of Ivo of Chartres*, Cambridge Studies in Medieval Life and Thought, Fourth Series 76 (Cambridge: 2010), esp. chapters 6-8.

ity of this book',[42] and around 1100, Sigebert of Gembloux also commented on Burchard as the ultimate authority at synods.[43] Both collections were also very frequently employed for the compilation and reworking of new collections well into the twelfth century; the *Panormia* was an important formal source for both recensions of Gratian; and Burchard provided the next generation with about one in two of the *paleae*. In the case of very many pre-Gratian collections, Burchard and the *Panormia* not only provided material, but were important models for the very structure of many of these works.[44] This also implies that the arguments based on the structure of the two collections studied here does indeed apply to many, perhaps even most collections that were compiled in the century before Gratian.

In the context of the present work, two aspects are important. First, the *Panormia* contained a short section gathering incest prohibitions as part of its seventh book. The book has no proper title, but is introduced by a *capitulatio* that indicates the subject matter of the whole book. As had become relatively common, kin marriages are called 'incestuous' here. This does not mean that the *Panormia* compiler was particularly concerned with incest; rather, both the division of material and the wording mainly indicate how widely Burchard's innovations were accepted by c. 1115. Secondly, the *Panormia* goes beyond Burchard in the conflation of what I have described as the 'two models of incest' in the first part of this paper. The overall impression is that it is less concerned with purity and pollution than Burchard had been. The compiler retained only a few of the relevant early medieval proof-texts, the rubrics do not highlight 'incest' as much as Burchard had done, and none of the texts refers to Leviticus. At the same time, the famous *City of God* chapter discussed above plays an important role, as an excerpt from it is placed at the head of the most important sub-section defining the prohibited degrees. The *Panormia* is one of the first collections to contain this passage, and the first to give it such prominence.[45] This, however, should not be described as a change from 'old' to 'new' justifications of the prohibited degrees. Despite the marked difference from Burchard, the *Panormia* conflates both traditions as he had done, and in so doing justifies the very doctrine that Burchard had so elegantly introduced into canon law.

42. O. Meyer, 'Überlieferung und Verbreitung des Dekrets des Bischofs Burchard von Worms', *Zeitschrift der Savigny-Stiftung für Rechtsgeschichte, kanonistische Abteilung* 24 (1935), 141-83, at 153, n. 2.
43. *De scriptoribus*, cap. 143, *Catalogus Sigeberti Gemblacensis monachi de viris illustribus: Kritische Ausgabe*, ed. R. Witte (Bern: 1974), 91.
44. Fowler-Magerl, *Clavis*; Rolker, *Canon Law*, ch. 2.
45. *Panormia* vii, 52 is taken from Ivo's *Decretum* viii, 39. As the very precise (and correct) inscription 'Augustinus in libro de civitate Dei XV' suggests, Ivo took the text from Augustine, not some florilegium. The *Panormia* compiler was apparently less familiar with the source, as the inscription in all known manuscripts gives the incorrect book number also found in two *Decretum* manuscripts.

Again, it is not so much textual manipulation that is at play here, but rather the art of abbreviating and re-contextualizing ancient proof-texts.

Let us take a closer look. In the original context, it is clear that Augustine is talking about how to make sense of certain passages of the Old Testament, discussing for example the age at which the Old Testament patriarchs had reached puberty. In the passage on the marriages of the children and grandchildren of Adam and Eve, he discusses endogamy and makes some references to his own time, including his disapproval of marriages between first cousins. However, he does not call these unions incestuous, and correctly notes that they were not forbidden by divine law; as for secular law, Augustine mentions that cousin marriages had recently been banned.[46] In any case, it was custom rather than law that changed first, as pagans avoided the sibling marriage allowed to them and Christians refrained from cousin marriage even when it was allowed. Divine law, human law and custom all changed, and crucially, all three (most of the time) were at variance as to which marriages were acceptable and which not.

To any later reader, these passages could have served as a reminder that marriage prohibitions are a complex issue and that they had changed several times both before and after the time of Augustine. However, all this is true only if one reads the *City of God*. In the *Panormia*, the reader is presented with a slightly different text in a very different context. All references to cousin marriages as (formerly) legal, and also the remarks on changing law and custom are omitted here; even Augustine's statement that the first men were allowed to marry their sisters is removed. Only the argument why exogamy is favourable for the distribution of *caritas* remains. The new context, as already indicated, is a section on incest. The *City of God* excerpt here is followed by Roman law fragments that condemn incest as a horrible crime.[47] What these excerpts from Justinian's *Code* do not tell the reader is that its thundering rhetoric is actually referring to a very narrow set of prohibited degrees. In the original at least, cousin marriage is explicitly allowed; in the version found in the *Panormia*, this stance is subverted by a '*non*' inserted in the relevant passage.[48] To remove all doubt, after a short passage from Ambrose on uncle/niece marriages as violating

---

46. See above (n. 15).
47. *Panormia* vii, 53, ultimately taken from *Codex Justiniani* (C. J. 1, 10, 1) via Ivo, *Decretum* ix, 1 (see the note following).
48. The '*non*' is already found in the *Panormia*'s formal source (Ivo, *Decretum* ix, 1): 'Duorum autem fratrum sororumve liberi, vel fratris et sororis iungi non possunt.' What Ivo's formal source looked like is not easy to decide. The absence of the '*non*' from both London, British Library, Add. Ms. 8873, fol. 57v and Paris, Bibliothèque de l'Arsenal, ms. 713, fol. 158r seems to suggest that it was added by Ivo himself; on the other hand, both manuscripts are later copies of material that was available to Ivo, not the manuscripts he worked with. On the collections, see Brett, 'Creeping up' and Fowler-Magerl, *Clavis*.

divine law the *Panormia* has the famous letter of Alexander II on the seventh degree of kinship. Most of this material is 'new' in the sense that in c. 1115 it was not widely found in canon law collections and had never been combined before. Yet as in Burchard, not the 'new' content but the arrangement is crucial, as it suggests that all texts refer to the same crime of 'incest'. In the form the *Panormia* presents its material, Augustine provides a general argument why endogamy should be avoided and that kinship extends very far; the Roman law adds to the impression that this endogamy is indeed incest; and the decretal gives precise instruction on how to determine exactly which marriages are incestuous.

As in Burchard, the selection, abbreviation and arrangement of canons in the *Panormia* serves to create the impression that the prohibited degrees are supported by a very uniform tradition including biblical incest prohibitions (as alluded to by Ambrose), natural law (as argued by Augustine) and both secular and ecclesiastical law from Roman antiquity to the recent past (Justinian and Alexander II, respectively). As so often,[49] and not unlike Burchard,[50] the *Panormia* compiler achieved considerable doctrinal unity of his texts by selecting and re-arranging his material. While neither Augustine nor Justinian would have called cousin marriages 'incest', in this context they work very well as authorities supporting the extreme marriage prohibitions of the eleventh and twelfth centuries. Such an argument would have been impossible to make in a chronologically arranged collection of canon law, but in the systematic collections, the very structure of the work could be used to challenge or to affirm the *status quo* of marriage legislation.

As the analysis of Burchard's *Decretum* and the *Panormia* suggests, pre-Gratian canon law collections went far beyond simply making certain proof-texts fit; it is the absence of the original context, the arrangement of material and not least the choice of the 'right' title that could substantially change the law and at the same time very strongly suggest that the law as presented in these collections had never changed. As Augustine remarked on sibling marriage, the custom of turning away from this practice was so strong that eventually it became unimaginable that it once had been allowed.[51] In the case of the systematic canon law collections, however, it is not so much custom but rather the conscious decisions of the compilers that made certain legal traditions invisible, and indeed not only suggested that

---

49.   Rolker, *Canon Law*, ch. 7.
50.   Austin, *Shaping Law*.
51.   *De civitate Dei* xv, 16 (eds. Dombart and Kalb, CCSL 48, 477-78): 'Quod humano genere crescente et multiplicato etiam inter impios deorum multorum falsorumque cultores sic observari cernimus, ut, etiamsi perversis legibus permittantur fraterna coniugia, melior tamen consuetudo ipsam malit exhorrere licentiam, et cum sorores accipere in matrimonium primis humani generis temporibus omnino licuerit, sic aversetur, quasi numquam licere potuerit.'

marriages in the seventh degree were forbidden but made it appear as though they had never been legal.

Of course, this does not mean that arguments based on the changing nature of positive law were impossible to make in the eleventh and twelfth centuries. First of all, canon law was not uniform. Some compilers of canon law collections, such as Ivo of Chartres, made very different choices and did not strive for doctrinal unity.[52] Other pre-Gratian canonical collections, for example the famous *Collection in 74 Titles*, contained little marriage law and as a consequence had not much to say about endogamy or incest. However, given the striking success of Burchard's *Decretum* and the *Panormia*, both directly and indirectly, it is fair to say that mainstream canon law collections before Gratian presented the reader with a view of the law that defined marriage even to very distant kin, if implicitly, as 'incest'. Development over time, internal contradictions and differences between different kinds of 'incest' was precisely not what the reader would find in these collections.

7. 'Nunc licere, nunc non licere': Theologians and marriage laws

Thus, if we are searching for different interpretations of the tradition, we have to turn away from these systematic collections. As I want to argue in the last part of this paper, the theologians of the late eleventh and early twelfth centuries were the ones who developed the arguments that later (mainly after 1215) would become legal dogma. Much earlier than the compilers of canon law collections, the theologians argued that there were different reasons for different kinds of incest prohibitions, that the prohibited degrees had changed over time, and that different prohibitions were of different quality. This kind of argument can already be found in the writings of Hrabanus Maurus († 856), who insisted that divine law prohibited only a very limited number of relations as incestuous.[53] He was very clear that any extension was based on human law, if indeed it was 'law' and not merely presumptuousness.[54] In the eleventh and twelfth centuries, this line of argument was taken up again by the theologians. This is most visible in an abundance of treatises and *sententiae* collections dealing with marriage that emerged in the milieu of the cathedral schools of northern France. The attribution of authorship and the dating of this material is complicated; in the context of the present paper, no attempts will be made to address these ques-

---

52.   Rolker, *Canon Law*, ch. 7.
53.   *Expositiones in Leviticum* (PL 108, 245-86).
54.   Ubl, *Inzestverbot*, 308-16.

tions. I will concentrate on a number of relatively well-known texts from around 1100 to the 1130s: the tract *De nuptiis consanguineorum* attributed to Anselm of Canterbury,[55] the *Sententiae magistri A.*[56] and the sentences attributed to Peter Abelard.[57] The largest amount of material is associated with the so-called school of Laon.[58] The sentences on marriage from this milieu have been thoroughly studied,[59] including the material gathered in the famous *Liber Pancrisis*[60] and the marriage tract *In primis hominibus*.[61]

A first difference between the theological material and the canon law collections concerns the vocabulary employed. While marriage is a prominent topic, and the prohibitions are regularly discussed, the term 'incest' (and related vocabulary) is remarkably absent. In the sentence collection of the so-called school of Laon, for example, the term rarely is used at all, and is applied only to very specific sexual offences.[62] Most strikingly, none of the very numerous *sententiae* and none of the various marriage tracts from

55. PL 158, 557-60. I have no reason to believe that the attribution to Anselm is correct.

56. The relevant section on marriage is edited by Reinhardt, *Ehelehre*, 167-244; for the full text, see P. H. J. T. Maas, *The Liber sententiarum Magistri A.*, Middeleeuwse Studies 11 (Nijmegen: 1995).

57. *Sententie magistri Petri Abelardi*, ed. D. E. Luscombe, CCCM 14 (Turnhout: 2006).

58. V. I. J. Flint, 'The "School of Laon": A Reconsideration', *Recherches de Théologie ancienne et médiévale* 43 (1976), 89-110, remains fundamental.

59. O. Lottin, *Psychologie et morale aux XIIe et XIIIe siècles*, 6 in 8 vols. (Gembloux: 1948-1960); H. Zeimentz, *Ehe nach der Lehre der Frühscholastik: Eine moralgeschichtliche Untersuchung zur Anthropologie und Theologie der Ehe in der Schule Anselms von Laon und Wilhelms von Champeaux, bei Hugo von St. Viktor, Walter von Mortagne und Petrus Lombardus*. Moraltheologische Studien, Historische Abteilung 1 (Düsseldorf: 1973); H. J. F. Reinhardt, *Die Ehelehre der Schule des Anselm von Laon: Eine theologie- und kirchenrechtsgeschichtliche Untersuchung zu den Ehetexten der frühen Pariser Schule des 12. Jahrhunderts*. Beiträge zur Geschichte der Philosophie und Theologie des Mittelalters N.F. 14 (Münster: 1974). For Bliemetzrieder's works, see the note following.

60. In addition to the works cited above, see those of F. P. Bliemetzrieder, especially *Anselms von Laon systematische Sentenzen*. Beiträge zur Geschichte der Philosophie des Mittelalters 18 (Münster: 1919), 'Trente-trois pièces inédites de l'œuvre théologique d'Anselme de Laon', *Recherches de Théologie ancienne et médiévale* 2 (1930), 54-79; and 'Paul Fournier und das literarische Werk Ivos von Chartres', *Archiv für katholisches Kirchenrecht* 115 (1935), 53-91 (with incorrect attribution of authorship, 62-66). From the modern literature, see most recently C. Giraud and C. J. Mews, 'Le *Liber Pancrisis*, un florilège des Pères et des maîtres modernes du XIIe siècle', *Bulletin du Cange* 64 (2006), 145-91. Giraud's Ph.D. thesis on the *Liber Pancrisis* was not avaiable to me.

61. The tract is edited by B. Matecki, *Der Traktat* In primis hominibus:*Eine theologie- und kirchenrechtsgeschichtliche Untersuchung zu einem Ehetext der Schule von Laon aus dem 12. Jahrhundert*. Adnotationes in Ius Canonicum 20 (Frankfurt and New York: 2001). While it is conventionally dated to the 1120s, any precise dating would require a new study of the formal sources. Matecki suggested, but in my opinion did not prove, a use of the *Panormia* and the slightly later *Collection in Ten Parts*.

62. Reinhardt, *Ehelehre*, 115-17.

this milieu calls marriages within the prohibited degrees 'incestuous'. Turning from the vocabulary to the actual content, the difference between *sententiae* and canon law collections is equally manifest. Not surprisingly, the theologians turned more frequently to the Old Testament than contemporary canon law collections did. Yet while the latter quoted Leviticus (if only via the Council of Toledo) mainly to justify the legal *status quo*, the theologians rather stressed the difference between Old Testament and Christian times. Several *sententiae* and marriage tracts made explicitly clear that the prohibitions in Leviticus were limited to the relatives listed there.[63] Burchard, by contrast, had quoted Leviticus 18:6 in such a way as to suggest strongly that the general ban on kin marriages had a biblical foundation. For the theologians, it was commonplace to assert that kin marriage (never called 'incest') was allowed in Old Testament times but was now forbidden.[64] Only the Old Testament prohibitions are sometimes called 'natural' or 'natural law'; by contrast, kin marriage according to the *Sententiae Anselmi* was no violation of natural law but of ecclesiastical statutes,[65] an argument widely disseminated by Honorius Augusto-dunensis.[66] The prohibitions going beyond those found in Leviticus were referred to as newly established in Christian times ('institutio temporis gratiae'),[67] and more specifically as ecclesiastical statutes.[68] Some authors comment that many marriages are truly marriages, but their validity was subject to change ('nunc licere, nunc non licere'), both because of changing laws and because of changing practices of dispensation.[69] In any case, the difference between Old Testament precept and later legislation is made very clear. Rather than justifying contemporary legisla-

---

63. E.g. *De nuptiis consanguineorum*, after having quoted Lev. 18:6 (PL 158, 558): 'Deinde ex sequenti ordine proximos illos sanguinis, ad quos non sit accedendum nec revelanda eorum turpitudo.'

64. *De nuptiis consanguineorum* (PL 158, 558); *Cum omnia sacramenta* (ed. Bliemetzrieder, *Anselm von Laon*, 141); *In primis hominibus* (ed. Matecki, *Traktat*, 13*); *Liber Pancrisis* (ed. Bliemetzrieder, 'Paul Fournier', 76).

65. *Sententiae Anselmi* (ed. Bliemetzrieder, *Anselm von Laon*, 151): 'Sacerdotium enim non videtur auferre coniugium, cum Greci sacerdotes habeant uxores, sed ecclesie institutio et patrum prohibitio. Non enim esset contra legem nature, sed contra precepta ecclesiastice institutionis. Sed violat legem benivolentie, que tendit ad perfectionem ecclesie, sicut coniugium inter cognatos non est contra legem nature, sed contra precepta institutionis ecclesie.'

66. Honorius Augustodunensis, *Elucidarium* ii, 16 (PL 176, 1146): 'Discipulus: Est grave peccatum, ducere cognatam? Magister: Secundum naturam, nullum, sed secundum statutum Ecclesiae magnum.'

67. *In primis hominibus* (ed. Matecki, *Traktat*, 13*).

68. *Sententie magistri Petri Abelardi* (ed. Luscombe, CCCM 14, 124): '[...] ecclesia [...] constituit propter propagationem caritatis'; for a full quotation, see below (n. 71).

69. *Liber Pancrisis* (ed. Bliemetzrieder, 'Paul Fournier', 76): 'Confiteri igitur debemus hec omnia esse coniugia, sed secundum diversas ecclesie institutiones nunc licere, nunc non licere.'

tion by biblical parallels, the theologians time and again stressed the difference between them.

A similar observation can be made for the passage from the *City of God* discussed above. Augustine's model, so important for Peter Damian and the *Panormia* compiler, was indeed widely known and discussed among the theologians, too.[70] However, the latter used it to reach very different conclusions. In particular, they took up Augustine's original argument that already the divine precepts on kin marriage had been subject to change, and that human legislation, whether secular or ecclesiastic, was both different from biblical incest prohibitions and itself changeable. Augustine's model was thus not conflated with the discourse on incest as an abomination, as it was in the canonical collections. Rather, in the theological discussion it is linked to human, not even specifically Christian legislation, and the vocabulary of purity and pollution is lacking. Moreover, in the *sententiae* attributed to Peter Abelard at least, the Augustinian argument is explicitly described as having been adopted by the Church from the Romans.[71] While this (quite correctly) highlights Augustine's role in merging pagan and Christian arguments, it is striking to see that no such connection is made between church law and Old Testament precept. Whether adopting Roman law principles or issuing genuinely new laws, the Church according to the early twelfth-century theologians was making laws that were fundamentally different from the incest prohibitions in Leviticus.

Stressing the differences between biblical prohibitions, patristic reasoning and current legal dogma rather than conflating them, the theologians made quite clear that most marriage prohibitions were ecclesiastical statutes and thus subject to change. While pre-Gratian canonists would certainly have agreed in general, they nonetheless compiled, used and spread collections that at least in the case of incest conveyed a different picture. Collections like Burchard's *Decretum* made it extremely difficult to see that the marriage prohibitions were changing legislation based on variable legal concepts. Much of this was to become common stock among canonists of the late twelfth and early thirteenth century, and Gratian's *Decretum* cer-

---

70. *De nuptiis consanguineorum* (PL 158, 558); *Liber Pancrisis* (ed. Bliemetzrieder, 'Paul Fournier', 76); *Sententie magistri Petri Abelardi* (ed. Luscombe, CCCM 14, 124). Augustine is quoted verbatim in *In primis hominibus* (ed. Matecki, *Traktat*, 13*).

71. *Sententie magistri Petri Abelardi* (ed. Luscombe, CCCM 14, 124): 'Preceptum etiam erat eis ut unusquisque de tribu sua uxorem duceret, ne tribus commiscerentur et ne transiret possessio unius tribus in possessionem alterius, quia terra per tribus divisa erat. Nunc autem non licet, sed de aliena gente, quod ecclesia (post Christum) constituit propter propagationem caritatis, quod a Romanis ecclesia accepit. Romani enim quando amicitiam cum aliis civitatibus facere volebant, uxores ex eis ad confederationem amicitie ducebant. Similiter ecclesia instituit ut non de sua sed de aliena prosapia uxorem quis ducat, quia non putavit hoc sufficere ad dilatationem caritatis; quia per uxorem quam accipit totam illam progeniem diligit.'

tainly was an important step in that direction.[72] However, before Gratian this line of argument is found mainly with theologians. Thinking about the history of salvation, these scholars were aware of the very historicity of canon law that was obscured in the most up-to-date genre of canon law collections of their time.

8. Conclusions: A law that can and cannot change

As the analysis of the 'two models of incest' has shown, in the Middle Ages there were at least two very different ways to talk about ecclesiastical prohibitions of kin marriage. For both, venerable and well-known authorities were available, and the way in which medieval authors followed one or the other (or combined both) was to a considerable degree a matter of choice. This is all the more true as the same texts could be read in very different ways. Quotations from Leviticus in the early Middle Ages served to justify the slowly expanding incest prohibitions, but for the theologians of the early twelfth century they showed how very different biblical and human legislation was. Likewise, for centuries Augustine's reasoning on exogamy was not thought to have much to do with incest, but in the *Panormia* and other twelfth-century collections it served to justify an excessive set of marriage prohibitions. Again, the theologians read and quoted Augustine differently, paying much more attention to his arguments on the changing nature of law and custom. Above all, it is crucial to see that these traditions were normally kept separate before Burchard of Worms chose to combine them in his canon law collection. Only this conflation of both discourses made it possible to justify an unheared-of expansion of marriage prohibitions, and paved the way for later radicals like Peter Damian.

These and other examples help to illuminate the differences between early and high medieval canon law, and also those between theological and canon law debates of the early twelfth century. These differences, in my opinion, have relevance beyond understanding the change of dogma or the growing distinction between canon law and theology. Indeed, despite all differences, it is the interaction between these textual traditions that sheds light on the canon law tradition itself as a law 'that can and cannot change'.[73] After all, while canon law and theology grew further apart in the twelfth century, there was also considerable interaction. Not only did theologians study the same authorities and use the same textbooks as the canon-

---

72. See, above all, C.35, q.1, d.p.c.1: *Decretum magistri Gratiani*, ed. E. L. Friedberg (Leipzig: 1879), cols 1262-63.
73. The phrase is borrowed from J. T. Noonan, *A Church That Can and Cannot Change: The Development of Catholic Moral Teaching*, Erasmus Institute Books (Notre Dame, IN: 2005).

ists;[74] it seems also plausible that their debates contributed to the re-examination that ultimately allowed Innocent III to change the ecclesiastical rules on marriage so dramatically in 1215, seemingly without much controversy. At the present state of research, the silence surrounding this decision, which made many 'incestuous' unions perfectly acceptable marriages, still calls for a satisfactory explanation. Had the pre-1215 rules relied on a belief that all marriages within the prohibited degrees were incest, even contemplating such a dramatic change would have seemed highly unlikely. While it is clear how campaigns against 'incest' would often result in an expansion of the prohibited degrees, a 'campaign for incest' seems unimaginable. However, the theologians helped to discuss these issues in calmer terms and at the same time provided solid arguments why marriage prohibitions could indeed change.

While this development cannot be studied in the context of the present article, it is clear enough that the development of canon law ultimately was not restricted by the various efforts to present the laws of marriage as unchangeable. While some compilers clearly presented their material in ways that made certain interpretations more likely than others, they rarely envisioned and certainly never achieved a definite law code. Even the more selective compilers confronted their readers with material that potentially challenged the legal *status quo*, and had only limited control of how their collections were read, used, re-worked and added to by others. Burchard and others in their collections had greatly reduced the divergence of canonical marriage prohibitions, and glossed over the remaining discrepancies. However, while thus reducing the confusion resulting from the long process of expanding marriage prohibitions, the new model also produced a new kind of confusion among readers who looked beyond the collections and compared them to other texts – be they the original sources (Leviticus, Augustine) or some other canon law collection. Without too much effort, any twelfth-century scholar could quickly find canons from various centuries banning quite different degrees, divergent justifications for these prohibitions, very different trees of consanguinity, and several ways of calculating the prohibited degrees. He would certainly find many authorities supporting the current legislation, but also many others who did not; with some luck, he could even find canon law collections that included texts allowing the marriage of first cousins.[75]

Whatever the intentions of this or that compiler may have been, they all passed on traditions much richer and more complex than any 'tendency'

---

74. The *Panormia* was among the most important sources for the reception of patristic material among twelfth-century theologians. See C. Munier, *Les sources patristiques du droit de l'église du VIIIe au XIIIe siècle* (Mulhouse: 1957), 27-52.
75. See above (n. 47) on the twelfth-century manuscripts London, BL, Add. Ms. 8873 and Paris, Arsenal 713.

established by modern scholarship. Conflict and confusion surrounding the medieval law on marriage posed and continues to pose problems to any reader of this material; yet it is precisely this confusion that is indicative of the dynamic traditions of canon law.

Re-defining Marriage Impediments
– Tolerating Dubious Marriages through a Special
Declaration from the Apostolic Penitentiary
in the Late Middle Ages

Kirsi Salonen

1. Introduction

The regulations of canon law regarding different marriage impediments
were mainly defined by the mid-thirteenth century, but this did not mean
that no development in the interpretation of these regulations took place
thereafter. There were still, in the fifteenth and sixteenth centuries, many
dubious marriage cases which did not exactly fit within the categories of the
marital impediments specified in canon law. Sometimes these dubious cases
caused problems for couples who intended to marry or whose marriage was
at stake, because their union was suddenly considered void. We have traces
of such dubious cases in ecclesiastical court records because local ecclesiastical courts occasionally dealt with them. In principle, the court had to decide whether there was a question of an impediment forbidding a marriage
or not, and whether such dubious marriages could be tolerated or not. In this
paper these cases are called 'toleration cases', following the wording used in
the medieval court records of the consistory court of Freising.[1]

If the local ecclesiastical authorities could not, or did not want to, resolve dubious marriage cases, one possibility for solving the problem was to

---

1. Concerning the records of the court of Freising, see K. Salonen, 'The Consistory
    Court of Freising in the Late Middle Ages', *Zeitschrift der Savigny-Stiftung für
    Rechtsgeschichte, Kanonistische Abteilung* 96 (2010), 226-57, at 247-48; K. Salo-
    nen, 'Marriage Disputes in the Consistorial Court of Freising in the Late Middle
    Ages', in M. Korpiola (ed.), *Regional Variations in Matrimonial Law and Custom
    in Europe, 1150-1600* (Leiden and Boston: 2011), 189-209.

pass their handling to the apostolic authority. This is why the archives of the Apostolic Penitentiary contain petitions related to dubious marriages, even though these kinds of cases did not fall within its normal powers. This essay examines what kinds of cases supplicants presented to the authority of the Penitentiary and what kinds of details they contain regarding the application of canon law.

2. What was the Apostolic Penitentiary?

The Apostolic Penitentiary was a papal office whose competence included all matters that concerned sin and breaking the norms of canon law. Christians could turn to this office when they had issues of conscience or canon law to resolve. In principle the Penitentiary had apostolic authority to grant four different types of grace:

1) Absolutions for those who had broken the regulations of canon law in such a serious matter – as for example with clerical homicide – that the local father confessors or even the local bishops had no powers to absolve them.

2) Dispensations that allowed Christians to act against the regulations of the Church – for example, to marry a close relative or to become a priest despite an impediment such as illegitimacy, minority, or bodily defect.

3) Licenses that allowed Christians not to observe certain ecclesiastical norms in matters that concerned mainly the exercise of one's Christian faith: for example, confessing to a priest other than one's own parish priest or consuming meat during Lent.

4) Official declarations in various matters. The Penitentiary could, for example, declare that a cleric was not guilty of murder despite an (unjust) murder accusation. Similarly, it could declare a marriage or a monastic profession void, if the supplicants had a legitimate reason, or could issue a declaration of tolerance with respect to a dubious marriage.[2]

According to these powers, the Penitentiary could grant graces in numerous different matters including marriage, illegitimacy, priestly ordina-

---

2. For the history, functioning and competence of the Penitentiary in the Middle Ages, see for example E. Göller, *Die päpstliche Pönitentiarie von ihrem Ursprung bis zu ihrer Umgestaltung unter Pius V.* Bibliothek des Königl. Preuss. Historischen Instituts in Rom 3-4, 7-8 (Rome: 1907, 1911); L. Schmugge, P. Hersperger and B. Wiggenhauser, *Die Supplikenregister der päpstlichen Pönitentiarie aus der Zeit Pius' II. (1458-1464).* Bibliothek des Deutschen Historischen Instituts in Rom 84 (Tübingen: 1996); K. Salonen, *The Penitentiary as a Well of Grace in the Late Middle Ages: The Example of the Province of Uppsala 1448-1527.* Suomalaisen Tiedeakatemian Toimituksia – Annales Academiae Scientiarum Fennicae 313 (Saarijärvi: 2001); K. Salonen and L. Schmugge, *A Sip from the 'Well of Grace': Medieval Texts from the Apostolic Penitentiary* (Washington D.C.: 2009).

tion, violence, apostasy, and confessing. Of these, marriage cases formed one of the biggest groups of petitions directed to the competence of the Penitentiary. The medieval records of the office are divided into seven different categories: *de matrimonialibus* (about marriages), *de diversis formis* (concerning various types of cases), *de declaratoriis* (about declarations), *de defectu natalium* and *de uberiori* (matters related to illegitimacy), *de promotis et promovendis* (about ordinations), and *de confessionalibus* (licence to choose a personal confessor).[3]

The category *de matrimonialibus* includes registered petitions for graces (in the form of a dispensation and/or absolution) from couples who wanted to marry – or had already married – despite the existence of a marital impediment. Without such a grace the couple could not have married, or if they already were married, they would have been obliged to separate from each other.[4] In addition to these standard petitions, some more particular petitions regarding marriage matters are registered in the *de declaratoriis* category. These cases are the subject of study in this essay.

3. Penitentiary and marriage declarations

Declarations regarding marriages were the third most common type of declarations granted by the Penitentiary, after homicide and monastic issues.[5] Most of those who petitioned for a letter of declaration related to a marriage from the Penitentiary did so because they wanted to nullify a marriage they had been forced to contract *per vi et metu* or because they needed an official document stating that their marriage was considered void due to an existing impediment. An apostolic declaration of nullity was crucial for the petitioners, because a nullified marriage meant automatically that they had the right

---

3.   The Penitentiary registers, which (in almost all types of instances) contain abbreviated copies of the incoming and approved petitions, are internally divided into different sections, each of them with a specific title. All categories contain petitions concerning certain types of matters. Registering the different types of instances under specific titles is a technique that can only be found in the Penitentiary registers, not in the other medieval papal register series. The division of the cases into different petition categories was probably made for practical reasons. Such a division made it easier to record and to find the decisions of the office, if there was need to consult the records later. Concerning the registers of the Penitentiary, see for example Salonen and Schmugge, *A Sip*, 3-7, 17-20.

4.   More about the Penitentiary graces in marriage matters, L. Schmugge, *Ehen vor Gericht: Paare der Renaissance vor dem Papst* (Berlin: 2008).

5.   Concerning the *de declaratoriis* petitions in the Penitentiary registers, see for example Salonen and Schmugge, *A Sip*, 49-56.

to remarry – unlike those who had received a sentence of separation from the local ecclesiastical courts.[6]

Christians did not request declarations only when they wanted to liberate themselves from an unwanted marital union, however. The Penitentiary also handled 'toleration' cases, in which the supplicants wanted a declaration – as distinct from the dispensation and/or absolution requested in standard marriage petitions – authorizing them to marry or to remain in their already-contracted marriage despite rumours about an existing impediment. These cases often involved situations where there was no certainty of the impediment. In similar cases handled by the local courts, the court often examined whether there was a fourth or fifth degree of consanguinity or affinity between the petitioners, for example. A fourth degree constituted an impediment, and a marriage was not possible. If, on the other hand, the court found that there was an affinity or consanguinity of the fifth degree, no impediment was involved and a legal marriage could take place. The main difference between toleration cases handled by local ecclesiastical courts and cases handled by the Penitentiary was that the latter were usually more complicated from a legal point of view.

Two features of the letters of declaration granted by the Penitentiary are of particular importance here. First, if the petition was composed correctly and the matter fell within the authority of the office, the Penitentiary always decided in favour of the supplicant – but in a conditional form, so that local authorities had to examine the case before the grace was valid. In practice this meant that the letters of grace granted by the Penitentiary were always referred to local ecclesiastical authorities (usually to the local bishop or to his *vicarius in spiritualibus*), whose task it was to check that all details provided by the supplicant and mentioned in the letter of grace were right. If everything was found to be correct, the bishop could execute the letter of

---

6. Although the Catholic Church considered a marriage to be an inseparable union, in a few specific cases it allowed a couple to separate. This could take place in two different ways: First, a couple could be separated from each other so that they did not have to endure each other's company. In this case they were not allowed to remarry after their separation. This practice is known as *divortium a mensa et thoro*, divorce from bed and board. According to canon law a divorce from bed and board could take place because of domestic violence, adultery or spiritual fornication (apostasy or heresy) and it had to take place through a decision of the local ecclesiastical court – of which we have numerous medieval testimonies from throughout Christendom. The other possibility to divorce, *divortium a vinculo*, meant in practice that a marriage between two persons was declared void. Since this implied in legal terms that the marriage had never been legally contracted, the spouses were free to marry someone else. For getting one's marriage annulled, there had to be a strong legal motivation which officially caused the union to be void. Concerning separation, R. H. Helmholz, *Marriage Litigation in Medieval England* (London and New York: 1974), 13.

grace. On the other hand, if something was found to be wrong, the local executor could simply declare the grace granted by the Penitentiary to be void.

Another thing I wish to stress is that the declaratory matters often tended to be relatively complicated, and therefore the cases needed the approval of an expert in canon law. Hence, all entries in the *de declaratoriis* category contain a reference to consultation with one of the legal experts in the papal curia called *auditores*.[7] It was their task to check all details mentioned in the petition and to ensure, first, that the Penitentiary could take a decision in such a matter and second, that the decision taken by the Penitentiary was correct in terms of canon law.

4. Toleration declarations among the Penitentiary entries

What kinds of toleration cases were brought before the Penitentiary? The corpus of all petitions handled by the office during the pontificate of Pope Pius II (1458–1464) consists of about 15.700 petitions, of which almost 4200 petitions were standard marriage graces in the *de matrimonialibus* category.[8] Only a minimal portion of all petitions – 12 cases, all registered in the *de declaratoriis* category – concerned toleration matters. In the following I will analyse these cases and answer these questions: Where did the petitions come from? When did the Penitentiary handle such petitions? Who made the decisions in the Penitentiary? Who were the supplicants in need of such graces? And last but not least, which were the impediments that induced the supplicant to turn to the Penitentiary? Obviously we must keep in mind, when analysing the material statistically, that no strict conclusions can be drawn on the basis of such a small corpus. Nevertheless the numbers can show some general trends, and it is worth looking at them.

Provenance
Table 1, which presents the provenance and quantity of the toleration petitions, shows which parts of Christendom those supplicants came from who turned to the Penitentiary for resolving issues concerning marriage toleration. The numbers allow us to observe whether such matters were more of an issue in some areas of Christendom than elsewhere.[9]

---

7. An *auditor* was a judge at the Sacra Romana Rota. See for example G. Dolezalek, 'Audientia sacri palatii' and 'Auditor', *Lexikon des Mittelalters* I, 1192-96.
8. Archivio Segreto Vaticano (hereafter ASV), *Penitenzieria Ap., Reg. Matrim. et Div.*, vols 7-11, 13.
9. Christendom is divided into seven different territories according to the principles set forth in G.-R. Tewes, *Die römische Kurie und die europäischen Länder am Vorabend der Reformation*, Bibliothek des deutschen historischen Instituts in Rom 95 (Tübingen: 2001), 13-17. The same division is used in K. Salonen, 'The Penitentiary under Pope Pius II: The Supplications and Their Provenance', in G. Jaritz, T.

Table 1. The provenance of toleration petitions

Territory	Cases	%
British Isles	0	0 %
Eastern Europe	1	8 %
France	3	25 %
Germany	4	33 %
Italy	3	25 %
Scandinavia	0	0 %
Spain/Portugal	1	8 %
Total	12	100 %

Source: ASV, *Penitenzieria Ap.*, *Reg. Matrim. et Div.*, vols 7-11, 13, passim.

The few cases in the corpus of this study are distributed relatively widely throughout Christendom. There are four cases from German territory, three cases from France and Italy, and one petition each from Eastern Europe and the Iberian Peninsula. On the other hand, no cases originate in the British Isles or Scandinavia. Such a division does not indicate that any particular European region had special problems in toleration matters, but it shows that they occasionally became problematic all over Latin Christendom.

Distribution on a time-axis

Table 2 presents the yearly distribution of toleration petitions, indicating whether such cases were regularly brought to the attention of the Penitentiary or whether they became an issue within a specific time period.

Table 2. The distribution of toleration petitions on a time-axis

Year	Cases	%
1458	0	0 %
1459	0	0 %
1460	3	25 %
1461	0	0 %
1462	2	17 %
1463	4	33 %
1464	3	25 %
Total	12	100 %

Source: ASV, *Penitenzieria Ap.*, *Reg. Matrim. et Div.*, vols 7-11, 13, passim.

Jørgensen and K. Salonen (eds.), *The Long Arm of Papal Authority: Late Medieval Christian Peripheries and Their Communication with the Holy See*. CEU Medievalia 10 (Budapest: 2005 – 2nd edn), 11-21 as well as Salonen and Schmugge, *A Sip*.

The numbers in Table 2 demonstrate that there are no significant differences in the yearly distribution of the toleration cases. Although the annual number of cases seems to increase a bit over the course of Pius II's pontificate, this apparent 'tendency' results in part from lacunae in the source material: from the year 1458 there are no Penitentiary records preserved at all, and the Penitentiary registration from the first three months of 1459 is incomplete. Therefore it is not totally correct to talk about a tendency for the annual number of cases to increase during the latter part of this period. What we can conclude is that such petitions came in relatively frequently, but not in great quantities – and that such cases were certainly not part of the daily business of the Penitentiary.

Decision-makers

More evidence that graces regarding dubious marriages were anything but routine or mass-produced emerges when we study the persons to whose authority the resolving of these matters was referred. According to the powers of the Penitentiary, these cases could be resolved not only by the Cardinal Penitentiary, who was the head of the Penitentiary office, but also by his deputies ('regents'). Examining the signatures on the petitions for toleration graces shows that the Cardinal Penitentiary – who during the pontificate of Pius II was Filippo Calandrini – signed the great majority of them, 11 out of 12 cases. Only one decision was taken by the regent of the office, Galeottus de Oddis, a papal prothonotary who acted as regent from November 1459 until November 1463.[10] The fact that so many decisions in these cases were taken by the cardinal himself indicates that they were considered relatively unusual, since for more routine questions the cardinal did not necessarily have to take part in the decision-making but could leave delegate it to his deputies.

As previously noted, the content of the declaratory cases was usually checked by a competent jurist, *auditor*, before the letters of grace were sent off to their recipients. Ten of the twelve toleration cases were committed to the competence of one man, Agapitus Cenci Rustici, who was not only a Rota *auditor* but also the bishop of Ancona (from April 1460) and Camerino (from August 1463).[11] In the remaining two cases there is no sign that a jurist was consulted. That so many of these cases were referred to the competence of one of the leading jurists in the papal curia provides more

---

10. For the Cardinal Penitentiaries and other officials of the Penitentiary, see Göller, *Die päpstliche Pönitentiarie* II, 1, 9-11; and Schmugge, Hersperger and Wiggenhauser, *Die Supplikenregister*, 33-36.
11. C. Eubel, *Hierarchia Catholica Medii Aevi, vol. II ab anno 1431 usque ad annum 1503* (Münster: 1914) (hereafter Eubel II), 87, 116; W. von Hofmann, *Forschungen zur Geschichte der kurialen Behörden vom Schisma bis zur Reformation. Band. II: Quellen, Listen und Excurse.* Bibliothek des Königl. Preuss. Historischen Instituts in Rom 13 (Rome: 1914), 23, 27, 131-32.

evidence that the decision-making in these cases really was concentrated in the hands of a very few professionals.

The letters of grace also had to be checked by local authorities before they could be executed. The referral of the cases to the competency of local authorities is always mentioned in the Penitentiary entries. In one of the 12 cases the entry says only '*Committed*', without specifying the authority or person to whom the case was referred. Most probably this means that the case was committed to the local bishop, but because of the incomplete reference we cannot be totally sure about this. Ten cases were referred to the authority of the bishop of the home diocese of the supplicant(s), expressed in the documents with words: '*committatur ordinario*'. In only one case was the final decision referred to a bishop other than the *ordinarius*. In this case the male and female petitioners came from two different dioceses, Siena and Sutri respectively. However, their case was referred neither to the bishop of Siena nor to that of Sutri, but to the bishop of Viterbo (Petrus Francescus[12]). Unfortunately, the commission does not indicate any specific reason why the case was referred to the authority of the bishop of Viterbo. Certainly there is no question of possible incompetence on the part of the local bishops in the matter, since the bishop of Sutri, Baptista Pontinus de Marsi, was a learned man who held the title of *decretorum doctor*.[13] Why the bishop of Siena, Franciscus Todeschini-Piccolomini (a relative of Pope Pius II and later himself Pope Pius III) was not involved might be explained by the fact that after March 1460, when he was appointed cardinal, he held the episcopal see only in the role of an administrator and was probably not present in his diocese to take care of such matters.[14]

Petitioners

Before going on to the content of the supplications, let us consider the question of gender in these petitions. The fact that a Christian marriage was always a union between a man and a woman did not mean that the petitions were necessarily made by the couple together. In fact, we have many examples – especially in declaration cases where the supplicant asked for an annulment of a marriage – where one supplicant acted alone. But how stands the matter in these 12 cases?

Since the intention of these petitions was that the supplicant(s) could marry or remain in their already-contracted marriage, it is logical to assume that the couples acted together – and so it was in 11 cases. In one case the petitioner was a single man, Mariotus Johannis, who wished to marry the

---

12. The name of the bishop is not mentioned in the document, but the bishop of Sutri at that time was Petrus Francescus. Eubel II, 269.
13. Eubel II, 244.
14. Eubel II, 13, 235.

widow of a certain Dominicus Bertrami but feared that there could be a question of the impediment of *compaternitas* between them.

Impediments and requests

Finally, we come to the question of the impediments that prompted the need to turn to the papal curia in these matters. All of the petitioners in these cases asked for a declaration that they could marry or remain in their marriage, even though there existed or might exist a marital impediment between them. Canon law stipulates numerous different marriage impediments, such as consanguinity, affinity, spiritual relationship, adoption, and so on. The toleration cases handled by the Penitentiary, however, do not include the whole spectrum of impediments but only some of them. In my opinion, this indicates that the regulations of canon law with respect to some impediments (those that are absent from the toleration cases) were clear to all Christians, while the regulations concerning some other impediments (those that are present among the toleration cases) were ambiguous and therefore led to doubts as to whether a legal marriage could be contracted or not.

But which were these less clear impediments that needed to be clarified by the Penitentiary? The answer is very clear. Whereas the majority of petitions, 11 in total, concern spiritual relationship, only one case is about something else, namely affinity (incest). Table 3 shows the percentages of different marital impediments in cases handled by the Penitentiary during the pontificate of Pius II. First come the distributions for the standard marriage petitions registered in the *de matrimonialibus* category (4193 petitions), and then the same is shown for the toleration cases within the *de declaratoriis* category (12 petitions). Because of the disparity in the total number of cases in these two categories there is no way to make a strict statistical analysis, but these numbers nevertheless highlight a very significant difference.

Table 3. Main impediments in standard marriage petitions and in toleration cases

Impediments found in standard marriage petitions (*de matrimonialibus*)	%	Impediments found in toleration cases (*de declaratoriis*)	%
Consanguinity & affinity	85 %	Consanguinity & affinity	8 %
Publicae honestatis iustitia	5 %	*Publicae honestatis iustitia*	0 %
Spiritual relationship	9 %	Spiritual relationship	92 %
Other	1 %	Other	0 %

Source: ASV, *Penitenzieria Ap.*, *Reg. Matrim. et Div.*, vols 7-11, 13, passim.

If we look at the numbers in Table 3, we notice immediately that the percentages of different impediments relating to standard marriage graces (dispensations, or absolutions and dispensations) found under the heading *de matrimonialibus* and to the toleration-type graces (declarations of tolerance) found under the heading *de declaratoriis* differ widely from each other. Among the standard marriage cases, the impediments of consanguinity and affinity are without doubt the most common: in almost nine marriage petitions out of ten there is a question of one or both of these impediments. The third most common impediment, spiritual relationship, gets a share of about 8%, and the *impedimentum publicae honestatis iustitiae* just under 5%. In toleration cases, on the other hand, the impediment of spiritual relationship is dominant.

It is noteworthy that those impediments which are the most common among the typical Penitentiary marriage cases are so little present among the toleration cases. This supports my argument that certain impediments were so precisely defined in canon law that they were clear to everyone, and that in such situations no doubts could arise which would require toleration-type declaration from the Penitentiary. At the same time, it seems that the regulations related to the impediment of spiritual relationship were significantly less clear. As a result, there were questions as to whether there was an impediment in this or that case, and these questions were then brought to the authority of the Penitentiary. In order to identify which questions were particularly tricky, I will present the twelve cases one by one.[15]

5. The case involving affinity (incest)

The single case involving affinity – or actually, incest – differs from the other 11 cases not only in its content but also in another respect: the supplicants did not ask for a declaration of tolerance, but for absolution and a dispensation that would allow them to continue in their marriage legally. Despite this the petition is registered among the declaratory cases – probably because of the very special character of their request, which did not fit in the typical marriage dispensation category either.

---

15. Since the entries in the Penitentiary registers are abbreviated copies of original petitions, they tend to have the form of a supplication, but the syntax of the phrases was often damaged when the entries were copied into the registers. The entries are edited here as they appear in the Penitentiary registers without linguistic comments, and only evident errors of the scribes have been corrected if necessary for understanding. In a few cases words or letters have been added in order to make incomplete phrases or words understandable. The additions are indicated by angle brackets < >. The variation between v/u has been normalized so that 'u' is used for the vowel.

The petitioners, Claudius Aubrieti and Johanneta, daughter of Johannes Belie, from the French diocese of Besançon, explained that they were married *per verba de presenti* but had not consummated their union immediately. Claudius, instead, had had a sexual relationship with Johanneta's mother. The local ecclesiastical authorities had learned about this offence and summoned the couple before the *officialis*. By then the couple had already consummated their marriage and wished to continue in it despite what had happened. Hence they petitioned together for absolution from the excommunication they had incurred in the course of events and for a dispensation which would allow them to remain in their marriage despite incest.[16]

In this case there is thus a question about whether the sexual relationship between a man and his mother-in-law caused an impediment. According to canon law, committing incest after a marriage had been contracted did not dissolve the union.[17] This regulation was very clear and no doubt should have arisen. What could then be the reason behind the doubt in this case? Possibly Claudius had had sex with his mother-in-law *before* the couple had consummated their marriage. This would raise the possibility that someone could have thought that a non-consummated marriage was equal to a *sponsalia de futuro*, which according to canon law was dissolved by supervening affinity. In this case the Penitentiary took the position – by granting them absolution and dispensation – that the incest committed by Claudius did not dissolve his marriage with Johanneta.

16.   ASV, *Penitenzieria Ap., Reg. Matrim. et Div.*, vol. 10, fol. 214r (dated in Rome 8.3.1462): 'Claudius Aubrieti laicus et Johanneta filia quondam Johannis Belie mulier coniuges Bisuntin. dioc. exponunt quod ipsi alius matrimonium per verba de presenti publice secundum mores patrie contraxerunt et carnali copula operam dederunt et matrimonium minime inter se consumarunt. Postmodum prefatus exponens quandam Parrenetam matrem dicte eius uxoris actu incestuoso pluries carnaliter cognovit, propter quod ipse Claudius et Perrenete ad instantiam ordinarii seu eius officialis cum eodem officiali fuerunt citati et moniti quatenus infra certum tunc expressum terminum eisdem prefixum non comparuerunt fuerunt per eundem officialem excommunicati. Et cum dictus Claudius demum uxorem suam predictam pluries carnaliter cognoverit et in suo matrimonio remanere intendat et inquitas huiusmodi predicte Jo<han>nete nocere non debeat supplicatur e. s. v. pro parte dictorum Claudii et Parrenete quatenus ipsos a dicta excommunicatonis sententia et reatu incestus quam propter ea incurrerunt absolvi et cum ipsis Claudio et Johanneta ut in eorum matrimonio libere remanere possint dispensari. Com<c>itatur ordinario qui post absolucionem agat secundum canonicas sanctiones, Phi. S. Laurentii in Lucina. – Videat eam dominus Anconitanus, Phi. – Comictatur ordinario prout de iure.'

17.   For example, *X* 4.12.1-2, *Corpus Iuris Canonici, pars secunda, Decretalium collectiones*, ed. E. Friedberg (Graz: 1959 – 2nd edn), 696-97 (hereafter Friedberg II). See also J. A. Brundage, *Law, Sex, and Christian Society in Medieval Europe* (Chicago and London: 1987), 337-38.

6. Cases involving spiritual relationship

Johannes Verbraken and Elizabet vander Bemde from the diocese of Cambrai had contracted a *sponsalia per verba de futuro*, after which they had had sexual intercourse and procreated children. They wished to celebrate their marriage *in facie ecclesie* but doubted whether they could do this legally, because Johannes had earlier had a sexual relationship with Elizabet's goddaughter, Katarina. In order to legally precede with their marriage plans, they needed a declaration that they could marry each other without problems – which they got from the Penitentiary.[18] Although the regulations of canon law concerning spiritual relationship do not mention anything about whether a sexual relationship between a man and the goddaughter of his spouse could constitute an impediment, nevertheless this couple had doubts about the legality of their possible marriage. The Penitentiary liberated them from this doubt and granted them the requested letter of declaration stating that no impediment existed between the spouses as a result of the sexual relationship between Johannes and Katarina and that they could marry without any problems.

Another similarly doubtful case was the one alluded to above between Mariotus Johannis from Siena and Lucrecia Antonelli from Sutri. Mariotus had once promised to Lucrecia's late husband, Dominicus Bertrami from the diocese of Padua, that he would be happy to become the godfather of Dominicus's and Lucrecia's child. Nevertheless, since Dominicus had died before the couple had any children, no direct spiritual relationship was formed. Some kind of doubt about the issue had evidently arisen, however, because their case was handled by the Penitentiary twice. The case was brought to the attention of the Penitentiary for the first time on 31 March 1463, when Mariotus alone petitioned to the office. He told the above story and pointed out in his petition that he wanted to marry Lucrecia but needed

---

18. ASV, *Penitenzieria Ap.*, *Reg. Matrim. et Div.*, vol. 8, fol. 202r-v (dated in Mantua 6.1.1460): 'Beatissime pater, exponitur s. v. pro parte devotorum vestrorum Johannis Verbraken laici et Elizabet vander Bemde mulieris Cameracen. dioc. quod ipsi olim desiderantes prout ad huc desiderant invicem matrimonialiter copulari sponsalia inter se per verba de futuro contraxerunt carnali copula inter eos subsecuta et prole procreata. Sed antequam predicti exponenti sponsalia contraherent dictus Johannes quandam Katherinam Vils quam dicta Elizabet exponens de sacro fonte levavit actu fornicario pluries carnaliter cognovit. Cum autem pater sancte ab aliquibus simplicibus et iurisignaris ac ipsorum exponentium forsan emulis asseritur propter premissa matrimonium in facie ecclesie ut moris est patrie invicem contrahere non posse ad ora talium igitur ac emulorum suorum obstruenda dignetur s. v. dictos exponentes premissis non obstantibus matrimonium invicem posse libere contrahere et in eo postquam contractum fuerit licite remanere declarare, prolem subceptam et subcipiendam ex /202v/ exinde legitimam decernentes. Fiat ut infra, G. prothon. de Oddis, regens. – Videat eam dominus Agapitus, G. – Commictatur et constito de assertis si aliud non obsistat declaretur et declaretur ut petitur.'

a declaration stating that the earlier promise to her late husband did not constitute an impediment. The Penitentiary agreed with his request on the condition that no scandal would arise.[19] After receiving this grace, Mariotus and Lucrecia must have married (since in the second petition they are described as a married couple), but apparently there were doubts about the validity of their marriage notwithstanding the grace Mariotus had earlier received from the Penitentiary,[20] because the couple – this time together – turned to the Penitentiary on the 30 May 1464 and requested a declaration that they could remain in their marriage despite the promise.[21] The crucial point in their case was whether a verbal promise between the two men constituted a legally valid pact that would have made the men *compatres* and thus would have created an impediment between the men and their families.[22] In this

19.	ASV, *Penitenzieria Ap., Reg. Matrim. et Div.*, vol. 11, fol. 266r-v (dated in Rome 31.3.1463): 'Mariotus Johannis laicus Montiscilmen exponit quod cum ipse verba amicabilia cum quodam Dominico Bertrami laico castri Citadelle /266v/ Paduan. dioc. haberet eidem Dominico promisit quod quamprimum opportunitas interveniret eum in eius compatrem assumeret et compaternitatem cum eodem contraheret. Et post antequam huiusmodi compaternitas sortita fuisset effectum dictus Dominicus diem suum clausit extremum. Verum quia dictus exponens certis de causis matrimonium cum uxore dicti Dominici contrahere desiderat nonnulli simplices asserere volunt exponentem et Dominicum predictos compatres premissorum occasione esse et per inde desiderium adimplere non posse igitur ad obstruendum ora talium supplicatur e. s. v. pro parte dicti exponentis quatenus nullum inter ipsum et dictam uxorem impedimentum premissorum occasione esse sed matrimonium inter se posse libere contrahere declarari misericorditer mandare dignemini. Fiat ut infra, Phi. S. Laurentii in Lucina. – Videat eam dominus Anconitanus, Phi. – Comictatur ordinario et si vocatis vocandis premissa esse vera constiterint et quod scandalum non sequatur ita quod communi reputacione tales non reputentur compatres declaretur ut petitur.'
20.	Unfortunately the Penitentiary entries do not shed light on the question of what happened in the interim, or why the couple had to petition the Penitentiary again on the same issue. Only the surviving local source material – if such exists – could tell us more details concerning their case.
21.	ASV, *Penitenzieria Ap., Reg. Matrim. et Div.*, vol. 13, fol. 370v-371r (dated in Rome 30.5.1464): 'Mariotus Johannis laicus Senen. et Lucrecia Antonelli mulier Sutrin. exponunt /371r/ quod cum ipse Mariotus cum quadam Dominico de Padua marito dum viveret dicte Lucrecie quadam die amicabiliter confabularetur Dominicus ipse Marioto predicto dixit quod primum filium quem a dicta Lucrecia susciperet idem Mariotus illum de sacro fonte levaret cui exponens respondit "Sum contentus". Et demum mortuo dicto Dominico nullo filio ab eadem Lucrecia eius uxore procreato exponentibus predictis in eius morte minime machinantibus, exponentes ipsi matrimonium inter se contraxerunt et consumarunt. Verum quia dictus Mariotus predicta verba Dominico predicto "sum contentus" dixit, nonnulli simplices asserere possent inter coniuges predictos impedimentum cognationis spiritualis existere et perinde in eorum matrimonio remanere non posse igitur ad obstruendum ora talium supplicatur quatenus nullum ex premissis inter eos esse impedimentum declarari sed in eorum matrimonio remanere posse dignemini. Fiat ut infra, Phi. S. Laurentii in Lucina. – Videat eam dominus Camerinen., Phi. – Comictatur episcopo Viterbien. et si vocatis vocandis premissa vera esse constiterint et aliud impedimentum non sististat [sic, recte: existat] declaretur ut petitur.'
22.	See *X* 4.11.1-3, edited in Friedberg II, 693-94.

case the Penitentiary answered in the negative – probably because the officials considered that no legally valid *compaternitas* had been formed by an oral agreement.

The remaining cases all hinged on the possibility of a spiritual relationship created by the sacraments of baptism or confirmation. The relationships in question, however, were not direct ties of spiritual relationship between the man and the woman who wished to marry or to continue in their marriage. In fact, in two cases the existence of a spiritual relationship was clearly in doubt:

Michael Cachon and Maria, daughter of Fernandus Martini, from the Spanish diocese of Osma, had a problem related to a possible spiritual relationship created by baptism. Maria had been the wet-nurse of Michael's son and therefore she had been present at his baptism, although not in the role of his godmother. After the death of his wife Michael had married Maria, but they were not sure whether their marriage was legal or not in light of the prior connection between Maria and the boy. They therefore petitioned the Penitentiary for a declaration that their marriage was legal.[23] The Penitentiary granted them such a declaration; and its decision was certainly correct, because according to the ecclesiastical regulations mere presence at a baptism did not constitute the impediment of spiritual relationship.

The question whether presence at the administering of a religious sacrament could constitute an impediment is found in another of the twelve petitions as well. Rudinus, son of Petrus Inholcz, and Margareta, daughter of Petrus Thome, from Rottenburg in the German diocese of Konstanz, doubted whether their marriage was valid because Margareta's father had been present at Rudinus's confirmation and afterwards had taken a piece of cloth away from his forehead at exactly the place where he had been anointed with chrism ('paniculum in fronte dicti Rudini supra crismam positum de ipsius fronte levavit'). They too asked for a declaration which would make clear that no impediment of spiritual relationship existed between them. The Penitentiary gave its consent conditionally and instructed the local bishop to investigate how long after confirmation the act had taken place, so that there might be no question that that Margareta's father could

---

23. ASV, *Penitenzieria Ap.*, *Reg. Matrim. et Div.*, vol. 8, fol. 217r-v (dated in Siena 8.4.1460): 'Michael Cachon et Maria Fernandi Martini coniuges Exanen. [sic] dioc. exponunt quod dum quidam puer quem dicta Maria lactavit babtisaretur qui ex altera muliere ipsius Michaelis erat quem dicta Maria non tenuit in babtismo quia presens fuit in eodem nonnulli simplices asserere possent ipsos in dicto matrimonio non posse stare. Ad obstruendum igitur ora talium, supplicatur pro parte eorundem exponentium quatenus ipsos premissis non obstantibus in eodem matrimonio inter eos contracto et consumato libere et licite posse remanere /217v/ libere et licite remanere [sic] possint prolem legtimam decerenentes. Comictatur ordinario qui constito sibi de premissis et quod vera sint declaret ut petitur, Phi. S. Laurentii in Lucina.'

have participated in the act of chrism and thus indirectly have been Rudi-nus's godfather.[24]

In the rest of the cases there existed some kind of spiritual relationship between the petitioners, but the main point in these petitions was whether the relationship was so distant that it did not constitute an impediment.

In two of these the problem lay in the fact that the first wife of the male supplicant had been godmother to a child of the female supplicant and present at its baptism. Both Johannes de Olde and Ahelis Pelgrinis from the diocese of Utrecht[25] and Hereminus Zsthaubuch and Jonota Tristanni from the diocese of Lausanne[26] turned to the Penitentiary because of such a

24. ASV, *Penitenzieria Ap.*, *Reg. Matrim. et Div.*, vol. 13, fol. 364r (dated in Petrioli, diocese of Siena 17.4.1464): 'Rudinus filius Petri Inholcz laicus et Margareta filia Petri Thome de villa Rotenburg mulier coniuges Constancien. dioc. exponunt quod ipsi desiderantes copulari matrimonium inter se contraxerunt et consumarunt. Demum ad eorum devenit noticiam quod pater dicte Margarite dicto Rudino paniculum in fronte dicti Rudini supra crismam positum de ipsius fronte levavit. Ob quod nonnulli simplices asserere volunt exponentes ipsos in eorum matrimonio remanere non posse impedimento cognacionis spiritualis obstante igitur ad obstruendum ora talium supplicatur e. s. v. pro parte dictorum exponentium quatenus nullum inter eos esse impedimentum premissorum occasione declarari misericorditer mandare dignemini. Fiat ut infra, Phi. S. Laurentii in Lucina. – Videat eam dominus Camerinen., Phi. – Comictatur ordinario et si vocatis vocandis premissa vera esse constiterint et quod post confirmacionem ex intervallo non ad huiusmodi finem ut contraherent cognacionem spiritualem levaverit declaretur ut petitur.'A summary of this case is edited in *Repertorium Poenitentiariae Germani-cum IV. Verzeichnis der in den Supplikenregistern der Pönitentiarie Pius' II. vor-kommenden Personen, Kirchen und Orte des Deutschen Reiches 1458-1464*. Text bearbeitet von Ludwig Schmugge mit Patrick Hersperger und Béatrice Wiggenhau-ser. Indices bearbeitet von Hildegard Schneider-Schmugge und Ludwig Schmugge (Tübingen: 1996) (hereafter RPG IV), no. 1841.
25. ASV, *Penitenzieria Ap.*, *Reg. Matrim. et Div.*, vol. 8, fol. 220v (dated in Siena 2.6.1460): 'Johannes de Olde et Ahelis Pelgrinis laici coniuges Traiecten. dioc. ig-norantes aliquod impedimentum inter eos existere matrimonium inter se contraxe-runt et consumarunt. Et quia quondam Margarita Stapes prima uxor dicti Johannis antequam matrimonium cum dicto Johanni contraheretur filium sive prolem dicte Ahelidis de sacro fonte levavit propter quod a nonnullis dubium trahitur cognacio-nem spiritualem inter eos existere, igitur ad obstruendum ora talium <supplicant> ipsos premissis non obstantibus in dicto eorum matrimonio remanere posse et nul-lam cognationem spiritualem inter <eos> existere declarari mandare dignemini. Comictatur ordinario qui constito de assertis declaret ut petitur, Phi. S. Laurentii in Lucina.' A summary of this case is edited in RPG IV, no. 1778.
26. ASV, *Penitenzieria Ap.*, *Reg. Matrim. et Div.*, vol. 10, fol. 220v-221r (dated in the abbey of S. Salvatoris, diocese of Chiusi 2.8.1462): 'Hereminus Zsthaubuch laicus et Joneta Tristanni mulier coniuges Lausanen. dioc. exponunt quod ipsi non obstante quod quondam Anna uxor dum viveret dicti Hermini antequam cum dicto Hermino matrimonium contraheret quendam puerum dicte Jonete de /221r/ sacro fonte levasset et demum sicut Deo placuit suum diem clausisset extremum matrimonium inter se per verba de presenti publice contraxerunt et illud carnali copula consuma<ve>runt. Verum quia dicta quondam Anna antequam ut prefertur matrimonium cum dicto Hermino contraheret puerum dicte Jonete de sacro fonte levavit nonnulli simplices et iuris ignari ac forsan eorum emuli asserere possent impedimentum cognationis spiritualis inter se existere et proinde in eorum

doubt. In both cases the Penitentiary granted the requested grace – thus stating that no spiritual relationship existed between the spouses – but in both cases the Penitentiary also committed the case to the local bishops who were supposed to examine that a real spiritual relationship did not exist between the petitioners. This decision (despite the inversion of the genders) can be seen as contrary to the decretal of Pope Clement III, which stated that a spiritual relationship between the father of the baptized child and the first wife of its godfather was considered an impediment.[27]

Petruspaulus Benedicti and Margareta, daughter of Bartholomeus Lippi, from Camerino, could not marry without a declaration from the Penitentiary that would make their marriage legally valid, since Margareta's father was godfather to Petruspaulus's daughter. Although the couple was clearly tied by spiritual relationship, the Penitentiary nevertheless granted them a declaration that they could marry. It thereby indicated with this decision that the relationship in question was considered too distant to constitute an impediment between the two. However, the Penitentiary made its decision with the condition that this would not be against the local customs and it would not create a scandal.[28] Hence, here we can see a clear reference to different local ways of interpreting what constituted a too-close spiritual relationship and what did not. This statement too is a clear reference to the regulations of canon law stating that the local customs had to be respected in these cases.[29]

Nicolaus de Fugy and Elena, widow of Valentinus Fugi, from the Hungarian diocese of Nagy-Varad had a similar problem, e.g. whether the

matrimonio remanere non posse. Igitur ad obstruendum ora talium supplicatur quatenus inter ipsos nullum cognacionis spiritualis impedimentum esse sed eosdem in eorum sic contracto matrimonio libere remanere posse declarari misericorditer mandare dignemini. Fiat ut infra, Phi. S. Laurentii in Lucina. – Videat eam dominus Anconitanus, Phi. – Comictatur odinario et si vocatis vocandis premissa constiterint esse vera et non reputentur communi opinioni pro compatribus adeo quod scandalum sequatur declaretur ut petitur.' A summary of this case is edited in RPG IV, no. 1815.

27.   *X* 4.11.4, edited in Friedberg II, 694.
28.   ASV, *Penitenzieria Ap., Reg. Matrim. et Div.*, vol. 11, fol. 262v-263r (dated in Rome 6.2.1463): 'Petruspauli [sic] Benedicti laicus et Margareta filia Bartholomei Lippi mulieris Camerinen. exponunt <quod> ex certis causis desiderantes copulari sed. quia dictus Batholomeus pater eiusdem mulieris per quatuordecim annos et ultra post eius nativitatem quandam dicti Petripauli filiam de sacro fonte levavit, timent ne aliqui simplices asserant impedimentum cognationis spiritualis inter eos existere. Ob quod supplicatur pro parte eorundem quatenus non obstantibus premissis matrimonium inter se contrahere ac postquam contractum fuerit in eodem remanere prolem exinde suscipiendam /263r/ legitimam decernentes declarari posse dignemini ut in forma. Fiat ut infra, Phi. S. Laurentii in Lucina. – Comictatur ordinario et si vocatis vocandis premissa constiterint esse vera et sine consuetuda sit in contrarium aut scandalum ex hoc resultaret declaretur ut petitur. – Videat eam dominus Anconitanus, Phi.'
29.   *X* 4.11.3, edited in Friedberg II, 694.

spiritual relationship between them was too close for marriage. The second wife of Nicolaus's father had been the godmother to Elena's son by her late husband. They too needed a declaration stating that such a distant spiritual relationship did not impede them from remaining in their marriage.[30] The Penitentiary could agree with their request because the regulations of canon law do not expressly forbid that.

A closer spiritual relationship existed between Leonardus Cervalt and Anna, daughter of Clos Heydese, from the German diocese of Mainz. Because Leonardus was godfather to Anna's sister or brother, the couple doubted whether they could remain in their marriage and requested a declaration stating that they could continue together legally. The couple – who claimed to have been ignorant of the spiritual relationship when their clandestine marriage was contracted *per verba de presenti* and consummated – received from the Penitentiary the needed grace, on condition that everything they had asserted was true.[31] The reference to the truth was probably especially meant to address the issue of whether they had been ignorant about the impediment or not. It seems that the spiritual relationship had not been very tight, particularly since the petitioners (or their procurator at least) could not specify whether Leonardus had been godfather to a boy or to a girl, and therefore used the expression 'a certain brother or sister of Anna's'. This detail might have helped the couple obtain the desired result from the Penitentiary.

30. ASV, *Penitenzieria Ap.*, *Reg. Matrim. et Div.*, vol. 11, fol. 269r-v (dated in Rome 4.5.1463): 'Nicolaus de Fugy laicus et Elena relicta quondam Valentini Fugi mulieris [sic] coniuges Varadien. dioc. exponunt quod alius matrimonium per verba de presenti clandestine contraxerunt et carnali copula consumarunt. Et quia 2a uxor patris /269v/ ipsius exponentis unum puerum ipsius Elene et dicti quondam Valentini de sacro fonte levavit, nonnulli assere\<re\> possent impedimentum cognationis spiritualis inter eos existere et proinde in eorum matrimonio remanere non posse. Igitur ad obstruendum ora talium supplicatur e. s. v. pro parte dictorum exponentium quatenus nullum inter eos premissorum occasione esse impedimentum declarari mandare dignemini. Fiat ut infra, Phi. S. Laurentii in Lucina. Et absolvatur ab excommunicatione, G, regens. – Videat eam dominus Anconitanus, Phi. – Comictatur ordinario et si vocatis vocandis premissa esse \<vera\> constiteri\<n\>t declaretur ut petitur.'

31. ASV, *Penitenzieria Ap.*, *Reg. Matrim. et Div.*, vol. 13, fol. 360v (dated in Siena 22.3.1464): 'Leonardus Cervalt laicus et Anna Clos Heydeses dochter coniuges Maguntin. dioc. exponunt quod ipsi ignorantes quod dictus Leonardus quendam fratrem sive sororem ipsius Anne de sacro babtismate levaverat matrimonium inter se contraxerunt et consumarunt. Postea ad eorum devenit noticiam quod dictus Leonardus ipsius Anne per prius quendam fratrem sive sororem de sacro fonte levavit. Dubitant igitur iidem coniuges propter nonnullorum assercionem in eorum matrimonio remanere non posse. Igitur ad obstruendum ora talium supplicatur quatenus premissis non obstantibus in eorum matrimonio libere remanere posse declarari mandare dignemini. Fiat ut infra, Phi. S. Laurentii in Lucina. – Videat eam dominus Camerinen., Phi. – Comictatur ordinario et si vocatis vocandis premissa vera esse constiterint declaretur ut petitur.' A summary of this case is edited in RPG IV, no. 1838.

Jacobus de Labeca and Margarita, widow of Johannes de Mande, from the diocese of Cambrai, in their turn had faced the problem that Margarita was godmother to the son of a woman with whom Jacobus had earlier had a sexual relationship. Therefore they doubted whether they could be married or not. In this case there was obviously question as to whether Margarita was the godmother of Jacobus's own child, since the Penitentiary resolved the case by referring the case to the local bishop and instructed him particularly to investigate whether the baptized child was Jacobus's. If it was his son, an impediment existed and Jacobus and Margarita could not get married; if not, then they were free to marry each other.[32]

7. Conclusions

What can we learn from these cases? One important point is that they are only very few in number, which indicates that the problems they address cannot have been particularly problematic. That they exist at all, however, demonstrates that there were sometimes doubts, and that interpreting the canon law regulations regarding marital impediments was not always unproblematic. In fact, these tolerance cases show that even as late as the second half of the fifteenth century some marital regulations of canon law were still considered ambiguous which resulted with the need to turn to the authority of the Penitentiary for resolving these issues. The corpus of this analysis seems to point towards problems with two particular issues:

First – as we saw in one of the cases – there seem to have been regional variations in how the regulations were interpreted; and from looking at the regulations stipulated in canon law it is clear that they actually allowed the existence of variation. Second, some impediments, in particular

---

32. ASV, *Penitenzieria Ap.*, *Reg. Matrim. et Div.*, vol. 11, fol. 261v (dated in Rome 30.1.1463): 'Jacobus de Labeca clericus et Margarita relicta quondam Johannis de Mande mulier coniuges Cameracen. dioc. exponunt quod ipsi olim postquam ipsa Margarita quendam puerum cuiusdam mulieris quam pluries dictus Jacobus actu fornicario cognoverat de sacro fonte levaverat desiderantes ad invicem matrimonialiter copulari sponsalia inter se contraxerunt. Et licet ipse exponens matrem dicti pueri ut prefertur actu fornicario pluries cognoverit dictus tamen puer ipsius exponentis filius minime fuit. Sed quia a nonnullis exitari posset dictum puerum dicti exponentis fuisse filium et propter hoc exponentes huiusmodi matrimonium inter se contrahere non posse. Igitur ad obstruendum ora talium supplicatur e. s. v. pro parte dictorum exponentium quatenus premissa ordinario commicti et se si puer eiusdem exponentis erat se informari et si puerum huiusmodi suum fore minime reperierit nullum inter eosdem exponentes esse impedimetum declarare. Fiat ut infra. – Videat eam dominus Anconitanus, Phi. – Comictatur ordinario et si vocatis vocandis premissa vera esse constiterint declaretur ut petitur.'

the spiritual relationship, were clearly more ambiguous than others such as consanguinity or affinity.

The Penitentiary sources show too that a number of couples from different parts of Christendom had turned to the Penitentiary because they wanted to ensure through a papal declaration that their marriages were legally valid even though some kind of impediment existed between them. This demonstrates that in dubious cases the opinion of the papal curia – and in particular of the Penitentiary – was what counted when it came to interpreting the regulations of canon law. In practice this means that the Penitentiary – and the few but qualified persons working for it – was still redefining the marital impediments as late as the mid-fifteenth century.

Wills as Testimony
of Marriage Contracts
in Late Medieval Krakow

Jakub Wysmułek

1. Source characteristics – definition of wills[1]

Wills are sources of information with a complicated nature that hides in
seemingly definite content. A will's wealth of details is lost in the vague-
ness of what it refers to; its personal and genealogical data and the relationships it suggests are silent in the face of the near-anonymity of the people it
mentions; its motives and purposes are obscured by convention and formulaic language.

These problems are apparent even in simply defining what wills are,
since they are envisaged differently in canon law, municipal law, and land
law as well as in applied local practice. Steven Epstein has given this extremely broad definition, for example: 'The testament was an act made by
an individual at a specific time and place, for personal motives'.[2] This definition, despite its undoubted accuracy, could be applied to almost every
form of human activity, and therefore it does not reveal the specific and
unique character of the phenomenon of wills. Rather, it shows the chal-
lenges that face the researcher in analyzing a type of source that is difficult
even to define.

---

1. In this article I am using the terms 'will' and 'testament' interchangeably, as syn-
    onyms, not like, for instance, in English legal system, where there is a division of
    meaning of those terms. No differentiation of meaning of 'will' and 'testament' is
    chosen in accordance with the practice of medieval testators and Polish law tradi-
    tion.
2. S. Epstein, *Wills and Wealth in Medieval Genoa, 1150-1250* (Cambridge, MA, and
    London: 1984), 38.

Jakub Wysmułek

Previous research suggests that we will find it useful to define wills more specifically, as the donation made by one person to another, or to a group or institution, which transfers rights over property after the donor's death. (In this case *donatio mortis causa* acts are also treated as wills.) By this definition the term 'wills' embraces a wide range of donations, including pious bequests, reciprocal bequests between spouses (*mutua donatio*) and bequests to close family, relatives, and non-relatives. All of these forms of bequests appear in medieval Krakow wills, which local sources usually designate as 'testaments'. If it is difficult to differentiate one type of bequest from another – and it is – the question then arises whether modern scholars cannot grasp distinctions that were quite obvious at the time they were made, or whether in fact the flexibility of the regulations or even unawareness of statutory law led to inconsistency in everyday practice. For the moment this is an open question.

2. Reasons for writing wills

The data contained in wills are usually used in statistical analyses to investigate religious practices, genealogy, material culture and circulation of members among elite. This approach does not take into account the specific and individual character of the source, however.[3] In order to delve deeper into the nature of the source and to avoid generalization, a researcher must try to understand the testator's motives in undertaking such a relatively uncommon enterprise. As in any attempt to determine motives for human actions or decisions the answer is found on different levels, which the performers may or may not be aware of, and which they may or may not address directly. In some cases the testator explicitly mentions in the preamble of the document the purpose for writing it. Instances of this are rare in Krakow sources, and appear primarily from the second part of the fifteenth century. Although the language itself is formulaic, this type of preamble is nevertheless valuable for determining the testator's religious or secular motiva-

3. For example: P. Baur, *Testament und Bürgerschaft: Alltagsleben und Sachkultur im spätmittelalterlichen Konstanz* (Sigmaringen: 1989); J. Majorossy, *Church in Town: Urban Religious Life in Late Medieval Pressburg in the Mirror of Last Wills* (Ph.D. diss. CEU University: 2006); B. Możejko, *Rozrachunek z życiem doczesnym: Gdańskie testamenty mieszczańskie z XV i początku XVI wieku* (Gdańsk: 2010); E. Piwowarczyk, *Legaty testamentowe 'ad pias causas' w XV-wiecznym Krakowie: Z badań nad pobożnością miejską* (Kraków: 2010); M. Riethmüller, '*To troste miner sele': Aspekte spätmittelalterlicher Frömmigkeit im Spiegel Hamburger Testamente (1310-1400)* (Hamburg: 1994); U. Sowina, 'Najstarsze sieradzkie testamenty mieszczańskie z początku XVI w. Analiza źródłoznawcza', *Kwartalnik historii kultury materialnej* 39/1 (1991); U. M. Zahnd, 'Spätmittelalterliche Bürgertestamente als Quellen zu Realienkunde und Sozialgeschichte', *Mitteilungen des Instituts für österreichische Geschichtsforschung* 96 (1988).

tions. The most commonly cited reasons for writing wills are the fear of damnation and the hope of ensuring salvation.[4] Some testators also express their wish to prevent quarrels within the family when the property is divided.[5] Sometimes the writing of wills was also prompted by an imminent pilgrimage, long trip or military expedition, in which case both religious and secular motivations were possible.[6] Other more or less consciously realized factors that could prompt testators to write a last will include the wish for prestige within a social group, sympathy and antipathy towards particular family members or other persons, fear of death and a desire to ensure some type of permanent memorial, and a wish to compensate for past wrongdoing.

3. Dower and concept of wills

In addition to the above-mentioned possibilities, sometimes the reasons for writing wills were quite prosaic, connected with the social and legal obligations of the individual in a municipal community. Among them I would like to bring to light the intent of writing wills as a record to ensure and guarantee the performance of the obligations stated in a marriage contract. Wills in those cases served to confirm the dower promised to the wife, as well as specifying the distribution of property between spouses (and their children) in case the husband or wife should die.

Evidence of this can be found in the Krakow municipal records, which suggest that some wills were written shortly after a first or second mar-

---

4. 'In ciuitate Cracouiensi, In presencia mei notarij et testium infrascriptorum personaliter constituta honesta domina Clara relicta Iacobi Rolle, In domo sua, sana corpore et bone racionis, zelo pietatis ardenter cupiens facultates suas ad cultum diuini numinis disponere, quippe qui saluberrimum sit operum caritatis, ac pro gracia et amore amantissimi datoris et remuneratoris omnium bonorum et in remedium et salutem anime sue atque dicti quondam eius mariti, qui decedens testamentum aliud non fecit, nisi quod ipsum disponendum eius fideli reliquit voluntati, Voluit dari et mandauit de bonis suis [...]' (1419), *Kodeks Dyplomatyczny Miasta Krakowa 1257-1506*, III, ed. F. Piekosiński, *Monumenta, Medii Aevi Historica, Res Gestas Poloniae Illustrantia*, Tomus VII (Kraków: 1882), 532-34. In the quotations of the above-mentioned edition of Krakow sources I am remaining faithful to the way of transcription used in it, which treats, for example, letter 'v' as 'u'.
5. 'Margaretha Czypserynne licet egra tamen bene racionis et bene deliberata, volens ut post mortem suam inter pueros eius, quos ex tribus maritis habuit videlicet Zalcz, Czipser et Johanne Lovicz, nulla esset dissensio et controversia, ideo fecit suam ultimam voluntatem et testamentum suum in hunc modum qui sequitur[...].' Liber Testamentorum (Archiwum Państwowe w Krakowie, ms. 772), 165.
6. 'Hannos Lode unsir mitburger wellende czyen wedir dy ungetrawen finde der Cristenlichen glaubins dy Turken vor sitczendem Rate machende seyn testament frisch und gesint bey guttir vornumft in solchen worten[...].' Liber Testamentorum, 37.

Jakub Wysmułek

riage.[7] The motive for writing these wills and validating them in court seems above all to have been to legally regulate the new circumstances relating to property and familial connections as they might affect all interested parties. This can be observed in the structure of the record, which often begins with a detailed description of the position of one of the spouses after the death of the other and then proceeds to calculate the survivor's property share and the means of inheriting it, as well as the procedures to be followed in the event that the marriage produced children. For instance, the assessor and then councilman Mikolaj Strelich stated in his will in 1393 that his wife was to have his whole estate, but then added that were they to have children, then the wife would have a rich dower and the estate would be divided into equal shares, so the wife and each of the children would have the same portion.[8] Likewise, in 1396 the Krakow citizen Piotr Puczk specified the sum which his wife had brought into the marriage, but stipulated that if they were to have children, an amount less than this would be returned to her upon his death.[9] In some wills it was also *expressis verbis* mentioned that the record was being made to protect the rights of a second wife of the testator and to divide the estate between her, their future children and the children from the first marriage.[10]

7.   This similarity was also observed by B. Klosterberg, *Zur Ehre Gottes und zum Wohl der Familie: Kölner Testamente von Laien und Klerikern im Spätmittelalter* (Bonn: 1992), 207.

8.   *Acta scabinalia Cracoviensia 1365-1376 et 1390-1397*, ed. S. Krzyżanowski (Kraków: 1904), no. 1645.

9.   'Petrus Puczk testamentum voluntatis sue ultimo condidit in hunc modum: Ich Petrus von Puczk mache meyn testament, ab ich abginge, adir meyne eliche husfraw Praxedis, das wir von frunde vnser beyde vngehindirt bleiben, yn alsotin worten: **ab ich sturbe ane fruchte**, zo bekenne ich das meyne husfraw egenannte czu mir hat brocht LXXXI mrc. gr., dy sal man ir lassen volgen mit der tat vnd L mrc. gr., dy ich ir hab gemorgengobt, **adir ap vns got fruchte gibt mitenandir** vnd bleibt se witwe, zo sullin dy kinder by ir bleibin vnd das gut, was ich habe vnd habin werde mitenandir, an hindirniss meynir vnd ir frunde, yn alsotener vndirscheit, ap se sich wurde vorandirn, zo sal man ir gebin C mrc. gr. vor das, dasse czu mir brocht hat vnd vor morgengabe, vnd meynen kindern das andirn; reservat etc., tutores Nicolaus Leymiter et Johannes institor et si etc ab ich sturbe ane fruchte [...] adir ap uns got fruchte gibt mitenandir.' *Acta scabinalia Cracoviensia*, no. 2354.

10. 2070. (8.1.1395) 'Johannes Michilwicz testamentum suum in cedula papirea conscriptum ydeomate teutonico presentavit, cuius dispositio testamenti sequitur in hec verba: Ich bekenne das ich Katherin meyner elichin husfrawen gemorgengobt habe XXX mrg., dy sal se nemen noch meynem tode von meyner varnden habe, dorczu ir gerade, dy ir mit rechte geboren mag, also verre, als se, mich obirlebt, auch gebe ich Margarethen meyner tochter, dy ich vor gewinnen habe **mit meyner ersten frawen** Dorothea genant, XXX mrc. groschin in meyn gut erbe vnde varnde czuvor vs czu hebin vor allir teylunge, doch also, **wurde mir got kinder geben mit desen frawen adir mit andirn**, ap ich dy haben wurde, das dy czukunftigen kinder mit der vorgenanten Margriten myn guth vnd meyn erbe czu gleichim teile nemen sullen, vs genomen dy XXX mrg. dy Margaretha czuvor vs hebin sal, auch also, ap das got fugen wurde, das ich abeginge vnde nicht me kinder lisse, wenne dy vorgenannte Margarite, so sal dy selbe Margaretha meyn erbe vnd meyn gut, das

184

In terms of the responsibility undertaken by the husband to administer the common estate, the most important part of the marriage contract was setting the dower (*morgengeld, morgengabe, dotalicium, donatio propter nuptias*), the amount that the husband left to the wife for her maintenance after his death. Originally an oral undertaking that was part of concluding the marriage contract and was confirmed by the presence of witnesses, the dower settlement came to be put into written form as a result of the development of municipal bureaucracy and the pressure of municipal authorities. This evolution is reflected in particular in resolutions of the city council. It is stated in the municipal constitutions (German *Willekur*) from the second part of the fourteenth century (1378 and 1397) that 'if a husband gives his wife the *morgengeld*, he, with his bride, his relatives or by himself must come to the councilors four days before the marriage and declare the exact value of the *morgengeld* so that what is planned can take place and disputes between relatives can be prevented'.[11] The later Krakow municipal constitution from 1468 and 1487, containing and readjusting 'resolutions of the city gathered from ancient records', expands this period to include the eight days after the marriage.[12] Although from the beginning of the fourteenth century in the Krakow municipal books dower was sometimes mentioned in a general way, the first record that specified the exact sum of the dower appeared in 1338 and even later, in the second half of fourteenth and in the fifteenth century, records with declaration of amount of dower are quite rare.

ich lossen wurde noch meynem tode, gancz vnde gar hebin vnd nemen, vsgenomen dy vorgeschreben XXX mrg., dy ich Katherinen meyner husfrawen gemorge(n)gobt habe, doch das mit namen doryn genomen, was ich kinder wurde lossen noch meynem tode, ap der eyns adir me desen nochgeschreben vormunden nicht gehorsam wurde seyn, das dy selbin Vormunden irkenten, das meyn guth an em nicht bestat were, so sullen se volle macht haben deme vngehorsamen kinde seyn gut czu entwenden vnde das teil wenden an dy werk der barmherczigkeit noch willin der vormunden vnd. ap ich nicht kinder wurde lassen noch meynem tode, so gebe ich desen nochgeschrebenen vormunden volle macht meyn erbe czu vorkawfen vnde andir myn guth vnd das gelt czu geben armen leuthin, wo en das allirbeste geballen wirt; des mach ich mechtige schaffer Swarczpeschken, Petrum Girhardisdorf vnde Kunczonem Habirgeyst vnd Johannem vom Skawin, also ap eyner abeginge, wy ofte das geschege, das dy andern mogen czu en kysen, wer en gefallen wirt, doch wil ich eyn herre seyn meynis gutis, als vor.' *Acta scabinalia Cracoviensia,* nr. 2042.

11. *Najstarszy zbiór przywilejów i wilkierzy miasta Krakowa,* ed. S. Estreicher (Kraków: 1936), part II, no. 15.
12. *Kodeks Dyplomatyczny Miasta Krakowa,* 1257-1506, II, ed. F. Piekosiński (Kraków: 1882), no. 334.

4. The unification of establishment of dower with the act of last will

Beginning at the end of the fourteenth century an interesting phenomenon can be observed in the Krakow municipal chancellery records, namely the emerging tendency to think of specifying dower arrangements as one of the functions of wills. Indeed, in this period information about the amount of dower, as well as the specifics of how the estate was to be divided between the heirs, became the predominant element of medieval last wills. An example of this is the will of the Krakow patrician Jan Bozemecz (1394), which states only that his wife should receive as her dower one-third of all his property after his death.[13] Bozemecz's will is noticeably similar to the one made by the tailor Dinko (1396), who acknowledged in the presence of his daughters that after his death his wife Elżbieta should receive one-third of the house.[14] Likewise other, more complex wills of that period concentrate mainly on declaring the dower and regulating the division of the estate after the death of the husband. In contrast to the earlier wills, which appeared mainly to have been written for religious motives, they do not include any pious bequests. They were also not written at the deathbed, but were brought to the court on the cards and are often in German. The merger of both forms of document can be seen in the title of the first volume of Krakow wills (no longer extant), founded by the municipal council in 1396, the 'Liber Testamenti et Dotaliciorum'.[15] Similarly, the will of Piotr Scharf (1432) – the second-earliest will in the surviving book, the 'Liber Testamentorum' (which starts at 1427, although it was compiled in 1450) – is dedicated to transferring all his goods to his wife Anna, if she survives him, and also excludes all other relatives from the inheritance.[16] Though the majority

---

13. 'Johannes Bozemecz testamentum suum condidit in hunc modum, ita videlicet, quod domina sua Agnes pro dotalicio et omnibus aliis terciam partem in omnia ipsius bona hereditaria et mobilia habere debet post mortem suam et tenere, reservat etc.' *Acta scabinalia Cracoviensia*, no. 1914.
14. 'Dinko sartor terciam partem domus sue in plathea sancti Floriani circa domum Jlkusserinne, presentibus Katherina, Agnete et Margareta filiabus suis et pro Nicolao Wislicia consencientibus, pro dotalicio et omnibus aliis ipsam concernere valentibus Elyzabeth conthorali sue resignavit; reservat dominium.' *Acta scabinalia Cracoviensia*, no. 2278.
15. *Kodeks dyplomatyczny miasta Krakowa, 1257-1506*, II, no. 334.
16. 'Anno ... XXXII feria secunda diei sancti Mathie apostoli Scharf Peter institor pauper fecit testamentum coram dominis Consulibus Cuncze Korsner et Johanne Crancz. Anne uxori sue legavit omnia bona sua que habet post mortem suam habenda cum plena faciendi et dimittendi potestate Exclusis omnes suos consangwineos propinquos et amicas. Sin autem ipse supervivent moriente uxore extunc ipse mulieris quam sua habere cum plena potestate ut super exclusis eciam omnibus propinquis et amicis eiusdem uxoris. Et in hanc ordinacionem testamenti Anna prefata praesentialiter constituta plenarie consensit suscipiens eam pro grato. Neutra presencium reservavit dominorum.' Liber Testamentorum, 3.

of fourteenth-century wills are far more complex, due to changes in their form and the growing quantity of their records, from the end of the fourteenth century the declaration of the amount of dower to safeguard the wife's position after her husband's death becomes the most consistently found element of wills made by married testators.

5. *Donatio mortis causa* records

The other popular way of regulating inheritance property was by recording a short note (*donatio mortis causa*) stipulating that upon the death of one spouse, the entire estate should go to the survivor. This sometimes took the form of an acknowledgment made by the husband on his wife's behalf[17] and sometimes that of a mutual donation in case of death, referred to in the sources as *mutua donatio*.[18] An annotation is often added specifying that all relatives and others are excluded from the inheritance.[19] Although usually in the notes themselves neither the word 'dower' nor the word 'testament' appears, it seems that they served the same function. Primarily, they are contractual records made between the spouses. A similar phenomenon in German sources is called *geschefft*, a term whose etymology (contemporary spelled Geschäft) underlines its consensual and transactional nature.[20] The same word also appears in Krakow sources together with the words *testament* and *zelgerethe*.[21]

These notes were a way to distribute goods and to regulate inheritance in favour of a spouse (usually the wife), who, after the relatives were disinherited, stood to inherit the whole property. In some of the notes the chil-

17. 'Georgius cirologus omnia bona sua mobilia et immobilia, que habet vel habere poterit, domine Elizabeth conthorali sue legitime post mortem suam libere resignavit, volens esse dominus, quamdiu vixerit.' *Acta scabinalia Cracoviensia*, no. 1483.
18. 'Andreas Werzingi omnia bona sua mobilia hereditaria, pecuniaria et quecumque habet vel habuit, domine Anne consorti sue iure hereditario assignavit cum plena faciendi et dimittendi facultate et eadem consors sua eidem Andree, Caspar pro tutore recepto, similiter resignavit.' *Acta scabinalia Cracoviensia*, no. 1475.
19. (1396) 'Nicolaus Gleywicz gladiator resignavit uxori sue omnia sua bona, exclusis omnibus amicis.' *Acta scabinalia Cracoviensia*, no. 2227.
20. Other terms used are *schikung, vormackung, gestifte, letzter wille, ordnunge* and *seelgerethe. Wiener Stadtbücher 1395-1430. Teil 1: 1395-1400,* ed. W. Brauneder and G. Jaritz (Wien and Köln: 1989), 17-21.
21. 'Lucas Bochner mit gezundem leibe und guter vornunfft hat gekorn gesaczt und gemacht dy erbarn Casparn Krugiln und Nicolaum Platener czu vormunden schaffern und zundirlichen vorwesern, alzo das se seyn **gescheffte, testament und zelgerethe**, ab an em off dem wege icht geschege, vorwesen, volbrengen und schaffen sullen czutun und czulasen In allir mose und weyse, als se in eyme papirn brife den her en vorsegilt antwortin wirt, werden finden beschrebin.' *Consularia Cracoviensia. Inscriptiones* (Archiwum Państwowe w Krakowie, ms. 427), 240.

dren (either born or expected[22]), grandchildren or siblings are mentioned, to whom some part of the estate has to be given.[23] An example of ensuring the dower combined with a mutual donation is the record of 30 marks made by Jan Steynbach to his wife Klara in 1396, in which she also transmitted to him all her possessions.[24] Given the growing popularity of this kind of short form of exchange of goods between the spouses starting from the middle of the fourteenth century (around 400 of them are found among four-teenth-century entries), it can be assumed that at least some of them served as the protection of dower that municipal authorities required to be made right after the marriage. The notes which have a more complex character, and include stipulations about inheritance of property by children and the procedures to be followed if the spouse remarries, are even more similar to the 'testaments' of that period.[25]

6. When was the will written?

Taking into consideration all of the above-mentioned examples and obser-vations, the relationship between wills and marriage contracts seem to be probable. However, in order to prove that connection, information about the

22. (1393) 'Niclos Jegirdorf et Dorothea ipsius Nico consors legitima, Johanne Czop-chin sibi ibidem pro tutore recepto, omnia bona sua mobilia, hereditaria, que habent aut habituri fuerint, sibi invicem mutuo seu alterutrum, sub submissis condicioni-bus resignaverunt ita, si sine prole decederent, si autem pueros procrearent, tunc pueri consimilem porcionem debent habere et possidere, premissis non obstan-tibus.' *Acta scabinalia Cracoviensia*, no. 1671.

23. (1395) 'Nicolaus Weydnow domine Margarethe conthorali sue in omnia bona sua hereditaria et mobilia equalem uni puerorum suorum post mortem suam tribuit por-cionem, et si pueri morirentur, pars ipsorum ad dominam derivetur; si autem domina moriretur, extunc pars ipsius ad pueros devolvatur, exclusis omnibus ami-cis ipsius Nicolai.' *Acta scabinalia Cracoviensia*, no. 2209.

24. 'Johannes Steynbach domine Clare contorali sue post mortem suam XXX mrc. monete tunc currentis pro dotalicio suo et omnibus aliis, ipsam concernere valen-tibus, resignavit et ipsa sibi omnia bona econverso.' *Acta scabinalia Cracoviensia*, no. 2358.

25. 'Nicolaus Hungerkaste requisivit, in sentencia [...] Idem Nicolaus domine Agneti consorti sue legitime domum suam in plathea Hospitalis, circa domum Nicolai Bo-chner relicte, post mortem suam contulit et donavit, ita quod ipsa domina pauperi-bus hospitalis sancti Spiritus in Cracovia dare debet II mrc. annis singulis, quamdiu vixerit et in viduitate permanserit, tenendam et omnia bona sua mobilia et suppel-lectilia domus omniaque parafernalia, que *rade* wlgariter dicuntur, tali condicione, quod si bona mobilia [ita bona] quemadmodum ipsius domine dotalicium, quod idem Nicolaus recongnovit facere XXX mrc., non forent, extunc in hereditate pre-dicta, ipsa domina predictum dotalicium poterit recuperare, si autem ipsa domina maritum duceret, aut permittente domino moriretur, extunc domus predicta ad proximos dicti Nicolai, prout de iure debet, devolvatur, qui singulis annis III mrc. dabunt ad hospitale predictum et hoc XXX annis, quousque dicta domus pro XC mrc. fuerit persoluta; reservat dominium [...].' *Acta scabinalia Cracoviensia*, no. 1967.

age of the testator at the time of writing his will is also needed. Preliminary prosopographical research suggests that at least of some of the testators made their wills at the beginning of their professional careers and their lives as independent adults. A typical example is the Krakow burgher Mikolaj Strelich, who in 1390 recorded a bequest to his wife Jadwiga of all his goods with all the rights to dispose them after his death.[26] Two and a half years later he made a similar record, this time specified as a 'testament', which added details about the succession to his property: what should be done if his widow remarried or did not; and if the marriage produced children, how she should choose guardians (*tutores*) for the children and when she should convey their portion of the property to them.[27] Prosopographical research reveals that Mikolaj Strelicz was just beginning his professional career when he wrote these wills. During the years 1392-1396 Mikolaj was a member of the municipal jury. In 1397-1404 he became a Krakow city councilor,[28] and in a document from 1407 he appears as mayor of the town of Nowy Sącz.[29] In 1421 he handed down the house with the brewery and a

---

26. 'Strelicz omnia bona sua domine Hedwigi eius consorti legitime post mortem suam cum plena etc. resignavit', *Acta scabinalia Cracoviensia*, no. 1259
27. 'Nicolaus Strelicz requisivit in sentencia, utrum cum bonis etc. et fuit adiudicatum, quod sic, tandem ipso Nicolaus omnia bona sua mobilia et immobilia, nichil excipiendo, domine Hedwigi conthorali sue legitime post mortem suam habenda, si ipsum sine prole decedere contigerit, cum plena faciendi et dimittendi facilitate contulit et donavit, si vero pueros ex se procreaverint, tunc ipsa domina debet habere principaliter C sexag. gr. prag. et cum eisdem derelictis suis pueris equalem uni ipsorum in predicta bona omnia porcionem, quod si predicta sua conthoralis, viventibus pueris, alium duxerit maritum et prefatos derelictos pueros circa se tenere voluerit, tenebitur et debebit tutoribus suorum puerorum infrascriptis certos ponere fideiussores, quod bona mobilia vel immobilia, ipsis pueris devoluta, vel eosdem ex dicti Nicolai Strelicz patris eorum successione legitime concernencia, non debeant minorari, nec quomodolibet peyorari. Quibus, in quantum eos predictus Nicolaus cum uxore sua procreaverit pueris, cum ad annos debite etatis, videlicet, si masculus ad XX annos, si femella, quousque cum voluntate matris maritata fuerit, pervenerint, debebit predicta Hedwigis, mater ipsorum, cuilibet suam, capitalem et devolutam dare et assignare porcionem, nichil pro expensis per predictos pueros infra predicta tempora factis et sumptibus eisdem pueris penitus computando, si autem prefata Hedwigis in ordine viduitatis permanserit, non tenebitur ipsis [...] tutoribus aliquos de minoracione seu peyoracione bonorum predictorum ponere fideiussores, sed solummodo ipsis notiflcare, que bona prescriptorum puerorum circa se fuerit habitura; constituit insuper predictus Nicolaus Strelicz presentis sue ultime voluntatis sive testamenti certos executores et tutores: Rudolfum Saxonem et Nicolaum Loslaw, dans eisdem plenam et omnimodam auctoritatem, alium post discessum alterius ipsorum vel alios eligendi, relinquens sibi nichilominus dominium huiusmodi sue voluntatis ultime, quamdiu vita fuerit sibi come.' *Acta scabinalia Cracoviensia*, no. 1645.
28. Maciej Starzyński, *Krakowaka rada miejska w średniowieczu* (Kraków: 2010), 251; Jacek Laberschek, 'Strelicz Mikołaj', *Polski Słownik Biograficzny* XL (Warszawa-Kraków: 2007), 16-17.
29. *Consularia Cracoviensia. Inscriptiones* (Archiwum Państwowe w Krakowie, ms. 427), 298.

rent and a stall to his elder son, Jan,[30] probably because Jan had reached adulthood.[31] Mikolaj's death was recorded three years later. After he died, the property was shared between his son Jan (who became the new major of Nowy Sącz), and his daughter Barbara, the wife of a Krakow patrician.[32]

7. Conclusions

This analysis of the sources draws attention to the hitherto rarely noticed connection between, on the one hand, wills and other notes providing for the distribution of property after death and, on the other hand, marriage contracts – in particular as they related to dowers. If we assume that at least some of the wills and other legal documents for the disposition of property after death were made not because of reflection on and preparation for an impending and inevitable death, but rather right after marriage, metaphorically at the beginning of a new life, this changes the way we understand and perceive them. Perhaps last wills should be thought of not as originating in the abstract fear of death, but rather as part of the cycle of human life. This observation, of course, can be made only in reference to the surviving medieval wills from a specific time and place. Nevertheless, it is important because it helps us to avoid oversimplifying the character of wills in general and considerably enriches our understanding of these documents which are so important for historical research.

30. *Scabinalia Cracoviensia. Inscriptiones* (Archiwum Państwowe w Krakowie, ms. 5), 34.
31. Two years later, in 1423, Jan gave that property to his wife Agnes as her dower: *Consularia Cracoviensia. Inscriptiones* (Archiwum Państwowe w Krakowie, ms. 428), 197.
32. *Scabinalia Cracoviensia. Inscriptiones* (Archiwum Państwowe w Krakowie, ms. 5), 88.

Widows' Opportunities to Continue Craft Trade in Northern Baltic Cities during the 15ᵀᴴ and 16ᵀᴴ Centuries

Maija Ojala

1. Introduction

The household was the cornerstone of society in cities of the Northern Baltic Sea area during the late Middle Ages[1]. It formed the basic unit for craft production in which the work contributions of both husband and wife were needed for sustenance.[2] This ideal balance was disturbed when the husband died. For the community this created a problematic situation: should the ideal norm be restored by encouraging the widow to remarry, or should the community accept a different form of enterprise led by a single adult? The craft organizations of the cities took a stance on this matter in their ordinances by regulating the ways in which widows could continue in their trade.

This article studies the marital and survival strategies of widows in four late medieval cities, namely Lübeck, Riga, Tallinn and Stockholm, thus provides for the first time an extensive comparison of craft widows' status

---

1. The period covered by this study, 1400-1600, can be described as 'late medieval', 'early modern', or both, depending on how one chooses to define these terms. To simplify matters, I will use the term 'late medieval' to categorize the entire period under investigation.
2. M. Keniston McIntosh, *Working Women in English Society 1300-1600* (Cambridge: 2005), 4.

in the cities bordering the Baltic Sea.[3] I argue that the regulations in the craft ordinances relating to widows' status gave them various possibilities to carry on with their trade, and that therefore the regulations were not merely restrictions against female labour, as is often suggested in the literature, but must be seen as opportunities. I will first use quantitative methods to pinpoint how important the definition of the widows' rights and obligations within the crafts was. Thereafter I will analyze in detail the various possibilities open to craft widows, in order to get a clearer picture of the position they occupied within the craft after their husbands died. In addition, I will discuss the relationship between norm and practice – that is, whether the craft regulations were actually followed in everyday life. While inheritance, dower and such external factors as economic status also affected widows' ability to continue their trade, here the focus is on the regulations found in the craft ordinances.[4]

2. Sources and terminology

Artisans, craftsfolk, were organized in late medieval cities in such a way that usually those who practised one particular trade, such as shoemakers, formed one 'craft'. Each craft had its own rules (Middle Low German *schra*), which in research are usually called craft ordinances.[5] Each craft ordinance included dozens of different articles. The craft ordinances regulated above all the actual work of the artisan, but they also touched upon other aspects of life such as craft festivities and religious participation. They were intended to guarantee the monopoly of the trade to the craft members, to ensure equal privileges and obligations for the members and to assure the quality of the goods produced. Because the city council 'lent' the ordinance to the craft and confirmed or amended it periodically, craft ordinances served as a way for city governments to exercise control over craft production.[6]

3. For extensive comparison in German-speaking areas, see the pioneer work of P.-P. Krebs, *Die Stellung der Handwerkerswitwe in der Zunft vom Spätmittelalter bis zum 18. Jahrhundert* (Diss., Universität Regensburg: 1974).
4. For inheritance and women's legal status in general see, for example, B. Hanawalt, *The Wealth of Wives: Women, Law and Economy in Late Medieval London* (Oxford: 2007); M.C. Howell, *The Marriage Exchange* (Chicago: 1998); M. Korpiola, *Between Betrothal and Bedding: Marriage Formation in Sweden 1200-1600* (Leiden, Boston: 2009).
5. In this article the guild rules are called guild *statutes*, as distinct from craft *ordinances*. However, in research the term 'statutes' can refer both to guild and craft rules.
6. Tallinna Linnaarhiiv / Tallinn City Archives (hereafter TLA), coll. 190, inv. 2, no. 555, 1r (*Schmiede* 1459): 'Do vorleneden uns unse heren Borgemeister und Radtmanne to Reuell eyne schraa […]'. In this article the TLA documents are

It is important to clarify the nomenclature here, because in research the far more familiar term 'guild' is often used synonymously with 'craft' to refer to any merchants' or artisans' organization with specific economic, political, social and religious functions. As if this were not confusing enough, other terms such as 'confraternity' or 'brotherhood' can be used to designate different urban organizations. In this article the following tripartite classification is used: 1) The term 'guild' refers primarily to merchants' organizations, which often had a leading economic and political position in cities. The term additionally was used in Tallinn and Riga for two composite artisan guilds, St Canute's Guild and St Olaf's Guild, which united various smaller crafts. 2) The term 'craft' refers to an organization of artisans who practised the same trade and were united to ensure their privileges in a specific field of craft production. 3) Finally, the term 'devotional guild' is used for the religious organizations which were dedicated to their patron saint(s), their main function being religious participation and charitable work.[7] Generally guild statutes and the statutes of devotional guilds make no reference to women's rights to carry on with their trade after becoming widows. This underlines the differences between the various guilds and craft organizations, whose ordinances regulated above all daily work. Thus it validates the explicit distinction of the organization types. Furthermore, in devotional guilds men and women from different estates could be members, whereas in crafts and in merchants' and artisans' guilds the membership base was far narrower.[8]

This article focuses on crafts because it was precisely these organizations that defined the opportunities for a widow to carry on her professional activity after her husband had died. A wide-ranging study of widows' rights in the Baltic Sea area is possible because of the quantity of surviving craft ordinances. Altogether 152 ordinances survive from c. 1400-1600, the period chosen for this study:[9] 19 from Stockholm (1450-1604),[10] 34 from Tal-

---

numbered in accordance with A. Margus, *Katalog des Stadarchivs Tallinn, Archiv der St. Kanutigilde* (Tallinna: 1938).

7. In literature these organizations are mainly called 'brotherhoods' or 'confraternities'. However, drawing on the terms used in the original source material (*gild, gille*) they are referred to here as 'devotional guilds'.

8. A. Mänd, *Urban Carnival: Festive Culture in the Hanseatic Cities of Eastern Baltic, 1350-1550* (Turnhout: 2005), 29-31, 39-40; C. Anz, *Gilden im mittelalterlichen Skandinavien* (Göttingen: 1998), passim; A. Margus, *Katalog*, Einleitung. See also M. Escher-Aspner (ed.), *Mittelalterliche Bruderschaften in europäischen Städten/ Medieval Confraternities in European Towns* (Frankfurt a.M., New York: 2009).

9. Some craft ordinances have been preserved from before this period, and their number explode after 1600.

10. Stockholm craft ordinances are edited in *Skrå-ordningar*, ed. G. E. Klemming (Stockholm: 1856) and in *Småstycken på forn svenska*, ed. G. E. Klemming (Stockholm: 1868-1881).

linn (1394-1600),[11] 43 from Riga (1375-1619)[12] and 56 from Lübeck (1400-1599).[13] The majority of craftsfolk were members of the middle class, with citizen rights, but some belonged to the lower class. In Livonian cities craftsfolk were mainly German-speaking people, whereas in Stockholm they were Swedes and Germans. Whether the widows' rights applied to masters' widows only is unclear, but often this seems to have been the case. The craft ordinances are normative source material, which has to be taken into account. Nevertheless, they offer an insight to past everyday life in an urban milieu.

3. Widows' rights in the craft ordinances

Quantitative analysis makes evident that the crafts regarded it important to define the position of a widow within their organization. In late medieval towns widowhood and remarriages were common,[14] which partly explains the quantity of articles related to widows' rights in the ordinances. The following table shows that at least 30 percent of the craft ordinances in each city had an article related to widows' rights, rising to 44 percent in Tallinn.

These results fit well with the common perception that the nuclear family/household was the cornerstone of late medieval urban society. In the craft milieu, they indicate that the household was also the basic unit for craft production, and that both spouses worked in the family workshop to earn the family's living.[15] After the death of the business partner the question was whether the community should try to get back to the 'normal' and 'ideal' state of the nuclear family and encourage the surviving spouse to remarry, or should instead accept a different form of enterprise, a craft workshop led by a single adult instead of a married couple.[16] Because the

11. Tallinn craft ordinances are preserved in, TLA, in coll. 190 Archiv der St Kanutigilde, inv. 2 Handwerksämter and in coll. 230 Der Revaler Magistrat, inv. 1. Some craft ordinances are edited in *Beiträge zur Kunde Est-, Liv- und Kurlands*, ed. Estländische Literärische Gesellschaft. Some craft ordinances can be found edited in *Liv-, Est- und Kurländisches Urkundenbuch* (hereafter LECUB).
12. Riga craft ordinances are edited in *Schragen der Gilder und Ämter der Stadt Riga bis 1621*, ed. W. Stieda and C. Mettig (Riga: 1896).
13. Lübeck craft ordinances are edited in *Die älteren lübeckischen Zunftrollen*, ed. C. Wehrmann, (Lübeck: 1872).
14. Lager-Kromnow, *Att vara stockholmare på 1560-talet* (Stockholm: 1992), 85; Hanawalt, *The Wealth of Wives*, 96; C. Fairchilds, *Women in Early Modern Europe 1500-1700* (Harlow, New York: 2007), 105.
15. Fairchilds, *Women*, 149; Hanawalt, *The Wealth of Wives*, 70, 180.
16. Family ideal, the male as head of the household and subordinate status of wives, was promoted by moralists and the clergy. See for example L. Roper, *The Holy Household: Women and Morals in Reformation Augsburg* (Oxford: 1989), 17, 22, 31; R. M. Toivo, *Witchcraft and Gender in early Modern Society* (Aldershot: 2008), 10; S. Katajala-Peltomaa and R. M. Toivo, *Noitavaimo ja neitsytäiti: Nais-*

relevant articles in the craft ordinances have been seen from the point of view of the craft community, led by male masters, the articles related to widows' status have hitherto been interpreted by scholars as strengthening a patriarchal system and restricting female labour.[17] Nevertheless, as I argue, looking at the regulations in the craft ordinances from the point of view of the widows themselves leads to another interpretation, one which paints a brighter picture of their situation.

City	Number of extant ordinances	Ordinances with widows' rights article	Percentage of ordinances with widows' rights article
Lübeck	56	17	30 %
Riga	43	17	40 %
Tallinn	34	15	44 %
Stockholm	19	6	32 %

Table 1. Number of surviving ordinances c. 1400-1600 and share of widows' rights articles in numbers and percentage
(Note: In this table a widows' rights article in an ordinance has been counted as one unit
even though one such article might have several paragraphs and give a widow multiple
options. Sources: See footnotes 10-13)

The status of widows raised many questions.[18] Should the widow have the same rights and obligations as a craft member as male masters did? For example, were widows to be allowed to attend the craft assemblies? In most cases the ordinances do not mention whether women in general were allowed to participate in the crafts' official assemblies and in more unofficial celebrations. The common view of scholars is that women did not attend the official assembly but could participate in some festivities.[19] However, the

ten arki kesiajalta uudelle ajalle (Keuruu: 2009), 34-37; Hanawalt, *The Wealth of Wives*, 105.

17. M. S. Hartmann, *The Household and the Making of History* (Cambridge: 2004), 169; J. M. Bennett, *Ale, Beer and Brewsters in England: Women's Work in a Changing World, 1300-1600* (Oxford: 1996); M. E. Wiesner, *Working Women in Renaissance Germany* (New Brunswick, N.J.: 1986), 32-34. Cf. also Hanawalt, *The Wealth of Wives*, 180-83.

18. Margaret Pelling has highlighted the differences between female and male widow-hood, arguing that the status of widower did not pose any challenge to society's norms and customs because it did not alter a man's civic, legal or occupational status. See M. Pelling, 'Finding Widowers: Men without Women in English Towns before 1700', in S. Cavallo and L. Warner Harlow (eds.), *Widowhood in Medieval and Early Modern Europe* (New York: 1999), 37-54, at 42. See also Fairchilds, *Women*, 107.

19. A. Schmidt, 'Women and Guilds: Corporations and Female Labour Market Partici-pation in Early Modern Holland', *Gender and History* 1 (2009), 170-89, at 175;

situation was not so straightforward. The 1546 craft ordinance of the Riga masons clearly states that if a widow wanted to stay in the craft she was to pay two shillings as a membership fee, and if she wanted to participate in *druncke*, the craft's assembly, the payment would be three shillings.[20] The 1502 ordinance of the Stockholm carriers forbade any wife to represent her husband in the craft's assemblies,[21] which suggests that up until then women had been present at them. Thus it varied from town to town and from craft to craft whether women, that is wives or widows, were present at festivities and meetings.

Another important question was the widow's competence in dealing with journeymen and apprentices. Usually the training of apprentices and hiring of journeymen was permitted and, as far as the actual performance of the work was concerned, widows were seen as equal to male members.[22] Tallinn hemp weavers considered widows to be as capable of training young people in the profession as male masters, for example.[23] Nevertheless, some crafts were concerned about the fate of the workshops' personnel after a male master's death. The carriers in Stockholm ordained that the widow must keep the same workers until the next Michaelmas (29 September), which marked the start of the new working year.[24] It seems that in Riga some apprentices in the chamois leather tanners craft had left a widow's workshop, because an ordinance stipulated that young trainees had to stay with the widow if they wanted to continue in the same trade.[25] Some craft ordinances took widow's side against uncooperative apprentices. For example the masons in Stockholm decreed that the apprentices were to be obedient to the mistress of the house if her husband died.[26] A series of city books, called *tänkeböcker*, are preserved from Stockholm in which various legal acts of the city council are recorded. To my knowledge the *tänkeböcker* re-

---

Keniston McIntosh, *Working Women in English Society*, 38; Fairchilds, *Women*, 150; Hanawalt, *The Wealth of Wives*, 175.

20. *Schragen*, ed. Stieda and Mettig, no. 82, 429 (*Maurer* 1546): 'item so einer frowen ere meyster afftervet will desulvige in diesser cumpanye bliven, so sall geven 2 sch. Unnd so se mede in den druncken drinken will, sall se geven 3 sch. [...].'
21. *Skrå-ordningar*, ed. Klemming, 199 (*dragare* 1502).
22. Schmidt, '*Women and Guilds*', 175; S. Ogilvie, *A Bitter Living: Women, Markets and Social Capital in Early Modern Germany* (Oxford: 2006 [2003]), 232, 325-26.
23. TLA, coll. 190, inv. 2, no. 642, 5v (*hanfspinner* 1462).
24. *Skrå-ordningar*, ed. Klemming, 203 (*dragare* 1502). From late medieval London the evidence shows that apprentices and journeymen sued the widows for neglecting their training and selling the late husband's property (Hanawalt, *The Wealth of Wives*, 176). For widows as mistresses and female apprenticeship, see Keniston McIntosh, *Working Women in English Society*, 133-39.
25. *Schragen*, ed. Stieda and Mettig, no. 121, 651 (*Semischgerber* 1579). If this had been just a single episode or whether it had happened repeatedly is unclear.
26. *Skrå-ordningar*, ed. Klemming, 85 (*murare* 1487). Riga tailors ordained that the other masters were not allowed to appropriate the best, hardest-working journeyman from the widow's workshop. *Schragen*, ed. Stieda and Mettig, no. 98, 501 (*Schneider* 1500s).

cord no cases in which widows were sued for improper training. It is possible that if some disagreements came up they were not handled at the city level, but in the craft assemblies. Another possibility is that such problems did not come up. One could also claim that perhaps widows did not train apprentices and journeymen at all. Since death was a common visitor in the house, the later explanation is doubtful, however. It was likely that at some point the responsibility for training was left to a widow, at least for a time.

4. Survival strategies of widows

The craft ordinances offered five different possibilities for a widow to carry on with her trade after the husband's death. The following table illustrates the various possibilities mentioned in the craft ordinances and the number of cases in each of the four cities. In the first option the widow was allowed to continue a certain period of time, usually for one year, after which she usually had to either remarry or give up her trade. In the second option she could carry on by hiring a *knecht* (either a journeyman or a skilled male worker). The third option was to continue the trade with her children. The fourth was to carry on until she had finished working with the materials purchased before her husband's death. Finally, in some cases a widow was permitted to carry on her trade without any restrictions.

City	Time limit	With *Knecht*	With Children	Complete work with previously purchased materials	No Res-tric-tions
Lübeck	7	5	4	3	2
Riga	10	0	0	0	7
Tallinn	10	1	6	1	5
Stockholm	5	0	0	0	1

Table 2. Widow's opportunities to continue the craft trade and number of cases in craft ordinances
(Notes: In this table each different paragraph within a widows' rights article has been counted as one unit. Therefore the number of units, or cases, can exceed the total number of widows' rights articles mentioned in table 1. For example Tallinn hemp weavers gave a widow three different options in their widows' rights article, each of which has been counted as one unit in this table.[27] Sources: See footnotes 10-13)

In 7 of the 17 ordinances from Lübeck which had articles about widows' rights, a time limit was bestowed to the widow. In 5 cases the widow could

27.   TLA, coll. 190, inv. 2, no. 642, 5v (hanfspinner 1462).

carry on by hiring a *knecht*; and in 4 cases she could carry on with the children. In 3 cases she could carry on as long as she could continue production with already purchased materials, and in 2 cases she was allowed to carry on without any restrictions. Moreover, in Lübeck the same ordinance usually gave widows a choice of two or three different options. In table 2 every single option has been counted as one case.[28] Therefore the total number of Lübeck cases, 20, exceeds the number of ordinances with widows' rights article, 17, presented in table 1. For example the ordinance of the pursemakers stated that if a widow had children she could carry on with her profession as long as she wanted, but if there was no children then she was bound by the one-year limit.[29]

Tallinn, where one widows' rights article within one craft ordinance often gave the widow multiple options, had similarities with Lübeck. These similarities may be explained by the tight connections between these two cities. When established in 1248 Tallinn was granted the Lübeck city law, and the Lübeck craft ordinances also served as exemplars for the Tallinn ones.[30] Many Tallinn ordinances emphasized the importance of children: In 6 cases of a total of 15 the possibility of a widow to carry on her trade with her children was one option mentioned in widows' right article. But then again, in 10 cases a specific time limit was defined for a widow. In 5 cases a widow was allowed to continue the trade without any restrictions. Interesting is that both the Tallinn smiths and the locksmiths first gave a widow the option to carry on with children (and if childless the one-year limit would be applied), which the two crafts then later changed to the 'no restriction' option.[31]

In contrast to Lübeck and Tallinn in Riga there was only one option mentioned in each ordinance: either a widow had the one-year limit as stated in 10 ordinances, or she could carry on with no restrictions, as in 7 cases. The same approach was also taken in Stockholm, where 5 ordinances mentioned the one-year limit and in only a single case was the widow allowed to carry on with her trade without any restrictions. From these two

---

28. The different options mentioned in widows' rights articles could be written in ordinances as one entirety where the different options were mentioned within one paragraph or a widows' rights article might be divided into paragraphs each including one option. In both cases they are counted as one widows' right article (as in table 1) and each option has been counted as one case (as in table 2).
29. *Zunftrollen*, ed. Wehrmann, no. 9, 187 (Büdelmaker 1459). Both options are counted as individual cases in table 2.
30. E. Somelar, 'Circumstances of Criminality in Medieval Reval', in J. Kivimäe and J. Kreem (eds.), *Quotidianum Estonicum: Aspects of Daily Life in Medieval Estonia* (Krems: 1996) 80, 83.
31. TLA, coll. 190, inv. 2, no. 555, 5v, 6v (*smede* 1459-1528); no. 149, 8v, 9v (*schlosser* 1459-1549).

cities there is no mention of the other three possibilities, and multiple options are not mentioned either.

As the statistical analysis shows, the majority of ordinances allowed a widow to carry on her trade without any limitations for a certain period of time, at least for one year after her husband had died. Table Three demonstrates how dominant the timely limit was in terms of percentages.

City	Number of ordinances with widows' rights article	Time limit, number of cases	Percentage of the time limit cases from all cases
Lübeck	17	7	41 %
Riga	17	10	52 %
Tallinn	15	10	67 %
Stockholm	6	5	83 %

Table 3. The number and percentage of time limit cases in the craft ordinances
(Sources: See footnotes 10-13)

In previous research this option is often called one-year limit or one-year rule. However the one-year limit was not fixed and rigid, but could be modified in various ways. Therefore in the tables I use more descriptive term 'time limit'. For example the chest makers in Lübeck gave the widow two years to find a new husband.[32] In Tallinn coopers gave the widows three years' time to find a new partner.[33] The wheel makers in Lübeck ordained that the widow could ask additional time from the craft's aldermen if no suitable new husband had been found.[34] In Riga, goldsmiths' widows were allowed to negotiate with the craft's aldermen about the one-year limit.[35] The bakers in Stockholm put the widow on a one year and six weeks trial period: if she proved skilful and craftworthy, she could carry on the trade as long as she wanted.[36]

Quite often other additions were made to the widow's rules as well. A common addition was that if the new husband was from a different craft from that of her late husband, the widow would have to give up her old trade. It is very hard to say whether this rule was followed in real life. Presumably this was based on city councils' decrees which allowed artisans to

32. *Zunftrollen*, ed. Wehrmann, no. 26, 256 (*Kistenmaker* 1508).
33. TLA, coll. 190, inv. 2, no. 473, 7r (*Böttcher* 1515); no. 474, 105v (*Boddecker* 1556).
34. *Zunftrollen*, ed. Wehrmann, no. 45, 368 (*Rademaker* 1508).
35. *Schragen*, ed. Stieda and Mettig, no. 32, 302 (*Goldsmede* 1542).
36. *Skrå-ordingar*, ed. Klemming, 212 (*bagare* 1506).

practice only one trade.[37] A situation in which practitioners of two closely related but officially distinct trades married one another would be problematic, because then the different work stages could have been performed in the same workshop. This of course would lower the production costs and give the couple an advantage over the other producers. Apparently some disputes arose, since the regulation was written into the ordinances to address the issue.

According to craft ordinances from all four cities, a journeyman was often given benefits if he should marry a widow. The glaziers in Riga, for example, stipulated that if a journeyman married a master's widow or daughter he would be admitted to the craft after only two years instead of the normal three.[38] The benefit could also be a lower entrance fee.[39] Sometimes marrying a widow or master's daughter was the only way for a journeyman to become a master and a member of the craft.[40]

The craft ordinances also regulated the transfer of craft rights in remarriages. Often the widow could transfer the craft rights to her new husband. Especially if a widow remarried a master widower from the same craft they could enjoy the membership free, as they had done previously. In Stockholm the masons' and shoemakers' craft ordinances mentioned three husbands in the widows' rules. According to the shoemakers' ordinance, a widow's third husband had to meet the membership requirements if her second husband had not been from the shoemakers' craft.[41] In other words, if a widow first remarried outside the craft but then remarried a widower from the 'original' craft, the couple could not automatically enjoy the craft's membership.

5. Possibilities or restrictions?

Many scholars have argued that since the late sixteenth century demographic change, industrialization, accumulation of capital in fewer hands, the professionalization of crafts and strengthened patriarchalism led to the restrictions against female labour and, in some cases, even to the exclusion

---

37. *Stockholms stads tänkeböcker* (hereafter SST) *1474-1483, samt burspråk*, ed. E. Hildebrand (Stockholm: 1917), bursråk 1462 § 30 s. 445. See also G. Dahlbäck, *I medetidens Stockholm* (Stockholm: 1988), 180.
38. *Schragen*, ed. Stieda and Mettig, no. 24, 285 (*Glaser* 1541).
39. *Schragen*, ed. Stieda and Mettig, no. 45, 351 (*Hutmacher* 1595).
40. *Schragen*, ed. Stieda and Mettig, no. 98, 501 (*Schneider* 1500s).
41. *Skrå-ordningar*, ed. Klemming, 86 (*murare* 1847); 17 (*skomakare* 1474); In Stockholm three marriages seem to have been common during the late Middle Ages. See Lager-Kromnow, *Att vara stockholmare*, 85.

of women from crafts.[42] In the source corpus of this study most of the articles related to widows' rights appear into craft ordinances after the mid-fifteenth century, whereas only six cases can be found from previous decades. Furthermore the majority of articles relating to widows date from the sixteenth- century ordinances. Indeed, the time span during which articles related to widows appeared into craft ordinances cohere with the prevailing conception of scholars. Additionally within this framework, the late medieval widow's right to continue the trade has been interpreted as just a continuation of her husband's trade activities, aimed only at securing the widow's living and preserving the business for the children, and has been contrasted with the fourteenth century, when widows continued *their own trade*, the trade they had pursued as wives.[43] At first sight the craft ordinances from the Baltic Sea region seem to support this emphasis on saving the family business for the next generation. In 10 cases the widow had the right to carry on the trade with her children.[44] In 7 cases this possibility was combined with the one-year limit: if there were no children, then the one-year limit would be applied.[45] Here regional variations occur, since this possibility was mentioned only in the ordinances from Lübeck and Tallinn. The Lübeck ordinances also favoured sons, for in 3 cases it was explicitly mentioned that the widow was allowed to carry on the trade with her sons.[46]

However, a wider perspective must be taken. First, the temporal distribution of ordinances from each of the four cities is not equal. The source corpus from Riga includes a few ordinances from the very end of the fourteenth century, whereas from Stockholm no ordinances have survived prior to the 1450s. No long-range change over time can therefore be observed in the Stockholm material.[47] Second, it must be asked how the widows experi-

---

42. Keniston McIntosh, *Working Women in English Society*, 30, 40-41; M. E. Wiesner-Hanks, *Gender in History* (Malden, Mass.: 2001), 66-67; Bennett, *Ale, Beer and Brewsters*, passim; Ogilvie highlights the nature of craft organizations as closed social networks, which favored male members and tried to limit women's economic options. See Ogilvie, *A Bitter Living*, 258-63.

43. Bennett, *Ale, Beer and Brewsters*, 57.

44. Lübeck *Zunftrollen*, ed. Wehrmann, no. 6, 171 (*Bekermacher* 1591); no. 12, 201 (*Dreyer* 1507); no. 46, 372 (*Gürtler* 1414); no. 51, 403 (*Sadelmaker* 1502). Tallinn, TLA, coll. 190, inv. 2, no. 511, 5v (*Schroter* 1413-1650); no. 555, 5v (*Smede* 1459-1528); no. 642, 5v (*hanfspinner* 1462); no. 121, 4r (*Knochenhauer* 1509); no. 149, 7v (*Schlosser* 1459-1528); and LECUB, Abt. 1, Band 4, MCCCLXV, *Knochenhauer* 1394, cols 21-24.

45. Lübeck: cup-makers *(Bekermacher)* turners *(Dreyer)*, and girdlers *(Gürtler)*; Tallinn: tailors *(Schroter)*, smiths *(Smede)*, hemp-weavers *(Hanfspinner)* and locksmiths *(Schlosser)*. See preceding footnote for detailed references.

46. *Zunftrollen*, ed. Wehrmann, no. 6, 171 (*Beckermacher* 1591); no. 12, 200-01 (turners/*Dreyer* 1507); no. 46, 372 (girdlers/*Gürtler* 1414).

47. In contrast to Stockholm, surviving craft ordinances from Riga and Tallinn enable a temporal comparison. The preliminary findings from these cities suggest that no large scale change occurred in widow's right during fifteenth and sixteenth centuries.

enced this situation, a challenging task since the craft ordinances, among other normative sources, are frequently silent about individual experiences. The household-based craft production system needed the work contribution of both spouses to sustain it. Furthermore the married couple often formed a joint economy. Consequently it would be hard to imagine that the husband thought the business to be solely *his*; or that the widow would have thought herself as only a means to keep the household business going until the children would come of age. Besides, as family business strategy it would be only natural to try to ensure the continuation of trade activity to the next generations. Further in English towns widows were actually expected to continue the business, as recent studies point out.[48]

Third, as Danielle van den Heuvel convincingly argues, in some trades specialization and commercialization during the early modern period created new business opportunities for women.[49] Generalizations about a widow's right to carry on her trade must therefore be avoided. Because so much depended on the organization of the trade, on the craft itself and economic fluctuation the evaluation of articles related to widows' rights simply as 'good' or 'bad' is unfruitful.[50] Instead, when looking at the possibilities for widows to continue their trade we must take into consideration a system that was influenced by external factors such as current economic, political and demographic situation, varied from town to town and craft to craft and, as the additions to the craft ordinances illustrate, left room for negotiations.[51]

None of the craft ordinances in Stockholm, Tallinn, Riga or Lübeck explicitly forbade widows to carry on their profession. In approximately two-thirds of the ordinances, in fact, there is no mention of widows' rights at all. The craft ordinances' silence on this issue can be interpreted to mean that widows were not allowed to carry on with their work. On the other hand, the absence of references to widows in the craft ordinances could also be interpreted to mean that the crafts did not feel the need to restrict participation of these women in the trade.[52] This interpretation suggests that there may have been a change in policy over time: The widows' rights that began to appear in the craft ordinances from the mid-fifteenth century onwards in

48.   Keniston McIntosh, *Working Women in English Society*, 29.
49.   Van den Heuvel, 'Partners in Marriage and Business? Guilds and the Family Economy in the Dutch Republic', *Continuity and Change* 23 (2008), 217-36, at 219, 228, 231.
50.   Cf. van den Heuvel, 'Partners in Marriage', passim.
51.   Dutch scholars have emphasized the flexibility of the craft and guild system and underlined the geographical variations. See for example A. Schmidt, 'Women and Guilds', passim, and M. Prak et al. (eds.), *Craft Guilds in the Early Modern Low Countries: Work, Power and Representation* (Aldershot: 2006).
52.   G. Ingendahl, *Witwen in der Frühen Neuzeit: Eine kulturhistorische Studie* (Frankfurt a.M.: 2006), 152.

significant numbers can be seen as a means of restricting widows' work opportunities, whereas the prior absence of references to widows could indicate that there was greater toleration of their participation in an earlier era.[53] However, as I suggest here, the appearance of widow related articles into craft ordinances does not automatically mean they were solely restrictions to widows. Certainly when studying widows' rights the current economic situation must be taken into account in any event. During periods of economic growth it is quite possible that widows were allowed to run workshops. On the other hand, decline meant tightening competition, during which the craft organizations, led by men, would not necessarily sanction widows' activities as independent entrepreneurs.[54] Pestilence and wars could also have an effect; for instance, in London the remarriage rate increased after plague epidemics.[55]

Detailed analysis of a widow's options for carrying on with her trade clearly shows a range of possibilities. The craft ordinances also left room for negotiations and took notice of diverse circumstances. Yet it must be pointed out that while craft ordinances established official regulations for the trade, a widow's opportunities in real life depended to a great extent on her economic situation, including such things as her ability to obtain credit and manage property. The legal status of women rendered them less creditworthy than men. Poorer widows may not have had enough capital to pay the journeymen, apprentices and maids essential for household workshops. Although in general in towns the inheritance laws were favourable to widows, men often inherited more property.[56] These were the restrictions that real life imposed. Though to modern eyes the one-year limit may seem harsh, it must be interpreted within the context of its own era. Taking economic and population changes, war and pestilence into account, as well as the fact that the majority of townspeople married more than once in their lifetime,[57] remarriage appears to have been a good option, or even the best.

53. Wiesner, *Working Women in Renaissance Germany*, 157-59. See also Fairchilds, *Women*, 151.
54. In Stockholm the number of masters was limited in many crafts. See Lindström, *Skrå, stad och stat, Stockholm, Malmö och Bergen ca. 1350-1622* (Uppsala: 1991), 195. Cf. Keniston McIntosh, *Working Women in English Society*, 121.
55. Hanawalt, *The Wealth of Wives*, 107.
56. Keniston McIntosh, *Working Women in English Society*, 10-11, 37-38, and ch. 4 on credit ability; Bennett, *Ale, Beer and Brewsters*, 53-55; Wiesner, *Working Women in Renaissance Germany*, 158. For creditworthiness as social capital see also D. Lindström, 'Oärliga mästare och kivande makar: Ett och annat om rättskipning, kriminalitet och normsystem i 1500-talets Norden', *Svenskt Historisk Tidskrift* 124 (1994), 513-54, at 540.
57. Hartman, *The Household*, 66-67; Hanawalt, *The Wealth of Wives*, 96, 106-07.

6. Win-win-win situation

When set within the framework of late medieval urban market production, remarriage should be regarded as a win-win-win situation. From the widows' point of view, there are multiple reasons why remarriage would be a suitable option. For economic reasons, in fact, a remarriage must have been the best option. Remarriage increased economic security by providing new resources: economic capital such as rents, workshops, labour, cash, materials and tools, as well as social capital and social networks. A young, skilled journeyman who already knew the trade could also offer an attractive opportunity. If a widow had children, the need for a business companion might be considerable. Despite these advantages, it must be noted that marriage could also involve drawbacks such as domestic violence, conflicts with step-children and the loss of capital if business went badly. Some widows never remarried.[58]

From the point of view of the men, both widowers and journeymen, widows were often eligible marriage partners. A widow could provide the social and economic capital essential for a flourishing business, and besides her work contribution, she could offer an easy means of access to the craft.[59] In towns or trades where the number of masters was limited, marriage with a master's widow could be the only way to mastership.[60] The daughters and widows of Tallinn master goldsmiths tended to marry other master goldsmiths who also became crafts aldermen.[61] There is, for example, the case of Frau Ramborghe, who – to judge from references in a Tallinn city book (*Denkelbuch*) and other sources – seems to have climbed up the social ladder and acquired wealth by remarrying strategically. Of her first husband we know only his name, Hans Moller. Her second husband was Michel Swabbert, a master goldsmith, whose purchase of a house in 1486 is mentioned in a city book. Ten years later he was the craft's alderman. He later died, in 1503. The widow's third husband was also a master goldsmith, Lambert Hostkamp, who was the craft's alderman twice, first in 1514-1518 and then in 1529-1531. According to the city's *Denkelbuch* Lambert and Ramborghe

---

58. On potential negative sides of (re)marriage see, for example, Bennett, *Ale, Beer and Brewsters*, 39; E. Foyster, 'Marrying the Experienced Widow in Early Modern England: The Male Perspective', in Cavallo and Warner (eds.), *Widowhood*, 108-24, at 113; Fairchilds, *Women*, 109. Because of the lack of systematic source material such as censuses, remarriage rates and patterns are often hard to analyse in demographic terms. Cf. Pelling, 'Finding Widowers', 45.
59. Cf. Hanawalt, *The Wealth of Wives*, 96; Foyster, 'Marrying the Experienced Widow', passim. Widowers remarried more often and more quickly than their female counterparts: Fairchilds, *Women*, 105-06.
60. Lindström, *Skrå, stad och stat*, 195.
61. The tendency of craftsfolk to marry within the same craft, especially in case of widows' remarriages, predominated in London. Cf. Hanawalt, *The Wealth of Wives*, 114.

were married by 1509; and in 1524, Lambert bought the house of Michel Swabbert, his wife's late husband.[62] During the years of her widowhood, c. 1503-1509, Ramborghe seems to have managed the business and property well, because she was a suitable match for another master goldsmith as her third husband. On the other hand, it is also possible that what helped the new husband to become the alderman of the most prosperous craft in the city was precisely his marriage with Ramborghe. Wealth could also have some side-effects, as well-to-do widows might have experienced pressure from family and community to remarry.[63]

Finally, from the community's point of view remarriage was favourable. The maintaining of the household-based production system, with the nuclear family at its core, was preferred for several reasons. For one thing, it corresponded to the societal ideal set by moralists and the clergy.[64] Also, with a successful marital policy the craft would become a clan, or a network of closely related families who would protect each other's privileges. Keeping the widows and their assets within the same craft was a form of protectionism, because it would strengthen the craft's cartel and trade secrets would not leak out. Moreover, in times of tightened economic competition the number of masters would not increase if a master's widow married a journeyman, who would become a master.[65] This protectionism is in part visible in the additions made to widows' rights in the craft ordinances. In 5 cases, if the new husband was from a different craft the widow had to give up her trade.[66] In 4 cases, the ordinance clearly stipulated that the new husband was to be from the same craft.[67] The protectionism can be interpreted also as a form of mutual aid and old-age benefit, because crafts tried to protect widows from poverty.[68] In short, with remarriage the proper social order would be restored.[69]

62. A. Friedenthal, *Die Goldschmiede Revals* (Lübeck: 1931) 65, 67; TLA, coll. 230, inv. 1, no. Aa7, 95r (Denkelbuch); TLA, coll. 190, inv. 2, no. 76, 95 (Goldsmede Protocollbuch).
63. J. Kermode, *Medieval Merchants* (Cambridge: 1998), 90-91.
64. Fairchilds, *Women*, 109.
65. Hanawalt, *The Wealth of Wives*, 109; Wiesner, *Working Women in Renaissance Germany*, 161-62.
66. From Tallinn there are three cases: TLA, coll. 191, inv. 2, no. 24, 7r (*Shuster* 1481-1530); no. 555, 5v-6r (*Smede* 1459-1528); and no. 149, 8v (*Schlosser* 1459-1528); from Riga, one case: *Schragen*, ed. Stieda and Mettig, no. 39, 342 (*Gürtler* 1512); from Stockholm, one case: *Skrå-ordningar*, ed. Klemming, 87, (*murare* 1487).
67. From Riga, one case: *Schragen*, ed. Stieda and Mettig, no. 34, 311 (*Goldsmede* 1582); from Lübeck, one case: *Zunftrollen*, ed. Wehrmann, no. 51, 403 (*Sadelmaker* 1502); from Stockholm, two cases: *Skrå-ordningar*, ed. Klemming, 212 (*bagare* 1506) and 17 (*skomakare* 1474).
68. Ingendahl, *Witwen in der Frühen Neuzeit*, 160; Sandra Bos has pointed out that widows were not always able to use remarriage as a survival strategy in Dutch cities, where the surplus of women diminished their marital prospects. See S. Bos, 'A

7. Girdlers, saddle-makers and turners

Judging from the craft ordinances that regulated widows' rights in the Baltic Sea region, there was no strict sexual division of labour between male and female trades. One might assume that in the crafts which are traditionally perceived as women's professions, such as textile work and small retailing, widows would have been granted the right to carry on. Nevertheless, this was not the case in this area, and in fact many crafts that required a great deal of physical strength regulated the widows' rights. For example, the masons' craft in Stockholm gave masons' widows the one-year limit.[70] In Riga and Tallinn, a smith's widow was allowed to carry on for one year, with some additional terms.[71] One might of course speculate whether it was possible for a female to practice professions that were so physically demanding. However, as the examples reveal, the physical demands of the work were not the decisive factor for widows in whether to continue or not.[72] In Stockholm, the city council stipulated in January 1496 that carriers' widows be allowed to stay in their trade still for still one year, following the old tradition.[73] At least in this case women were able to manage the hard work.

The listing of various crafts that regulated widows' rights shows no general pattern whereby the same craft would have ordinances related to widows in all four cities. Only the shoemakers' craft took a stance on the widows' position across the board: in each city shoemakers' widows were bound by the one-year limit. Other crafts that regulated the position of widows included hucksters/stallholders, turners, wheel-makers, girdlers and cloth-dyers in Lübeck; painters, hat-makers, linen-weavers and carpenters in Riga; hemp-weavers, butchers and boatmen in Tallinn; and bakers, coppersmiths and carriers in Stockholm. The crafts that regulated widows' rights in two of the towns considered here were saddle-makers (Riga and Lübeck), coopers (Tallinn and Lübeck), tailors (Riga and Tallinn), locksmiths (Riga and Tallinn) and barbers (Stockholm and Riga). In three cities – Lübeck, Riga and Tallinn – the goldsmiths regulated widows' rights in their ordi-

---

Tradition of Giving and Receiving: Mutual Aid within the Guild System', in Prak et al. (eds.), *Craft Guilds in the Early Modern Low Countries*, 174-93, at 186-87.

69. Cf. Fairchilds, *Women*, 151.

70. *Skrå-ordningar*, ed. Klemming, 87 (*murare* 1487).

71. In Riga the widow was to hire a *knecht* for her help: *Schragen*, ed. Stieda and Mettig, no. 91, 476 (*Schmiede* 1587). In Tallinn the one-year limit was valid if the couple had had no children, whereas if there were children, there were no restrictions. Later it was added that widows could carry on without restrictions regardless of whether they had children. TLA, coll. 190, inv. 2, no. 555, 5v, 6v (*Smede* 1459-1528).

72. Cf. Ogilvie, *A Bitter Living*, 228-29, for the situation in early modern Germany.

73. SST 1492-1500 III, ed. J. A. Almquist (Stockholm: 1930), 267.

nances. The option was either the one-year limit as in Tallinn,[74] the one-year limit with additional terms and negotiation with the craft's aldermen as in Riga[75] or negotiation with the craft's aldermen about possible new marriage with the craft's *knecht* as in Lübeck.[76] This supports the argument that the possibilities for widows varied from craft to craft and from town to town. The question of whether we are dealing with a phenomenon that was specific to the Baltic Sea area requires more study, since scholars have different views about widows' rights in 'male' or 'female' professions.[77] Some scholars argue that widows were generally cut out of trades that were dirty or required physical strength,[78] whereas others assert that in most 'male' or 'heavy' trades, widows enjoyed the right to continue the business.[79]

8. Law and enforcement

The majority of the articles in the craft ordinances included as penalty a fine, which was to be paid either in money or in goods such as wax or beer. Were the penalties carried out, or were they just a dead letter? We have some strong evidence indicating that the penalties were indeed carried out. The Tallinn city archives contain the protocol book of the goldsmiths' craft, recording mainly financial matters that were handled in the craft's assemblies.[80] However, often only the payer and the sum were mentioned. The personal notebook of the same craft's alderman Hans Ryssenberg has also survived.[81] In various craft assemblies he noted down the financial matters of the craft: who was in debt to the craft, who paid money into the craft fund and who made donations to the craft's altar in the parish church. Probably some of the payments mentioned in the protocol book and in the notebook were penalties, which the members paid to the craft. Stockholm's city books, or *tänkeböcker*,[82] include many cases in which craftspeople were involved. Some of the cases relate to the same kinds of issues that were

74. TLA, coll. 190, inv. 2, no. 70, 1r (*goltsmede* 1453); TLA, coll. 230, inv. 1, no. Ac5 Schragen-Codex, 67v (*goldsmede* 1537).
75. *Schragen*, ed. Stieda and Mettig, no. 32, 302 (*Goldschmiede* 1542).
76. *Zunftrollen*, ed. Wehrmann, no. 16, 219 (*Goltsmede* 1492).
77. Cf. Lager-Kromnow, *Att vara stockholmare*, 81-82, where she lists burgher women's professions in sixteenth-century Stockholm; and the discussion in Fairchilds, *Women*, ch. 7.
78. Hanawalt, *The Wealth of Wives*, 175; Keniston McIntosh, *Working Women in English Society*, 40.
79. Ogilvie, *A Bitter Living*, 228-29; Bennett, *Ale, Beer and Brewsters*, 57.
80. TLA, coll. 190, inv. 2, no. 76 (Goldsmede Protocollbuch).
81. TLA, coll. 190, inv. 2, no. 82 (Denkelbuch des Amts ältermann Hans Ryssenberg 1518-1522).
82. Various legal acts of the city council, such as execution of wills and conviction of crimes were recorded into tänkeböcker.

regulated in the craft ordinances, such as serious insults against fellow members or the requirement to show evidence of one's honourable birth when claiming membership. In these cases the penalties correspond with the penalties written into the craft ordinances, and the fines which the city received are noted.[83] More research is needed to ascertain whether behaviour changed after paying a fine or if craftsfolk, having paid their fines, carried on just as before.

What about widows' rights then? In Stockholm's *tänkeböcker* there is only one case concerning the widow's right to carry on her trade after her husband had died. In January 1496, as we have seen, the city council stipulated that carriers' widows should be allowed to stay in their trade still for a year.[84] The exact same paragraph can be found in the carriers' ordinance.[85] The majority of cases in the city books involving artisan widows are those which concern property transactions. Quite often the widow handed over the property to her daughter and son-in-law. Some of the property transactions recorded in the city books are likely to have been purely commercial ventures which could have been related to the widows' trade.[86] This leads to the question of why no such civil cases were handled in the Stockholm city court. There could be several reasons. First, we might argue that there were no disputes about widows' rights. This argument is implausible, however, because the fact that the widows' rights were written into the ordinances suggests that there had been some grounds for dispute. Second, if there was no fine involved, the case might not necessarily have been written down in the city's book, because the city received no payment and therefore the case had no effect on the city's bookkeeping.[87] This argument might hold in some cases.

The main reason, however, lies in the diversity of medieval legal systems. In late medieval towns, various kinds of legal systems co-existed – not just the official city court led by the council but also, complementary to it, unofficial arbitration/settlement procedures and customary law.[88] It seems

83. SST 1578-1583 VI, ed. J. A. Almquist (Stockholm: 1945) 335-36, 526-27 (Hans Schwalbe och sämskmakare); cf. Lindström, 'Oärliga mästare', 536; Dahlbäck, *I medeltidens Stockholm*, 175, 180.

84. SST 1492-1500 III, ed. J. A. Almquist (Stockholm: 1930), 267: 'Samma dagh sades, tet dragere hustrvn bliffue j deris embete æn nw ith aar epter gambel plechsidh'.

85. *Skrå-ordningar*, ed. Klemming, 203 (*dragare* 1502).

86. SST 1483-1494 I-IV, ed. G. Carlsson (Stockholm: 1921): 8 November 1484, tailor's widow Katerina sold a stone house, 70; 14 March 1491, goldsmith's widow Cecilia conveyed a stone house to her daughter and son-in-law, 517. For London, see Hanawalt, *The Wealth of Wives*, 166-67; and Keniston McIntosh, *Working Women in English Society*, 126.

87. Lindström, 'Oärliga mästare', 530.

88. M. Taussi Sjöberg, *Rätten och Kvinnorna, från släktnakt till statsmakt I Sverige på 1500- och 1600-talen* (Stockholm: 1996), 38-42; Lindström, 'Oärliga mästare',

very likely that disputes about widows' rights were settled in the crafts' official assemblies, where smaller disputes between craft members were usually solved,[89] or in private. This kind of arbitration was cheaper, and the issue of avoiding publicity could also be a decisive factor.[90] Maybe the craft assembly was a better place to aim at compromise. Unfortunately, extant medieval source materials from craft assemblies are rare. However, at least one case concerning remarriage of a widow can be found in the protocol book of the Tallinn goldsmiths. In January 1542 the apprenticeship test of Christopher Feltstede was evaluated in the goldsmiths' assembly. He was accepted as master on condition that he would marry the widow of a master goldsmith, Peter Wardeheil.[91]

How often widows took advantage of the possibilities to which craft ordinances entitled them is hard to estimate. The Tallinn tax rolls include independent widows, who were liable to taxation and had male employees. The tax roll of 1375 lists 466 burgher households, of which 35 were households of independent widows. The tax rolls of 1527/38 list 468 burgher households, of which 32 were households of independent widows. The Munster-Rolle of 1688 list 541 households headed by males and 61 households of widows, who were active in the market economy.[92] By converting these numbers to percentages, it can be perceived that in both the fourteenth and sixteenth centuries widows made up only around 7 percent of the taxable citizen households, whereas in the seventeenth century their proportion had risen to 11 percent. This is significant, because it contradicts the argument that the possibilities for widows diminished during that century.[93] In addition, the Tallinn tax rolls do not list widows living on their own without male employees,[94] widows who could have participated in the market economy on a small scale. The pestilences only partly explain the number of independent widows.[95] Tallinn was spared from the war of 1656-1658, and

530, 550. For Tallinn legal practices see *Alte Criminalchronik Revals*, ed. E. von Nottbeck (Reval: 1884); and E. Somelar, 'Circumstances of Criminality'.

89. TLA, coll. 190, inv. 1, no. 76 (Goldsmede Protocollbuch).

90. In early modern Sweden, economic reasons were often the motive for private settlements: Taussi Sjöberg, *Rätten och kvinnorna*, 42-43; Cf. Hanawalt, *The Wealth of Wives*, 98-99; and Keniston McIntosh, *Working Women in English Society*, passim, for processes in medieval London.

91. TLA, coll. 190, inv. 2, no. 76, 113 (Goldsmede Protocollbuch).

92. H. Von zur Mühlen, 'Schosslisten der Stadt Reval 1396-1372', *Jahrbuch für Geschichte Mittel- und Ostdeutschlands* 48 (2002), 117-218, at 205-09.

93. Keniston McIntosh, *Working Women in English Society*, 30, 40-41; M. E. Wiesner-Hanks, *Gender in History* 66-67; Bennett, *Ale, Beer and Brewsters*, passim; Ogilvie, *A Bitter Living*, Introduction, 258-63. See also the discussion under the heading 'Possibilities or Restrictions?' in this article.

94. Von zur Mühlen, 'Schosslisten', 205.

95. P. Johanssen and H. von zur Mühlen, *Deutsch und Undeutsch im mittelalterlichen und frühneuzeitlichen Reval* (Köln and Wien: 1973), 275.

the years of famine did not take place until the 1690s,[96] hence external factors do not explain the large percentage of widows. For a fuller picture of how often widows continued in their trade, other kinds of source material must be added to the study. Wills, tax rolls and archaeological evidence, among other things, would enlarge our knowledge about widows' activities. Additionally, extant court records and property inventories could be used as sources.

10. Conclusions: various opportunities

The late medieval craft ordinances from the Baltic Sea region gave women several different possibilities, along with a number of variations and combinations, for continuing the family business after being widowed. Contrary to previous research, in which these widows' options have often been seen as restrictions, I have proposed another interpretation whereby the articles in the craft ordinances should also be regarded as possibilities. Also, craft ordinances left room for negotiations. They were not static but flexible, and adjustments were made to correspond to the current situation. In addition, the opportunities for widows varied from craft to craft and town to town. The one-year limit, after which time the widow was expected to have remarried, was the most common widows' right mentioned in the ordinances. This indicates that the crafts compelled widows to remarry. Yet in the framework of urban market production, remarriage must have been the best option from both the individual's and the community's point of view, and there were rational arguments to support it. Because the craft ordinances are normative source material, the question arises of how closely they were adhered to in real life. The evidence, especially from Stockholm, suggests that only few disputes about widows' rights were handled at the city level. However, more archival research is needed to get a fuller and clearer picture.

The study of emotional aspects of remarriage would enhance the study of late Middle Ages: In this case it could bring new insights to everyday life in urban settlements and into the choices people made. Additionally, new empirical studies would enrich our knowledge about how often widows used the opportunities extended to them in craft ordinances. As Sheilagh Ogilvie has pointed out, individual decisions of how to allocate one's time were of utmost importance in the shift from household production to the industrial world.[97] As this study reveals, although some local variation in the widows' opportunities did exist, in general craft ordinances were rather similar. Preliminary geographical comparison suggests that widows' rights

96.   S. Zetterberg, *Viron historia* (Helsinki: 2007), 180, 188, 214.
97.   Ogilvie, *A Bitter Living*, passim.

in late medieval and early modern craft ordinances may have been quite consistent, not only in the Baltic Sea region but Europe-wide. More research is required to confirm these findings.

COMPETING FOR DOWER IN THE ENGLISH THIRTEENTH-CENTURY ROYAL COURTS

Paul Brand

1. Introduction

In Michaelmas term 1297 one Alice, claiming to be the widow of Simon Constable, brought an action of dower in the Common Bench, the main royal court for the hearing of civil litigation at Westminster. She asserted her right to a third share of a considerable property holding at West Halsham in Holderness in the East Riding of Yorkshire. The tenant of this land and defendant to this action was a woman whom Alice's writ named as Katherine, the daughter of Philip of Weelsby.[1] In a previous term Katherine, in response to the same claim, had stated that she held the property for her life by the grant of Robert, the son of the same Simon Constable, and had vouched him to warranty. He now appeared and asked Katherine to show whatever evidence she might possess to prove that he was indeed obliged to warrant the 'manor' of West Halsham. Katherine produced an indented deed. This was enrolled, virtually in full, in the record. The deed had been made at Everley in the North Riding of Yorkshire at the feast of St Margaret the Virgin (20 July) in 1294. At the time it was made, as it shows, Katherine had herself also been claiming to be the widow of Simon Constable (evidently this same Simon) and had been claiming her own dower share of his land. The writing also indicates that Robert was not just Simon's son but

---

1. The National Archives [of the United Kingdom], Kew, London (hereafter TNA), CP 40/118, m. 66. The holding consisted of thirty messuages, three hundred acres of arable, eighty acres of meadow, sixty acres of moor and ten pounds of rent with appurtenances.

also his heir. Under the terms of this agreement Katherine had quitclaimed all right to dower in what had been Simon's lands (whether held by Robert or by others) in return for a life interest in the manor of West Halsham,[2] and a rent of 100s payable by the priory of Sixhills in Lincolnshire. Robert had promised to warrant this holding, and Katherine had reserved a right of action to claim her dower if she was ever impleaded for the manor and lost it for lack of Robert's warranty or was otherwise impeded in its enjoyment. Robert's initial response was to impugn the voucher on the grounds that Katherine had claimed a life estate in court when vouching him but that the writing supposed she had dower. A year later, however (in Michaelmas term 1298), the court held that he was indeed obliged to warrant his grant. Robert then tried to plead his only other possible response: that at the time Simon had married Alice he already possessed a wife named Katherine, who had been Simon's wife for ten years by then. The court, however, probably prompted by Alice's own lawyers, noted that the bishop of Norwich had previously certified in separate litigation that Alice had been joined to Simon in lawful matrimony and that Robert had also previously surrendered to Alice her dower in respect of other lands, and thus the exception did not lie. It adjudged that Alice recover her dower. Because of the warranty Robert had previously been held to owe Katherine, the court decided that Robert should provide lands of an equivalent value to the dower claimed from other lands still in his possession. Only if he did not have enough lands should any of the land come from the lands in Katherine's possession which Alice had been claiming.[3]

The suit brought by Alice directly against Robert had been pleaded one year earlier, in Michaelmas term 1296. It had been a claim to one third of further extensive holdings in fourteen other places in Holderness.[4] Robert

---

2. The manor also included lands in East Halsham, Otteringham and Keyingham.

3. A report of the pleading in this case (which manages to confuse the names of the parties) helps us to understand in detail the pleading of the parties' lawyers. It is to be found in British Library, London (hereafter BL), MS. Hargrave 375, fols 42v–43v.

4. TNA, PRO, CP 40/115, m. 40. The claim was to one third of seventeen messuages, three hundred acres of arable, fifty acres of meadow, sixty acres of woodland, twenty acres of marsh, ten acres of turbary and a rent of ten pounds in Burton Constable; of twenty messuages, two hundred acres of arable, twenty acres of meadow, ten acres of turbary and a rent of one hundred shillings in Newton Constable; of eighteen messuages, one hundred acres of arable, ten acres of meadow, and a rent of forty shillings in Marton; of twenty acres of arable in Sproatley; of a rent of sixty shillings in Paull Fleet; of ten messuages, sixty acres of arable and a rent of forty shillings in Paull; of a rent of twenty shillings in Paull Holme; of one messuage in East Halsham; of a rent of forty shillings in Keyingham; of six messuages and a rent of 40 shillings in Tharlesthorp (in Patrington, but now in the Humber); of one messuage and one bovate in Waxholme; of one messuage and one bovate in Tunstall; of one messuage, forty acres of arable and one thousand acres of turbary in 'Morhamwyk'; and of one messuage in Ravenser.

had also denied here that Alice had ever been joined to Simon in lawful matrimony and Alice had asserted that she had been married to Simon at East Winch in Norfolk (close to King's Lynn) within the diocese of Norwich. The bishop of Norwich had therefore been instructed by the court to make enquiries and to report back the following Hilary term (of 1297). However, before the bishop of Norwich had made any certification in regard to the alleged marriage Robert had agreed to surrender almost all the dower Alice had claimed.[5]

The episcopal certification of Alice's marriage had been given in a third suit, also pleaded, like the first case, in Michaelmas term 1297. It had been brought by Alice against Katherine daughter of Philip of Weelsby and against Alan son of John Hagheman and his wife Radegund and was for a dower third of a less substantial holding at Tharlesthorp, again in Holderness.[6] Katherine had denied holding any of the land, but Alan and Radegund (evidently under age) had answered as sole tenants through their guardian, probably a guardian *ad litem*. They said that Alice was not entitled to her dower, since she had never been joined to Simon in lawful marriage. Alice again asserted that she had married Simon at East Winch, and so instructions were given to the bishop of Norwich to make enquiries. The bishop reported back two weeks after Trinity Sunday in 1298 that Alice had indeed been lawfully married to Simon. After a further delay the court awarded Alice the dower she had been claiming in Michaelmas term 1298.

Simon Constable, the late husband of these two widows, is an interesting figure from what was evidently a well-established Yorkshire gentry family. Almost certainly he can be identified with the man of the same name who had been a member of the group of royal justices commissioned to hear assizes in the northern counties of England between 1285 and 1290.[7] He had died not long before 1 March 1294. Since he was a tenant in chief an inquisition post mortem was held into his holdings. These were the Yorkshire lands mentioned in the dower litigation and the rent owed by Sixhills priory in Lincolnshire, plus a house in the city of Lincoln.[8] From other evidence it is known that he had died in possession of quite valuable chattels: those in

5. The land he surrendered was now given in aggregate as one third of seventy-six messuages, two bovates, seven hundred and twenty acres of arable, eighty acres of meadow, sixty acres of woodland, twenty acres of marsh, one thousand and twenty acres of turbary and twenty seven pounds of rent in the same villages: TNA, PRO, CP 40/116, m. 72.

6. TNA, PRO, CP 40/118, m. 93. The claim was to one third of ten messuages, one hundred and sixty acres of arable, twenty acres of meadow, forty acres of pasture and a rent of forty shillings.

7. *Calendar of Close Rolls, 1279-1288*, 365. He had been replaced shortly before 2 June 1290: TNA, PRO, C 66/109, m. 28d.

8. *Calendar of Inquisitions Post Mortem*, iii, no. 193. Their seizure was ordered on 1 March and their release to Robert as his son and heir on 23 April 1294: *Calendar of Fine Rolls, 1272-1307*, 336, 337.

Yorkshire were worth over £366 and those in Lincolnshire over £74. There were also chattels in Nottinghamshire worth £29 and chattels of unknown value in Norfolk.[9] His had not, however, been a quiet or an easy death. In the 1293-1294 Yorkshire eyre he had been indicted of a number of serious criminal offences: procuring the poisoning of his first wife Joan by a servant named Beatrice de Vere; stealing twelve oxen from the prioress of Swine (in Holderness); stealing two horses from one John of Danthorpe; and abducting John's wife Katherine and John's goods against John's wishes.[10] As will be seen, this Katherine can be identified with Simon's own future wife of that name. The indictment seems to have been made by the Holderness jury during November 1293. Simon refused to put himself on the verdict of a jury when accused of these crimes and so (under the provisions of the Statute of Westminster I [1275], c. 12) had been adjudged to a 'strong and hard imprisonment' (*prisone forte et dure*) to induce him to change his mind, and his chattels had been declared forfeit.[11] He had died, apparently in prison, during the course of the eyre and probably from the harsh imprisonment. The fact that he had not been convicted, however, preserved his lands for his son Robert and the dower for his two widows.

Katherine, as has been seen, was the sole heiress of her father Philip of Weelsby, who died in 1286, her two sisters having already died by then.[12] During his lifetime her father had granted her by final concord at the 1282 Lincolnshire eyre a substantial holding at Weelsby and five other places in Lincolnshire, probably by way of pre-mortem transfer of the major part of her inheritance.[13] In 1275 her future husband Simon Constable had confessed to committing 'sins of the flesh' with her while she was still married to John of Danthorpe knight and had been made to abjure her company and to agree a penalty of £100 if he reoffended. This was to be spent on a pilgrimage to the Holy Land by Simon or to pay the expenses of sending a suitable knight in his place.[14] Her first husband was dead by 1280, when the dean of Holderness was ordered to have Katherine, the widow of John of

9.   TNA, PRO, JUST 1/1098, part II, m. 80d.
10. TNA, PRO, JUST 1/1098, part II, m. 80d.
11. *Statutes of the Realm*, I, 29. On the background to this chapter see H.R.T. Summerson, 'The Early Development of the Peine Forte et Dure', in E. W. Ives and A. H. Manchester (eds.), *Law, Litigants and the Legal Profession* (London: 1983), 116-25.
12. TNA, PRO, JUST 1/578, m. 44d
13. It consisted of a mill, two carucates of arable and a rent of fifty-four shillings and two pence and a pound of cumin in Weelsby, Little Cotes, 'Sutholm', Thorpe, Bradley and Hale: TNA, PRO, JUST 1/1085, m. 48. A note had been made preparatory to the levying of the fine but no fine been issued.
14. *The register of Walter Giffard, Lord Archbishop of York, 1266-1279 / Diocese of York*, ed. W. Brown. Publications of the Surtees Society 109 (Durham: 1904), 282.

Danthorpe, and Simon Constable excommunicated for their contumacy.[15] Although an eyre was being held in Yorkshire between 1279 and 1281 there was no attempt, it seems, at this time to accuse Simon of abducting Katherine against John of Danthorpe's will, although this must have taken place prior to 1280,[16] nor any suggestion then been made that John of Danthorpe's death had been anything other than natural. By the time of the 1293-1294 Yorkshire eyre, however, it was to be alleged, as has been seen, that Simon had abducted Katherine and that she had arranged the poisoning of her first husband John as well as of Simon's first wife Joan (something in which Simon was also said to be implicated); and in June 1294 she was pardoned for these deaths as well as for the death of one Henry of Thorley.[17] Simon married Katherine after John's death. This was sometime between Hilary term 1282, when she alone levied a final concord with her father,[18] and June 1282, when the archbishop of York, who had doubts about the marriage contracted between Simon and Katherine and had therefore called them to court, pronounced the marriage 'just' after canonical proof had been provided.[19] So the Church (in the person of the local ordinary, the archbishop of York) had concluded in 1282 that Simon and Katherine were lawfully married to each other, presumably through a marriage contracted in the archbishop's own diocese.

Of Katherine's rival as Simon's widow, Alice, less is known. It seems likely that she came from Norfolk since that was where Simon married her. What is certainly known is that sometime prior to her second marriage to the erstwhile Common Bench serjeant and (by then) royal justice William Howard, also a Norfolk man, around 1300 she had been granted a sizeable holding of land at Beechamwell in Norfolk by Nicholas of Cressingham.[20] He was probably a relative and perhaps her father, and this was perhaps also

15. *The register of William Wickwane, Lord Archbishop of York, 1279-1285 / Diocese of York*, ed. W. Brown. Publications of the Surtees Society 114 (Durham: 1907), 93-94. Katherine was also presented during the 1279-1281 Yorkshire eyre by the jury of the wapentake of Holderness as John's widow whose marriage was in the king's gift and whose land was worth ten marks: TNA, PRO, JUST 1/1070, m. 46.

16. Simon and Katherine were, however, at this time among those appealed by Richer of Arnold of the death of his son John: TNA, PRO, JUST 1/1070, m. 46d. The appeal was subsequently disowned by Richer and both of them acquitted at the king's suit.

17. TNA, PRO, JUST 1/1098, part II, m. 95; *Calendar of Patent Rolls, 1292-1301*, 76.

18. Above, n. 13.

19. *The register of William Wickwane*, 282-3.

20. It was in 1300 that lands in East Winch and Middleton were settled jointly on them, though she is not then specifically identified as Howard's wife: TNA, PRO, CP 25/1/161/118, no. 802. By 1305 William Howard and Alice his wife were suing for her dower share of a moiety of a messuage in the suburb of Lincoln and the tenant said he held a life estate by the grant of Robert, the son and heir of Simon Constable: TNA, PRO, CP 40/155, m. 78.

prior to her first marriage.[21] If what Robert said in the 1297 litigation was true, her marriage to Simon had taken place ten years after Simon's marriage to Katherine, and thus perhaps as recently as 1292.

This suggests that it was still possible in later thirteenth-century England for a fairly prominent member of the gentry in northern England to go through at least a form of formal marriage with two women at an interval of no more than about ten years, despite the fact that the second wife was still alive at the time of marriage to the third. There is nothing in our evidence to suggest that the second marriage had been annulled. We know that it had been specifically affirmed by the archbishop of York shortly after it was made, and it is difficult to believe that Simon's son Robert, who in 1294 was said to be aged either 29 and more or 24 and more,[22] and who must therefore have been the son of Simon's first wife Joan, would not have known of its annulment and so would not have mentioned it when impleaded by Katherine for dower in 1294. We can only speculate about how, and why, Simon's two marriages happened and were possible. Simon Constable must have known what he was doing and can hardly have thought it legal or permissible. He must have thought he could get away with it. Neither of the wives need to have known about it until after Simon's death. The second marriage probably took place in Yorkshire and the third in Norfolk, and the distance between them may simply have meant that news of the third did not reach Katherine in Yorkshire and that Alice knew nothing of Katherine. There is no evidence to suggest that Katherine had initiated any process to undo the third marriage prior to Simon's death. What the litigation also shows is that it might pay a son and heir (especially the son and heir of a putatively murdered first wife) to be very careful before making any kind of settlement with a woman claiming to be his father's widow and seeking dower. It was the terms of Katherine's settlement which allowed her to retain the substantial holding she had been allocated in satisfaction of her claim to dower, but not specifically as dower, while Alice also succeeded in enforcing her own separate claim to dower from the same husband. The court did not save Robert from his folly. He therefore found himself providing dower for both his father's wives.

2. Obtaining the dower

Simon Constable was by no means the only English thirteenth-century landowner to die leaving two competing widows with claims to dower from

---

21. *Year Books 3&4 Edward II (1309-1311)*, ed. F. W. Maitland and G. J. Turner. Publications of the Selden Society 22 (London: 1907), 14-15.
22. *Calendar of Inquisitions Post Mortem*, iii, no. 193.

his lands. There are at least ten other such instances in the surviving official records and unofficial reports of the period, and there are probably more to be discovered. Those which have been found are, however, unevenly distributed over time. Four out of these ten instances occurred during the 1220s. In 1221 two women both claimed dower as widows of William of Dowdeswell;[23] in 1222 there was litigation between two women claiming dower as widows of Robert of Acton;[24] in 1223 the records show two women both claiming to be entitled to dower as widows of John fitzHugh;[25] in 1226 two women both asserted their dower rights in the lands of Thomas of Fulston.[26] In the second quarter of the century two women claimed dower as widows of William son of Walkelin of Passenham, one in 1239-1240 and the other c. 1250.[27] There are two further instances from the 1250s. In 1250 Robert Foliot had two competing widows both seeking dower;[28] in 1254 John Cordeboef.[29] John de Arundel had two competing widows claiming dower in litigation with each other in 1260.[30] Two further instances come from the early 1270s. In 1271 there were two women claiming dower as widows of Richard fitzWymer;[31] in 1272 two women claiming dower as widows of Ranulph le Poer.[32] The only instance known from the reign of Edward I (1272-1307) is the case of Simon Constable's two rival widows, though there is also one so far unidentified early fourteenth-century case between two women both claiming to be widows of Henry Conan, known only from a report that belongs to the chief justiceship of Ralph Hengham. This may belong to any date between 1301 and 1309.[33]

It is only the Simon Constable case which shows two women, two widows, managing, in effect, to ensure that they both obtained dower from

23. *Rolls of the Justices in Eyre: being the rolls of pleas and assizes for Gloucestershire, Warwickshire and Shropshire, 1221, 1222*, ed. D. M. Stenton. Publications of the Selden Society 59 (London: 1940), no. 267.
24. *Bracton's Note Book: A Collection of Cases decided in the King's Courts during the reign of Henry III*, ed. F. W. Maitland, 3 vols (Cambridge: 1887), pl. 1564 (and cited in *Bracton: On the Laws and Customs of England*, ed. G. E. Woodbine and trans. and revised by S. E. Thorne, 4 vols (London: 1968-1977), iii, 383-84).
25. *Curia Regis Rolls*, xi, no. 54 [= *Bracton's Note Book*, pl. 1573].
26. *Curia Regis Rolls*, xii, no. 1835 [= *Bracton's Note Book*, pl. 1703].
27. For references to the initial successful claim by one widow see *Curia Regis Rolls*, xvi, no. 934; TNA, PRO, JUST 1/614B, m. 21. There seems to be no record of the claim by the second widow, but there are references to it in the *Summa Parva* of Hengham (*Radulphi de Hengham Summae*, ed. W. H. Dunham, Jr. [Cambridge: 1932], 57) and in *Casus Placitorum* (*Casus Placitorum and Reports of Cases in the King's Courts, 1272-1278*, ed. W. H. Dunham, Jr., Publications of the Selden Society 69 [London: 1952], 43-44).
28. *Curia Regis Rolls*, xix, no. 2224; *Curia Regis Rolls*, xx, no. 1516.
29. TNA, PRO, KB 26/152, m. 4d.
30. TNA, PRO, KB 26/169, m. 59d.
31. TNA, PRO, KB 26/202, m. 33.
32. TNA, PRO, KB 26/208A, m. 20d.
33. Cambridge University Library, MS. Ee.6.18, fols 88v-89r.

the same husband's heir. Indeed, in a number of these cases third parties (apparently the husband's heir(s) or their guardians) specifically asked the court for judgment when facing a claim for dower as to whether they were, or could be, obliged to provide dower for two wives or widows.[34] In the case of the competing widows of Simon Constable one widow, Katherine, was evidently quicker off the mark than her rival Alice. Katherine had initiated her dower claim against Simon's son Robert in the same year that Simon died (1294) and had also settled it that same year; Alice, however, did not bring her litigation until 1296 and 1297. This is not an uncommon phenomenon. In a majority of cases one widow had already obtained her dower by the time the second began her action for dower. In at least three instances it is not clear how much earlier this had happened or how the first widow had obtained her dower. This is true, for example, of Isabel, the widow of Robert of Acton, against whom a second widow, Agnes, brought her action of dower in 1222;[35] of Isabel de Curton, who had already obtained her dower as widow of Thomas of Fulston before a second widow, Juliana, made claim against the heirs of Thomas in 1226;[36] and of Katherine Esturmy, who was already in possession of dower as widow of John Cordeboef when Galiena was suing for her dower as his widow in 1254 in the court of King's Bench.[37] In two instances dower is known to have been assigned to the first widow by the king as guardian of the husband's heir. In Hilary term 1223 Gunnora de Bendenges claimed dower as widow of John fitzHugh. The tenant (Peter fitzHerbert), who was the grantee of the king's wardship rights over John's infant heir Geoffrey, said that Maud de Berners had already obtained her dower from the same land by the king's order.[38] That assignment can only have been relatively recent. John fitzHugh's death while on Crusade was known in England by early March 1222, when orders were given by the king for the seizure of his lands, and the assignment of dower to Gunnora must have taken place shortly thereafter.[39] In May 1245 the sheriff of Devon was instructed to assign dower to Christine, the widow of Robert Foliot, from Robert's lands that were in the king's hands. It was not until 1250 that she and her second husband, John de Seccheville, and Ralph de Gorges, the guardian of Robert's lands and heir, faced a claim to dower from a second woman claiming to be Robert's widow, named

---

34. This objection was made by an heir's guardian in 1223 in *Curia Regis Rolls*, xi, no. 54 [= *Bracton's Note Book,* pl. 1573]; apparently by the husband's heirs in 1226 in *Curia Regis Rolls*, xii, no. 1835 [= *Bracton's Note Book*, pl. 1703]; again apparently by the husband's heir in 1254 in TNA, PRO, KB 26/152, m. 4d.
35. *Bracton's Note Book*, pl. 1564 (and *Bracton*, iii, 383-84).
36. *Curia Regis Rolls*, xii, no. 1835 [= *Bracton's Note Book*, pl. 1703].
37. TNA, PRO, KB 26/152, m. 4d.
38. *Curia Regis Rolls*, xi, no. 54 [= *Bracton's Note Book*, pl. 1573].
39. *Bracton's Note Book*, pl. 1120; *Fine Rolls, 6 Henry III*, no. 125.

Emma.[40] In a further case the first widow to obtain her dower did so through litigation. In 1239 Albreda (of Bassingbourn) claimed a share of the North-amptonshire manor of Passenham as the dower of which William son of Walkelin of Passenham had endowed her against the guardian of William's heir; and she eventually recovered it by a judgment in the 1239-1240 North-amptonshire eyre.[41] Ten years later or more Alice de Vernay also came and claimed her dower from the same land as the widow of the same man.[42]

Only in a minority of these instances did the two competing widows bring their dower litigation at the same time. In 1221 Clemence, the widow of William of Dowdeswell, was seeking her dower against John of Dowd-eswell. John said that he was not obliged to answer her since Maud, who also claimed to be William's widow, had brought a prior writ claiming dower against him and the case had been adjourned to a later eyre.[43] When in 1260 Clarice, claiming to be the widow of John de Arundel, brought a writ of dower against tenants who vouched two women and their husbands (probably as the heiresses of John), they said that Isabel was also impleading them in the same court for her nominated dower from the same husband.[44] Alice the widow of Richard fitzWymer claimed a dower third of a fairly substantial holding against master John of Ashby in 1271, but he was also facing at the same time a parallel claim from a second woman named Avice, who also called herself Richard's widow. The two women were then left to plead against each other.[45] In a fourth case heard the following year Joan, claiming to be the widow of Ranulph le Poer, asserted her entitlement to a dower third of various holdings against four different tenants, and there was also a rival claim to the same holdings from a second alleged widow, Albreda (Aubrey). Here too the court decided that the two widows should plead against each other.[46]

40. *Close Rolls, 1242-1247*, p. 307; *Curia Regis Rolls*, xix, no. 2224; *Curia Regis Rolls*, xx, no. 1516.
41. *Curia Regis Rolls*, xvi, no. 934; TNA, PRO, JUST 1/614B, m. 21.
42. No record of this litigation seems to survive, but for references to it in legal litera-ture see above, n. 27. Alice's son by William brought mort d'ancestor in the 1247 Northamptonshire eyre against Albreda for the land she had recovered and against Henry Mauveisin for what looks like the non-dower share of the same inheritance. The answers of both reveal that as yet Alice had made no claim: TNA, PRO, JUST 1/614B, m. 21. By 1252 Alice was bringing litigation against William in respect of lands at Passenham: *Close Rolls, 1251-1253*, 192.
43. *Rolls of the Justices in Eyre*, no. 267.
44. TNA, PRO, KB 26/169, m. 59d.
45. TNA, PRO, KB 26/202, m. 33. The competing claims were to a third of a mes-suage and half a carucate.
46. TNA, PRO, KB 26/208A, m. 20d.

3. Settling cases on dower

How then were these cases between rival widows determined? The last two cases (of 1271 and 1272), which are exceptional because they show two rival widows pleading directly against each other in court before either had obtained her dower, stand out as exceptional also in that they are cases where the question of entitlement was put to a lay jury. In the 1271 case Alice asserted that she had been married to Richard 'in the face of the church' and had long been with him as his wife, and that he had died seised of her as his wife. Avice, however, denied that Richard had ever married Alice 'in the face of the church'. She asserted that he had married her and had remained with her, and that their marriage never been annulled. Initially the court decided to entrust the decision as to which was the rightful widow to the archbishop of York (the local diocesan), but almost at once (and without any recorded explanation) this was changed to an enquiry by a jury. No outcome is recorded.[47] In the 1272 case Joan asserted that Ranulph had been 'seised' of her at his death and had been with her continuously for seventeen years before his death; Albreda that he had been 'seised' of her at the time of his death. This too was sent to a jury, evidently to be decided on the basis of which of them had been in Ranulph's seisin as his wife at the time of his death. Subsequently, however, Albreda quitclaimed all right in the dower, apparently admitting defeat.[48] These are not the only cases where one or both of the claimants or a third party asserted a widow's entitlement as resting at least in part on her husband's 'seisin' of her during his lifetime and at the time of his death, for something similar was also asserted in at least five other cases between 1222 and 1254.[49] In none of these other cases, however, was this claim to possession of the husband, or assertion of the husband's possession of the wife, in the end decisive.

The normal way of settling such cases was through a determination by the relevant ecclesiastical authorities. In some instances, this was a prior determination which had been made during the husband's own lifetime. In the 1250 case involving the two competing widows of Robert Foliot one widow, Emma, was suing the guardian of Robert's heir and lands, Ralph de Gorges, for her dower. Ralph objected that R.[50] bishop of Exeter had previously given sentence against Emma in a matrimonial cause by papal authority. He was told to bring the bishop's letters attesting that sentence, though

---

47. TNA, PRO, KB 26/202, m. 33.
48. TNA, PRO, KB 26/208A, m. 20d.
49. *Bracton's Note Book*, pl. 1564 (and cited by *Bracton*, iii, 383-84); *Curia Regis Rolls*, xi, no, 54 [= *Bracton's Note Book*, pl. 1573]; *Curia Regis Rolls*, xii, no. 1835 [= *Bracton's Note Book*, pl. 1703]; *Curia Regis Rolls*, xix, no. 2224 and *Curia Regis Rolls*, xx, no. 1516; TNA, PRO, KB 26/152, m. 4d.
50. This must be Richard Blund, who was bishop of Exeter from 1245 onwards.

there is no evidence that he did.[51] The following Michaelmas term Emma brought suit against both Ralph and the rival widow Christine and her second husband, John de Secchevile. Emma said that Robert had initially been married to her but had then abandoned her to marry Christine. She said that she had impleaded him before the archdeacon of Barnstaple and had obtained a sentence in her favour, presumably one affirming her marriage to John. When he had refused to accept her back as his wife she had secured his excommunication, and he had then died excommunicate. Christine denied that Robert had ever been married to Emma. Emma was told to produce proof of her marriage, presumably letters testimonial from the archdeacon, for the following Hilary term. There, however, the trail of evidence ends.[52] In the 1254 Suffolk case brought by Galiena as widow of John Cordeboef against John's heir Thomas and the rival widow, Katherine Esturmy, Katherine admitted that Galiena had once been married to John but asserted that the marriage had been annulled before the bishop of Norwich for consanguinity. John had then married Katherine and had held her as his wife the whole of his life. Galiena said that she and John had been married for fifteen years, but the bishop had then wrongfully annulled the marriage for consanguinity. She had appealed to the provincial, the archbishop of Canterbury. His official had examined the case and quashed the annulment and then sent letters to the bishop telling him of the sentence and mandating him to compel John to cohabit with Galiena and treat her 'with marital affection'. Although Katherine could say that her late husband had launched an appeal to the Holy See and had obtained a commission to the bishop of Ely to re-examine the matter prior to his death, she could not deny that the most recent sentence had been in Galiena's favour. The court adjudged that Galiena was to recover her dower against Thomas and he was then to recover the dower Katherine had wrongly been given.[53]

In rather more cases, even if prior activity in the church courts during the husband's lifetime is sometimes mentioned, it was a post-mortem determination that was apparently decisive, or intended to be so. The first of these cases is the 1222 case where Agnes, who was claiming to be the widow of Robert of Acton, sued the rival widow Isabel for her dower share of land at Acton in Middlesex. Isabel conceded that Agnes had indeed once been married to Robert, but asserted that she had been separated from Robert for consanguinity by an ecclesiastical judgment at St Paul's in London and that on Agnes's own initiative. Robert had then, she alleged, ceremonially married Isabel in London without any contradiction by Agnes. Agnes denied there had been any such decision by a church court. She

51. *Curia Regis Rolls*, xix, no. 2224.
52. *Curia Regis Rolls*, xx, no. 1516.
53. TNA, PRO, KB 26/152, m. 4d.

agreed that she had been living apart from her husband for the previous seven years at Winchester but asserted that this had been by her husband's wishes. The bishop of London was instructed to make enquiries.[54] There is, however, no record of the outcome.

The second is the Michaelmas term 1223 case where Gunnora de Bendenges, one of the two rival widows of John fitzHugh, claimed her dower against Maud de Berners. Maud asserted that John had been her husband and that any association her husband may have had with Gunnora had been adulterous. The court decided that Gunnora should have a writ of enquiry to the bishop of Winchester, in whose diocese she claimed to have contracted the marriage.[55] Later that same term Gunnora produced letters patent from the bishop attesting that she had been joined to John in lawful matrimony and so recovered her dower.[56] Matters did not rest there, however. Both widows had produced children by John. The wardship of Geoffrey fitzJohn, his heir by Maud, and of his lands had been granted to Peter fitzHerbert in the name of the infant king Henry III in April 1222 in return for a payment of 40 marks.[57] Despite Gunnora's recovery Geoffrey's body remained in the king's wardship and the king's grantee in possession of some, but probably not all, of his father's lands.[58] When Geoffrey came of age, probably in 1234, he took possession of those lands. It was not until 1234-1235 that Gunnora's daughter Juliana and her husband Adam fitz-Hervey were able to sue Geoffrey in King's Bench for her father's lands in both Norfolk and Berkshire. This was on the basis of the prior certification by the bishop of Winchester of the validity of Gunnora's marriage to her father and the consequent illegitimacy of Geoffrey.[59] Later still, in 1236-1237, Geoffrey brought mort d'ancestor, claiming to be the son and heir of John, against Gunnora in King's Bench, asserting his right as John's heir to the dower she had recovered in Berkshire. She objected that her daughter Juliana was John's heir. Geoffrey answered that he was the son of John's

---

54. *Bracton's Note Book*, pl. 1564; *Bracton*, iii, 383-84.
55. *Bracton*, iii, 382-83.
56. *Curia Regis Rolls*, xi, no. 1037 [= *Bracton's Note Book*, pl. 1649] and for an earlier stage see no. 713.
57. *Fine Rolls 6 Henry III*, no. 154. The heir is unnamed in this grant, but only Geoffrey was under age.
58. In May 1224 Adam fitzHervey, the husband of Juliana, made fine with the king in 100 shillings for relief for one knight's fee in Tidmarsh, held in chief: *Fine Rolls 8 Henry III*, no. 190. In November 1224 they were granted the Norfolk manor of Ormesby St Margaret in fee farm which John fitzHugh had held by the bail of king John for sixteen pounds a year: *Fine Rolls 9 Henry III*, no. 20; and in July 1227 Adam made fine in thirty marks for a confirmation of the manor to himself and Juliana and her heirs. But in July 1233 this manor was committed to an unrelated third party instead: *Fine Rolls 17 Henry III*, no. 260. In February 1234 Geoffrey, the rival heir, secured it for a proffer of only ten marks: *Fine Rolls 18 Henry III*, no. 161.
59. *Curia Regis Rolls*, xv, nos 1267, 1369 [= *Bracton's Note Book*, pl. 1120].

lawful wife, and that any plea between his mother and Gunnora should not prejudice him as he had then been below age. Eventually it was adjudged before the king (at Marwell) that any decision about Gunnora's entitlement to dower should be postponed until a definitive decision had been made about which of the two competing heirs was John fitzHugh's rightful heir.[60] The rivals seem subsequently to have reached a settlement in the court of King's Bench early in 1239 which divided the inheritance equally between them.[61] Evidently any initial decision as to which of the two widows was entitled to dower was without prejudice to any subsequent decision on which of the two heirs by the two competing wives was entitled to succeed to their father's inheritance.

In both of these cases the earliest surviving evidence reveals at once the existence of two competing widows. This was not so in the third of these cases. In 1239 Albreda of Bassingbourn claimed her dower share of the Northamptonshire manor of Passenham as widow of William son of Walkelin of Passenham. William de Ferrers, earl of Derby, the guardian of William's heir, objected that she had never been lawfully married to William and so was not entitled to dower, but the bishop of Lincoln subsequently certified she had been married. She recovered dower by judgment in the 1239-1240 Northamptonshire eyre.[62] There is no mention here of any second widow. The first we hear of her is in 1247 when William's son by a second woman, Alice de Vernay, another William, brought mort d'ancestor against Albreda for one-third of a knight's fee in Passenham and against Henry Mauveisin for two-thirds of it. Albreda objected that she had recovered her third in the presence of his mother and she had proved she was William's wife, and so was not obliged to answer. Henry likewise objected that since William had been born of another woman after Albreda's marriage he must be illegitimate. Eventually in 1249 William was non-suited against Albreda.[63] It was only some time after 1249 that Alice de Vernay brought suit for her dower against Albreda. Albreda seems to have objected that Alice had never been lawfully married to William, but a second reference to court Christian produced the certification that Alice was indeed the

---

60. *Bracton's Note Book*, pl. 1176.
61. There is what seems to be a draft of their agreement in TNA, PRO, CP 25/1/282/6, no. 73. (noted in *King's Bench and Common Bench in the Reign of Henry III* , ed C. A. F. Meekings and D. Crook. Publications of the Selden Society, Supplementary Series, 17 [London: 2010], 29 and n. 23). The eventual agreement made between them was probably a revised version of this, for a case heard in the 1248 Berkshire eyre suggests that the two rival heirs divided the inheritance between them, as the draft had envisaged: *Roll and Writ File of the Berkshire Eyre of 1248*, ed. M. T. Clanchy. Publications of the Selden Society 90 (London: 1973), no. 372 (and see nos 360, 376).
62. *Curia Regis Rolls*, xvi, no. 934; TNA, PRO, JUST 1/614B, m. 21.
63. TNA, PRO, JUST 1/614B, m. 21; *Curia Regis Rolls*, xix, no. 1049.

lawful wife and that the bishop had been deceived in his prior certification.[64] Presumably this then led to an unscrambling of the original assignment of dower to Albreda.

In the fourth of these cases, heard in 1260, Clarice was suing third parties for her dower as widow of John de Arundel. Their warrantors, who were probably the heiresses of John de Arundel, alleged that John's marriage to Clarice had been annulled during his lifetime before the dean and chapter of Wells in Wells cathedral when Philip d'Aubeny had come and claimed Clarice as his own wife; and John had then subsequently married Isabel. Clarice denied that any of this had happened, and the case went to the bishop of Bath and Wells to make enquiry. In Easter term 1261 he reported back that he had found by knights and other creditworthy persons that Clarice had indeed married John 'in the face of the church' and he had then cohabited with her for eighteen years and that their marriage had never been annulled. Clarice duly recovered her dower.[65]

4. Two wives, two widows

These cases suggest some possible answers to the question of how it was possible for a husband to find himself married to two different women and to leave two competing widows, despite the absence of divorce in the modern sense in thirteenth-century England. Sometimes it seems likely that the second 'wife' was the victim of deceit on the part of her 'husband', that she was an unwitting victim of what we would now call a bigamist. One probable example is provided by the 1260 case where Clarice and Isabel made competing claims to be the lawful widow of John de Arundel. It was John's heirs who told what sounded a convincing story of the annulment of John's first marriage to Clarice in Wells cathedral before the dean and chapter for precontract, although the bishop of Wells subsequently found that there had never been any such annulment. This sounds like the story that John had told to Isabel and others and that Isabel and others had believed, which however was untrue. Another example is provided by the 1222 case where Agnes and Isabel both claimed to be widows of Robert of Acton. In this case Isabel conceded that Agnes had once been married to Robert but asserted that Agnes had been separated from Robert for consanguinity by an ecclesiastical decision at St Paul's in London on Agnes's own initiative; and that Robert had then married Isabel in London. Isabel said she had subse-

64. No record of this litigation seems to survive, but there are references to it in the *Summa Parva* of Hengham (p. 57) and in *Casus Placitorum* (pp. 43-44). By 1252 Alice was bringing litigation against William in respect of lands at Passenham: *Close Rolls, 1251-1253*, 192.
65. TNA, PRO, KB 26/169, m. 59d.

quently lived with him for seven and a half years and he had died at Acton with her as his wife. Agnes denied there had been any such decision by a church court but agreed that she had been living apart from Robert for the previous seven years at Winchester. This had been by her husband's wishes, although he was living at Acton. The most likely explanation is that Robert had lied to Isabel, claiming to have been the victim of an annulment procured by his first wife, sending that first wife away to live in Winchester and then going through a form of marriage with Isabel, with whom he co-habited for the seven years before his death. Simon Constable's marriage to Alice may also fit into this category.

Other sets of rival widows seem to have been the product of the complicated and lengthy appeal structure of the church in matrimonial causes. Take the two widows of John Cordeboef in the 1254 case. Galiena had been John's first wife, but their marriage had been annulled by the bishop for alleged consanguinity after fifteen years of marriage. It had only been after this that John had married Katherine. Only Galiena's successful appeal to the archbishop of Canterbury had invalidated this second marriage and only John's death before a further appeal could be heard left him married to Galiena and not to the wife with whom he had been cohabiting until the time of his death. Something similar may also have happened in the case of the two widows of Robert Foliot in 1250. It also happened in one final unidentified but early fourteenth-century case heard before chief justice Hengham in the Common Bench, in which Margaret and Elizabeth both claimed to have been the widows of Henry Conan.[66] An account of the facts of this case gives the circumstances. Henry had initially married Margaret under the age of seven, when he was unable to give valid consent. Once he came of age he dissented and sued an annulment before Oliver bishop of Lincoln and obtained one. Margaret had then sued an appeal to the Court of Arches. In the meantime Henry had married Elizabeth and fathered a son and heir. The annulment was quashed as erroneous before the Court of Arches. Henry had appealed to Rome but had died while the appeal was pending. It was easy for a man who thought his marriage had been annulled to enter into a second marriage, only to find himself once more married to his first wife.

5. Conclusion

When a male landowner died in thirteenth-century England, there was normally only a single widow to claim her dower share of the lands which had been held by her husband at the time of their marriage or had been acquired

---

66. Cambridge University Library, MS. Ee.6.18, fols 88v-89r.

since then. This is, indeed, what we would expect. Canon law did not allow a man (or a woman) to be married to more than one partner at a time, and secular law, too, expected that marriage would be monogamous. A second marriage was normally possible only if the first partner had died or if the first marriage had been formally annulled by the judgment of a competent ecclesiastical court. Yet what should not have happened clearly did happen. In the period between 1220 and 1311 there were at least eleven instances where the king's courts were faced with the problem of competing widows, two women both claiming to have been validly married to the same deceased husband and asserting their right to a dower share of his landed property.

In only one of these cases (the quite exceptional case of the two widows of Simon Constable) did both rival widows in effect manage to secure their dower from their husband's heir, and then only because of the inadvisable wording of the out of court agreement by which the heir had given one of the widows property in lieu of dower. In all the other cases the clear assumption is, as might have been expected, that only one of the 'widows' could be entitled to dower. In a minority of cases (two), both heard in the early 1270s, the courts decided that the decision as to which of them was entitled was to be based on a jury verdict, perhaps in both cases on the basis of the position at the time of the husband's death. In the remainder the courts followed their more general policy of deferring to the church courts in questions of marriage.

In two of these cases the courts sought guidance from sentences given in the church courts during the husband's lifetime. In the 1250 case of the rival widows of Robert Foliot no final determination is recorded, but initially the defendants were given the opportunity to produce written evidence of the annulment of Emma's marriage to Robert and then (when they failed to do so) Emma given the opportunity of producing written evidence of the sentence she alleged had been given in her favour upholding her marriage before the archdeacon of Barnstaple. In the second case, involving the two rival widows of John Cordeboef, heard in 1254, it seems to have been questioning by the court and pleading by the parties, without any recorded production of the relevant documents, that established that, even if John's marriage to Galiena had been initially annulled for consanguinity and this had been followed by his marriage to Katherine, Galiena had subsequently succeeded in having the annulment reversed on appeal. Katherine had then to admit that, although John had taken steps to reverse this second sentence through obtaining the appointment of a papal judge delegate this had not led to a further judgment in his lifetime. So judgment was given in Galiena's favour.

In four cases the courts asked the relevant bishop to enquire into the matter and report back. In the first of these cases (in 1222) the two rival widows of Robert of Acton could not agree as to whether Robert's marriage to his first wife Agnes had been annulled for consanguinity at her suit, and the bishop of London was asked to enquire. In the second (in 1223), where Gunnora de Bendenges was suing for her dower (but a second wife Maud de Berners had already been assigned dower on the king's behalf), the bishop of Winchester was instructed to enquire whether or not she had been joined to John fitzHugh in lawful marriage. He reported back that she had been, and she recovered her dower. In the third of the cases (where proceedings started in 1239), involving two rival widows of William son of Walkelin of Passenham, the guardian of William's heir initially objected that Albreda of Bassingbourne had never been lawfully married to William but the bishop of Lincoln certified that she had been. The same bishop, however, ten years or so later found that Alice de Vernay had actually been William's lawful wife and that he had been deceived in his first certification. In the fourth case (in 1260), in which Clarice claimed her dower as widow of John de Arundel, the defendants claimed that their marriage had been voided in earlier proceedings when a third party had claimed Clarice as his wife, and that John had then married Isabel. Clarice denied this and the bishop of Bath and Wells then certified that it was indeed not the case.

In only a minority of these cases does it look as though one of the 'wives' was the victim of her husband's deception, that he may have consciously, deliberately and recklessly been engaging in what we would now describe as 'bigamy'. This seems likely to be the case with the second marriage of Robert of Acton (in the 1222 case) and John de Arundel (in the 1260 case) and probably in the 1296 case of Simon Constable. In rather more cases it looks as though the second marriages were entered into in good faith by husbands whose first marriages had been annulled, before that annulment was in turn overturned on appeal. This seems to be the case with the second marriages of John Cordeboef and Robert Foliot that we hear about in the 1250s and in the early fourteenth-century case of Henry Conan. In the other cases we have too little to know for sure.

'Bigamy' ought not to have been possible in thirteenth-century England, but it certainly happened, and probably in rather more instances than the research done for this paper has uncovered. This paper has, in general, dealt only with the consequences of such bigamy in creating two claimants to dower and the need to decide which of two rival widows was entitled to it. In one instance at least (that of the two wives of John fitzHugh) we have also noted the problems this might also raise for inheritance and seen how the decision as to which was the rightful widow did not also automatically determine who was the rightful heir. There are also instances in the thirteenth and early fourteenth century of the reverse case of 'bigamy', of women with two living husbands, but they deserve to be the subject of a separate paper.

DOS NON TENEAT LOCUM LEGITTIME: DOWRY AS A WOMAN'S INHERITANCE IN EARLY QUATTROCENTO FLORENCE

Thomas Kuehn

1. Introduction

In the cities and towns of central and northern Italy in the Middle Ages, dowered women were commonly excluded by local law and custom from the inheritances left by their fathers, brothers, and sons. To take the example of Florence – both as a leading city and as the site of the case we will examine – the statute redacted in 1415 governing intestate succession stipulated with regard to daughters that

> no woman, nor even any man born of the female line, can succeed on intestacy to her father, grandfather, or great grandfather, or other paternal male ascendant, if there is alive any male child born of the deceased person whose inheritance is in question, or any grandsons or great grandsons from a son or sons, or other male descendants in said line, or a full brother or nephew from a full brother, or father or paternal grandfather. Yet such women excluded from succession in any of the aforesaid instances, if they have not been dowered, can and should be conveniently and competently dowered from the goods of the father, grandfather, or whatever other ascendant whose succession is being dealt with, according to the condition and faculty of the father, grandfather, or great grandfather and other ascendants.[1]

1. *Statuta communis Florentiae anno salutis mccccxv*, 3 vols. (Freiburg [Florence]: 1778-1783), vol. 1, 224 (Book 2, rubric 129): 'Et nulla mulier, nec etiam natus ex linea feminina, possit patri, avo, vel proavo suo, vel alteri ascendenti masculo paterno ab intestato succedere, existente aliquo filio masculo nato ex defuncta persona, de cuius hereditate agitur, vel aliquibus nepotibus vel pronepotibus ex filio, vel filiis, vel aliis descendentibus masculis ex dicta linea, vel fratri carnali, seu

A dowered woman could seek no more at her father's death on intestacy and, if he died testate and left her something more, she had to remain content with that and not pursue what legally would have fallen to her by her rights in Roman law. By and large this Florentine statute was unexceptional. It was in line with those of many other communities.[2] It was part of a general tendency in local law and customs that Cardinal de Luca in 1684 would claim was 'universal'.[3]

The legal origins of these statutes have been broadly examined.[4] Awareness of these rules now forms part of the elementary understanding of the social history (including family and gender) of Italian communities in the Middle Ages and Renaissance. The problem for historians is determining the significance and consequences of the statutory exclusion of dowered women from inheritance (the *exclusio propter dotem*). Above all, was dowry simply their share of the inheritance (delivered ante mortem and probably not equivalent to shares left to male heirs)? This paper will demonstrate that in legal theory and forensic practice reliant on that body of theory dowry was not equated with a legitimate inheritance share for a woman, no matter the undeniable economic effect of such statutes. This was not simply an empty theoretical categorization, but a legal distinction that could have important practical consequences, just some of which can be appreciated from study of a single case. And more generally, consideration of dowry in the context of inheritance alerts us to the fact that in dowry the 'costs of marriage' did not all accrue at the time of marriage or necessarily in material form.

nepote ex fratre carnali, vel patre, vel avo paterno. Possint tamen, et debeant tales mulieres excluse a successione in quolibet casu predictorum, si non fuerint dotate, convenienter et competenter dotari de bonis patris, avi, seu cuiuslibet alterius ascendentis, de cuius successione tractatur, secundum conditionem, et facultatem patris, avi, vel proavi, et aliorum ascendentium'. The language was much the same in earlier versions. See T. Kuehn, *Law, Family, and Women: Toward a Legal Anthropology of Renaissance Italy* (Chicago: 1991), 238-57.

2. F. Niccolai, *La formazione del diritto successorio negli statuti comunali del territorio lombardo-tosco* (Milan: 1940), 65-108, provides a still useful survey of the language of the statutes of numerous localities. See also A. Romano, *Famiglia, successioni e patrimonio familiare nell'Italia medievale e moderna* (Turin: 1994); T. Kuehn, 'Person and Gender in the Laws', in . J. A. Brown and R. C. Davis (eds.), *Gender and Society in Renaissance Italy* (New York: 1998), 87-106.

3. Cf. G. Pomata, 'Family and Gender', in J.A. Marino (ed.), *Early Modern Italy, 1550-1796* (Oxford and New York: 2002), 69-86.

4. For now, see M. Bellomo, *Ricerche sui rapporti patrimoniali tra coniugi: Contributo alla storia della famiglia medievale* (Milan: 1961); L. Mayali, *Droit savant et coutumes: L'exclusion des filles dotées xiième-xvème siècles*, Ius Commune, Sonderhefte: Studien zur Europäischen Rechtsgeschichte 33 (Frankfurt a.M.: 1987); also M. T. Guerra Medici, *I diritti delle donne nella società altomedievale* (Milan: 1986).

2. Exclusion from inheritance

Statutory exclusions of dowered women were consequent on the combination of Lombard customs of marriage and marital property transfers and those of Roman law, which became resurgent in the course of the eleventh and twelfth centuries.[5] Against a daughter's right in late Roman law to succeed her father equally with her brothers (as represented in the *Corpus iuris civilis*),[6] the statutes of numerous places generally eliminated dowered women from inheritance from men (as opposed to women). At the same time, in adopting the Roman law system of dowry (goods from a wife's family handed to her husband at marriage), in preference to the Lombard *morgengabe* (an endowment upon the wife from her husband, supposedly on the morning after the nuptials), the statutes excluding women from paternal inheritance seemed to have substituted dowries for their Roman law inheritance claims, while also eliminating the Lombard *quarta* that the *morgengabe* supposedly contained.[7]

This impression is confirmed when one examines jurisprudence and finds discussion of the rule that a girl's dowry be *congruens* with the value of her father's holdings. This was not only an academic rule devised on the texts of Roman law; it was a rule stated in some of the statutes otherwise excluding dowered daughters from inheritance.[8] The Florentine statute used the terms *convenienter* and *competenter* to much the same effect, adding the qualifier 'secundum dignitatem et facultatem patris'.[9] *Congruitas*, however, was never precise in the law or in practice. It remained nebulous in relation to the value of the entire patrimony from which a dowry was carved out. The reigning impression among historians, as we will see, is that by and large women's dowries were not on a par with the inheritance shares that fell to their brothers. Such a disparity makes sense in the presence of statutes otherwise excluding dowered women from inheritance. In that connection there seems to be a real advantaging of the claims of male heirs.

There is consequently a broad tendency among scholars to equate dowry, however much diminished, with inheritance for a woman. At the

---

5. This is not the place to rehearse a large literature on a topic peripheral to the one treated here. For an interesting recent investigation that also looks more closely at litigation than at legal instruction, see C. Wickham, *Legge, pratiche e conflitti: Tribunali e risoluzione delle dispute nella Toscana del xii secolo* (Rome: 2000).
6. Generally on Roman succession law, see M. Kaser, *Roman Private Law*, trans. R. Dannenbring (Durban: 1968 – 2nd edn), 278-328.
7. Bellomo, *Ricerche*, 1-18.
8. Here, in addition to Niccolai, *Formazione*, see M. Bellomo, 'Dote (diritto intermedio)', *Enciclopedia del diritto* 14 (Milan: 1965), 8-32.
9. *Statuta*, vol. 1, 224. This language was consistent in Florence and can be found in the earlier statutes: *Statuti della repubblica fiorentina*, ed. R. Caggese, 2 vols., vol. 2: *Statuto del podestà dell'anno 1325* (Florence: 1921; rpr. Florence: 1999), 128.

beginning of his intensive study of Florentine marriage alliances, as one example, Anthony Molho states that 'dowry established rules on the intergenerational transmission of property to a family's female offspring, in the form of antemortem transmission'.[10] Molho recognizes that dowry was only one mechanism that could convey property to both genders of the younger generation, and his interest is in matrimonial alliances of families more than in dowry per se. Still, his perspective is in line with that of others who have been equally disposed to see dowry as female inheritance. Stanley Chojnacki, for example, has examined gender relations in Venetian families and utilized in his research 'the principle that a girl's dowry represented her share of the patrimony'.[11] And it has to be conceded that there was a legal basis to this linkage of dowry and inheritance. 'The words *dos* and *dote* were used in legal documents and opinions as a synonym for a woman's patrimony'.[12]

Dowry functioned as an important tool of social alliance in cities such as Florence and Venice. Molho's important book notably employs the term in its title, as does that of Lorenzo Fabbri. John Padgett and Paul McLean have argued that such alliances became increasingly important for the Florentine patriciate following the Ciompi Revolt of 1378 and its aftermath. Part of that importance can be tracked in an evident inflation of dowry values in Florence, as dowry also served as start-up capital for the diversifying interlocking partnerships that also became vital to the elite.[13] So there was genuine upward social pressure on dowry values that can lead one to wonder it they were not indeed *congruens* at least some of the time.

Having established alliances, moreover, dowry then took on a household economic function. As it was said in law, dowry was destined to cover the 'burdens of married life' (*onera matrimonii*). Gregory Hanlon, in a study of early modern Tuscan society from an anthropological or sociological perspective, thus terms dowry an 'adaptive mechanism making it possible for parents to transfer wealth to their daughters at the time of their peak fertility' to ensure survival of offspring. In this light, though the exact proportion of an estate represented by a dowry can only remain unknown, he

---

10. A. Molho, *Marriage Alliance in Late Medieval Florence* (Cambridge, MA: 1994), 12.

11. S. Chojnacki, *Women and Men in Renaissance Venice: Twelve Essays on Patrician Society* (Baltimore: 2000), 137.

12. J. Kirshner, *Pursuing Honor While Avoiding Sin: The 'monte delle doti' of Florence* (Milan: 1978), 4.

13. J. F. Padgett and P. D. McLean, 'Organizational Invention and Elite Transformation: The Birth of Partnership Systems in Renaissance Florence', *American Journal of Sociology* 111 (2006), 1463-1588; J. F. Padgett, 'Open Elite? Social Mobility, Marriage, and Family in Florence, 1282-1494', *Renaissance Quarterly* 63 (2010), 357-411.

declares that 'it appears to have been substantial'.[14] In his sense of dowry it is a well-timed premortem inheritance that served to protect biological continuity.

3. Anthropology and history

The British anthropologist Jack Goody has advanced an influential position on the effects of dowry as a form of intergenerational property transfer. Working from functionalist hypotheses, Goody looked at dowry as premortem diverging devolution in a bilateral kinship system. The married woman took some male property into her new marital home, with the consequence that her marital choices were also more likely to be under tight parental control. Limiting her inheritance to dowry ensured that her property claims did not dissipate family property unduly where property went to both sexes.[15] Thus dowry correlated, in his thinking, with bilateral kinship, the existence of distinct socio-economic strata, delayed marriage for women, and patrivirilocal residence.[16] Another feature of Goody's view is the association of dowry with Mediterranean societies, although more recent research has tended to complicate the picture and blur distinctions between Mediterranean societies and others in Europe.[17]

Studies of dowry, it must be said, have also seen it as serving as much more than a form of female inheritance. Not least in such studies, anthropological and historical, has been the trend to point to the important symbolic meanings of dowry in relation to notions of honor prevalent in many Mediterranean and other societies.[18] More was at stake than property; more was inherited than material resources. Indeed, among others, Molho has pointed

---

14. G. Hanlon, *Human Nature in Rural Tuscany: An Early Modern History* (New York: 2007), 114.
15. J. Goody, *The Development of the Family and Marriage in Europe* (Cambridge: 1983), 240-61; but see also his earlier *Production and Reproduction: A Comparative Study of the Domestic Domain* (Cambridge: 1976), esp. 9-22; and 'Inheritance, Property and Women: Some Comparative Considerations', in J. Goody, J. Thirsk, and E. P. Thompson (eds.), *Family and Inheritance: Rural Society in Western Europe, 1200-1800* (Cambridge: 1976), 10-36.
16. Cf. C. B. Brettell, 'Kinship and Contract: Property Transmission and Family Relations in Northwestern Portugal', *Comparative Studies in Society and History* 33 (1991), 443-65, at 444.
17. Cf. G. Augustins, 'La position des femmes dans trois types d'organisation sociale: La lignée, la parentele et la maison', in G. Ravis-Giordani (ed.), *Femmes et patrimoine dans les sociétés rurales de l'Europe méditerranéenne* (Paris: 1987), 25-37; and B. Martinelli, 'Matrimoine et patrimoine: Sur les fonctions successorales des femmes dans quelques exemples provençaux', ibid., 75-87.
18. On this theme, see generally P. Bourdieu, *Outline of a Theory of Practice*, trans. R. Nice (Cambridge: 1977), and for Florence specifically, Kirshner, *Pursuing Honor*, passim.

to the important symbolic functions of dowry as a barometer of a family's honor and standing in a community and the consequent upward pressure that placed on dowries' monetary values.[19] Julius Kirshner has examined, beyond numerous legal dimensions of assembling, using, and retrieving dowries, the ways in which it and other forms of marital property served to express family honor, denote sexual attraction, and serve as a 'gilded cage'.[20] There was always more than economic assets and legalities involved in dowries and the marriages they underwrote.

Dowry clearly was a multivalent social, economic, and legal institution. It was about inheritance; it was about honor; it was about kinship and marital strategies. It was also (and this was clearly of concern to Goody) about control over women. It is largely from this perspective that other scholars have come to dispute or minimize the equation of dowry and female inheritance, notably so for Florence. Perhaps the first to contest Goody's views was Diane Owen Hughes; her work has been vigorously seconded, expanded, and nuanced by Christiane Klapisch-Zuber and more recently by Isabelle Chabot.[21] Klapisch-Zuber pointedly stated her disagreement with Goody in a well-known 1982 essay:

> For Goody the dowry was equivalent to the daughter's share of the inheritance. When she brought it to her husband, she effected a transmission of goods from the male lineage. One of the results of the system was that it worked in favor of a greater social diversification, since each negotiation of an alliance redistributed the cards economically and redefined the rank and status of the partners. It is difficult, unfortunately, to apply this attractive theory to late medieval Europe, where bilateral filiation had been obliterated both in law and in practice, and where the principle of male transmission of goods – land in particular – had been adopted. Here the dowry was not considered a female share in inheritance; to the contrary, it worked to exclude its beneficiary from inheritance. In Florence, daughters, dowered or not, could inherit from their fathers, in the absence of brothers or nephews, only up to one-quarter of the father's estate, the remainder going to agnatic kin. Needless to say, heiresses were rare.

19. Molho, *Marriage Alliance*, 16-17.
20. Kirshner, *Pursuing Honor*; J. Kirshner, 'Li Emergenti Bisogni Matrimoniali in Renaissance Florence', in W. J. Connell (ed.), *Society and Individual in Renaissance Florence* (Berkeley: 2002), 79-109; J. Kirshner, 'Materials for a Gilded Cage: Non-Dotal Assets in Florence 1300-1500', in D. I. Kertzer and R. P. Saller (eds.), *The Family in Italy from Antiquity to the Present* (New Haven: 1991), 184-207; also J. F. Bestor, 'Marriage Transactions in Renaissance Italy and Mauss's *Essay on the Gift*', *Past and Present* 164 (1999), 6-46.
21. D. O. Hughes, 'From Brideprice to Dowry in Mediterranean Europe', *Journal of Family History* 3 (1978), 263-96; 'Struttura familiare e sistema di successione ereditaria nei testamenti dell'Europa medievale', *Quaderni storici* 33 (1976), 929-52; and on her work, see S. K. Cohn, Jr., *Women in the Streets: Essays on Sex and Power in Renaissance Italy* (Baltimore: 1996), 10-11.

In Florence, then, the dowry system functioned counter to modern anthropological theory. What is more, it functioned badly, created unbearable
tensions, and aroused innumerable complaints on the part of those involved
with it on a daily basis.[22]

Such complaints there undoubtedly were. They are well known. They reso-
nate from the pages of Dante and the accounts of Florentine fathers anx-
iously trying to arrange marriages and assemble dowries, or having to return
them when a marriage ended.[23] Ultimately they underlaid the foundation in
Florence in 1425 of a public fund to help fathers accumulate sufficient funds
for their daughters' dowries.[24]

Klapisch-Zuber appreciates, as did Goody, that dowry was part of a
whole set of marital exchanges and transactions, and she has examined them
in exemplary fashion. Her insistence that dowry was not female inheritance,
but rather a form of disinheritance, has met with widespread recognition, if
not always approval. For her part, Chabot has looked closely at the language
of Florence's statutes and argued that the differentiation of male and female
lines and male and female property forecloses any sense of bilaterality and
diverging devolution for that society.[25] Women were instead genealogically
invisible, and generally materially insignificant, as 'Florentines of the Renaissance had difficulty conceiving of the goods of both parents diverging to
their daughters'.

A key element of this position is the sense, accurate enough for the
vast majority of cases, that a woman's dowry, while required by law to be
'congruent' or 'suitable' in terms of paternal resources, need in no way have
been equal to or even approximate the value of the shares her brothers took

---

22. Ch. Klapisch-Zuber, 'The Griselda Complex: Dowry and Marriage Gifts in the
     Quattrocento', in *Women, Family, and Ritual in Renaissance Italy*, trans. L. Coch-
     rane (Chicago: 1984), 213-46, at 216-17. For a critical perspective on her work, see
     J. F. Bestor, 'The Groom's Prestations for the *Ductio* in Late Medieval Italy: A
     Study in the Disciplining Power of *Liberalitas*', *Rivista internazionale di diritto
     comune* 8 (1997), 129-77.
23. Cf. Kirshner, *Pursuing Honor*, 4-6.
24. J. Kirshner and A. Molho, 'The Dowry Fund and the Marriage Market in Early
     Quattrocento Florence', *Journal of Modern History* 50 (1978), 403-38.
25. I. Chabot, 'La loi du lignage: Notes sur le système successoral florentin (xive-xve,
     xviie siècles)', *Clio: Histoire, femmes et sociétés* 7 (1998), 51-72, at 66. Her posi-
     tion concerning the lineage-based and gender-based nature of inheritance and
     dowry in Florence, in comparison to other Italian societies, is traced out in addition
     in her 'Seconde nozze e identità materna nella Firenze del tardo medioevo', in S.
     Seidel Menchi, A. J. Schutte and T. Kuehn (eds.), *Tempi e spazi di vita femminile
     tra medioevo ed età moderna* (Bologna: 1999), 431-60; and 'Lineage Strategies
     and the Control of Widows in Renaissance Florence', in S. Cavallo and L. Warner
     (eds.), *Widowhood in Medieval and Early Modern Europe* (London: 1999), 127-44.
     See also Ch. Klapisch-Zuber, 'La femme et le lignage florentin (xive-xvie siècles)',
     in R. C. Trexler (ed.), *Persons in Groups: Social Behavior as Identity Formation in
     Medieval and Renaissance Europe* (Binghamton: 1985), 141-53.

from the paternal estate. There was no legal standard or test of proportionality. Chojnacki stresses this point, noting the fact that scholars like Chabot and Klapisch-Zuber thus see women as disadvantaged and legally powerless: 'Patrilineal imperatives led the families that sent their daughters into marriage to treat the dowry as a way of honoring the girls' inheritance rights in appearance but denying them in substance'.[26] His own thrust, in contrast, is to show that dowry was in fact a woman's *patrimonium*, to be returned to her or transferred to her chosen heir at the end of the marriage. In Venice at least, in contrast to Florence, things for women were, says Chojnacki, more 'unambiguously positive'.[27] Chabot has responded that dotal provisions were in fact 'inelastic' and rarely adequate to the number of girls in a family.[28]

The kinds of evidence unearthed by Molho, among others, show that there were considerable difficulties in negotiating the amounts for dowries, in assembling those assets, and even in finally delivering them. Congruent or not to the daughter's putative share in an estate, a dowry could still amount to a substantial investment for a family. Klapisch-Zuber's perspective, wrapped around the image of Griselda, who was endowed in fact by her husband and not her penurious father, may underplay the extent of assets transferred.

At least one alternative view exists, and it is worth taking the trouble to examine it briefly. Maristella Botticini takes a different approach in looking at dowries in a Tuscan community (Cortona) under Florentine rule. From a statistical comparison of dotal contracts with household assets (using Florence's *catasto* of 1427), she concludes that things were not so bleak. Fathers, according to her construction, 'acted altruistically' in dowering their daughters, adjusting the size of the dowry in light of the girl's age at marriage and the socio-economic status of the groom.[29] Her attention is entirely on the marriage process. Inheritance concerns are not for her, as they were for Goody, at the center of the dowry's social functionality.

One could also note that as a premortem transmission, dowry's proportional value to the entire estate was subject to change. If the father was alive at the time of his daughter's marriage, then by the time he died, his patri-

---

26. Chojnacki, *Women and Men in Renaissance Venice*, 95.
27. Ibid., 96, 157.
28. I. Chabot, 'A proposito di "Men and Women in Renaissance Venice" di Stanley Chojnacki: Ricchezze femminili e parentela nel Rinascimento: Riflessioni intorno ai contesti veneziani e fiorentini', *Quaderni storici* 118 (April 2005), 203-29, at 214.
29. M. Botticini, 'A Loveless Economy? Intergenerational Altruism and the Marriage Market in a Tuscan Town, 1415-1436', *Journal of Economic History* 59 (1999), 104-21; see also J. Kirshner, 'Family and Marriage: A Sociolegal Perspective', in J. Najemy (ed.), *Italy in the Age of the Renaissance* (Oxford and New York: 2004), 82-102.

mony's value could have risen or fallen. It could be that, in a drastic instance of the latter, sons could find themselves realizing less from the estate than the value of dowries previously carved out for their sisters. Conversely, a seeming sacrifice for a family at the time of marriage could dwindle into relative insignificance by the point at which a successful father died.

The crux of the problem historically was whether dowries typically were of sufficient economic value to function as an effective share of the patrimony of the woman's family. But added to that is the problem of whether legally dowry was the woman's share of the patrimony, for if it were, and provided the dowry was typically not of sufficient value to be a share of the estate, then law and practice truly would have functioned so as to shortchange women in comparison to their brothers.

There is thus a range of disagreement about the relation between dowry and inheritance, as well as on related issues (bilaterality of kinship versus patrilinearity, control over women's property and marital choices). Goody's functional equilibrium model of reproduction stands in contrast to Klapisch-Zuber's assertion that the dotal regime functioned badly for both fathers and daughters. Klapisch-Zuber, however, remains aware of the degree to which women were increasingly destined for convents and that monachization required a smaller dowry than a marital alliance.[30] At the heart of the matter is the presumed value of the dowry in relation to the entire paternal estate. What is much less discussed, but nonetheless important for understanding dowry, are the legal parameters of dowry in regard to inheritance.

4. The problem in law

That Florence's rules of intestate inheritance and Florentines' inheritance practices, testamentary and not, were biased to male and agnatic connections is not in doubt.[31] That dowry was part of that process is also clear. Even within learned law it was accepted and repeated that family was its property (*substantia*), that family was preserved through its sons (*conservetur per prolem masculinam*), and that sons were the basis of the family

---

30. Cf. J. G. Sperling, *Convents and the Body Politic in Late Renaissance Venice* (Chicago: 1999); S. T. Strocchia, *Nuns and Nunneries in Renaissance Florence* (Baltimore: 2009); P. R. Baernstein, *A Convent Tale: A Century of Sisterhood in Spanish Milan* (New York and London: 2002).

31. Beyond the work of Klapisch-Zuber and Chabot, see S. K. Cohn, Jr., *The Cult of Remembrance and the Black Death: Six Renaissance Cities in Central Italy* (Baltimore: 1992).

(*fundamentum domus*).[32] The dowry fund initiated in Florence in 1425 was an extension of the ideal and practice of keeping real property in the hands of agnate males.[33] The Florentine statute quoted above, when it allowed women to inherit along with more distant agnates (than those agnates it mentioned as excluding women), provided them only with one-quarter of the property or 500 *lire* (roughly 125 florins), whichever was less; and that portion was not to include houses or buildings.[34] If the legislators acted on the presumption that such a woman already had a dowry, they were willing to concede her only a modest amount in addition.

At the same time, while daughters could clearly be disadvantaged in the distribution of patrimonial resources in comparison to their brothers, concerns for family honor also drove a desire to make a good marital match, which required money. The socio-economic status of the family was on display along with a new bride. The cultural motivations behind dowry were so strong that they called into being numerous forms of charity, fueled by testamentary bequests in most instances, to provide dowries to deserving poor girls, including those in foundling homes.[35] Perhaps then differences in the amount and content of dowries of girls in comparison to the inheritance shares of boys are not enough on which to base a categorical statement that dowry was not inheritance but an exclusion from it?

Legal history presents another perspective. One of the prominent historians of the law of family, Manlio Bellomo, treats dowry as a substitute for legitim, the portion of an estate designated as reserved to one's children, the 'necessary' heirs. The Roman civil law set a minimum quota of the deceased's property as a suitable portion for the children. That portion, generally one-third, could rise to a half if it was to be divided among more than four children. Failure to provide that quota was grounds for overturning a will as unduteous (*inofficiosum*), rendering the succession intestate.[36] The claims of children to legitim were that powerful in law. As Bellomo has it, as an obligation falling in first order on a father to provide his daughter with a 'congruent' share of his goods, dowry effectively replaced her claims to legitim. Statutes excluding dowered women were thus also affirmations of

32. Cf. T. Kuehn, '*Memoria* and Family in Law', in G. Ciappelli and P. L. Rubin (eds.), *Art, Memory, and Family in Renaissance Florence* (Cambridge: 2000), 262-74.
33. Cf. Kirshner and Molho, 'The Dowry Fund and the Marriage Market', 435.
34. *Statuta*, vol. 1, 223.
35. Cf. I. Chabot and M. Fornasari, *L'Economia della carità: Le doti del Monte di Pietà di Bologna (secoli xvi-xx)* (Bologna: 1997), esp. 13; Cohn, *Cult of Remembrance*, 66-67; Molho, *Marriage Alliance*, 275-78; T. Kuehn, *Illegitimacy in Renaissance Florence* (Ann Arbor: 2001); P. Gavitt, *Charity and Children in Renaissance Florence: The Ospedale degli Innocenti, 1410-1536* (Ann Arbor: 1990), 210-11.
36. For the Roman law on this, see Kaser, *Roman Private Law*, 301-03.

legitim for daughters in the form of dowry obligations. However, Bellomo also notes that there were no rigorous criteria of proportionality applied to dowries.[37] Nor was failure to constitute a dowry sufficient to overturn a testament. The obligation to establish one would simply pass to the new heir(s) of the estate upon which the dowry obligation rested.

Laurent Mayali, whose work is more directly dedicated to the dowry exclusion, offers the reinterpretation that Roman dowry tempered the harsh exclusion of women from inheritance contained in Lombard law. 'Let us reserve for now,' he says, 'that despite its imperfections this statutory disposition established for the first time a link between dowry and succession, even if the means of this interdependence are not clearly set forth'.[38] Thus, though the early glossators treated *dos* in relation to the *onera matrimonii* shared with her husband, rather than as a girl's share of her father's estate, the equation of dowry and inheritance quickly gave sense to egalitarian imperatives in the law with a view to the necessities of family life. *Dos patrimonium filie est proprium* became a legal aphorism, which also carried the sense of the irreversibility of the dowry (as unrecoverable by father or brothers by a process other than standing as heir to a woman).[39] Thus also the rule that a *dos* be *congrua* was interpreted to mean that it not be less than the legitim a daughter would have received by the rules of Roman law.[40]

Still, the equiponderance of dowry and legitim in some doctrinal interpretations did not mean that statutes could be simply swept away by interpretation or that inheritance practices followed doctrinal lines. Mayali himself cites the example of the Sienese jurist Mariano Sozzini (d. 1467), who denied that a dowered daughter, under statutory terms, could seek a supplement to her legitim/dowry. Thus any compromise between the Roman law's imperative of equality of heirs of both sexes and the statutory goal of family preservation through males proved untenable; 'the reference to legitim had above all a symbolic value. [. . .] It was in effect admitted that the statutory rule could diminish the legitim yet without removing it'.[41]

There were other indications, even within legal doctrinal writings, that dowry could not be equated simply with legitim. Julius Kirshner's study of disinheritance finds that 'the prudent course for mothers as well as fathers who wanted to avoid a *querela inofficiosi testamenti* [litigation over the validity of a will] is to leave daughters something beyond the dowry in the

---

37. Bellomo, *Ricerche*, 169, 176, 178.
38. Mayali, *Droit savant*, 24.
39. Ibid., 51, 58.
40. Ibid., 88-89.
41. Ibid., 90. On the seeking of a supplement in law, see Kaser, *Roman Private Law*, 303.

testament'.[42] At least for purposes of effective disinheritance, the equation of dowry and legitim was precluded by such provision of a token amount. Conversely, Kirshner also found that, in the absence of sons, a daughter could claim her legitim with her dowry, only returning the latter to be thus included in the calculation of what was due her.[43] At best we might conclude that in certain legal circumstances there was a distinction between dowry and legitim; legitim could include more than dowry, but dowry would always be part (if not all) of legitim.

5. The case

All this was not just doctrinal legal sophistry. Real and practical results could hinge on the meanings of such terms, as we can see from the following case. From it dowry emerges as both less and more than legitim, whatever its amount. The surviving *consilium* gives no specifics regarding persons, amounts, or other factors that can allow us to place it in time. It was probably placed before the jurist in a denuded form to reduce it maximally to its legal issues (while eliminating nonlegal ones that might influence the jurist). The *consilium* also survives in a copy, and the process of copying may further have encouraged the dumping of detail, rendering it less useful to subsequent readers who might exploit its argumentation for their own purposes. But the copy carries two signatures, with the second seemingly vouching for the accuracy of the copy.[44] The lawyer was Filippo di Tommaso Corsini (1334-1421). This member of an old Florentine clan was the foremost native Florentine lawyer of his era (one in which numerous, more prestigious outsiders graced Florence's streets, courts, and lecture halls as legal practitioners and teachers). Corsini was a singularly powerful and influential figure in law and politics in Florence from the 1360s to his death.[45] His stature may say something about the importance of the litigants as well as of the legal issues.

---

42. Kirshner, 'Baldus de Ubaldis on Disinheritance: Contexts, Controversies, *Consilia*', *Ius Commune: Zeitschrift für Europäischen Rechtsgeschichte* 27 (2000), 119-214, at 140.
43. Ibid., 163.
44. Biblioteca Nazionale Centrale, Florence, (hereafter BNF) Landau-Finaly 98, fol. 297r-v. The final signature reads 'Facio fidem ego Phylippus de Corsinis quod illud quod supra scriptum est consilavi, subscripxi, et sigillavi'.
45. On him, see L. Martines, *Lawyers and Statecraft in Renaissance Florence* (Princeton: 1968), 482. Corsini held the chief political office in Florence, that of Gonfaloniere di Giustizia, as early as 1368 and four other times, as well as periods in the Dodici Buonuomini and the sixteen gonfalonieri di campagnia: see *Florentine Renaissance Resources: Online Tratte of Officeholders, 1282-1532*, machine-readable data file, ed. D. Herlihy, R. B. Litchfield, A. Molho and R. Barducci (Providence: 2000), www.stg.brown.edu/projects/tratte, 31 Dec. 2001.

The case facts were simple. A man with four sons and two daughters died with a testament, leaving the girls dowries (stated in precise monetary sums) and giving the rest to the boys as universal heirs, with clauses of substitution among them if any should die without sons of his own. All in all, an unexceptional example, practically and normatively, of a Florentine father's will. The legal complication entered in later, however, when one of the four sons died without sons. His testament named only one of his three brothers as his universal heir. The other two brothers sought their shares of his estate, citing the terms of the *fideicommissum* in the paternal will, versus their brother's omission of them in his. The one who had been named heir wanted to keep the legitim from his brother's estate (which had been part of what came to the brother from the father), claiming that it did not fall subject to a conditional *fideicommissum*. This right to legitim was not contested. The problem was determining what share of the paternal inheritance constituted the legitim in this instance. In other words, did the girls count? Did they affect the size of and the number of shares in the legitim?

Corsini's strategy in composing his response to the question before him was not to seek out areas of broad doctrinal agreement, or else he could not find any. He began instead by noting that he faced a difficult area of law, studded with varying opinions, including those of local figures of modest reputation whom he named – Giovanni Pagliaresi of Siena and Griffolo da Montepulciano. Those two had advised in a case put before them that daughters counted in establishing the size of the share of the estate that had to be set aside as legitim and that bequests to them (here, their dowries) took the place of legitim ('cedat loco legittime'). If the bequest to the daughters amounted to less than their legitim, the difference accrued to the sons; although Corsini noted that his own highly esteemed teacher, Bartolo da Sassoferrato (1313-1357), had said the opposite. In the same vein, he continued, 'many other things also can be brought forth which I omit because their *consilium* exists and according to this the legitim should be half of the entire estate, less what is owed others and funeral expenses'.[46]

Corsini went on to cite Bartolo and Dino del Mugello (d. 1303?) as also backing the view that legitim amounted to half the estate. Still, he immediately departed from them all (and supposedly from others that he did not name) to declare that legitim was only one-third. The civil law rule he invoked from one of Justinian's *novellae* was that four or fewer children were reserved a legitim of one-third; more than four saw an increase to half. In the case before him he was not counting the two dowered daughters, only the four sons. His reasons are illuminating.

---

46. BNF, Landau-Finaly 98, fol 297r: 'Super quo ipsi allegant pro et contra, et plura etiam allegari possent que obmicto, quia extat consilium eorum et secundum hoc legittima esset medietas totius hereditatis deducto ere alieno et funeris impensa'.

He argued that daughters were excluded by statute, and the bequest of a dowry in the paternal testament was not a *quota hereditaria*. They could not seek legitim or even be counted in it.[47] Thus, while he made an equivalence between the daughters' exclusion and their total nonexistence, he refused to equate a dowry bequest with a quota of the estate. It was instead specified as a quantity of money, not as a portion of a whole as a legitim, not a *portio legitima*. He also rejected Bartolo's view that a dowered daughter excluded from inheritance could seek a supplement to her legitim. Corsini's argument rested on the distinction that here the exclusion derived not from a will but from a statute, which was *potentius*.[48] A disinherited son could still hope to contest the will that removed him, and so his potential recourse to litigation argued to count him in setting legitim, whereas statutory exclusion of dowered girls was incontestable.

A counterargument had to be confronted and resolved – namely 'that a bequest to daughters for a dowry seems to be counted as legitim' ('quia relictum filiabus pro dote videtur censeri legittima'). After all, it was for that daughters were prohibited from contesting a will, as if they had received their legitim. The legal viewpoints that Bellomo and Mayali have uncovered thus did not escape Corsini's notice, but he slid past them in the concluding section of his *consilium*.

> To that I respond that this proceeds because by *ius commune*, although she be instituted [in a testament] in a certain quantity as a dowry, she still has rights to a full portion of the legitim; but in our case the statute blocks any supplement, saying that she must be content with any bequest and cannot seek any more. Nor is it indistinctly true that dowry entirely takes the place of the legitim, for even if a daughter is disinherited and excluded by law from legitim, the dowry is still hers and remains with her [. . .] for it is the daughter's own patrimony. [. . .] And so the bequest for dowry be equivalent to legitim, it may not be conditional nor can a delay be placed on it.[49]

47. Ibid.: 'Sed filie feminine ab intestato nullam quotam portionem hereditatis habuissent ex eo quia per statutum communis Florentie existentibus masculis a successione hereditatis excluduntur, et quamvis fuerit eis relictum per patrem pro dote illud est relictum quantitatis non quote hereditarie, ergo non possunt petere legittimam, nec quo ad legittimam computantur, nec in ea sive quo ad eam partem faciunt'.

48. Further, Corsini distinguished 'in questione Bar[toli], licet exheredatus non haberet partem, quia ab illa erat exclusus, ipsam sperabatur habere, nam habebat ius veniendi contra testamentum saltem spe per querelam inoffi[ciosi] testamenti, unde tunc facit partem et alteri aliter, qui non admicitur ad partem, et sic loquitur l. papinianus ' siquis ex hiis de inoffi. te. Sed predicte filie non sperant aliud habere quia statutum resistit eis' (ibid., fol. 297v).

49. Ibid.: 'Ad quod respondeo quod istud procedit quia de iure commune, licet sit instituta in certa quantitate pro dote, tamen iura supplent sibi quotam legittime, sed in casu nostro statutum obviat supplemento, dicens quod debeat esse contenta quoquo relicti titulo et plus petere non possit. Nec est indistincte verum quod dos omnino teneat locum legittime, nam etiam si filia esset exheredata et a legittima de iure ex-

The claim to a dowry, as set forth in the statute, was thus stronger even than a claim to legitim. Even a disinherited daughter retained a dowry. Thus Corsini could call it a *patrimonium*, following the usage common in many doctrinal texts. While there is a paradox that such a strong claim could not overturn a paternal testament, at least by the terms of the statute, it was so strong a claim that no exclusion or even disinheritance would work against it. In law, then, for Corsini dowry was related to and even part of inheritance, but it was also clearly something else as well.

6. Conclusion

One assumes that Corsini's opinion carried the court, if it was indeed submitted to aid the judge's deliberations. In the immediate particular context for the litigants, it had a decisive effect. By eliminating the daughters from legitim, he had reduced it, as a portion of the paternal patrimony, to a third. So the share of the estate that fell as legitim to the deceased brother, and then on to the one brother he had favored as heir in his will, was a fourth of a third—one-twelfth. Had Corsini allowed the girls to be counted, the legitim would have amounted to half, with the portion for one brother being one-eighth. His decision thus favored the one brother less. It kept as much equality among the brothers as was possible in light of one brother's favoritism, and it did so by distinguishing them from their sisters.

The wider legal effect of this *consilium* is harder to determine. Corsini's opinion about the daughters' weight in computing legitim does not seem to have received exceptional notice. At least the statute commentary of the Florentine lawyer Alessandro Bencivenni (1385-1423), which covered the new redaction of 1415 and was composed shortly before his death, did not mention Corsini's *consilium* when it touched on the problem in discussion of the statute excluding dowered women. Bencivenni made reference only to Bartolo's commentary and to portions of it, for that matter, not cited by Corsini.[50] Still, Bencivenni had his own agenda and needs in composing

---

clusa dos consolidaretur in eam et sibi remaneret ut dicta l. unica ' videamus de re. uxor. ac. Est enim proprium patrimonium filie ut l. iii ' sed utrum de mino. ff. et ibi pomponius filadelphus fa. here. Et sic ideo equiparetur legittime relictum pro dote non esset conditionale nec posset in eo apponi dilatio, cuius contrarium tenet Bar[tolus] in l. titio ' titio gerio de condi. et demo., quamvis contrarium teneat Ia[cobus] Buct[rigarius] in l. quoniam imprioribus de inoffi. testamento'. On the rule that even a disinherited daughter retained her claim to a dowry, see Bellomo, *Ricerche sui rapporti patrimoniali*, 174-75.

50. BNF, Fondo principale, II, iv, 435, fol. 72v: 'In ' nulla mulier nec natus. Nunquid iste mulieres que possunt succedere ascendentibus computent in numero aliorum filiorum quo ad computationem legitime portionis, vide Bar[tolum] in l. i ' si pater ff. de coningen. cum eman. liber. et vide per d. in l. unica ' in primo C. de caduc. tollen. ad plenum'.

his commentaries, and his neglect of Corsini's *consilium* does not defini-
tively prove that it was of no effect or notoriety in the legal community of
Florence.

A later Florentine lawyer, Antonio di Vanni Strozzi (1455-1523), who
left several volumes of a glossary on terms and problems of law, made a
weak equation of dowry and legitim:

> A statute where it decrees that a woman does not inherit when males are
> alive has to be understood such that her dowry consist of at least as much as
> falls to her legitim. So if such a woman otherwise cannot marry a suitable
> man, unless she deliver the entire paternal estate as dowry to her husband,
> there not being any male children, the entire estate is said to be a congruent
> dowry.[51]

He did not legally equate dowry with legitim, so in a sense he respected the
distinction Corsini had maintained about a century earlier. Yet he kept the
legal sense that, in order for dowry to preclude a woman's inheritance, it
had to take the place of her legitim. A careful ambiguity was kept in place,
nonetheless. One never sees a simple statement to the effect that 'dos est
legitima filiae'.

For our purposes, against the context of historical research on women
and dowry and their relation to inheritance processes, Corsini's reluctance
to equate dowry and legitim – shared with the rest of his profession – is instructive. His *consilium* reinforces Mayali's interpretation that dowry was
not simply equated with legitim. The two were distinct, if confused at times.
Dos as *patrimonium filiae* was not the same as legitim, which she might
share with her brothers. In Florence and elsewhere it was only in the absence of the close male heirs who excluded her from receiving more than
her dowry that a woman could look for a supplement to her share that would
be calculated in terms of legitim.[52]

In this regard Corsini's *consilium* was in conformity with one by a
much more illustrious contemporary, also active in Florence, Angelo degli
Ubaldi (1325-1400). In a case arising in Cortona and involving its statute
excluding dowered daughters from inheritance, Angelo rehearsed the arguments in favor of equating dowry and legitim (even admitting that the for-

51. Archivio di Stato, Firenze, Carte strozziane, 3rd ser., 41/18, fol. 389r: 'Statutum
ubi viget quod existentibus masculis femina non succedat sed dotetur debet intelligi
quod dos constituatur ad minus quantum capit legitima, ut in auc. res que C.
Comunia de lega. Item si talis mulier aliter viro condigno nubere non possit nisi totam paternam hereditatem in dotem viro tradat aliis non existentibus liberis masculis ipsa universa hereditas dicitur congrua dos ita not. Jo. de Bel. in auc. de restitu.
et Bal. in d. auc. res que in i col'.
52. Cf. ibid., fol. 73v: 'In ' si vero testatus, in ver[bo] masculis. Sed si ipsi non sint sed
alii agnati non excluditur a supplemento legitime sed remanet dispositio l. omni-
modo C. de inoffi. testa. Alex[ander]'.

mer might well be less than a real share of legitim) and thus militating toward counting daughters with sons in computing legitim;[53] but in the end he concluded that dowered girls were rendered 'dead' and unable to inherit by the statute and thus were not counted in the computation of how large a share of the estate fell into the category of legitim.[54] Angelo did not make the sweeping statements about dowry and legitim that Corsini did, but he could have agreed with them.

Thus in law, leaving aside the size of the dowry relative to the entire paternal patrimony, the dowry might take the place of legitim but it was not equated with it. Rather it had a more powerful, less contingent quality as *patrimonium filiae*. In most wills, therefore, like the one behind the case we have examined, dowries were left as specific bequests stated in monetary amounts. They came out of the estate before the universal heirs divided or shared the rest. They may not always have been 'congruent' by some criteria, but they had an undeniable priority. Here then we can understand some of the frequent complaints of Florentines and others about either constituting the dowry in the first place or having to 'return' it (or retrieve it) following the woman's death. Meanwhile the married woman, rendered a widow, had a statutory right of *tornata* by which she could return to her natal family and expect shelter and support.[55] Here, in contrast to dowry, which she owned but could not direct the use of, she had a right of use in *tornata* but no ownership. Perhaps here too we can understand another medieval legal innovation regarding dowry – namely, the rule that a woman guilty of adultery lost her dowry. Adultery was powerful enough to strip her of her *patrimonium*.[56] She could lose it to her (cuckholded) husband where she could

---

53. Angelo degli Ubaldi, *Consilia* (Frankfurt: 1575), *cons.* 300, fols. 213ra-va: 'licet ergo hae filiae dote debeant esse contentae (quae forsan minor est legitima, quae defertur de iure civili) tamen integram legitimam habere dicuntur: potest enim minui et augeri per statutum. [. . .] Et sic ex praedictis videtur debere concludi quod licet alia sit legitima filiarum, alia legitima filiorum; tamen quia omnes ad legitimam invitantur, in computatione omnium tam masculorum quam foeminarum ratio est habenda' (fol. 213rb).

54. Ibid., fol. 213rb-va: 'Praeterea dos succedit in locum dictae legitimae (ut est dictum) tamen considerato quod filia dotata excluditur in successione favore et contemplatione masculorum, per quos agnatitia proles et familiarum dignitas conservatur [. . .] et quicquid eis aufertur impugnare debet masculorum portionem: alias nullus versaretur favor eorum, quibus statutum voluit providere [. . .] sic enim determinat statutum, ut persistente masculo non invitaretur ad successionem filia, sed ad sui sustentationem aliquid concedebatur. [. . .] Praeterea quantum ad succedendi potentiam filia habetur pro mortua: licet non quo ad alia. [. . .] Sed in proposito statutum reddit filiam dotatam inhabilem ad succedendum: ergo suae personae consideratio nullatenus est habenda'.

55. Chabot, 'Lineage Strategies', 132-35.

56. This is not to deny a double standard in treating adulterous acts of men and women. The Roman law text at the base of the medieval rule was *Codex* 5.17.8,5, which decreed an adulterous lose half her dowry and one-third her property. But medieval jurists like Jacopo Bottrigari († 1348), in his *Tractatus de dote*, offered the simple

not ostensibly lose it to her father. In this regard the functional legal definition of dowry as sustaining the burdens of marriage came into play, it
seems. Her adultery undercut the marriage, cuckholded her husband, and in
that way, perhaps, she deservedly lost her *patrimonium filiae* to him, as forfeit for her indiscretion.

That dowry functioned as a form of inheritance is clear, but the legal
practitioners at times had to maintain a distinction between dowry (female
property) and legitim (male property, becoming female only in the absence
of male heirs). The claim to a dowry was powerful but remained distinct
from the right of an heir to a legitimate portion (and symbolic meanings
were also attached to that word): a right that could be invoked to set aside a
paternal will, a right precluded dowered daughters by statute in Florence
and elsewhere.[57] Dowry was not unambiguously an inheritance, as Goody
has seen it. At the same time, while it was probably often not near the value
of the share left her brother, a woman's dowry was a powerfully enforced
claim that, *pace* Klapisch-Zuber, was immune from disinheritance in law, if
not in reality.

rule that a wife guilty of adultery lost her dowry to her husband (*Tractatus universi
iuris* [Venice: 1585], vol. 9, fols 448v-49r, n. 26).
57.   The chief meaning or consequence of legitim in law seems to have been its capacity to define a testament as insufficiently appropriate for heirs. See W. M. Gordon,
'Succession', in E. Metzger (ed.), *A Companion to Justinian's 'Institutes'* (Ithaca:
1998), 80-126, at 98-99.

Marriage Among the Land-owning Peasants of Southern Norway: A Device for Social Reproduction of the Peasant Elite

Lars Ivar Hansen

1. Introduction

The aim of this article is to throw light upon marriage practices and strategies within a segment of the Norwegian peasantry during the late medieval period and the beginning of early modern times. The investigation will deal with the peasants settled in the valley of Fyresdal in the upper, higher-situated parts of Telemark county, a region in the interior of southern Norway. The focus will be on a higher social stratum within the peasantry, a set of actors and kindreds who made up a local and regional elite. Even though most of the land in these inner regions was owned by the peasants themselves, these specific actors and kindreds comprised an economic elite because they figured among the wealthiest landowning peasants. And because at the same time they had at their disposal significant intellectual capabilities and resources, as well as network connections, which played a central role in the social life of the valley community, they must also be characterized as a 'social elite'.

One central goal will therefore be to study how strategic marriages within this societal segment formed a part of wider, more comprehensive strategies for social reproduction among the peasants. As I see it, these wider strategies cannot be fully explained without taking into consideration a set of given factors that made out the basic acting conditions for the un-

folding of the peasants' strategies for property accumulation and social reproduction. These are:

1) A bilateral way of reckoning kinship

2) The inheritance system, as established in the National Law Code for
the Norwegian realm in 1274, which primarily followed a bilateral pattern,
but with some patrilineal elements, giving a certain priority to male heirs
and kinship through male links

3) The so-called residence right – i.e., the priority held by the oldest
son to take over the main residence or patrimonial farm, while the other
heirs had to be satisfied with other, 'loose' shares of landed property or
movables, and

4) The so-called rent ownership system, which had been applied to the
whole of Norway during the high Middle Ages, and by which the property
right was primarily defined as the right to collect rent for farms rather than
having a decisive authority over how the farms should be cultivated in practice.[1]

In this endeavour to grasp and understand the actions and measures
taken by the Fyresdal peasants and their social elite, I will draw on the analytical approaches that are made available by Pierre Bourdieu's concepts of
'social space' and 'social field'. The marriage exchange processes which
took place between various kindreds and peasant actors were part of a wider
interplay, involving economic assets and land property, general social status
and relative positions as well as specific know-how and knowledge about
the local judicial and administrative system. Through their efforts to secure
landed property, to establish favourable marital relations and to promote
valuable social network connections, these peasant actors drew on a wide
set of resources, which correspondingly may be analysed using Bourdieu's
categories of 'economic', 'social', 'cultural', and 'symbolic' capital. In this
way, they appear to stand out as actors – or 'agents' – occupying different
positions with various kinds of access to resources – or 'capital' – who
steadily kept up relations with one another.[2]

The further structure of this article will be as follows: After presenting
some main characteristics of the area of investigation, I will give an over-

1. The term 'rent ownership system' – *skyldeie-systemet* in Norwegian – has been
   used by Norwegian historians in order to emphasize that the primary object of
   property within the domestic agrarian system of Norway during the Middle Ages
   was the right to collect rent, and that the landowners in most cases had a distant relation to the way farmsteads were run in practice. See A. Holmsen, *Nye studier i
   gammel historie* (Oslo, Bergen and Tromsø: 1976), 128; and H. Bjørkvik: 'Jordlei-
   ge, Norge', *Kulturhistorisk leksikon for nordisk middelalder* 7, cols 677-80.
2. See among others, P. Thomson, 'Field', in M. Grenfell (ed.), *Pierre Bourdieu: Key
   Concepts* (Stocksfield: 2008), 67-81; C. Sestoft, 'Felt: Begreber og analyser (kap.
   5.)', in A. Prieur and C. Sestoft (eds.), *Pierre Bourdieu: En introduction* (København: 2006), 157-84.

view of the surviving sources that reflect the role and actions of the upper social segment of the local peasant society. Then three examples of their kinship relations and marital practices will be highlighted, through a presentation of genealogical charts. Finally, I will focus upon how the conjunction of separate property parts in each farm, divided among various land-owning peasants, might be considered as 'nodes' or 'meeting places' for property relations, and the degree to which this criss-crossing network of reciprocal obligations might be understood as resulting from and expressing the workings within a 'social field' according to Bourdieu's conception.

2. The area of investigation

The valley which makes up the area of investigation, Fyresdal, is situated in the interior of southern Norway, making up the south-westernmost part of Telemark county. Fyresdal, a forested and mountainous area, lies between 280 and 700 metres above sea level. According to a survey from 1972, less than 1 percent of its total area (1278 square kilometres) consists of cultivated land (fields and meadows), while productive forest accounts for almost 19 percent, and the remaining 80 percent comprises lakes, mountains and 'outlying areas' ('*hei*' in the local Norwegian dialect).[3] Some grain could be grown on the farms, though the quantities were quite limited in comparison with the output of the best grain regions in Norway. – The *hei* areas, consisting of upland pastures, were however excellently suited for cattle grazing in the summer, for hunting and for the gathering of fodder and other resources. The use of mountain dairy farming was very intensive, and during the summer the peasants regularly moved their cattle out to the dairy units called *støyler* in the upland regions.

In line with the common pattern in Norway, settlement was based on a single-farm structure. According to earlier investigations, there might have been some 140 farms bearing individual names during the high Middle Ages, of which about 60 percent were deserted during the late medieval period as a result of the demographic effects of the Black Death and ensuing plague epidemics. Around 1600, the number of individual peasant holdings (that is, those used by one peasant family) might have been 80 to 90, increasing to 98 a half-century later and surpassing 120 in the 1660s.[4] Together with the neighbouring districts in the county of Agder, the remaining part of Upper Telemark and the valleys of Hallingdal and Valdres, Fyresdal

---

3. *Generalplan for Fyresdal kommune*, utarbeidd av: Fyresdal commune, formannskapskontoret [= local municipal office], mars/juni 1972.
4. L. I. Hansen, *Markebol og ødegårder. Bosetning og økonomiske forhold i Fyresdal ca. 1300-1660* (Oslo, Bergen and Tromsø: 1980).

is included in a broader zone of southern Norway in which a very substantial percentage of the land was owned by the local peasantry. Whereas Norwegian peasants on average owned about one-third of the total landed property in the country during medieval times, the amount of peasant property in these areas reached quite other proportions, making up from 70 to 90 percent of the total landed property. As late as c. 1600, the peasants of Fyresdal owned between 94 and 97 percent of the land.[5] However, these peasants did not necessarily own the farms that they resided on and cultivated – at least not fully, in their totality. Instead, their property was distributed in the form of small ownership shares among several farms all over the valley and in some of the neighbouring valleys as well.

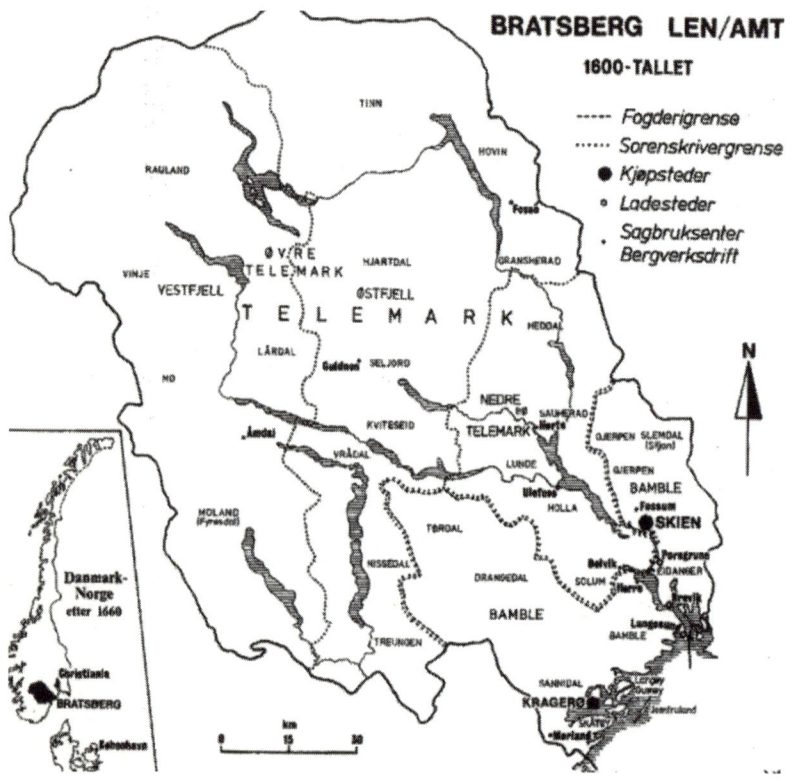

Fig. 1. The county of Telemark – formerly "Bratsberg amt"
(reproduced after Ø. Rian, *Bratsberg på 1600-tallet* (Oslo: 1997))

5.   L. I. Hansen, 'Arkaiske bønder eller alternativ sosial logikk? Om telemarksbøndenes forhold til stat, eiendom, kirke og helvete i middelalderen', in H. J. Orning, K. Esmark and L. Hermansson (eds.), *Gaver, ritualer, konflikter: Et rettsantropologisk perspektiv på nordisk middelalderhistorie* (Oslo: 2010), 117-59.

3. The upper social stratum of 'legal jurors'

Thanks to comprehensive written evidence – in the form of charters, sales contracts, title deeds, testimonies, probate cases, receipts for paid fines and reprieves – an upper social elite of locally resident, land-owning peasants can be followed throughout the period from the beginning of the fourteenth century until the end of the sixteenth century, and even further. These property-owning peasants occupied the positions related to administration and local government that were accessible to peasants, principally as legal jurors (*lagrettemenn*) in the local court system and sometimes also as local (peasant) bailiffs. As local jurors, they took their oath before the county judge of the province upon their appointment. They functioned as witnesses and took part in judging commissions at the local court (*thing* assembly) sessions and at various legal proceedings outside the formal court. They saw to it that legal documents such as sales contracts, title deeds, exchange agreements, inheritance probates and testimonies about kinship relations and inheritance issues were drawn up and sealed in a formally correct and legally prescribed manner. Furthermore, they carried out surveys of borders between farms and communities where disagreements occurred, and took part in evaluation of production potentials at certain farms, to establish the (relative) value of the farms, measured in land rent. Generally, they played an important role for the administration of justice and solving disputes at a local level. In this capacity, the jurors held a vast competence in technical, legal matters and judicial procedures, as well as practical know-how about farming and resource conditions, all of which was of high value to the local community.

From this perspective, it seems fruitful to consider this accumulated know-how as a form of 'cultural capital' (partly transformable into 'social' and 'symbolic' capital) according to Bourdieu's analysis.[6] At the same time, this stratum of local jurors was to a high degree involved in complex and entangled webs of kinship, which also must have served them as a great resource, and which also should be regarded as a social asset or 'social capital', but of another form. Finally, even if nearly all the land was distributed among the peasants in Fyresdal and neighbouring parishes, the social stratum from which these jurors were recruited seems to represent the wealthiest of the peasants.

Because the peasants in these interior regions were highly preoccupied with property and their ability to document and prove title and property rights, surviving documentary evidence is very suitable for following this upper stratum in their social functions. A large number of diverse docu-

6. See for instance P. Bourdieu, 'Social Space and Symbolic Power', P. Bourdieu, *In Other Words: Essays Towards a Reflexive Sociology*, trans. M. Adamson (Cambridge: 1990), 128.

ments relating to property, inheritance questions, conveyances, sales and barters has been preserved, since they served as legal title to various property relations. Apart from the ordinary dispositive letters recording an expression of will by a buyer, seller or mortgager of land, we find many letters of a type that represents a combined, intermediary form between the two classic document types, the *notitia* and the *charta*: the so-called testifying charter.[7] This was a testified and sealed public announcement, in which the issuers affirmed that they had been present and had observed as witnesses a legal, binding action concerning land sale, inheritance division, barter, proof presentation and the like. As witnesses, they testified and confirmed by their own seals, marks or signatures that they had observed 'real', legally binding practical actions: handshakes, prescribed formal utterances, and the formal handing over of significant objects such as 'the first and the last piece of the purchase price'. Since the local jurors possessed the relevant and requisite knowledge of the formal prescriptions necessary for making such transactions legally valid, they were used for such affairs to a great extent, and thus the chances of having their names preserved in these contexts was increased correspondingly.

Based on 126 charters dating from 1300 to 1600, 65 jurors have been individually identified from the years between 1389 and 1600. Investigation of property surveys from the end of the period indicates that the local jurors were recruited from the upper economic stratum. According to a tax survey from 1603, 12 persons serving or having served as legal jurors figured among the 17 wealthiest peasant landowners.[8] One of the highest ranking land-owners (in fact the second-wealthiest) at the beginning of the seventeenth century was Vetle Olavsson, who lived on the farm *Gåstjønn* in the annex parish of Skafså and served as a juror from 1583 to 1597 as well as being peasant bailiff for the twenty-two years between 1597 and 1619 (see table 3 in the attachment to the article). At the height of his prosperity in 1615, Olavsson held a total collection of property shares amounting to 23 barrels of grain rent,[9] an amount which at this time would correspond to the property of six of the greatest farms, with the best agricultural potential.

7. L. Hamre, *Innføring i diplomatikk* (Oslo: 2004 – 2nd edn), 62-68.
8. *Landskatt (munitions-skatt) martini 1603*, National Archives of Norway, *Rentekammeret, Lensrekneskap, Akershus, pk. 18 (1)*.
9. *Jordebog og regnskap over Leding og Skinnskatt m.v. – 1615*, National Archives of Norway, *Danske kanselli, Skap 14, pk. 14*; printed version by O. A. Helleberg, *Jordebok over Telemark (Bratsberg len) ca. 1615* (Kongsberg: 1991).

4. Kinship and marital relations among the local jurors

In order to highlight what kind of kinship relations existed and what kind of marriage strategies between various kindreds were practised by this social elite, I will present three genealogical charts, which involve persons with ties to eight farms and which cover the last part of the sixteenth century. Before this time, the available kinship data are unfortunately not sufficient to allow a detailed charting of marriage relations. Although we have to take as our starting point some people occupying positions at a set of particular farms, we shall see that specific attachment to one single farm is not a decisive factor. What seems to have been important was rather the significance of kinship ties, and attachment to a more broadly defined group of farms, namely the most productive and highest-ranking ones as measured by their assessment for rent.

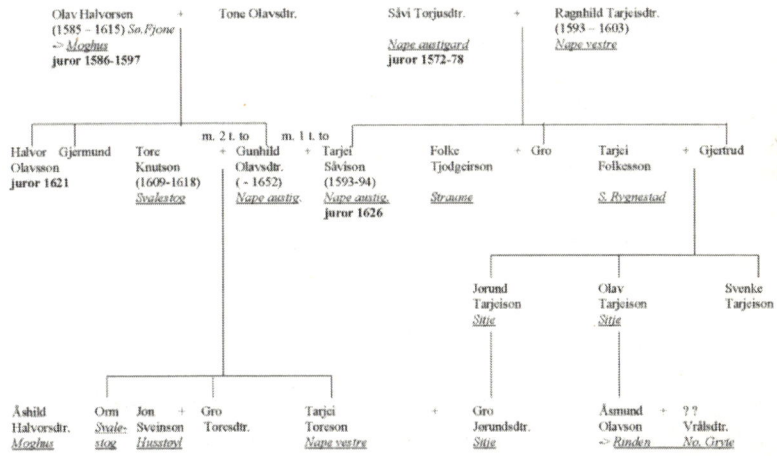

Fig. 2. Genealogical reconstruction for peasants attached to the farms Moghus and Nape

Figure 2 shows the descendants and marital relations between two kindreds attached to the central farms *Moghus* and eastern *Nape* in the last quarter of the sixteenth century and onwards. Olav Halvorsson at *Moghus* served as local juror in 1586-1597, and one of his sons, Halvord Olavsson, held the same office in the first decades of the seventeenth century. At the same time, a daughter of Olav Halvorsson, Gunhild, married Tarjei Såvison, who lived at eastern *Nape*. Tarjei was also a juror, as his father, Såvi Torjusson, had been before him. (Såvi's period of office preceded that of Olav Halvorsson.) Gunhild was soon left as a widow. Although she had no children with Tarjei, she had three children by her second husband, Tore Knutsson from the farm *Svalestog*. Both the sons from Gunhild's second marriage became local jurors in their time, after the middle of the seventeenth century. Thus, we can observe a clear tendency of descendants of jurors becoming jurors themselves. In the kindred attached to eastern *Nape*, we have an example of father and son holding the same kind of office, and in the kindred originally attached to *Moghus*, we have local jurors in three consecutive generations, mediated through one female link.

This tendency of holding the position of juror in several generations of the kindreds is even more clearly illustrated in Figure 3.

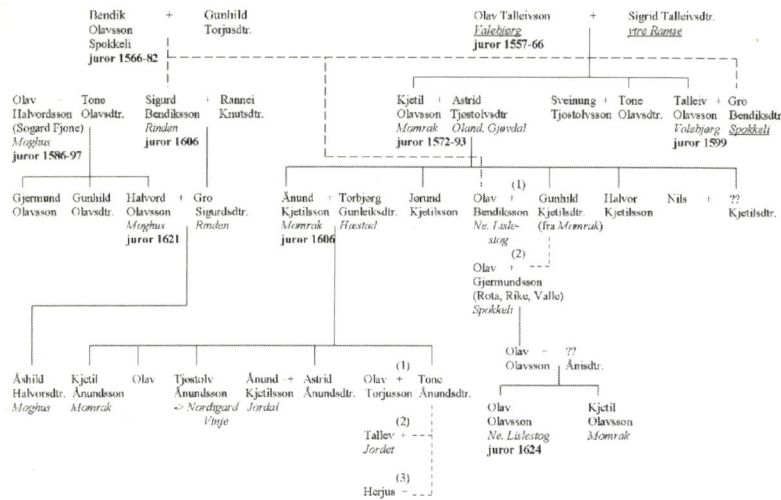

Fig. 3. Genealogical reconstruction for peasants attached to the farms
Valebjørg, Spokkeli and Momrak

While the point of departure here is kindred members who were attached to the farms *Valebjørg* and *Spokkeli*, as time went on descendants of these persons were also found at the farms *Moghus*, *Momrak*, *Rinden* and lower *Lislestog*. Olav Talleivsson at *Valebjørg* served as a local juror in 1557-1566, and two of his sons, Kjetil and Talleiv, took over as jurors in their turn towards the end of the century. Talleiv was married to Gro, a daughter of the former juror Bendik Olavsson at *Spokkeli*, who in his day was very likely the wealthiest peasant in Fyresdal, controlling a landed property that produced between 14 and 18 barrels of grain rent. (As we shall see later, two of his sons were also recruited to the position of juror, and one of his other daughters made an exceptionally good match in her marriage.) Kjetil Olavsson, for his part, had five children in his marriage with one Astrid Tjøstolvsdaughter from a neighbouring valley, and one of the sons, Ånund Kjetilsson, was appointed juror in the very first years of the seventeenth century. Thus, we have an example here of three generations of jurors, all descending through the male line. A sister of Ånund's, Gunhild Kjetilsdaughter, also married a son of Bendik Olavsson, but the marriage was childless. However, in a new marriage with a man from the neighbouring valley of Setesdal, she had a son, Olav, who in his turn had a son who served as juror in the 1620s. He lived at lower *Lislestog*, the residence of his grandmother. Following the line from Bendik Olavsson at *Spokkeli*, we can see that his son Sigurd, who took up residence at the farm *Rinden*, served as juror shortly after 1600. In his turn, he had a daughter, Gro, who married Halvor Olavsson, a man whom we met earlier (Figure 2) as a juror in the second decade of the seventeenth century and the son of the juror Olav Halvordsson at *Moghus*.

Perhaps the most interesting picture, however, is sketched out in Figure 4, where the children of Bendik Olavsson at *Spokkeli* are presented in detail along with marital connections between his offspring and the descendants of Olav Talleivsson at *Valebjørg*. As already mentioned, two of his sons, Kjetil and Sigurd, living at the farms *Rinden* and *Tarali* respectively, became local jurors. His daughter Sigrid for her part was married to a man from the annex parish of Skafså, Vetle Aslaksson at the farm *Storåsli*, who in his time was decidedly the richest landowner in the community. A taxation undertaken in 1603 records him as owning a landed property assessed for 20 barrels of grain rent, and in 1611 his wealth had increased to 26 barrels. He was actively engaged in the land market, buying and selling property shares, and amassed a great deal of property in this way himself. Still, a considerable part of the property recorded in his name probably stemmed from inheritance and dowry transferences from his wife's family, and thus had its origin in the property complex held by his father-in-law, Bendik Olavsson. As we have seen, in his time Bendik most probably was the wealthiest local peasant proprietor.

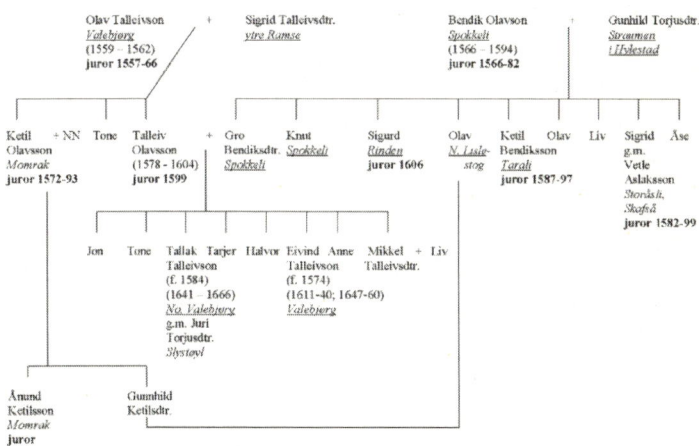

Fig. 4. Genealogical reconstruction for peasants attached to the farm Spokkeli

The descendants of Bendik Olavsson and the kindred having its point of departure in Olav Talleivsson at *Valebjørg* became affiliated by two marriages. In the first place, Bendik's daughter Gro was married to Olav's son Talleiv, who served as a local juror around the turn of the century, as we have seen. But then in the second generation counting down from Olav Talleivsson, a new link was established when the granddaughter of Olav married Gro's younger brother, Olav Bendiksson, residing at lower *Lislestog*. In other words, both Talleiv Olavsson and his brother's daughter married members of the same sibling group, the children of Bendik.

Another way that the kindred connections between local jurors can be ascertained is by charting those jurors who themselves were sons of former jurors. Out of 37 jurors serving during the latter half of the sixteenth century, 5 had such a direct relationship, as shown in the survey below. Some of the sons may even have taken over the office immediately after their father, or not many years after his period of tenure.

Fathers				Sons			
Forename	Patronymic	Location	Period	Forename	Patronymic	Location	Period
Gredgard	Bjørnsson	Loftsgrd. i Byrte	1483-1497	Åsmund	Gredgarsson	Loftsgrd. i Byrte	1516
Olav	Talleivsson	Valebjørg	1557- 1566	Ketil	Olavsson	Momrak	1572-1593
Olav	Talleivsson	Valebjørg	1557- 1566	Talleiv	Olavsson	Valebjørg	1599
Ledvord	Ledvorsson	Væting	1578	Sivord	Ledvorsson	Lislestog	1578-1595
Ledvord	Ledvorsson	Væting	1578	Gunnleik	Ledvorsson	Hæstad	1587-1597
Bendik	Olavsson	Spokkeli	1566-1582	Ketil	Bendiksson	Spokkeli	1587-1597

Table 1. Father–son relations among local jurors

These examples should suffice to show that at least some of the more resourceful[10] families with jurors in their midst did not allow marriages to be established haphazardly, but arranged them according to some kind of strategic thinking in order to establish or consolidate kinship ties with other families in the same position. Moreover, the strategic measures appear not to be confined to marriage exchange and the establishment of kinship networks solely, but also encompassed other resource assets as well – both 'social capital' of a more abstract nature, concerning experience and know-how

10. 'Resourceful' both because they possessed large amounts of property and because they were clever and capable in managing both these resources and their 'cultural capital'.

in juridical matters, and pure economic capital in the form of land ownership. Therefore, we must take a closer look at the mechanisms for distributing and transferring landed property.

5. Landed property as manifestation of relations between peas-
ants

The basic premises of the medieval Norwegian system of land tenure have
already been sketched out in the introduction. The so-called rent ownership
system not only emphasized the income aspect of landed property, irrespec-
tive of who the owner was, but also allowed for calculating and reckoning
with theoretical parts or proportions of a property, assessed for a fixed
amount of rent according to their production potential. This had significant
consequences for the division of the estate or property after the owner's
death, when the inheritance legislation prescribed that all heirs should have
their proportional shares. This included both men and women, although the
National Law Code of Magnus VI, 'The Lawmender' (1274) specified that
male heirs should have double the shares of female ones.[11] As a result of the
way in which the proportional shares of the farms' total rent were calculated, each of the heirs could have his or her legitimate share in the form of
a claim for a fixed yearly share of the total stipulated rent of the property
farms, while the eldest son was also guaranteed his 'residence right'. In
other words, the heirs who were not entitled to the main residence by birth
rank instead received proportional shares of annual rent obligations, which
the incumbent of the farm was obliged to pay them. This system avoided the
undesirable situation of splitting a farm or peasant holding into small portions or fragments that would have been unprofitable to cultivate separately.
At the same time, it resulted in a complex, criss-crossing network of different and partially reciprocal rent obligations. The land ownership cadastres
from the earliest years of the seventeenth century give ample examples of
such compound relationships, though we have to bear in mind that these
surveys give only a static picture of these fragmented, theoretical property
proportions at a specific moment of time, which is but a brief instant of an
ever ongoing, changing process.

To illustrate this point, we can turn to the so-called cadastre of allodial
lands from 1624.[12] As the following examples will demonstrate, this register

11. National Law Code of Magnus the Lawmender, Inheritance section, V, 7, *Norges
gamle Love, vol. II*, eds. R. Keyser and P. A. Munch (Christiania: 1848), 80-84; cf.
Taranger, *Magnus Lagabøters Landslov*, 80.
12. *Odelsjordebøker fra nokre vikværske len og Bratsberg Len 1624-26*, National Archives of Norway, Statthaldararkivet D IX – 9 (legg 4); printed version by O. A.
Helleberg, *Stattholderskapets jordebok over Telemark 1624* (Kongsberg: 2004).

gives a detailed survey of the various kinds of detailed and specified property relations that pertain to each farm.

Farm and Owner	Property share	Property title
Farm no. 81 – name: Hæstad		
Anund at Hæstad and his children	2,00 barrels	Marital property
Talleiv at Lundehall	0,50 barrels	By mortgage
Rolleiv at Døli, Skafså annex	2,00 barrels	Marital property
Farm no. 43 – name: Lislestog		
Torgeir at Lislestog (resident)	1,00 barrel	Allodial inheritance
Olluf at Lislestog	0,67 barrel	Bought property
Oluf at Taraldli	1,00 barrel	Allodial inheritance
Gunhild at Spokkeli and her children	0,67 barrel	Bought property
Åsmund at Veum	0,83 barrel	Marital property
Gro at Homme and her children (in the valley of Lårdal)	0,50 barrel	Allodial inheritance
Åsulv at Homme	0,50 barrel	Allodial inheritance
Farm no. 28 – name: Momrak		
Amund at Momrak (resident)	1,50 barrel	Allodial inheritance
Talleiv at Lundehall	0,50 barrel	Allodial inheritance
Gunnulv at Graver	0,50 barrel	Allodial inheritance
Nils at Songedal	0,50 barrel	Allodial inheritance
Gunhild at Spokkeli and her children	0,50 barrel	Allodial inheritance
Jørgen Vindsvoll (Åmotsdal)	1,00 barrel	Allodial inheritance
Farm no. 93 – name: Follsæ, in Veum annex parish		
Ulv at Follsæ (resident)	1,42 barrel	Allodial inheritance
Oluf at Tveito (in the valley of Lårdal)	0,67 barrel	Marital property
Vetle at Gåstjønn (in Skafså annex)	0,67 barrel	By mortgage
Farm no. 85 / 86 – Veum, in Veum annex parish		
Åsmund at Veum	1,00 barrel	Marital property
Bergit at Songedalstveit	0,67 barrel	Marital property
Vetle at Storåsli (in Skafså annex)	1,00 barrel	Allodial inheritance
Vetle at Gåstjønn (in Skafså annex)	1,00 barrel	Allodial inheritance

Table 2. Property survey of 1624, by farm

These few examples from the 1624 survey illustrate the complex ownership structure of the individual farms. Each farm has a set of owners, primarily living in the valley of Fyresdal, but the fact that peasants residing on and cultivating farms in the neighbouring valleys are also included demonstrates that kinship and marriage ties also extend beyond the valley. Furthermore, the peasant residing on and cultivating the farm is not necessarily the owner of the greatest property share in the farm. In the examples above, the resident farmer's share comes out to 25, 27, 33, 54 and 80 percent respectively. For all the 69 farms recorded in the 1624 survey, the average proportion of shares held by the residing peasants ranges from 0 to 100 percent, with an average of 55 percent.

Furthermore, since the 1624 records are very precise and detailed concerning the title or mode of acquisition of each property part, we can observe that every farm appears as a kind of 'node' or 'meeting place' for peasant landowners who have acquired their rights in different ways, or through various mechanisms or measures. In some cases, share-holders meet who have acquired their parts by way of inheritance (allodial inheritance), by marriage (dowry), by purchase, or by money-lending against a share in the farm (mortgage). Other farms appear with property shares stemming from allodial inheritance only, but dispersed among several heirs, as in the case with the farm *Momrak*. According to Norwegian law, 'allodial property' was land which had been passed on through the same (bilateral) kinship group for a certain minimum of time, and to which members of this kindred had certain rights of redemption, in case the property should be offered for sale. It is interesting to observe that the allodial lands in this case – and in fact in the whole Upper Telemark region – are not confined to the property shares owned and cultivated by the peasant residing on the farm in question. In fact, many peasants held property shares in farms cultivated by others, because their allodial rights stemmed from diverse inheritance settlements. As a result, about 70 percent of the total amount of property held by allodial rights in the valley was cultivated by the owners themselves, while 30 percent consisted of allodial property shares held in farms tilled by others. Consequently, allodial property belonging to a single owner could be dispersed among several farms. The widow Gunhild Olavsdaughter had been married to the resident peasant at eastern *Nape* and held half the farm after his death – probably as her part of a conjugal joint ownership – but at the same time had her own allodial shares in the farms *Svalestog*, *Snarteland* and *Moghus*.[13] The peasant Knut Tallaksson at *Slystøyl*, for his part, held allodial inheritance shares in the farms *Nesland*, *Skrei*, *Spokkeli* and *Strøm* in the valley of Setesdal, in addition to owning *Slystøyl* in its totality.

13. S. Marvik, *Fyresdal: Gards- og ættesoge, vol. II,* publ. by Fyresdal kommune (1992), 533.

This highly complex pattern was primarily due to the 1274 law code mentioned above, whereby every member of a sibling group had a right to proportional shares of the inheritance, though these were of varying size according to whether the heir was male or female.

Thus, at any given moment of time, an analysis of the property structure and ownership relations attached to each farm demonstrates how the farms – as property objects – appear as 'nodes' or 'meeting places' for networks of kindreds tied together by inheritance and marriage bonds. In view of this complex, criss-crossing pattern of obligations and partly reciprocal affiliations, it seems fruitful and relevant to follow those scholars who advocate that 'property' should be understood as a relational concept, a phenomenon which primarily expresses the relations between persons rather than between persons and objects. Attention should therefore primarily be directed at the various interpersonal relationships that are constructed by and through property, and not so much towards lists or catalogues that are focused solely on the amount of property in question.

In his analysis of family-based property and production in the village of Neckarhausen in southwest Germany, David W. Sabean gives the following relational definition of 'property':

> Property is nothing apart from the set of relations of which it is composed. That is to say, it is the complex totality of rights, claims, duties and obligations between people with regard to things. Although we loosely speak of things or objects as property, what makes them so is not the relationship between themselves and persons but that between persons.[14]

And in an article in the *University of Toronto Law Journal* from 2003, David Lametti states:

> Private property is a social institution that comprises a variety of contextual relationships among individuals through objects of social wealth and is meant to serve a variety of individual and collective purposes. It is characterized by allocating to individuals a measure of control over the use and alienation of, some degree of exclusivity in the enjoyment of, and some measure obligation to and responsibilities for scarce and separable objects of social wealth.[15]

The mechanisms leading to dismemberment and division of property complexes at inheritance, and the various measures applied in the aftermath to compensate for or to confirm the resulting distribution, might easily result

---

14. D. W. Sabean, *Property, Production, and Family in Neckarhausen, 1700-1870* (Cambridge: 1990), 184.
15. D. Lametti, 'The Concept of Property: Relations Through Objects of Social Wealth', *University of Toronto Law Journal* 53/4 (2003), 325-78.

in a state of affairs where a single land-owning peasant entered into double relations, both paying and collecting rent, sometimes even in a reciprocal relationship. A peasant might collect rent from property shares that he or she had inherited, bartered or bought, while being at the same time obliged to pay rent to siblings and co-heirs who had left their farm of origin but still held inheritance shares in it. An analysis of the peasants' rent paying and collecting which I have undertaken on the basis of the 1615 cadastre[16] illustrates this amply (fig. 5). This may also serve as an illustration of the real interpersonal nature of 'property relations'.

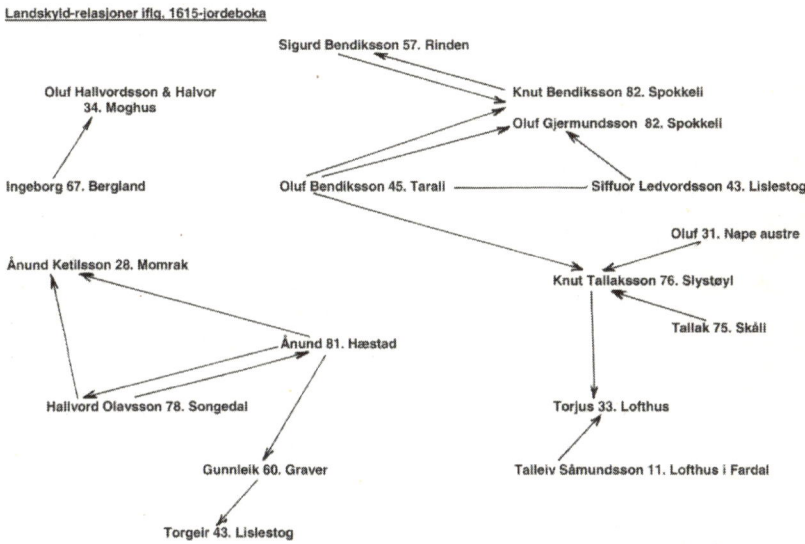

Fig. 5. Rent payment relationships according to the land cadaster of 1615

6. The peasants' preoccupation with questions of property transfers

As we have seen, an overwhelming proportion of the 126 letters issued in the parish of Fyresdal between 1300 and 1600 concerns questions of property such as inheritance matters, endowment, proofs of title, deeds and sales, and bartering of property shares, as well as corroboration of kinship ties. To highlight some of the questions which lay on the peasants' minds, a few typical examples can be cited:

16. Jordebog og regnskap over Leding og Skinnskatt m.v. – 1615: *Jordebok over Telemark ca. 1615*, 1991.

a) Clarifying kinship relations in connection with inheritance: In a letter issued in 1420 or 1421 at the farm *Kilan*, two local jurors pronounced the verdict that the paternal aunts of Audny Sveinungsdaughter and Tolv Gunnarsson had been legitimate daughters of the same father. The inheritance after them was therefore kept in custody until binding evidence could be produced.[17]

b) Redemption of property from the King / the representative of the King. In 1557 the two brothers Salmund and Tallak Berulvssons sold the farm *Brokke* in the region of Hegglandsgrend – which had been redeemed from the King – to their sister Helga and her husband Torbjørn Torgjulsson.[18]

c) Verdict in property case by the county judge in Skien, assisted by a committee of twelve jurors: Based upon a verdict by a committee consisting of twelve jurors, the county judge in Skien in June 1495 decided that Gunnulv Olversson, because of allodial rights, had the right to redeem the farm *Graver* from Torgeir Hallvardsson, who held it for the time being. Gunnulv was to appear on Graver on 15 September of the same year, produce witnesses to his allodial rights, and pay the purchase price to Torgeir.[19]

d) The consent of the relatives is required for the sale of a property part to a third party: In 1520, Olav Roaldsson on the farm *Kilan* sold a property part in the same farm to one Torgils Torvildsson. The four jurors who testified to it and produced a 'testifying charter' about it, emphasized that he did this with the consent of his mother, his stepfather, his three sisters as well as two brothers-in-law.[20] While in some ways resembling the continental practice of *laudatio parentum*,[21] this proceeding was probably triggered by an unfinished inheritance case, since all the mentioned relatives seem to belong to a group of relevant and possible heirs.

e) A case concerning dowry for married and non-married siblings, distinguishing between whole and half dowry: In 1599 a strife occurred about the size of the dowry and maternal inheritance for a group of nine siblings at the farm *Aslestad* in the northern part of the valley. Of the nine siblings, four had got married before their mother died, and they had all got full dowry. The remaining five unmarried siblings now demanded just as great a dowry as the first four, but according to the living father, his property would not suffice to give them so great a dowry. He would only manage to give the

17. *Diplomatarium Norvegicum* (hereafter DN), (Christiania/Oslo: 1847/1992), vol. X, no. 134.
18. *Diplomatarium Norvegicum, Series Topographica, Bygdesamlingar, Fyresdal i Telemark 1308-1708* (hereafter DN F), eds. A. Bugge and O. Kolsrud, (Kristiania: 1919), nos 58, 65.
19. DN VIII, no. 437.
20. DN IX, no. 500.
21. S. White, *Custom, Kinship, and Gifts to Saints: The* Laudatio Parentum *in Western France, 1050-1150,* (Chapel Hill and London: 1988), esp. 86-129.

remaining half as much. 6 jurors now made the verdict that the first, endowed four siblings must return what they had received, so that a new redistribution/ "new deal" could be made. One of the endowed daughters was however dead, and her children should be allowed to keep their maternal inheritance. All the other siblings should then be considered equal concerning dowry and maternal inheritance.[22] This verdict was in fact in concordance with the dowry regulations laid down in Magnus the Lawmender's National Law Code of 1274,[23] but it would also seem to correspond with some of the redistribution practices recorded from some parts of medieval France (Normandy, Brittany, Poitou).[24]

Marriage, kinship and property as relational elements of a 'social field' according to Bourdieu's conception

> Marriage has the primary function of ensuring the continuity of the lineage without compromising the integrity of the heritage.[25]

Clearly, marriage exchanges among the peasants – and in particular between the juror families – cannot be treated as isolated, but must be analysed in a wider context, taking several factors into consideration. These include not just the consequences for inheritance and property distribution but also the opportunity to establish or strengthen favourable kinship relations between resourceful families, to secure social status and relative positions within the parish community, and to convey specific knowledge about legal matters to new generations. In their aspirations for favourable marital relations, these peasant actors obviously had a set of goals in mind and drew on a broader set of resources. They were engaged in a 'relational game' concerning the mobilization and consolidation of resources, which can best be understood by Bourdieu's conceptualization of actors ('agents') who occupy certain positions within a 'social field'; that is, actors who fight for something which they have in common and recognize as such, and who have differential access to various kinds of resources. These resources may correspondingly be analysed using Bourdieu's terminology of 'economic', 'social', and 'cultural' as well as 'symbolic' capital.

To use 'social field' as an analytical tool for analysing social interaction is in Bourdieu's terms an approach for thinking relationally.[26] Accord-

---

22. DN F, no. 112.
23. National Law Code of Magnus the Lawmender, Inheritance section, V,1, *Norges gamle Love indtil 1387, vol. II*, 74-75; cf. *Magnus Lagabøters Landslov*, trans. A. Taranger (Oslo and Bergen: 1979 [1915]), 72-73.
24. J. Goody, 'Inheritance, Property and Women: Some Comparative Considerations', in J. Goody, J. Thirsk and E. P. Thompson (eds.), *Family and Inheritance: Rural Society in Western Europe 1200-1800* (Cambridge: 1979), 10-36.
25. P. Bourdieu, *The Bachelor's Ball* (Cambridge and Malden, MA: 2008), 12.

ing to Bourdieu, a 'social field' is a system of relations between positions occupied by specialized agents and institutions, who are contending for something they have in common.[27] A passage from his dialogues with Loïc Wacquant stands out as particularly instructive:

> In analytical terms, a field may be defined as a network, or a configuration, of objective relations between positions. These positions are objectively defined, in their existence and in the determinations they impose upon their existence and in the determinations they impose upon their occupants, agents or institutions, by their present and potential situation (situs) in the structure of the distribution of species of power (or capital) whose possession commands access to the specific profits that are at stake in the field, as well as by their objective relation to other positions (domination, subordination, homology etc.).[28]

The sociologist Richard Jenkins points out that an investigation of a social field entails three distinct operations:

> First the relationship of the field in the question to the 'field of power' (politics) must be understood. The field of power is thus to be regarded as the dominant or pre-eminent field of any society; it is the source of the hierarchical power relations which structure all other fields. Second, within the field in question one must construct a 'social topology' or map of the 'objective structure' of the positions which make up the field, and relationships between them in the competition for the field's specific form of capital. Third, the habitus(es) of the agents within the field must be analysed, along with the trajectories or strategies which are produced in the interaction between habitus and the constraints and opportunities which are determined by the structure of the field. The field is the crucial mediating context wherein external factors – changing circumstances – are brought to bear upon individual practice and institutions.[29]

Of special interest for this analysis is that Bourdieu repeatedly uses the metaphor of a card game to illustrate the acts of position-holders engaged in

---

26. P. Bourdieu and L. J. D. Wacquant, *An Invitation to Reflexive Sociology* (Cambridge and Malden, MA: 1992), 96-107; cf. P. Bourdieu, 'Structuralism and Theory of Sociological Knowledge', *Social Research* 35/4 (1968), 681-706 and P. Bourdieu, 'A Lecture on the Lecture', in *In Other Words* (Cambridge: 1990), 177-98.

27. D. Broady, *Sociologi och epistomologi. Om Pierre Bourdieus författarskap och den historiska epistemologin* (Stockholm: 1990), 270.

28. Bourdieu and Wacquant, *An Invitation*, 97; cf. the following definition in the chapter 'Quelques propriétés des champs' in P. Bourdieu, *Questions de sociologie* (Paris: 1984), 115: '[...] tous les gens qui sont engagés dans un champ ont en commun un certain nombre d'intérêts fondamentaux, à savoir tout ce qui est lié à l'existence du champ: de là une complicité objective qui est sous-jacente à tous les antagonismes.'

29. R. Jenkins, *Pierre Bourdieu* (London and New York: 2002), 87; cf. Bourdieu and Wacquant, *An Invitation,* 104.

keeping up relations within such a social field,[30] in particular the strategic and tactical considerations applied by families striving to establish the most ·favourable marriages for their children, given the social and economic assets at the family's disposal:

> Let us imagine that in the society under consideration here the marriage of each of its children represents the playing of a card in a card game. It is clear that the value of this 'move' (measured by the criteria of the system) depends both on the quality of the hand that the family has been dealt, whose strength is defined by the rules of the game, and on the greater or lesser degree of skill with which this hand is played. In other words, given that matrimonial strategies (at least in the most advantaged families) were always designed to bring about a 'good marriage' rather than just any marriage, that is, to maximize the profits and/or minimize the economic and symbolic costs of the marriage as a transaction of a very particular kind, these strategies are in every case governed by the value of the material and symbolic patrimony that can be committed to the transaction and by the mode of transmission of the patrimony, which established the systems of interests of the various claimants by assigning differential rights to the property to each of them according to sex and birth rank.[31]

7. The complex interactions among the landholding peasants of Fyresdal

Above, we have depicted the property relations centred at each farm and expressed in the complex of property shares belonging to various owners as they may be ascertained for any given moment of time, based for instance on analysis of property cadastres from the early seventeenth century. We will now adopt a more dynamic approach, focusing upon the continous flow of transactions that are taking place continually, and which to a great extent are triggered off by deaths and ensuing inheritance distributions. Such transactions are exactly the type that are recorded in the cited charter evidence, but obviously the preserved letters do only reflect a minor part of all the transactions that really are going on.

From a dynamic point of view, each generational shift – triggered by the death of a resident peasant – starts a wave of redistributing landed property. As soon as a resident peasant dies, a complex process of dividing and distributing property shares among the heirs begins. As soon as the distribu-

---

30. 'These objective relations are relations between the positions occupied in the distributions of resources which are or may become active, effective, like the trumps in a game of cards, in competition for the appropriation of the rare goods of which this social universe is the locus.' (Bourdieu, 'Social Space and Symbolic Power', in *In Other Words*, 128.)
31. Bourdieu, *The Bachelor's Ball*, 138.

tion after this settlement is clear, a new series of new operations begins, with the purpose of securing and guaranteeing the resulting distribution – or, as it might be perceived from the opposite perspective, quite contrary operations with the aim of defying or changing the new distribution and restoring the old one, or at least some of its main features. In this game, some kindreds have greater resources – more 'social capital' and 'economic capital' – to mobilize, or they are more clever in deploying them.

For each generational shift it was above all a question of securing the main residence for the oldest allodial heir, according to the National Law Code of 1274. But next, and almost equally important, it was also imperative to have the younger siblings – both sons and daughters – situated as well as possible, corresponding to their invested economic and social capital. This was partly done by way of strategic marriages, with the hope of making them able to control or redeem inheritance parts that had been distributed and dispersed. And partly by applying regulations in the same inheritance law, which secured all siblings a part of the inheritance, though with double as great shares for male inheritors as compared to female ones.[32]

Attachment

Table 3. Local jurors in Fyresdal ca. 1420-ca. 1600

Id.:	Forename	Patronymi-con	Period as juror	County	Farm	Son of id.no.:	Mentioned in trans-action concerning land or debt
00061	Gunnar	Petersson	[1389] – 1421				
00003	Bjørn	Auversson	[1389] – 1421				
00028	Torgrim	Lovardsson	1444 – 1450				
00027	Torgrim	Helgeson	1444 – 1462	Moland	35. Væting		
00005	Egil	Neridsson	1450 – 1462	Moland	45. Taraldlien		1459 (DN I, 848)
00041	Torgrim	Lavransson	1457	Moland	2. Vik		
00036	Åsmund	Folkeson	1457	Moland	60. Graver		
00066	Hallvard	Ulvsson	1457	Moland	Fardal		
00011	Hallvard	Reidarsson	1481 – 1483	Mo			
00022	Olav	Hergjulsson	1481 – 1493	Mo			1483 (DN VII, 493)
00017	Ketil	Ormsson	1481 – 1497	Skafså	43. Åsland		
00025	Svein	Arneson	1483 – 1492				
00008	Gredgard	Bjørnsson	1483 – 1497	Mo	3. Loftsgarden (i Byrte)		1483 (DN VII, 493), 1493 (DN VII, 510), 1497 (DN VII, 516)
00006	Gjermund	Torgjusson	1489				
00010	Gunnulv	Olversson	1489 – 1495	Moland	60. Graver		1495 (DN VII, 437) 1497 (DN X, 282)
00001	Are	Sæmundsson	1489 – 1506				
00013	Helge	Ulvsson	1489 – 1519	Moland [?]	35. Væting [?]		
00012	Hallvard	Steinulvsson	1491 – 1497	Moland	64. Metveit / 66. Kleivi		1462 (DN I, 857)
00007	Gjermund	Torgilsson	1506 – 1539	Moland			
00057	Torgeir	Avalsson	1515 – 1516	Skafså / Valle [?]			
00058	Tormod	Drengsson	1515 – 1526	Moland			
00063	Åsmund	Gredgards-son	1516	Skafså	3. Loftsgarden (i Byrte)	00008	1497 (DN VII, 516) 1515 (DN IV, 1070)
00047	Ånund	Gjermunds-son	1516 – 1525	Moland/ Skafså [?]			

00035	Øystein	Ulvsson	1525 – 1558				
00053	Tjøstolv	Torgeirsson	1526 – 1536	Skafså/ Moland [?]			
00048	Bjørgulv	Helgeson	1528 – 1536	Moland [?]	35. Væting [?]		1576 (DN F, 74 – Arvesk.)
00056	Tolleiv	Jonsson	1530 – 1539	Moland (Hegland)			
00067	Hallvard	Ulvsson [?]	1539 – 1550	Moland	Fardal [?]		1530-50 (DN X, 736) 1534 (DN F, 52)
00040	Tallak	Olavsson	1556 – 1557				
00044	Audun	Bjørnsson *	1556 – 1566	Skafså	46. Dølen		
00052	Torkell	Aslaksson	1557 – 1561				
00029	Torbjørn	Ånundsson **	1557 – 1561	Moland	34. Moghus		
00004	Bjug	Anundsson	1557 – 1566	Moland	85. Veum		
00051	Olav	Talleivsson	1557 – 1566	Moland	26. Valebjørg		
00033	Ulv	Arneson	1558 – 1578	Moland	14. Breivik no.		
00062	Eivind	Egilsson [?]	1566	Skafså	57. Storåsli		
00002	Bendik	Olavsson	1566 – 1582	Moland	82. Spokkeli		1580 (DN F, 77)
00023	Solve	Torjusson	1572 – 1578	Moland	29. Nape vestre		
00015	Ketil	Olavsson ***	1572 – 1593	Moland	28. Momrak	00051	1578 (DN F, 76)
00031	Tore	Torjusson	1576 – 1578				
00030	Torgeir	Torjusson	1578				
00018	Ledvord	Ledvordsson	1578	Moland	35. Væting		
00024	Sivord	Ledvordsson	1578 – 1595	Moland	43. Lislestog	00018	
00016	Knut	Arneson	1580 – 1597	Moland	38. Svalestog		
00034	Vetle	Aslaksson	1582 – 1599	Skafså	57. Storåsli		1603 (DN F, 120)
00065	Torgeir	Knutsson	1583	Mo	15. Åse		
00046	Olav	Niklausson	1583	Moland	19. Berge		
00032	Vetle	Olavsson ****	1583 – 1597	Skafså	65. Gåstjønn		
00019	Mikkel	Torjusson	1585 – 1587	Moland	62. Bondal nordre		
00020	Olav	Halvordsson	1586 – 1597	Moland	34. Moghus		1598 (DN F, 109)
00043	Tjodolv	Torkellsson	1587	Moland			
00014	Ketil	Eivindsson	1587 – 1590	Skafså	50. Bilstad [77. Aslestad]		1583 (DN F, 79)
00009	Gunnleik	Ledvordsson	1587 – 1595	Moland	81. Hæstad	00018	1572 (DN F, 71) 1601 (DN F, 116)

00045	Ketil	Bendiksson	1587 – 1597	Moland	82. Spokkeli	00002	1595 (DN F, 101)
							1595 (DN F, 103)
							1599 (DN F, 113)
00068	Olver	Gunnuvsson [?]	1589 – 1603	Skafså	69. Lauvvik		1601 (DN F, 116)
00042	Torkell	Tormodsson	1590				
00049	Gjermund	Olavsson [?]	1590 – 1599	Skafså	46. Dølen		
00050	Jon [?]	Tallaksson	1594 – 1599	Moland	35. Væting [?]		
00054	Talleiv	Såmundsson [?]	1597	Moland	11. Lofthus i Fardal		
00059	Sneri	Arneson	1599				
00060	Talleiv	Olavsson	1599	Moland	26. Valebjørg [?]	00051	1578 (DN F, 75)
00064	Jon	Nikulsson	1599	Mo	43. Åsland		

   *   Peasant bailiff 1553 – 1555 (DN XII, no. 652)
  **   Peasant bailiff 1561 – 1566
 ***   Peasant bailiff 1576
**** Peasant bailiff 1597 – 1619

271

Clandestine Marriage and Parental Consent in John Calvin's Geneva: The Gradual Synthesis of Theology, Statutes, and Case Law

John Witte, Jr.[1]

1. Introduction

John Calvin (1509-1564), the Protestant Reformer of Geneva, transformed the Western theology and law of sex, marriage, and family life. Building on a generation of Protestant reforms elsewhere in northern Europe, Calvin constructed a comprehensive new theology and jurisprudence that made marital formation and dissolution, children's nurture and welfare, family cohesion and support, and sexual sin and crime essential concerns for both church and state. Working with other jurists and theologians, Calvin drew

---

1.   This article represents work in progress on a multi-volume project initiated in collaboration with Robert M. Kingdon, *Sex, Marriage and Family in John Calvin's Geneva* published by Wm. B. Eerdmans Publishing Company. The first volume, subtitled *Courtship, Engagement and Marriage* (2005) is in print; the second volume, subtitled *The Christian Household*, will soon go to press. I wish to thank the late Professor Kingdon and Dr. Thomas A. Lambert for their expert commentary and criticisms, and Mr. M. Wallace McDonald for his diligent research and excellent translations of the Consistory cases in the Genevan archives sampled in the third section of this article.

I shall be using the following standard abbreviations throughout: CO – *Ioannis Calivini opera quae supersunt omnia*, ed. W. Baum, E. Cunitz and E. Reuss, 59 vols, *Corpus Reformatorum* series, vols 29-87 (Brunswick: 1863-1900); R. Consist. –*Registres du Consistoire de Genève au Temps de Calvin*, 21 vols, eds. R. M. Kingdon et al. (Geneva: 1996-); R. Conseil – *Les Registres du Conseil de Genève*, 13 vols, eds. E. Rivoire and V. van Berchem (Geneva: 1900-1940).

the Consistory and Council of Geneva into a creative new alliance to govern sex, marriage, and family life in the city. Together, these authorities outlawed monasticism and mandatory clerical celibacy, and encouraged marriage for all fit adults. They set clear guidelines for courtship and engagement. They mandated parental consent, peer witness, church consecration, and state registration for valid marriage formation. They radically reconfigured weddings and wedding feasts. They reformed marital property and inheritance, marital consent and impediments. They created new rights and duties for wives within the bedroom and for children within the household. They streamlined the grounds and procedures for annulment. They introduced fault-based divorce for both husbands and wives on grounds of adultery and desertion. They encouraged the remarriage of men and women who were divorced or widowed. They punished rape, fornication, prostitution, sodomy, and other sexual felonies with startling new severity. They put firm new restrictions on dancing, sumptuousness, ribaldry, and obscenity. They put new stock in catechesis and education, and created new schools, curricula, and teaching aids. They provided new sanctuary to illegitimate, abandoned, and abused children. They created new protections for abused wives and impoverished widows. Many of these reforms of sixteenth-century Geneva were echoed and elaborated in numerous Reformed communities, on both sides of the Atlantic, and a good number of these reforms found their way into our modern civil law and common law traditions.[2]

This chapter analyzes a small but important part of Calvin's reformation, namely, the doctrine of parental consent to a child's engagement and marriage. Parental consent was one of the bright flashpoints of confessional dispute between Protestants and Catholics in the Reformation era. In the first third of the sixteenth century, Protestant leaders like Martin Luther, Martin Bucer, Ulrich Zwingli, and others had championed mandatory parental consent as their biblical answer to the late medieval toleration of 'clandestine'[3] engagements and marriages. And Protestant magistrates soon insti-

---

2.   This is the thesis of Witte and Kingdon, *Sex, Marriage and Family in John Calvin's Geneva*.

3.   In Calvin's Geneva, the phrase 'clandestine marriage' generally meant marriages contracted without parental consent (and occasionally also without two witnesses). According to some recent studies, 'clandestine marriage' had a second meaning in the day: marriages between parties who married despite an absolute impediment (such as incest or precontract) that they knew but kept clandestine. Some case studies in France and Germany suggest that the second type of clandestine marriage was heavily litigated in late medieval church courts. See K. M. Linder, *Courtship and the Courts: Marriage and Law in Southern Germany, 1350-1550* (Th.D. Diss. Harvard: 1988), 126-28; B. Gottlieb, 'The Meaning of Clandestine Marriage', in R. Wheaton and T. K. Hareven (eds.), *Family and Sexuality in French History* (Philadelphia: 1980), 53; R. Lettmann, *Die Diskussion über die klandestinen Ehen und die Einführung einer zur Gültigkeit verpflichtenden Eheschliessung auf dem Konzil von Trent* (Münster: 1967). It was the first type of clandestine marriage that Calvin

tuted new marriage ordinances with a firm parental consent requirement built into their marital formation rules.[4] In 1563, the Council of Trent instituted similar requirements into the canon law of the Catholic Church.

Calvin and his Genevan colleagues ultimately carved out something of a *via media* between late medieval Catholic and early Protestant teachings on parental consent. In Calvin's Geneva, the consent of the couple was indispensable to the validity of both their engagement and their marriage. Without the free and full consent of both the man and the woman, the engagement and marriage contracts were void. The consent of parents (or guardians) was equally indispensable to the validity of a minor child's engagement and marriage. The consent of the father was sufficient; the consent of the mother counted only if the father was absent and other relatives concurred. In the absence of both parents, guardians would give their consent, again with priority for the male voice.

Clandestine engagements were presumptively void in Calvin's Geneva. Either fiancé(e), either set of parents, or even a third party (including a zealous minister or magistrate) could have these engagements annulled and the children punished. Clandestine marriages, however, were presumptively valid. Neither the couple nor their parents could have their marriages annulled just because they had been contracted without parental consent. Calvin came to this position on the validity of clandestine marriages only reluctantly in later life, aware that he was now closer to medieval Catholic teachings than to the teachings of some other Protestants, and even the Council of Trent.

As with several other topics on marriage and family life, Calvin first set out his legal views on parental consent in some detail in a lengthy Marriage Ordinance that he first drafted for the city of Geneva in 1545 and then revised with a committee in 1546.[5] Over the next fifteen years, he gradually

---

and his colleagues had in mind and that the Consistory adjudicated. The Consistory did occasionally encounter and punish parties who tried to keep their known impediments clandestine, but they did not apply the term 'clandestine' or 'clandestine marriage' to these instances.

4. See, among many others, S. Ozment, *When Fathers Ruled: Family Life in Reformation Europe* (Cambridge, MA: 1983); S. Ozment, *Ancestors: The Loving Family in Old Europe* (Cambridge, MA: 2001); L. Stone, *The Family, Sex, and Marriage in England, 1500-1800* (New York: 1979); R. M. Kingdon, *Adultery and Divorce in Calvin's Geneva* (Cambridge, MA: 1995); H. Selderhuis, *Marriage and Divorce in the Thought of Martin Bucer*, trans. J. Vriend and L. D. Bierma (Kirksville, MO: 1999); J. Witte, Jr., *From Sacrament to Contract: Religion, Marriage, and Law in the Western Tradition* (Louisville, KY: 2012 – 2nd ed.).

5. On 3 August 1545, the Council had commissioned Calvin and the four syndics to prepare a draft marriage ordinance. R. Conseil 40, 202v. A draft ordinance was completed on 5 November 1545, presented to the Small Council on 10 November, and to twelve representatives of the General Council on 13 November. It was commended but not formally approved, and circulated thereafter among ministers and magistrates of Geneva and beyond in slightly varying drafts. CO 10/1, 33n. On

laid out his theological rationale for these legal views and made modest legal refinements. From the start, the Geneva Consistory and Council, which together governed marriage and family law questions for the city, followed the 1546 Marriage Ordinance to the letter, helping to make the doctrine of parental consent a vital part of the Genevan Reformation.

2. The 1546 Marriage Ordinance and its interpretation

Like the medieval canonists before him, Calvin started with the principle of freedom of marital contract. Marriage, he insisted, depended in its essence on the mutual consent of both the man and the woman. Absent proof of consent by a fit man and a fit woman who had the freedom and capacity to marry, there could be no valid marriage. Calvin defended this principle repeatedly in his commentaries and sermons: 'While all contracts ought to be voluntary, freedom ought to prevail especially in marriage, so that no one may pledge his faith against his will.'[6] 'God considers that compulsory and forced marriages never come to a good end.... [I]f the husband and the wife are not in mutual agreement and do not love each other, this is a profanation of marriage, and not a marriage at all, properly speaking. For the will is the principal bond.'[7] When a woman wishes to marry, she must thus not 'be thrust into it reluctantly or compelled to marry against her will, but left to her own free choice'.[8] 'When a man is going to marry and he takes a wife, let him take her of his own free will, knowing that where there is not a true and pure love, there is nothing but disorder, and one can expect no grace from God.'[9]

Also like the medieval canonists, Calvin distinguished between contracts of engagement and contracts of marriage – or betrothals and espousals as he called them, following the tradition. Engagements were future promis-

---

11 November 1549, another committee, again led by Calvin, was convened to study existing marriage law and to recommend improvements to the Marriage Ordinance. R. Conseil 44, 261v. Calvin presented his report on 25 November, but complained on 20 January and, 17 and 24 February 1550 that still no official position had been taken on the Ordinance. R. Conseil 44, 273v, 306v, 324v, 329v. On 1 May 1551, Calvin again complained to the Council that the lack of clear guidelines led to much confusion over questions of marriage. It was not until 1561 that it finally received formal endorsement, now with a few more amendments. See detailed notes in CO 10/1, 33 n. The 1545 and 1546 draft is in CO 10/1, 33-44 and in *Registres de la compagnie des pasteurs de Genève au temps de Calvin*, 2 vols, ed J.-F. Bergier and R. M. Kingdon (Geneva: 1964), 1, 30-38. The final 1561 version is incorporated in *Les Ordonnances ecclesiastiques* (1561) in CO, 10/1, 91-124.

6.   Comm. Josh. 15:14.
7.   Serm. Deut. 25:5-12.
8.   Comm. Gen. 24:57.
9.   Serm. Deut. 25:5-12.

es to be married. Marriages were present promises to be married. But, unlike the medieval canonists, Calvin removed the need for the parties to use specific formulaic words: any clear indication of a future or present intent to marry would do. He softened the distinction and shortened the duration between engagements and marriages. He also insisted that the engagement contract be announced through public banns in the church and community and registered with the civil authorities, and that the marriage contract be celebrated in a mandatory church wedding.

The 1546 Marriage Ordinance took pains to ensure the free and full consent of both parties to the engagement and marriage contracts. It required that both sets of promises be made 'simply' and 'honorably in the fear of God'.[10] Engagements were to be initiated by 'a sober proposal' from the man, accepted by the woman, and witnessed by at least two persons of 'good reputation'.[11] Engagements clandestinely made, qualified with onerous conditions, or procured by coercion were automatically annulled – and the couple themselves, and any accomplices in their wrongdoing, could face punishment. Engagements procured through trickery or 'surprise', or made 'frivolously, as when merely touching glasses when drinking together', could be annulled on petition by either party.[12] Engagement promises extracted by or from children below the age of consent were presumptively invalid, though children could confirm them upon reaching majority. Engagements involving a newcomer to the city were not valid until the parties produced proof of the newcomer's integrity of character and eligibility for marriage. Absent such proof, the couple had to wait a year before they could marry.[13]

Normally, a Genevan couple, once properly betrothed, had little time to waste. Neither their publicly announced engagement nor the civil registration of their marriage was sufficient to constitute a marriage. A formal church wedding had to follow – within six weeks of engagement. If the couple procrastinated in their wedding plans, they would be reprimanded by the Consistory; if they persisted, they would be 'sent before the Council so that they may be compelled to celebrate it'.[14]

Not only the mutual consent of the parties, but also the consent of their parents was critical to the validity of an engagement and marriage contract. Calvin devoted no less than eight of the first ten articles of his 1546 Marriage Ordinance to the doctrine of parental consent. In the 1545 draft, Calvin had seemed so eager to maximize the rights of parental consent that he set the age of majority unusually high: Boys had to be 24, girls 20 before they

10. Item 11, 15, CO 10/1, 33ff.
11. Ibid., item 6.
12. Ibid., item 11.
13. Ibid., item 19.
14. Ibid., item 16.

could marry without seeking their parents' consent.[15] The 1546 Marriage Ordinance lowered these ages of majority to 20 and 18 for boys and girls respectively.[16] This was closer to the Protestant norm but still a bit high, and Calvin still advised that even fully emancipated children 'always be governed by the advice of their fathers'.[17]

The consent of the father was the most critical. The consent of the mother controlled only when the father was absent and no other relatives were present. If other relatives were at hand, the mother's views had to concur with theirs.[18] In his 1545 draft, Calvin had said that, in the absence of the father, the mother needed to have the concurrence only of the 'closest and most important' relatives to consent to a marriage.[19] He dropped this qualification in the 1546 version. Now it read that the mother's consent would count only if and until she had 'consulted one of the relatives if there are any' – without regard for their 'closeness' or 'importance' to the family. In the absence of both parents, guardians would give their consent to a child's engagement and marriage, again with priority for the male voice.

The 1546 Marriage Ordinance made clear that this parental consent was only a supplement to, not a substitute for, the consent of the couple themselves. Parents were prohibited from coercing their children into unwanted engagements, or withholding their consent or payment of dowry until the child chose a partner whom they favored.[20] Parents were further prevented from forcing youngsters into marriage before they were mature enough to consent to and participate safely in the institution. Children 'observing a modest and reverend spirit' could refuse to yield to their parents' insistence on an unwanted fiancé(e) or a premature engagement.[21] Other children, confronting a 'negligent or excessively strict' father, could 'have him compelled to give a dowry' in support of a marriage they contracted in spite of him.[22] The main goal of these provisions was to stamp out the medieval Catholic Church's toleration of what the 1546 Marriage Ordinance called private or 'clandestine promises' (*promesses clandestines*) – that is, engagements and marriages contracted without parental consent.[23]

The Ordinance made clear that clandestine *engagement* promises were 'void' (*nulle*).[24] This did not necessarily prevent a clandestinely engaged couple from going forward with their plans if they received their parents'

---

15. Ibid., item 1.
16. Ibid.
17. Ibid., item 10.
18. Ibid., item 2.
19. Ibid.
20. Ibid., item 8
21. Ibid.
22. Ibid., item 7.
23. Ibid., item 6.
24. Item 6, CO 10/1, 35.

consent after the fact. But, absent this parental consent, if anyone challenged this engagement because it had been clandestinely contracted, the engagement would be annulled regardless of what the couple wished. The Ordinance was not so clear about the legal status of clandestine *marriage* promises – especially if they had been celebrated and consummated, and had yielded children. The crucial statutory language was in item 3 of the 1546 Marriage Ordinance. There, Calvin provided:

> If it happens that two young people have contracted marriage by their own action, through folly or recklessness, let them be punished and chastened and such a marriage be dissolved at the request of those who have charge of them.[25]

It was clear from this language that children who entered such clandestine marriages would be punished. What was not clear was whether their marriage would be annulled if challenged by their parents.

A plain reading of item 3 suggests that parents could seek annulment of their children's clandestinely 'contracted marriage'. On this reading, while clandestine engagements were automatically 'void', clandestine marriages were voidable. They would be voided only if and when the children's parents or others 'who have charge of them' brought an action of annulment. But this reading does not pick up the studied ambiguity in the language of item 3. First, the opening phrase 'two young people' might well have meant only youngsters who were not only below the age of majority but also below the age of consent. Read as such, item 3 was only a statement of the familiar medieval impediment of infancy: that infants and youth may not enter marriage contracts, and when they do, their parents or guardians need to have those promises dissolved or at least postponed until the children reached an age where they could consent or dissent to them. This was, in fact, how that phrase came to be read by the Genevan Consistory in its case law.[26]

Second, the phrase 'if ... two young people have contracted marriage' (*contracté mariage*) could mean either (1) 'contracted to get married in the future' or (2) 'had already entered a marriage contract'. If the phrase meant the former, then item 3 would mean simply that parents had standing to bring an action to annul their child's clandestine engagement promise. These standing rights of the parents were not specified elsewhere in the statute. It made good sense to stipulate them, particularly since in 1546, when Calvin was drafting the Ordinance, the Consistory had no other rules

---

25.   Ibid.
26.   Witte and Kingdon, *Sex, Marriage, and Family,* 1, 202-19.

of civil procedure to guide them.[27] Even if the phrase 'contracted marriage' meant the latter (that the children 'had already entered a marriage contract') the matter was still not resolved. For final validity of the marriage turned on whether the couple had celebrated their marriage in a proper wedding liturgy in the church, not whether they had entered a marriage contract. In Calvin's Geneva, marriage contracts without church weddings were not valid – and those contracted clandestinely or without ceremonies outside of Geneva would have to be recontracted and celebrated in Geneva in order to be valid.[28]

Third, the two subsequent phrases of item 3 were also ambiguous. The phrase 'by their own action' (*de leur propre mouvement*) was separated by a comma from the next phrase, 'through folly or recklessness' (*par folie ou legierté*). These two phrases could be read separately. This reading would allow parents to seek annulment of the pending marriage either (1) if it was contracted clandestinely by the couple ('by their own action') or (2) if the marriage, even if done with the parent's consent, proved to be 'foolish' or 'reckless'. Alternatively, the two phrases could be read interdependently – with the second phrase understood as a qualification of the first. This reading would allow parents to attack a clandestine marriage only if it could be shown that the marriage itself not only was clandestinely contracted ('by their own action') but also was foolish or recklessly entered. This was not so easy a standard to meet. Children who married clandestinely sometimes did so not with recklessness but with elaborate plans to circumvent their parents. And many times their marriages, while not necessarily well advised, were hardly 'foolish', especially if they were motivated by a desire to get away from overbearing, abusive, or bickering parents.

All this close exegesis might seem like silly legal hairsplitting. But Calvin, who was well trained in law, may well have intended the language of the Ordinance to be a bit open-textured. For the legal status of parental consent and clandestine marriages was a divisive question at the time he was drafting the Ordinance. The first generation of Protestant reformers had required parental consent in an effort to counter the late medieval Catholic

---

27. What survives of Calvin's efforts to draft a code of civil procedure is in CO 10/1, 132-39, analyzed in detail in J. Bohatec, *Calvin und das Recht* (Graz: 1934), 209-79. Nothing in the fragmentary draft, however, addresses issues of standing in domestic litigation.

28. Calvin prepared a detailed marriage liturgy in 1542, which he revised substantially in 1545 and cosmetically in 1547, 1558, 1559, 1562, and 1563. The 1545 version is in CO 6, 203-08. Calvin included legal provisions mandating weddings in his 1541 Ecclesiastical Ordinances (CO 10/1, 26) and in his 1546 Marriage Ordinance (CO 10/1, 36-37). On the importance of his reforms of marriage liturgy, see H. Vuilleumier, *Histoire de L'Eglise Réformée du pays de Vaud sous le Régime Bernois,* 2 vols (Lausanne: 1927), 1, 310-14, 345-48; B. D. Spinks, 'The Liturgical Origins and Theology of Calvin's Marriage Rite', *Ecclesia Orans* 3 (1986), 195.

practice of tolerating clandestine engagements and marriages. All the leading Protestant reformers allowed parents to annul their children's clandestine *engagements*. The question that began to divide Protestants sharply after 1540 was whether parents could annul their children's clandestine *marriages*, too. Some reformers allowed parents to annul their clandestine marriages under any circumstances. Some allowed the same, unless the wife was pregnant or already had children. Some favored continuation of the clandestine marriage. Some insisted on it. The new Protestant laws of the day reflected these disparate views.[29] This issue became even more divisive in the 1540s and 1550s, when Catholics began accusing Protestants of frivolously dissolving marriages and foolishly catering to the tyranny of parents through their wooden application of the doctrine of parental consent.[30]

Calvin's 1546 Marriage Ordinance did not clearly answer the question whether parents could seek annulment of their children's clandestine marriages. In 1549, Calvin seemed inclined to allow such annulments. The occasion was Calvin's commentary on the *Adultero-German Interim* (1548), a new imperial law designed to establish the emerging Catholic teachings of the Council of Trent. The *Interim* insisted that even clandestine marriages were indissoluble because they were sacramental.[31] Calvin stood this argument on its head: If a marriage was indissoluble because it was sacramental, shouldn't its sacramental status turn on whether the couple had entered it properly, including their procurement of parental consent?

> Of marriages rashly contracted by young persons, let me just say this: It is as easy to deny a word as it is for our moderators to assert one. Who revealed to them that such marriages should be binding? [...] The dignity of the sacrament, they say, is to be preferred to a parent's right. [But] the more dignity there is in marriage, the more modesty and religion should attend those who enter it.[32]

29. See sources and discussion in J. Witte, Jr., *From Sacrament to Contract*, chaps. 5-7; H. Dieterich, *Die Protestantische Eherecht in Deutschland bis zur Mitte des 17. Jahrhunderts* (München: 1970), 123-27.
30. G. H. Joyce, *Christian Marriage: An Historical and Doctrinal Study* (London: 1948 – 2nd rev. edn), 116-24, 416.
31. Art. XXI.10 of the *Adultero-German Interim* read: 'Since the father's power justly yields to a union between the parties, you should not listen to those who now insist that contracted betrothals or marriages are dissolved and nullified if there is no consent of the parents. In this, we do not derogate from the obedience that children owe to their parents. But we do not wish parents to abuse their power by impeding or dissolving marriages. But, since we think it is good for children not to contract [marriage] without the advice and consent of parents, the preachers should carefully instruct them in their duty.' Translated in John Calvin, *Tracts and Treatises in Defense of the Reformed Faith*, 3 vols, trans. H. Beveridge (Grand Rapids, MI: 1958), 3, 220.
32. John Calvin, *Vera Christianae Pacificationis et Ecclesiae Reformandae Ratio* (1549), CO 7, 640.

A decade later, Calvin seemed inclined to regard clandestine marriages as ill-advised, but not subject to annulment by parents or anyone else. 'All good men properly disapprove of clandestine marriages which offer an opportunity and even, in fact, an open door to many disgraceful acts', he wrote in a 1557 *consilium*.[33] But even a clandestinely contracted marriage precluded a party from entering a second engagement or marriage – regardless of whether the parents or guardians of the doubly contracted child now consented to the second match.

By 1560, Calvin had settled the matter in his mind. Clandestine marriages, once contracted, celebrated, and consummated, could not be annulled absent proof of some other impediment. Neither a dissenting parent nor a distraught husband or wife could seek annulment of the marriage on grounds that it was clandestinely contracted. Indeed, if the marriage was unhappy, it was just what the clandestinely married couple deserved. As Calvin put it in a *consilium* of 1560:

> When an adolescent has married without his parents' knowledge, he should recognize that he is paying a just penalty for his heedless behavior if his wife is unresponsive to him. He did not offer God and his parents the obedience he owed them, and he should not be surprised if he gets his just reward in the form of his wife's defiance.[34]

This moved Calvin very close to what was the actual bottom line of the medieval canonists: clandestine marriages were formally prohibited, but when they occurred, the marriage should stand and the couple be punished. The medieval canonists used sacramental logic: even clandestine marriages could not be dissolved because they were sacramental. Calvin used prudential logic: even clandestine marriages could not be dissolved because that catered to parental tyranny, left despoiled virgins vulnerable to spinsterhood, and consigned any children of the union to the bane of bastardy.

3. Calvin's theological reflections

While Calvin dithered on the issue of whether parents could annul clandestine marriages, he was decisively in favor of the doctrine of parental con-

33. CO 10/1, 242-44, with translation in *Calvin's Ecclesiastical Advice*, trans. M. Beaty and B. W. Farley, ed. J. H. Leith (Louisville, KY: 1978), 135.
34. Consilium (Sept. 1, 1560), CO 10/1, 252-54. Calvin continued: 'Because it is not disagreement over religion which is tearing the marriage apart, he should fulfill his marital duty as long as he can live with his wife without danger. If greater force and necessity compel him to leave her, he should remain celibate until his wife recovers her senses or gives him cause to divorce her'. Ibid., using translation in *Calvin's Ecclesiastical Advice*, 147-48.

sent. In his 1546 Commentary on 1 Corinthians 7, published shortly after his Marriage Ordinance, Calvin argued that parental consent to marriage was a 'sacred right' of parents and a 'moral duty' of children.[35] It enabled parents to guide their children in this final fateful step toward adulthood, and it prevented children from choosing their mates imprudently or impetuously. Particularly when children were still young and vulnerable, it ensured that the marriage was formed by free, full, and mature consent on all sides. Parental consent, Calvin insisted, does not license 'parental tyranny' over children, nor can it substitute for the consent of the child to the marriage. The 'proper rule' of parental consent is that

> children should allow themselves to be governed by their parents, and that they, on the other hand, do not drag their children by force to what is against their inclination, and that they have no other object in view, in the exercise of their authority, than the advantage of their children.[36]

If parents abused their authority, and coerced their children into unwanted engagements or marriages, therefore, such contracts should be annulled.[37]

The doctrine of parental consent to marriage 'originated in the common laws of nature', Calvin argued in his same 1546 Commentary on 1 Corinthians.[38] Calvin adverted to these natural law origins of the doctrine several more times in later writings. 'Nature herself dictates that the authority of parents is necessary', he wrote in 1549. 'This has always been observed by the law of nations and is approved by the testimony of Scripture.'[39] In 1554, he wrote:

> [S]ince marriage forms a principal part of human life, it is right that, in contracting it, children should be subject to their parents, and should obey their counsel. This order [is what] nature prescribes and dictates.[40]

35. Comm. 1 Cor. 7:36-38.
36. CO 49, 425-26.
37. Calvin applied this principle of no parental coercion clearly in an undated *consilium* (CO 10/1, 238-39). The case sent to him for his advice involved a young woman named Marguerite. Her mother had tricked and forced her into marrying a young man named Jean. Jean's brother, aunt, and servant were apparently part of the conspiracy as well. Marguerite was trapped into going through with the wedding. But she was distraught throughout the ceremony and maintained consistently thereafter that she was not married. At least two witnesses testified that she did not say her wedding vows but was silent throughout the ceremony. The notary who recorded the marriage contract testified that the marriage 'was not of God' because Marguerite had not consented to it. Calvin concluded that because 'the girl was forced into it, no foundation for marriage exists'. A properly constituted court should examine Marguerite and her mother closely. If their testimony holds true, the court should annul the marriage, and leave the young woman free to marry another – and punish the mother and her conspirators for coercing the child.
38. CO 49, 425-26.
39. CO 7, 639-40.
40. Comm. Gen. 21:20, CO 23, 305-06. In his first edition of the *Institutes* (1536), Calvin condemned the Catholic canon law for allowing that 'marriages between

And again:

> [I]t is not lawful for the children of a family to contract marriage, except with the consent of parents. And, certainly, natural equity dictates that, in a matter of such importance, children should depend upon the will of the parents.[41]

Surprisingly, Calvin did not ground the doctrine of parental consent to marriage in the Fifth Commandment of the Decalogue: 'Honor thy father and thy mother' (Ex. 20:12; Deut. 5:16) and the amplification of the Commandment by St. Paul (Eph. 6:1-2; Col. 3:20).[42] Other Protestant Reformers had made the Fifth Commandment a critical source of the right of both fathers and mothers to give their consent to marriage, and the correlative duty of their children to seek the consent of both parents. This was part and product of their elaborate efforts to ground a whole new Protestant legal system in the Ten Commandments.[43] Calvin did not take this step, at least with respect to the doctrine of parental consent. He might well have been constrained by his insistence in the 1546 Marriage Ordinance that it was the father's, not the mother's, consent that was essential. It would have been hard for him to press the father's superior authority on the strength of a Commandment to 'Honor thy father *and thy mother*'.

This is not to say that Calvin had a narrow view of the Fifth Commandment or a restricted view of a parent's authority or a child's obedience. In his numerous pages of commentaries, sermons, and catechism entries on the Fifth Commandment, he regularly described parents, especially fathers, as God's vice-regents on earth, in whose title and office God has invested a measure of his being and power, making them 'something divine'.[44] He called upon children to render to their parents forms of 'reverence, obedience, and gratefulness' comparable to what they rendered to God – at least up to the point of violating the Bible and their conscience.[45] Calvin gave

minors contracted without parental consent should remain firm and valid', which he considered contrary to 'the laws of all nations and also against the ordinances of Moses'. CO 1, 194-95. Calvin repeated this charge almost verbatim in his 1559 *Institutes*. See John Calvin, *Institutes of the Christian Religion* [1559], ed. J. T. McNeill, trans. F. L. Battles (Philadelphia: 1960), 4.19.37 [hereafter *Institutes 1559*].

41. Comm. Gen. 24:1-3, CO 23, 329-33.
42. This is treated as the Fourth Commandment in Catholic and Lutheran traditions. On various traditions of numbering and dividing the Ten Commandments, see B. I. Reicke, *Die Zehn Worte in Geschichte und Gegenwart* (Tübingen: 1973); P. G. Kuntz, *The Ten Commandments in History* (Grand Rapids, MI: 2004).
43. J. Witte, Jr., *Law and Protestantism: The Legal Teachings of the Lutheran Reformation* (Cambridge: 2002), 113-15, 125-27, 169-74.
44. *Institutes* (1559), 2.8.35.
45. Ibid., 2.8.36-38. This caveat, of obeying up to the point of violating God's law, does not appear in his exegesis of the Decalogue in 1536 *Institutes*, chap. 1 or in Calvin's 1555 Sermons on Deuteronomy 5:16. It might well signal part of Calvin's emerging theory of resistance to tyrannical authority – whether parental, political,

many examples of the proper obedience that children should render to their parents in conformity with the Decalogue. Included was the duty of children, which Calvin rooted in the Third Commandment, to seek their father's consent to make 'a binding oath', and the duty of the father, in turn, not to withhold or condition his consent capriciously.[46] Calvin concluded that, 'if a daughter, while living with her father, has vowed anything without his knowledge, it is of no force'. This was the closest Calvin came to tying the doctrine of parental consent to marriage to the Fifth Commandment.[47]

To ground his doctrine of parental consent, Calvin was more content to point favorably to the examples in the Bible of how some early patriarchs participated in the marriages of their children. For Calvin these were examples, as well as counterexamples, of the natural law in operation.[48] Calvin saw in the biblical story of Abraham's pursuit of a wife for his son Isaac (Gen. 24:1-67) a particularly good lesson of how and why the natural law of parental consent should operate.[49] Abraham sought to ensure that his son Isaac, who had come of age, would marry a woman who was both spiritually and physically compatible with him. He sent out his servant to find just the right woman, armed with a clear recitation of the terms of the proposed marriage contract. The servant found a suitable woman in Rebekah. He sought the consent of Rebekah's father, uncle, and mother. He then put down a handsome bride price signified by rings and bracelets. All of this was done, Calvin noted, with full consideration of the consent of the two children, Isaac and Rebekah. The servant made sure that Isaac and Rebekah met together to ensure their compatibility before the contract was sealed.

Particularly notable for Calvin was that Rebekah's father, Bethuel, 'did not exercise tyranny over his daughter, so as to thrust her out reluctantly, or to compel her to marry against her will, but left her to her own free choice'.[50] This stood in marked contrast with many other biblical examples of fathers who contracted or coerced their children into marriage without consideration of their wishes. A good such counterexample was Caleb's crass indifference to his daughter Achsah.[51] Caleb was one of the spies whom Joshua had sent into the newly promised land of Israel. He was one of the few who had stood up against the majority of the people who had de-

---

or ecclesiastical. On this see J. Witte, Jr., *The Reformation of Rights: Law, Religion, and Human Rights in Early Modern Calvinism* (Cambridge: 2007), chaps. 1-2.

46. Comm. Harm. Law Num. 30:2-5.
47. See, e.g., Comm. Harm. Law Ex. 20:12; Serm. Deut. 5:15; Comm. and Serm. Eph. 6:1-4.
48. See, e.g., Comm. Gen. 21:20 (Hagar and Ishmael); Comm. Gen. 24:1-67 (Abraham and Isaac; Rebekah and mother); Comm. Gen. 34:12 (Schechem and Jacob re: Dinah); Comm. Harm. Law Ex. 21:7-11.
49. Comm. Gen. 24:1-3, 57.
50. CO 23, 339.
51. Comm. Josh. 15:14-17.

spaired about their ability to conquer Jericho and who wanted to return to Egypt (Num. 13:6, 30; 14:6). While God condemned the people of Israel for their unbelief, God spared Caleb: 'because he has a different spirit and has followed me fully, I will bring him into the land in which he went, and his descendents shall possess it' (Num. 14:24). After the conquest of Jericho, Joshua rewarded Caleb with an ample plot of land. But the land was still occupied (Josh. 14:6, 21:12). Caleb wanted his soldiers to claim the land and to kill its pagan leader. Whoever killed the leader, Caleb promised, could marry his daughter Achsah. Othniel killed the leader, and was given Achsah to marry (Josh. 15:16-17). Despite Caleb's noble place in Israelite history, Calvin condemned him roundly: 'How could Caleb presume to bargain concerning his daughter until he knew her wishes', Calvin wrote incredulously. It was no excuse that Othniel was a valiant warrior. That did not necessarily make him the right husband for Achsah. It also did not matter that Achsah ultimately accepted him as her husband or indeed that Caleb later obliged her by giving the couple a choice plot of land (Josh. 15:18-19). Caleb must have just forgotten to ask Achsah her wishes while 'in the heat of battle', Calvin concluded. But we have to assume that 'according to the common law the agreement implied the daughter's consent and was only to take effect if it was obtained'.[52]

Calvin's condemnation of Caleb was of a piece with his condemnation of other biblical fathers and guardians who sold their children into slavery or prostitution, or put their daughters on the marriage market as prizes to be sold to the highest bidder.[53] Even with the power of parental consent, no father was allowed to do this to his daughter. It was the mutual consent both of the husband and the wife, and of the parents and their minor children, that makes the marriage. As Calvin put it:

> Although it is the office of parents to settle their daughters in life, they are not permitted to exercise tyrannical power or to assign them to whatever husbands they think fit without consulting them. For while all contracts ought to be voluntary, freedom ought to prevail especially in marriage that no one may pledge his faith against his will.[54]

4. Consistory cases

The Genevan Consistory, on which Calvin sat as Moderator of the Company of Pastors, heard a number of cases raising disputes over parental con-

52. Comm. Josh. 15:14-17.
53. See, e.g., Comm. Gen. 29:18-27; Comm. Harm. Law Ex. 21:7-11, Lev. 19:29. But cf. Serm. 1 Sam. 18:22-30; Serm. 2 Sam. 3:14-16 (where Calvin does not criticize fathers for offering their daughters as prizes for valor).
54. CO 25, 529.

sent.[55] The Consistory generally followed the letter of the 1546 Marriage Ordinance. Clandestine engagements involving minor children were presumptively void, unless the parents would later consent. Clandestine marriages were presumptively valid, unless the children could demonstrate highly irregular circumstances. Parents who refused to give their consent were little questioned unless the Consistory suspected foul play. Guardians who refused consent were more closely questioned. Where the views of the fathers and mothers conflicted, the Consistory followed the father. Where the views of mothers and relatives conflicted, the mother prevailed. Parents or guardians who did consent to the engagement were responsible to see that the child was married properly and promptly. Such parents could neither leave the young couple to their own devices, nor seek to withdraw their consent once given.

In most cases, if either party to the engagement was a minor, the Consistory would insist on knowing whether their father or guardian consented – and would order postponement of the wedding until they were satisfied. In a 1552 case, for example, Louise Loup requested the Consistory to approve her marriage to Nicod des Planches, a minor.[56] The parties had been engaged before witnesses, and Nicod had given Louise an engagement gift. The Consistory wanted to know whether Nicod's father approved the match. When Nicod reported his father's dissent, the Consistory recommended annulment.

Similarly, in another 1552 case the Consistory summoned to them two minor couples, Jenon Ramou and Humbert Gallatin, as well as Françoise Tournier and Jean Berto.[57] The Consistory had learned that the two couples had become clandestinely engaged during a party together, each couple apparently serving as witnesses to the other's engagement. When confronted, the couples said this was all done in jest, and they would not want to marry without the consent of the parents. The Consistory called in their parents. The parents of the two girls dissented because of the manner in which the

---

55. In Calvin's day, the Genevan Consistory was something of a hearings court of first instance and a mediator of last resort in cases of sex, marriage, and family life (among many other subjects). It consisted both of local ministers (including Calvin) and members of the city council. The Consistory met once per week for several hours. Parties could petition the Consistory voluntarily or be subpoenaed to appear – often on the recommendation of a local pastor or magistrate. Pleadings were oral. Proceedings were recorded by a notary, which records have been preserved in the register sampled below. Though the Consistory followed the provisions of Calvin's 1546 Marriage Ordinance, it did not have formal legal power, only the power to administer spiritual sanctions. Cases or issues that required legal action or orders were referred to the city council for disposition. In such instances, the Consistory's findings of fact and recommendations of action were probative but not binding on the Council.
56. R. Consist. VII, 96r, 98r.
57. R. Consist. VII, 96r, 98r.

couples had become engaged. The Consistory sent the case to the Council with a recommendation that the engagements be annulled and the two young men punished for seducing the women. The two young women were sent home with a warning to exercise more care the next time.

If both children were minors, it was not enough that only one child had received parental consent. In a 1557 case, for example, Pierre Clerc asked the Consistory to approve the marriage of his minor daughter and Clement de Biffort, also a minor.[58] The parties had a notarized written engagement contract with mutually favorable terms. Pierre was eager to see his daughter get married and urged the Consistory's blessing. Clement, however, had not procured his father's consent. Even though Clement, too, wanted to marry, the Consistory refused to allow the marriage to go forward. Instead, they sent the case to the Council with a recommendation that the notary be punished for notarizing the contract without procuring the consent of one of the two fathers.

The Consistory heard a few cases where fathers and mothers differed over whether to consent to their child's engagement. Each time the Consistory sided with the father.[59] Typical was the 1547 case of Etienne de Lonnay and a young girl named Maxima.[60] Maxima's mother had consented to the union, and had signed an engagement contract that Etienne had prepared. When called before the Consistory, however, Maxima testified that she had not consented to the engagement. She reported further that her father, who was away at the time, also did not consent to the marriage. For the Consistory even this hearsay testimony of the father's dissent was enough to trigger an instant annulment. On the Consistory's recommendation, the Council annulled the engagement contract. They also imprisoned the mother both for perjury during trial and for consenting to the engagement, evidently in defiance of her husband's wishes for young Maxima.

The Consistory also occasionally heard cases raising conflicts between mothers and other relatives regarding the engagement of a minor child. In a 1545 case, for example, Girard Reveillet asked the Consistory to approve his forthcoming marriage to a young woman (unnamed in the record).[61] Girard testified that he had received the consent of his fiancée's uncle in the presence of several of her other relatives, and they had all toasted to confirm the engagement. When questioned, the woman's aunt confirmed this. The young woman, however, testified that she had not consented or toasted to the marriage, and pled with the Consistory to protect her from this unwanted

58. R. Consist. XII, 8r.
59. See several examples in C. Seeger, *Nullité de mariage, divorce et séparation de corps a Genève, au temps de Calvin: Fondements doctrinaux, loi et jurisprudence* (Lausanne: 1989), 361 ff.
60. R. Consist. III, 48r.
61. R. Consist. VII, 6r, 8v, 11r, 49v, 56r, 58r.

marriage. The Consistory ordered that she be given help in having her mother and brother come to Geneva to testify; her father was evidently not in the picture. The mother appeared the following week, and protested the engagement loudly. A local minister echoed her protest.

Confronted with this conflict between an uncle who consented and a mother who did not consent to the young woman's engagement, the Consistory sent the case to the Council. The Council discovered that Girard was already engaged to someone else in a Catholic territory. Girard returned repeatedly to the Consistory with documents testifying that his first engagement was dissolved, and indeed that his first fiancée had married someone else. The Consistory did not believe him. They became doubly suspicious when they learned that his prior fiancée was a Catholic and that Girard had a reputation for making frivolous promises. Though the record ends here, such a marriage could not have passed muster with both the young woman and her mother protesting the match.

What was left unclear in this case was what the Consistory would have done if both the young woman and her uncle wanted to go forward with the wedding, but the mother did not. The Consistory faced this question squarely in a 1561 case, and they sided with the mother.[62] Jean Casaux, a minor, had become engaged to Madeleine D'Agnon. Both Jean's brother and his guardian had consented to and helped facilitate the match. But none of the parties had consulted Jean's mother, who was a Catholic living in a distant town. It turned out that Casaux's mother refused to consent to any engagement until Casaux reached 25, even though she supported his decision to move to Geneva (and presumably also to convert to the Reformed faith). Though the case went down on different grounds, the mother's dissent was enough for the Consistory to annul the engagement, despite Casaux's brother's consent and despite the fact that the mother was a Catholic living well outside Geneva's jurisdiction.

Once parents or guardians had consented to an engagement, they were obliged to see that the parties were properly and promptly married. A Genevan father named Nicolas found this out in 1552.[63] About a year before, Nicolas had consented to the engagement of his daughter and her fiancé, Jaques d'Orléans. Jaques had given the young woman a ring and some property as an engagement gift. The couple had then apparently moved away from Geneva and had put off their wedding. The woman had returned the gifts temporarily until Jaques and her brother could work out more suitable property arrangements. Nicolas had apparently not known of, or had at least not objected to, this delay, though it was in clear violation of the 1546 Marriage Ordinance that required the couple to wed within six weeks of

62. R. Consist. XVIII, 135v, 136v-138r, 141r-v, 143r.
63. R. Consist. XII, 8r.

their engagement. Since Nicolas still wanted the wedding to go forward, the Consistory ordered him to try to persuade the couple to get on with their wedding plans. If that failed, the Consistory threatened to send them all to the Council to have them punished and the engagement annulled because of the untoward delay.

Once a father or guardian consented to his minor child's engagement, he could not withdraw it. Engagement contracts were serious business in Calvin's Geneva. The Consistory worked hard to ensure that the couples consented to them freely and fully – and, if they were minors, that their fathers, mothers, or other guardians consented to them freely and fully as well. But once these engagement contracts were made with free and full consent, neither the couple nor their parents could break them without proof of an impediment. A mere change of heart by any of the parties, or a dispute over property and dowry, was not sufficient grounds to seek annulment.

A Genevan father named Nepveur learned this lesson in 1556.[64] Nepveur had consented to the engagement of his daughter Jeanne to one Louis Blanchet. The parties had signed a written engagement contract, which specified the property payments that Louis was to make to Nepveur in consideration of the marriage. Shortly thereafter, Louis wanted to move to another town. Jeanne did not want to follow him. The parties agreed to dissolve their engagement by mutual consent. Louis had not delivered his promised payment to the Nepveurs, so father Nepveur decided to withdraw his parental consent to the engagement as well. Louis moved away. The Nepveurs then requested the Consistory for permission for Jeanne to be free to marry another. The Consistory denied their request. An unconditional engagement contract, they ruled, could not be broken either by the mutual consent of the couple or by the subsequent withdrawal of parental consent. Moreover, failure of a dowry payment was never a sufficient ground to annul an engagement. Jeanne was still bound by her engagement promise, unless she and her father could prove that Louis had actually deserted her – desertion being a separate ground for annulment in Geneva.

Similarly in another 1557 case, Jacques Gaudy had consented to his minor daughter Michee's engagement to Nicolas Millet.[65] Nicolas had promised to deliver an ample engagement gift to father Jacques, when Nicolas returned from a journey. Nicolas was delayed on his return, and then did not tender the full promised payment, causing Jacques to lose some land he had intended to buy with the promised funds. An angry Jacques declared that he was withdrawing his consent to the engagement, and forcibly took his daughter Michee back into his own custody. The Consistory sought to reconcile the parties, explaining to them that his post hoc withdrawal of

64. R. Consist. XI, 47r-v; XII, 5r, 24v-25r, 96r.
65. R. Consist. XII, 45r-v.

consent was ineffective. They also reprimanded Nicolas for his delinquency, and ordered him to make the full promised engagement gift. An enraged Jacques, however, said he would refuse the money if tendered because he now believed the young man to be dishonest and wanted him out of the family. After further attempts at reconciliation failed, the Consistory sent the matter to the Council for final disposition, recommending that 'such [engagements to] marriage should not be broken and may not be dissolved, for this would open the door to many others'.[66]

The Consistory reserved the right to second-guess the parents, especially when the cases involved young children or the Consistory suspected foul play. In a 1556 case, for example, the Consistory annulled the engagement of a fourteen-year-old young woman, Françoise Chastellain, who had a debilitating 'hump' that would preclude pregnancy and perhaps even intercourse.[67] Françoise had evidently consented to the union. Her father had approved the match, and had executed a prenuptial contract with her fiancé and his family. Françoise's father now insisted that the Consistory allow the marriage to go forward. The Consistory decided not only that the woman was too young to be married now, but also that her 'hump' was an absolute impediment to marriage altogether. They annulled the engagement contract, despite the loud protests by the father and fiancé.

In a 1547 case, the Consistory learned that Pierre Mestrazat had become engaged to a ten-year-old girl in another town.[68] Pierre had forced the girl's mother to give her consent to the engagement and allow him to marry the young girl as soon as she came of age. He was now threatening to take the child away to a Catholic territory. All this was 'scandalous', said the Consistory. They called upon the mother to testify. She confirmed that Pierre had not only threatened her but in fact had 'beaten her villainously' in order to extract her consent to her daughter's engagement. Yet, the mother said she was willing to accept Pierre as her 'son' if he promised to live by the Word of God. The mother was not just being pious and charitable. Pierre had evidently signed a contract to pay the costs of the girl's apprenticeship and maintenance in exchange for her later hand in marriage. With no mention in the record of any father, it was likely that this was a single mother doing the best she could to support her child.

Pierre intimated that he would be happy to cancel the engagement contract – and, by implication, cancel his contract to pay the girl's maintenance and support expenses as well. The Consistory would hear none of it. No doubt still scandalized by the evidence of Pierre's belligerence and his threat to take the girl to a Catholic home, the Consistory insisted on Pierre's

66. R. Consist. XII, 45v.
67. R. Consist. X, 81r.
68. R. Consist. III, 124r, 128r.

full performance of both the engagement contract and the maintenance contract. At the same time, they reserved the girl's right to rescind the engagement contract when she reached the age of consent, which was stipulated as fourteen years of age in this case. The Consistory thereby made Pierre the victim of his own hard bargaining. Pierre had forced the mother into accepting what was, in effect, an installment contract to marry a young virgin. The Consistory converted this into a mandatory child support contract with no guarantee of a bride in return. Indeed, there is no record that Pierre and the girl were ever married upon her reaching the age of consent.

The Consistory ruled similarly in a 1546 case involving the purported marriage of two nine-year-olds, Jean Dimier and Nicolarde du Pont.[69] This 'marriage' was a guardianship arrangement gone utterly amiss. Nicolarde's parents needed to find a place for her to live. They had arranged with Jean's father, Claude, to become a guardian to Nicolarde and to take her into his home. Claude promised to raise her as if she were his own child. Nicolarde's parents gave him funds for Nicolarde's maintenance and support. So far, there was nothing unusual in this arrangement.

But then, inexplicably, the parents had their local minister marry young Nicolarde to young Jean, Claude's son. Even more inexplicably, the minister married the youngsters without reservation. It is hard to know what was motivating the parties to take this unusual step. There was no obvious legal advantage for the couple to be married at this early stage of life. Whatever testamentary advantages might have been gained by the marriage were so remote that this could not have been the motivation. Perhaps Nicolarde's parents thought that Claude's duties of guardianship would be more effectively delivered if his ward Nicolarde were his daughter-in-law rather than just a stranger. Perhaps Claude and his wife wanted to have a daughter, and this arrangement gave them the benefits of effectively adopting a daughter without having to pay for her support. The record does not clearly say.

The record does make clear, however, that Jean's parents thought that the couple was married. Young Nicolarde and Jean were made to sleep together, albeit with father Claude present. But when Nicolarde wet the bed 'under him', Jean became 'disgusted' with her. Claude and his wife beat Nicolarde severely for her misbehavior and wanted her out of the house. A complaint about the minister from Nicolarde's home town brought this whole unusual arrangement to the Geneva Consistory's attention. The Consistory rebuked both sets of parents for their 'monstrous' impropriety. They questioned the children closely. It was obvious that neither Nicolarde nor Jean understood what marriage meant, nor considered themselves to be married. The Consistory thus asked the Council to remove Nicolarde from Claude's home and guardianship and to safeguard her assets. They also

69.   R. Consist. II, 63r.

asked the Council to declare the marriage contract 'void[able]' and to give the parties the right to confirm or deny the marriage when they reached maturity. Four years later, when the couple came of age, Nicolarde's father, no doubt still chastened by their earlier rebuke, asked the Council whether the couple could marry. Though Jean wanted to marry, Nicolarde dissented because of her earlier mistreatment by Jean's family. The Council thus dissolved the engagement contract and declared that the parties were free to court and marry others.

The Consistory maintained this position on arranged child marriages in later years. This can be seen in a 1557 case of Jaques Rosset and his fiancée Madeleine Lechiere.[70] The couple had become engaged when both were minors. Claude had apparently used ample gifts of liquor to induce the woman's family to consent to the engagement. Since then, he had fraternized rather freely with Madeleine, much to her family's chagrin. The couple had now reached the age of consent, and the issue was whether they should marry or could break their engagement with impunity. Upon learning of the couple's philandering, the Consistory ordered Madeleine to remain in her parents' home while the case was pending. They then ordered that the marriage could proceed only if both sets of parents would come to the Consistory to give their consent to the union. Claude's parents appeared the following week to protest the marriage. The Consistory thus removed the case to the Council, recommending annulment of the engagement and a permanent prohibition against the parties' seeing each other again. The Council ordered the engagement annulled and also imprisoned the couple for their evident fornication. Had this been a simple case of two youngsters promising marriage, the Consistory could have enforced the letter of the 1546 Marriage Ordinance, namely, that such promises were automatically void. But, it was the purported consent of the girl's parents, even though fraudulently procured, that must have given the Consistory pause.

In the absence of both fathers and mothers, the Consistory would turn to guardians to give their consent to a minor child's wedding. Unless the absent parent's last will and testament or a guardianship agreement stipulated otherwise, the views of paternal uncles and male siblings to the minor child were given priority. In their absence, paternal grandfathers, maternal uncles, and full sisters to the minor child were consulted. Paternal and maternal grandmothers, aunts, and more distant relatives were consulted only as a last resort. The guardian stood in the shoes of the absent parents and was generally free to consent to or dissent from a minor ward's engagement.[71]

70. R. Consist. XII, 13v, 17r.
71. See examples in Seeger, *Nullité,* 363-65.

The Consistory would inquire more closely, however, when a guardian neglected or abused his or her authority. An egregious example came in a 1546 case involving a young woman named Mademoiselle Fertz.[72] Fertz had just lost her parents to the plague. By their last will and testament, her parents had appointed one Pierre Gravier as her guardian. Shortly thereafter, Gravier began sleeping with Fertz. Fertz herself then became infected with the plague. She went to the hospital. There she met another man, Pierre Dolen. They, too, began sleeping together. A few days later, Dolen and Fertz became engaged. They kept the matter secret, evidently not wishing to seek the consent of Gravier, Fertz's guardian and first lover. But Dolen gave Fertz an engagement ring to wear. They also broke into Fertz's late parents' home and took some of the money and property they found there. They were imprisoned for their fornication and burglary, but thereafter continued to live together. They then sought to publish their banns of marriage, bringing them again to the attention of the Consistory.

The Consistory summoned Gravier, the guardian, to answer whether he consented to his ward Fertz's marriage. They learned more than they could have expected. Gravier would not approve the marriage. When they pressed him as to why, Gravier admitted to his earlier affair with Fertz. He also testified that to his surprise (and no doubt his pique), Fertz had suddenly become engaged to Dolen. Gravier did not consent to the engagement, but he also had done nothing either to care for Fertz or to safeguard the property she had inherited. For the Consistory, this nonfeasance was evidently more than enough to disqualify Gravier from his guardianship, for he faded from the story.[73]

The Consistory focused their attention on Fertz and Dolen. Because the couple had contracted and consummated a clandestine engagement, the Council, on the Consistory's recommendation, annulled their union and punished them severely for their flagrant fornication. Thereafter, they were left free to enter a new engagement contract – provided Fertz's closest relatives were found to give their consent, and provided further that the couple desist from future fornication and cohabitation until their wedding.

---

72. R. Consist. II, 86v, 88r, 100v.
73. Gravier may well have faced criminal prosecution as well. Even consensual sex between a guardian and ward was a serious crime in Geneva. A 1566 statute that codified the prevailing law provided that a 'guardian or trustee who has fornicated with his ward [...] will be proceeded against more severely, even to death if necessary, according to the severity and circumstances of their crimes, at the discretion of the judges'. *Les sources du droit du canton de Genève*, 4 vols, ed. E. Rivoire and V. van Berchem (Aarau: 1927-1935), vol. 3, no. 1065.

5. Summary and conclusions

Parental consent to engagement and marriage was one of the staples of early Protestant theology and law. In the first generation of the Reformation, Martin Luther, Martin Bucer, Ulrich Zwingli, and others had held up the doctrine of parental consent as their biblical answer to the late medieval toleration of clandestine engagements and marriages. Unless they had consented to their minor child's unions, parents could seek their annulment. Unless they could prove their parents' abuse, children would be punished for entering such contracts clandestinely. For many reformers, the requirement of parental consent was a moral right and duty anchored in the Fifth Commandment: 'Honor thy father and thy mother'.

Calvin and his colleagues in Geneva accepted much of the prevailing Protestant law of parental consent. They declared parental consent, like individual consent, to be indispensable to the validity of a minor's engagement. The Geneva Consistory inquired closely into the engagements of minors, and routinely dissolved them if their parents dissented. Not only the couple themselves, but also a parent, guardian, witness, or notary to an engagement contract could be punished if they failed to get the necessary consent from both sets of parents. Overbearing or officious parents or guardians would be punished for intruding on the consent of their children or wards. Once parents or guardians had given their consent to their minor children's engagement or marriage, they could not withdraw it. Only proof of another impediment would allow the parents to seek annulment of an engagement or marriage to which they had consented.

Calvin ultimately rejected the law of some Protestant communities that allowed parents to annul their children's clandestine marriages as well, a question he had left unresolved in his 1546 Marriage Ordinance. Initially, he was attracted to conventional Protestant arguments that unless parents could annul their children's clandestine marriages, the doctrine of parental consent would be a mere form of words that guaranteed nothing. Initially, he was also turned off by Catholic arguments that clandestine marriages could not be dissolved because they were sacramental. This, too, for Calvin was a mere form of words that proved nothing: If marriage was an indissoluble sacrament, why should its sacramental status not turn on whether it was properly formed by the couple and approved by their parents?

Calvin ultimately abandoned this early position and resolved that clandestine marriages once consummated could not be dissolved by anyone, including the couple and their parents. His concerns were in part prudential, relating to the dangers of parental tyranny and the costs of marital breakup to the couple and their children. His motivations were perhaps also pragmatic. After all, in a small city like Geneva, with its intensely active Consistory and its multi-step public marriage process, it would have been hard for a clandestinely engaged couple to sneak into marriage without discovery by parents or guardians. To be valid, their banns would have to be posted, their certificates publicly registered, their wedding publicly celebrated during a worship service. Throughout this time – and indeed until the very last step in the marriage liturgy when the pastor called 'if anyone has reason to object to this marriage' – anyone could protest the match, not least the parents or guardians of the couple. This objection would have automatically halted the process, and put the couple before the Consistory. If they were minors, the Consistory would require them to prove that they had their parents' consent. If they did not have it, their engagement would be annulled. With all these safeguards in place, Calvin must have concluded, it was best to leave clandestinely married couples to lie in their marital beds undisturbed. At that point, it was as much a consequence of the parents' and community's negligence as of their children's delinquency that the couple had been clandestinely married.

Calvin also accepted much of the prevailing Protestant theology of parental consent – but with two somewhat peculiar new accents. First, his concerns for daughters and mothers in the process of marital formation stood sharply juxtaposed. On the one hand, Calvin was surprisingly jealous to ensure that girls were as protected from tyrannical parents as boys were in their decision to marry. This was biblically counterintuitive. Both the stories in Genesis and the laws of Moses were filled with examples showing that young women had little voice and few rights in the decision to get married, especially vis-à-vis their fathers. Yet Calvin showed little patience with any of this. He repeatedly castigated biblical fathers who sold, coerced, or tricked their daughters into marriage. And he lifted up the one example of Bethuel and Rebekah as exemplary of what the natural law teaches about how a father is to care for his daughter's consent.

On the other hand, Calvin was surprisingly churlish about the role of the mother in consenting to her minor child's engagement and marriage. Her views counted only if her husband was absent, and then only if they concurred with that of other relatives. Even hearsay testimony of a father's wishes was given priority over a mother's contrary written and oral statements before the Consistory. This strong accent on the father's voice was, of course, typical of the stories in Genesis and the laws of Moses, and indeed of some of the New Testament household codes as well. But why should Calvin stick to the letter and spirit of Bible on the place of a wife, but not on the place of a daughter? Calvin did not say.

This first peculiarity may well be related to a second, namely, Calvin's reliance on natural law, rather than the Fifth Commandment, for the doctrine of parental consent. This was not unprecedented. But both the early Church Fathers and other early Protestants had seen the doctrine of parental consent as part and product of the Fifth Commandment: 'Honor thy father and thy mother'. Indeed, the rest of the Commandment seemed to underscore the wisdom of such obedience to parents for the future happiness of children: 'so that your days may be long in the land that the Lord your God gives you'.

For all his robust exegesis of the Decalogue as a source and summary of natural law on many other aspects of life, Calvin did not follow it on the issue of parental consent. Instead, he pointed vaguely and variously to natural law, the law of nations, common equity, and plain common sense to argue for the doctrine. It is hard to know what motivated Calvin in this choice of authority. Perhaps it came down to the simple fact that Calvin had written into his 1546 Marriage Ordinance that it was the consent of the fathers, not the mothers, that counted, and he was sticking to it. It would have been hard to square this provision with the Commandment to '[h]onor thy father and thy mother'. This was not Calvin's usual style, however. He was certainly firm and fierce in defending what he wrote, but he would sometimes change his mind, especially when the Bible charted a better way. On this issue, the Bible and the tradition did chart a more egalitarian way. Calvin did not follow it.

CONTRIBUTORS

PER ANDERSEN is an Associate Professor at the Department of Jurisprudence at the Law School, Aarhus University. His main research interests are legal changes in Denmark and Europe in the twelfth and thirteenth centuries, especially concerning legal procedure, and the interaction between learned law and local lawmaking.

PAUL BRAND is a Professor of English Legal History at the University of Oxford and a Senior Research Fellow and Senior Dean of All Souls College, Oxford. His main research interests are in the history of the English Common Law in the period from the twelfth to the fourteenth centuries.

DOMINIK BUDSKÝ is a PhD Student of Ecclesiastical History at the Catholic Theological Faculty, The Charles University of Prague. Currently he is preparing an edition of the treatise *Processus iudiciarius secundum stilum Pragensem*. His main research interests are history of canon law and canonries in the Late Middle Ages.

ANNE J. DUGGAN is a Professor Emerita of Medieval History at King's College London. Principally known for her extensive work on Thomas Becket, her interests include Roman, canon, and English common law and the twelfth-century papacy, with special emphasis on the so-called 'new law' of the decretals. Studies on Adrian IV and Celestine III have already appeared, chapters on Alexander III and Eugenius III are in press, and another on Innocent II is in preparation.

INGER DÜBECK is a Professor Emerita from Aarhus University and Doctor of Law from the University of Copenhagen. Her main research interests include legal history, especially family and marriage law.

LARS IVAR HANSEN is a Professor of Medieval and Early Modern History at the University of Tromsø. His main fields of research are economic and social history, with focus on resource rights, the role of social networks of alliance and inheritance practices, as well as the inter-ethnic relations between the peoples of northern Fennoscandia.

HANS HENNING HOFF is practising as a business lawyer in Hamburg, Germany, but also qualified to practise in Iceland. Having studied law, Scandinavian languages and medieval history, in both Germany and Iceland, his academic interest focuses on medieval Iceland and the foundations of civil and corporate law.

THOMAS KUEHN is a Professor of European History and Chair of the Department of History at Clemson University. His interests are in legal and social history, including gender, in late medieval and renaissance Italy, especially Florence. His most recent book is Heirs, Kin, and Creditors in Renaissance Florence (Cambridge University Press: 2008).

HIRAM KÜMPER is an Assistant Professor (Akademischer Rat) of Medieval and Early Modern History at the University of Bielefeld. Besides legal history his research and teaching interests include manuscript studies, the history of historiography, and the communication of history in the public sphere.

MAIJA OJALA is a PhD Student of General History at the School of Social Sciences and Humanities, University of Tampere. Her main research interests are the history of craft trade and religious reformation in the North European cities. Currently she is finishing her PhD studies on artisan crafts in the Baltic Sea Region in the period from the fifteenth to the seventeenth centuries.

PHILIP L. REYNOLDS is Aquinas Professor of Historical Theology at Candler School of Theology, University of Emory. He has studied Western Christian thought A.D. 400-1400 and has focused on scholastic theology and philosophy during the high Middle Ages (especially Bonaventure and Thomas Aquinas) as well as on the theology and canon law of marriage.

CHRISTOF ROLKER is a Postdoctoral Scholar at the Department for History and Sociology, University of Constance. Currently he is working on late medieval social history, especially concerning family and marriage. One of his main research interests is pre-Gratian canon law; he has recently published a major monograph on Ivo of Chartres († 1115).

JAN RÜDIGER is a Professor of Medieval History at the Goethe University, Frankfurt/Main. His main research interest is in the field of political cultures in the medieval West, including languages, élite polygyny, and medieval thalassocracies.

KIRSI SALONEN is a Senior Associate Professor (Docent) of General History at the School of Social Sciences and Humanities, University of Tampere and currently working as a research fellow of the Academy of Finland. Her main research interests include papal justice in the Late Middle Ages in the Christian West.

HELLE MØLLER SIGH is a PhD Student of History at the Department of History and Area Studies, Aarhus University. Her main research interests are in legal and cultural history, including gender, in medieval and early modern Denmark and Europe. Currently she is finishing her PhD thesis on Christianization of Marriage in Denmark from 1200-1582. Furthermore she has published articles on sexual crimes and the concept of guilt and on the creation of legal identities in relation to property rights in Danish medieval law.

HELLE VOGT is an Associate Professor of Legal History at the Faculty of Law, University of Copenhagen. Her main research topics are Nordic legal history and the interaction between local law and learned Christian legal ideology.

JOHN WITTE, Jr., is Jonas Robitscher Professor of Law, Alonzo L. McDonald Distinguished Professor, and Director of the Center for the Study of Law and Religion Center at Emory University. He has specialized in legal history, marriage law, and religious liberty.

JAKUB WYSMUŁEK is a researcher at the Department of History at the University of Warsaw. His main research field is the social and cultural history of cities in the Middle Ages, and currently he is working on the late medieval wills of Cracow.